Lecture Notes of the Institute
for Computer Sciences, Soci
and Telecommunications En

T0073488

Editorial Board

Christos K. Georgiadis   Hamid Jahankhani
Elias Pimenidis   Rabih Bashroush
Ameer Al-Nemrat (Eds.)

Global Security, Safety and Sustainability & e-Democracy

7th International and 4th e-Democracy
Joint Conferences, ICGS3/e-Democracy 2011
Thessaloniki, Greece, August 24-26, 2011
Revised Selected Papers

 Springer

Volume Editors

Christos K. Georgiadis
University of Macedonia
Department of Applied Informatics
156 Egnatia Street, 54006 Thessaloniki, Greece
E-mail: geor@uom.gr

Hamid Jahankhani
Elias Pimenidis
Rabih Bashroush
Ameer Al-Nemrat
University of East London
School of Architecture Computing & Engineering
Docklands Campus 4-6, University Way
London E16 2RD, UK
E-mails:
{hamid.jahankhani; e.pimenidis; r.bashroush; a.al-nemrat}@uel.ac.uk

ISSN 1867-8211   e-ISSN 1867-822X
ISBN 978-3-642-33447-4   e-ISBN 978-3-642-33448-1
DOI 10.1007/978-3-642-33448-1

Springer Heidelberg Dordrecht London New York

Library of Congress Control Number: Applied for

CR Subject Classification (1998): K.4.4, K.4.1, K.6.5, H.4.1, H.5.5, J.1, C.2.0-1, F.2.2

Typesetting: Camera-ready by author, data conversion by Scientific Publishing Services, Chennai, India

Printed on acid-free paper

Springer is part of Springer Science+Business Media (www.springer.com)

Foreword

The annual International Conference on Global Security, Safety and Sustainability is an established platform in which security, safety, and sustainability issues can be examined from several global perspectives through dialogue between academics, students, government representatives, chief executives, security professionals, and research scientists from the UK and from around the globe.

The three-day conference in 2011 focused on the challenges of complexity, the rapid pace of change, and risk/opportunity issues associated with modern products, systems, special events, and infrastructures.

In an era of unprecedented volatile political and economic environments across the world, computer-based systems face ever more increasing challenges, disputes, and responsibilities. Their role in facilitating secure economic transactions and maintaining steady and reliable sources of information that support politically stable and sustainable socioeconomic systems is becoming increasingly critical. Under such a spectrum of issues, the 7th International Conference on Global Security, Safety and Sustainability and the 4th Conference on e-Democracy were jointly organized.

The conferences provided coverage of a wider spectrum of related topics and enhanced incentives for academic debate with a sharply focused critical evaluation of researchers' results from innovative applications of methodologies and applied technologies.

ICGS3 2011 and eDemocracy received paper submissions from more than 12 countries in all continents. Only 37 papers were selected and were presented as full papers. The program also included three keynote lectures by leading researchers, security professionals, and government representatives.

September 2011   Hamid Jahankhani

ICGS3/e-Democracy 2011 Conference Organization

General Chair

Hamid Jahankhani   University of East London, UK

Local Organizing Chairs

Christos K. Georgiadis   University of Macedonia, Greece
Elias Pimenidis   University of East London, UK

Organizers

University of Macedonia, Department of Applied Informatics Thessaloniki, Greece
University of East London, School of Computing, IT and Engineering, UK
Scientific Council for Information Society, Greece

Organizing Committee

Devon Bennett   University of East London, UK
Vasilios Katos   Democritus University of Thrace, Greece
Panagiotis Katsaros   Aristotle University of Thessaloniki, Greece
Costas Lambrinoudakis   University of Piraeus, Greece
Sin Wee Lee   University of East London, UK
Ioannis Mavridis   University of Macedonia, Greece
Ioannis Stamatiou   University of Ioannina, Greece
Vasilios Zorkadis   Directorate of the Hellenic Data Protection
      Authority, Greece

Program Chairs

Ameer Al Nemrat   University of East London, UK
Rabih Bashroush   University of East London, UK
Ken Dick   Nebraska University Center for Information
      Assurance, USA

Program Committee

Talal Alkharobi	Kings Fahad University of Petroleum and Minerals, Saudi Arabia
Muhammad Ali Babar	IT University of Copenhagen, Denmark
Miltiades Anagnostou	National Technical University of Athens, Greece
Alexandros Chatzigeorgiou	University of Macedonia, Greece
Ali Chehab	American University of Beirut, Lebanon
Mohammad Dastbaz	University of East London, UK
Christos Douligeris	University of Piraeus, Greece
Orhan Gemikonakl	Middlesex University, UK
Christos K. Georgiadis	University of Macedonia, Greece
Wasif Gilani	SAP (UK), UK
George A. Gravvanis	Democritus University of Thrace, Greece
Valiantsin Hardzeeyeu	Ilmenau University, Germany
Ali Hessami	Vega Systems, UK
Lazaros Iliadis	Democritus University of Thrace, Greece
Christos Ilioudis	A. T. E. I. of Thessaloniki, Greece
Shareeful Islam	University of East London, UK
Hossein Jahankhani	University of East London, UK
Konstantinos Kardaras	Technical Consultant, Greece
Vasilios Katos	Democritus University of Thrace, Greece
Panagiotis Katsaros	Aristotle University of Thessaloniki, Greece
Petros Kefalas	City College/University of Sheffield, Greece
Panayiotis H. Ketikidis	City College/University of Sheffield, Greece
Costas Lambrinoudakis	University of Piraeus, Greece
George Loukeris	Scientific Council for Information Society, Greece
Ioannis Manolopoulos	Aristotle University of Thessaloniki, Greece
Konstantinos Margaritis	University of Macedonia, Greece
Ioannis Mavridis	University of Macedonia, Greece
Gianluigi Me	University of Rome Tor Vergata, Italy
Haralambos Mouratidis	University of East London, UK
Hamid R. Nemati	The University of North Carolina at Greensboro, USA
George Pangalos	Aristotle University of Thessaloniki, Greece
Elias Pimenidis	University of East London, UK
Despina Polemi	University of Piraeus, Greece
Kenneth Revett	The British University in Egypt, Egypt
Konstantin Sack	Cyber and Computer Forensic Investigation Unit, Police Headquarters of South Hesse, Germany
Ali Sanayei	University of Isfahan, Iran
Henrique M.D. Santos	University of Minho, Portugal

Alexander Sideridis	Agricultural University of Athens, Greece
Ioannis Stamatiou	University of Ioannina, Greece
Demosthenis Stamatis	A. T. E. I. of Thessaloniki, Greece
Amie Taal	Forensics Associate Director, Grant Thoronton, UK
Sérgio Tenreiro de Magalhães	Catholic University of Portugal, Portugal
Sufian Yousef	Anglia Ruskin University, UK
Irini Vassilaki	Scientific Council for Information Society, Greece
David Lilburn Watson	Forensic Computing Ltd., UK
George Weir	University of Strathclyde, UK
Michalis Xenos	Hellenic Open University, Greece
Vasilios Zorkadis	Directorate of the Hellenic Data Protection Authority, Greece

Publicity Chairs

Hossein Jahankhani	University of East London, UK
Despoina Polemi	University of Piraeus, Greece
Zoe Kardasiadou	Hellenic Data Protection Authority, Greece

Secretarial and Technical Support

Eugenia Papaioannou	University of Macedonia, Greece
Apostolos Provatidis	University of Macedonia, Greece
Nikos Vesyropoulos	University of Macedonia, Greece

Table of Contents

Transforming Vehicles into e-government 'Cloud Computing' Nodes

Dellios Kleanthis[1], Chronakis Aristeidis[2], and Polemi Despina[1]

[1] Department of Informatics, University of Piraeus,
80 Karaoli & Dimitriou St., 18534, Piraeus, Greece
[2] Intrasoft International, Software Engineer,
{kdellios,dpolemi}@unipi.gr,
Aristeidis.Chronakis@Intrasoft-intl.com

Abstract. Nowadays sophisticated vehicles can become autonomous e-government service providers by viewing them as "G-Cloud computing" nodes. By using web services technologies vehicles can offer e-government cloud computing services.

Keywords: vehicular, G-Cloud, e-government, web services, registry, discovery.

1 Introduction

Vehicles have evolved from basic assets into sophisticated devices produced by a conjunction of sciences such as architecture, mechanical and electronic engineering, telecommunications and computer science [1]. This kind of technological invocation continues seeking ways to transform vehicles into autonomous service providers.

Cloud Computing is giving us a new trend and form of technological resources and enterprise services of the Web [2]. Several efforts are being made by the automotive industry to exploit the cloud computing concept on vehicles [3] in order to provide end-users with new kind of services.

In this paper an architecture with which vehicles become Vehicular Service Providers (VSP), acting as G-Cloud Computing Nodes, is proposed utilizing Web Services and Cloud Computing technologies to provide and deliver e-government services whether they are public order vehicles (e.g. police vehicles, ambulances, fire trucks units) or commercial vehicles. This paper is structured as follows: Second section there is an introduction to the concept of cloud computing vehicular services; the third section presents an adaptation of Cloud Computing terms into vehicular terminology; the fourth section proposes a vehicular service discovery mechanism in order for vehicles to become cloud computing nodes. The paper concludes with future research directions.

2 Situation Awareness

Vehicle vendors focus in new technological developments addressing vehicular network requirements in order to enhance vehicular services [3]. Nowadays, web

H. Jahankhani et al. (Eds.): ICGS3/e-Democracy 2011, LNICST 99, pp. 1–8, 2012.

enterprises applications utilize in high extend the Web Services technologies over the "Cloud". Several efforts are being made by the automotive industry to exploit the "Cloud Computing" concept on vehicles in order to provide end-users with new kind of services. A powerful example is the partnership for research and development of Ford, Microsoft and Intel with the University of Michigan in order a vehicle to access Windows Azure "Cloud" Platform [4].

Such kind of services can be utilized to enhance e-government service information strategy. The combination of Cloud Computing and Web Services can provide government agencies with innovative creations of new set of services and applications, addressed to citizens, third party application developers and the automotive industry as a whole. Web Services technology can reduce the cost of integration and produce immediate financial advantages with the integration of new systems for deploying services. Additional functionality can be composed using Web Service messages mechanisms [5, 6]. The roles in the operational model of Vehicular Web Services (Fig. 1) are defined as follows: The VSP provides the environment for the deployment and operation of Web Services defines the vehicular services and publishes them.

The Vehicle Service Requestor (VSRq) refers to a Vehicle Client program, which invokes Web Services. The Vehicle Service Registry (VSRg) is responsible for the vehicular service registration.

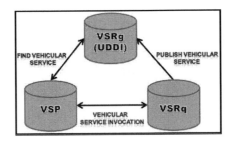

Fig. 1. Operational Model of Vehicular Web Services

The VSRg lists the various types, descriptions and locations of the vehicular services. During the publish service operation, the VSP registers Web Services information in VSRg. The VSRq finds in the Registry information such as service description, interface description and access point. Finally, the vehicle requestor finds the required vehicular service and executes it from the VSP.

This mechanism is a key to overcome actual implementation and standardization issues now that vehicles are becoming intelligent platforms and possess tremendous computational power, capable to host complex applications. Taking vehicles to the next level, is to consider them as computation "Clouds" providing services to other vehicles and various in-vehicle network-capable "terminals". This paper proposes a web service-based model, for offering vehicular services over the G-Cloud.

3   "Cloud Computing" Vehicular Services

In this paper, the term "services" in a vehicle computation G-Cloud, describes how a vehicle or any other network-capable electronic device can use on demand computation assets provided by other vehicles. Vehicles can provide the following Vehicular Cloud Services:

Hardware - Infrastructure as a Service: Is a type of service that can be available in a Vehicle Cloud Computing or G-Cloud. This kind of services offers the hardware infrastructure of a vehicle (e.g. on-board memory, GPS receiver), to users that do not have in their vehicles the same hardware capabilities.

Platform as a Service: A vehicle may provide more than infrastructure. A fully networked vehicle [3] could deliver an integrated set of software and hardware that a developer needs in order to build an application for both software development and runtime.

Software as a service: While vehicle applications are stand-alone applications, companies who want to offer portfolio of next generation, vehicle applications will increasingly rely on shared services between vehicles (e.g. governance, account management, workflow, single-sign-on, social networking).

Network - Internet as a Service: Vehicles with internet access can be used by vehicle users to obtain internet service (e.g. e-mail, RSS feeds) or even be the gateway for users to gain access to any other network or the Web.

Treating traditional vehicle services (e.g. such as navigation, traffic, warning and weather information), as vehicle cloud services, there will be an enhancement in terms of functionality, interoperability and cost effectiveness. Specifically this new view can enhance the notion of e-government such as traffic information and management (cooperative traffic information & forecasting, dynamic free parking space information, location based information and warning), safety and security (e.g. hazard warning, theft recovery, tracking and trace, emergency calls) or comfort (e.g. future adaptive cruise control systems and infotainment systems with music/video on demand or business information) enabling them to offer innovative next generation services. Cloud computing and web services can offer technological and financial advantages in government agencies.

4   Vehicular Service Registry Mechanism

The combination of cloud computing services and vehicles, state that a vehicle with less capabilities than others, could be able to request a service from vehicles that already are equipped with. In the various modes of Vehicle-to-Anything (V2X) communication, network capabilities are under consideration to support new applications and services.

In this paper a high level implementation mechanism that can be used by the contracting parts, is described for the exposure of various governmental vehicular services. These services are provided by the "G-Cloud" vehicles and their discovery is made by the client vehicles. Technologies used in Web Services play a key role to this operational model.

A Web Services Description Language (WSDL) document is used by the side of the service vehicle provider in order to describe the functional characteristics of its Web Service [5, 6]. The UDDI ver.3 protocol (Universal Description, Discovery and Integration) is an XML-based registry that is used to register and locate the services provided by the "cloud" vehicles. UDDI v3 protocol introduces the function of a service subscription. In this case, the service subscription function provides the service requestor vehicle with the ability to subscribe interested service information in the UDDI and receive notification of adding, updating and deleting operations [5, 6].

There can be three implementation mechanisms for service discovery over a high mobility cloud. In all service discovery mechanisms SOA Protocol (SOAP) messages are being exchanged between all vehicle-counterparts. SOAP is utilized for exchanging information between the VSP and the VSRq. The three secure discovery mechanisms are described as follows:

4.1   Case 1: Decentralized Service Discovery over a Vehicle (DSDV)

A Decentralized Service Discovery over a Vehicle (DSDV) (Fig. 2) can be applied in an environment where no centralized service infrastructure exists. A client node that requests services search for existing connections with other available online nodes.

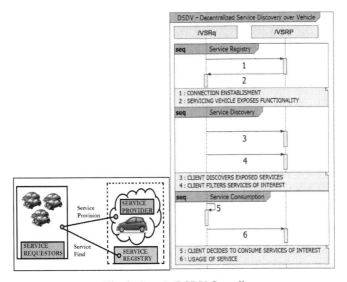

Fig. 2. Case 1- DSDV Overall

This action occurs until the client node finds another node capable to provide the required vehicular services. Every time that a VSRq node connects to another node always checks if a UDDI with registered vehicular services exist. If a UDDI exists the VSRq will filter the provided exposed vehicular services, to find and use a service of its interest. More specific DSDV takes place after the network communication between the VSP and the VSRq is established. A servicing vehicle having its services functionalities exposed is being discovered by the client by the exchange of SOAP messages. The VSRq filters the services that interests it and decides to use them. A connectivity status check process can be utilized, during all phases of nodes communication of DSDV.

4.2 Case 2: Centralized Service Discovery over Infrastructure (CSDI)

In the second case of a CSDI implementation mechanism a local region based dynamic UDDI infrastructure (Fig.3) holding all services is utilized.

After the registration of the service takes place the local UDDI infrastructure provides the VSRg with a security token. This security token is provided for authentication reasons once a connection between the VSP and the VSRq nodes is established. A client requesting services in that specific region will search the local UDDI for a VSP. The infrastructure will provide the client with a security token after the identification of the service occurs. This security token will be used by the client in order to be authenticated by the VSP. A connection will then be established with the VSP.

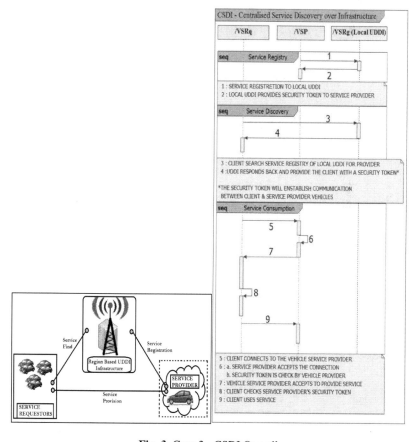

Fig. 3. Case 2 - CSDI Overall

For authentication reasons the VSP will check the VSRq security token in order to provide services. The VSP sends its security token for authentication by the client. Finally, the VSRq will authenticate the VSP and will use the service.

In CSDI, a connectivity status check process can be utilized during all phases of vehicle node communication.

4.3   Case 3: Centralized Service Discovery a Vehicle (CSDV)

The CSDV implementation mechanism is utilized due to the lack of a centralized region based infrastructure holding a UDDI. A number of vehicles capable to provide services are forming a group and decide which one will hold the UDDI. Once this phase is completed the rest of the CSDV mechanism is the same with the CSDI mechanism (Fig. 4). All VSPs will register their services to the vehicle holding the UDDI. The vehicle UDDI will generate a security token that will provide to each VSP.

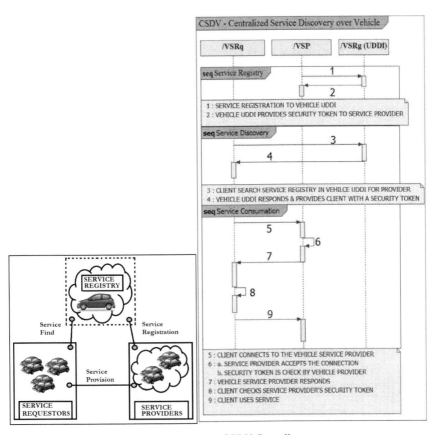

Fig. 4. Case 3 - CSDV Overall

When a VSRq establishes a connection with the vehicle UDDI will find that a UDDI exists and will search and find the desired vehicle service. If the services are not provided locally by the vehicle UDDI, the VSRq will receive a security token in order to be authenticated by the VSP. The VSRq will then establish a connection with the VSP. For authentication reasons the VSP will check the VSRq security token in order to provide services. After the authentication of the VSRq, the VSP will send its security token to the client vehicle. Finally, when the VSP's authentication is completed, the VSRq will consume the service. During all phases of CSDV mechanism a connectivity status check process can be utilized.

In addition, the vehicles, regardless of their role, are capable for transmission through an onboard or external network capable device. This way vehicle will be updatable and upgradeable.

5   Conclusions – Future Directions

Three implementation mechanisms for vehicular service discovery over a governmental cloud are presented in this paper. These mechanisms can be applied in cases that a client vehicle or a group of client vehicles request services. Provided on demand generic services such as navigation information, points of interests, road warnings and weather condition information via a computation cloud, next generation services are offered in vehicles.

Moreover, the second implementation mechanism can also be used in cases where the services are consumed from already existing road infrastructures that can host in the future the UDDI. This case of implementation also helps the appliance of cloud computing in vehicles in order to become stand alone cloud nodes.

Nowadays vision regarding vehicles is to be able to operate over functional oriented architectures and information-based services over packet based networks. Cloud computing in vehicles can not only offer new generation services, but also can provide system efficiency in high mobility environments, such the one that vehicles are operating.

Vehicular Safety also can be increased via a Vehicular G-Cloud Computing cooperative environment. In addition, a cloud computing notion, fully adopted in a high mobility environment such as the one that vehicles are operating, a vehicular service discovery mechanism plays a key role when applying the notion of cloud computing in vehicular services.

The presented Vehicular Service Discovery Mechanisms is a functional approach of a service finding model. A future enhancement approach for this implementation will be the construction of a more dynamic vehicular invocation framework. This framework can be specialized in vehicular high mobility environments along with new security mechanisms such as an embedded vehicular firewall.

References

1. Navet, N., Sommot-Lion, F.: Automotive Embedded Systems Handbook. Industrial Information Technological Series. CRS Press (2009)
2. Sullivan, J.D.: The Definitive Guide to Cloud Computing. Realtime publishers,
   http://nexus.realtimepublishers.com/dgcc.php
3. ITU: The Fully Networked Car, International Motor Show Workshop (2007-2010),
   http://www.itu.int/ITU-T/worksem/
   ict-auto/200903/programme.html
4. Ford Online: Ford, University of Michigan Reveal Student's Vision for Future of In-Car Cloud Computing Apps,
   http://media.ford.com/article_display.cfm?article_id=32572
5. Graham, S., Davis, D., Simeonov, S., Daniels, G., Brittenham, P., Nkamura, Y., Fremantle, P., König, D., Zentner, C.: Building Web Services with Java – Making Sense of XML, SOAP, WSDL and UDDI. Sams Publishing (2005)
6. W3C: Web of Services, http://www.w3.org/standards/webofservices/

Maximum Entropy Oriented Anonymization Algorithm for Privacy Preserving Data Mining

Stergios G. Tsiafoulis[1], Vasilios C. Zorkadis[2], and Elias Pimenidis[3]

[1] Hellenic Open University
Ministry of Public Administrative Reform and e-Government
Vasilissis Sofias Av. 15, 10674, Athens, Greece
stetsiafoulis@gmail.com
[2] Hellenic Open University
Hellenic Data Protection Authority Athens
Kifissias Av.1-3, 115 23, Athens, Greece
zorkadis@dpa.gr
[3] University of East London
e.pimenidis@uel.ac.uk

Abstract. This work introduces a new concept that addresses the problem of preserving privacy when anonymising and publishing personal data collections. In particular, a maximum entropy oriented algorithm to protect sensitive data is proposed. As opposed to k-anonymity, ℓ-diversity and t-closeness, the proposed algorithm builds equivalence classes with possibly uniformly distributed sensitive attribute values, probably by means of noise, and having as a lower limit the entropy of the distribution of the initial data collection, so that background information cannot be exploited to successfully attack the privacy of data subjects data refer to. Furthermore, existing privacy and information loss related metrics are presented, as well as the algorithm implementing the maximum entropy anonymity concept. From a privacy protection perspective, the achieved results are very promising, while the suffered information loss is limited.

Keywords: Privacy preservation, maximum entropy anonymity, k-anonymity, ℓ-diversity, t-closeness, maximum entropy, (SOMs), neural-network clustering.

1 Introduction

Data contained in databases may be personal, i.e. information referring to an individual directly or indirectly identifiable and therefore its processing should be restricted to lawful purposes. However, exploiting such personal data collections may offer many benefits to the community and support the policy and action plan development process and even contribute to prognosis and treatment of diseases [1]. To address these at first sight contradicting requirements, privacy preserving data mining techniques have been proposed [2-10].

A few years ago, the most common and simplest method to protect from privacy breaches was to remove the identifiers from the database. But an attacker can associate published databases from different sources and extract personal information of

H. Jahankhani et al. (Eds.): ICGS3/e-Democracy 2011, LNICST 99, pp. 9–16, 2012.
© Institute for Computer Sciences, Social Informatics and Telecommunications Engineering 2012

an individual. An attack of this kind is called "linking attack". A study held in 2000 linked a Massachusetts voter list with an anonymized database that contained medical records demonstrating that 87% of the population of the United States can be uniquely identified.

Existing privacy-preserving data mining algorithms can be classified into two categories: algorithms that protect the sensitive data itself in the mining process, and those that protect the sensitive data mining results [1]. The most popular concepts in the privacy preserving data mining research literature are k-anonymity, ℓ-diversity and t-closeness. All these concepts belong to the first category and apply generalization and suppression methods to the original datasets in order to preserve the anonymity of individuals or entities data refer to [15].

In this paper, the authors propose a new concept called maximum entropy anonymity concept. It is based on the idea of creating equivalence classes with maximum entropy with respect to the sensitive attribute values.

The paper is structured as follows. Section 2, provides an introduction to the proposed maximum entropy concept, while in section 3, anonymity and information loss metrics are briefly presented. In section 4, the algorithm that implements the proposed concept is presented and in section 5 the experimental studies and results are discussed.

2   Maximum Entropy Oriented Anonymity Concept

The concept of k-anonymity does not take into account the distribution of the sensitive attribute values in each equivalence class, thus leaving space for successful privacy related attacks, while the concept of ℓ-diversity reduces this risk by requiring at least ℓ different sensitive attribute values in each equivalence class. Finally, t-closeness aims at having sensitive attribute values, in each equivalence class, that follow the related distribution of the initial data table being anonymised in order to cope with background knowledge based attacks.

From the privacy protection perspective, the maximum entropy oriented anonymity concept sets a much more ambitious goal, namely that of building equivalence classes with possibly uniformly distributed sensitive attribute values, i.e., showing maximum entropy with regard to sensitive attribute values and thus maximizing the uncertainty of an aspiring attacker exploiting background knowledge. Background knowledge related attacks are radically encountered, regardless of the information an attacker may possess. However, maximum entropy may not be achieved in all equivalence classes, and depending on the initial distribution it may be restricted to only a few. For such a reason, the original goal may be reduced and the new requirement could be set for each equivalence class to have maximum entropy or at least equal entropy to that of the initial data collection. Noise must be constructed and introduced into those equivalence classes for which the defined goal cannot be achieved otherwise, while keeping the information loss to possibly negligible levels.

The algorithmic implementation of the maximum entropy oriented anonymity concept is attained by dividing the initial sensitive attribute distribution into possibly equivalence class uniform distributions, while minimizing the required noise and information loss.

3 Performance Evaluation

The anonymization process has two objectives, that of preserving privacy, in other words to achieve a high degree of anonymity, and, that of minimizing the resulting information loss. Therefore, any performance evaluation criteria should take into account the above two objectives [15].

Information theoretic anonymity metrics have been proposed mainly based on the entropy concept [15, 20]. The entropy $H(X)$ refers to an attacker's a priori knowledge regarding for instance possible senders of a message or a number of messages,

$$H(X) = \sum_{i \in X} p(x_i) \log_2 p(x_i) \tag{1}$$

while $H(X/C)$ is the conditional information quantity for an attacker after having received the anonymized table (published table), while exploiting available background The higher the entropies, the better the anonymity, i.e. the more uncertain the attacker is about data subject identities [15, 20].

From the information loss perspective, several criteria have been proposed so far in the literature [12, 13, 16, 22]. In most previous work that proposed group based ano-nymization, the relevant evaluation metrics used are: *Discernibility metric* [12, 13, 22], *Classification metric* [12, 16] and *Normalized Certainty penalty* (NCP)[13].

$$H(X/C) = \sum_{i \in X, j \in C} p(x_i, c_j) \log_2 p(x_i/c_j) \tag{2}$$

Discernibility metric assigns a penalty to each tuple based on how many tuples in the transformed dataset are indistinguishable from it. This can be mathematically stated as follows:

$$C_{DM}(g,k) = \sum_{\forall E s.t. |E| \geq k} |E|^2 + \sum_{\forall E s.t. |E| < k} |D||E| \tag{3}$$

where |D| the size of the input dataset, E refers to the equivalence classes of tuples in D induced by the anonymization g.

The Normalized Certainty penalty calculates the information loss introduced by the generalization depth incurred in every attribute value of each tuple, considering also the importance of each attribute by assigning them with a proper weight. If the attribute is a numerical one then the information loss is measured as follows

$$NCP_A(t) = w_i \cdot \frac{z_i - y_i}{|A_i|} \tag{4}$$

where $z_i - y_i$ is the range of the generalization to the tuple t on the values of the attribute A_i and $|A_i|$ is the range of all tuples on this.

4   The Maximum Entropy Anonymization Algorithm

In the beginning of the proposed algorithm, equivalence classes with distinct sensitive attribute values are being created. The algorithm that is presented in [15] with the proper modifications is being used to create those equivalence classes.

Input: A database T in a table format
Output: An anonymized table T^*
Variables: $E \leftarrow \{\}$, the set of the equivalence classes EQ
$QIC \leftarrow \{\}$, set of equivalence classes with similar quasi identifier set QI
$SAP \leftarrow \{\}$, set of tuples with same SA values

01. **Begin**
02. d=number of distinct values of the SA
03.   **While** d>2 **do** {
04.   *Cluster (T)*
05.   **For** every QIC set created from the clustering procedure **do** {
06.   Bucketize the tuples according the SA value to SAP sets
07.   **For** every SAP set **do** {
08.   **While** $|SAP|$>=d **do** {
09.   **Create equivalence classes** (SAP)
10. E=E **U** EQ
11.   **Return** E
                            }
                        }
                    }
                }
12. d=d-1
            }
13.   *Entropy_procedure (E)*
14. **End**

Fig. 1. The Main Algorithm

Input: Table T
Output: $QIC \leftarrow \{\}$, set of tables with tuples with similar QI sets

01. **Begin**
02.   Insert T to the neural network
03. $QIC= \{QIC1, QIC2, ..., QICm\}$
04.   Return QIC
05. **End**

Fig. 2. The Clustering Procedure

```
Input: SAP
Output: EQ

01. Begin
02.        Randomly selection of tuple tm from the smallest group
03.        EQ={tm}
04.              For p←1 until p=d-1 do {
05.                      Select a tuple tp that minimizes the NCP
06.                      EQ=EQ U tp
07.                      Remove tp from T
08.                      Remove tm from T
                      }
09.        Generalize the values in the EQ
10.        Return EQ
11. End
```

Fig. 3. The *"Create Equivalence Classes"* Procedure

```
Input: Table E
Output: set of EQ with entropy more than a threshold ε

01. Begin
02.        Until there is no EQ with entropy lower than ε do {
03.                Calculate the entropy to each EQ
04.                Create a table LE with the tuples that belong to
                   EQ classes with entropy lower than ε
05.                Delete those tuples from E
06.                Incorporate the tuples from LE to E
                   }
07. End
```

Fig. 4. The *"Incorporation"* Procedure

After the initial creation of equivalence classes, the *incorporate procedure* is undertaken. In this procedure, firstly the entropy of the created equivalence classes is calculated. Secondly, the tuples that belong to equivalence classes with entropy lower than the set threshold ε are removed from the temporary anonymized set and are incorporated to the *Low Entropy* table. Thirdly, for each tuple of this table, the equivalence classes with the most common quasi identifier set from the temporary anonymized table are searched. Finally, the tuple is incorporated to the class that does not contain the same value to the sensitive attribute field in order to achieve larger entropy value. The entropies of the created equivalence classes are calculated once more and the same procedure of the incorporating step is being repeated until there are no more classes with entropy lower than the threshold ε. The proposed algorithm is shown in the above Figures 1 – 4.

5   Experimental Data Set Up and Results

The Adult database from machine learning repositories offered by the California University has been used for the implementation of the suggested algorithm of this paper. This database includes 30162 tuples with 14 attributes. Eight out of those (age, work class, education, marital-status, occupation, race, sex, native-country) were chosen for the experimental part of this work. The attributes were represented in numerical form according to their distributions and their domain generalization hierarchy as stated in [16] and [23], respectively and extends by setting the restriction of the valid generalization [12]. For the categorical attributes "work class" and "marital status" the same taxonomy trees as those stated in [12] were used. To the categorical attributes "race" and "sex" a simple two level taxonomy tree was applied.

The mapping to numeric values from the categorical attributes was applied according to the valid generalization notion [12]. Age, education, occupation and native-country were considered as numerical attributes. The generalizations for the attribute age were defined through rounding to median while that to the former ones through total generalization. For the evaluation of the algorithm, total weight certainty penalty *NCP(T)* and the discernibility metric *CDM* that were discussed in section(3), are computed. The experiments were conducted under the Windows XP professional operating system on a PC with a 2.4 GHz AMD Athlon processor and 2 GB RAM.

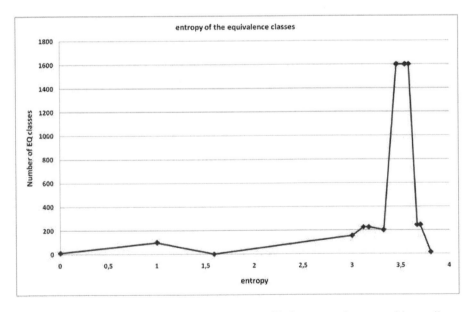

Fig. 5. Entropy of the created equivalence classes considering occupation as sensitive attribute

For the first experiment in this work, the set {*age, education, marital-status, occupation, race, sex, native-country*} was chosen as quasi indentifying set, while *work class* was considered as sensitive attribute. For the second experiment we choose the set {*age, work class, education, marital-status, race, sex, native-country*} as quasi indentifier set and *occupation* as the sensitive attribute. The distribution of this attribute is much closer to uniform than the previous one. Fig.5 shows the entropy values of the created equivalence. While the entropy of the initial dataset is 3.4, in the resulting intermediate equivalence classes, most of them consisting of 22831 tuples have entropy higher than 3.4. Noise is to be added into the rest of the equivalence classes in order to satisfy the above mentioned entropy threshold.

6 Conclusions

The maximum entropy anonymity concept was introduced and an algorithm that implements it was designed. The performance of our algorithm was measured with respect to privacy by the entropy of the sensitive attribute in each equivalence class and with respect to information loss by means of the *NCP* and discernibility metrics.

We conclude from our work that keeping the distribution of the sensitive attribute values in each equivalence class possibly uniform, or at least the same as the distribution of the initial table, leads to better privacy preservation. We intent to further explore the impact of introducing noise into the equivalence classes, in order to achieve almost perfect privacy preservation, while the resulting information loss is kept to a minimum.

References

1. Wickramasinghe Nilmini, B.R.K., Chris, G.M., Jonathan, S.: Realizing the Knowledge Spiral in Healthcare: the role of Data Mining and Knowledge Management. The International Council on Medical & Care Compunetics, 147–162 (2008)
2. Dalenius, T.: Finding a Needle In a Haystack or Identifying Anonymous Census Records. Journal of Official Statistics 2(3), 329–336 (1986)
3. Sweeney, L.: k-anonymity: a model for protecting privacy. International Journal on Uncertainty, Fuzziness and Knowledge-based Systems 10(5), 557–570 (2002)
4. Sweeney, L., Samarati, P.: Protecting privacy when disclosing information: k-anonymity and its enforcement through generalization and suppression. In: IEEE Symposium on Research in Security and Privacy (1998)
5. Meyerson, A., Williams, R.: General k-Anonymization is Hard. In: PODS 2004 (2003)
6. Ashwin Machanavajjhala, D.K., Gehrke, J., Venkitasubramaniam, M.: L-Diversity: Privacy Beyond k-Anonymity. ACM Transactions on Knowledge Discovery from Data 1(1), 52, article 3 (2007)
7. Li, N., Li, T., Venkatasubramanian, S.: t-Closeness: Privacy Beyond k-Anonymity and ℓ-Diversity. In: 23rd International Conference on Data Engineering, ICDE 2007, pp. 106–115 (2007)
8. Ye, Y., Deng, Q., Wang, C., Lv, D., Liu, Y., Feng, J.-H.: *BSGI*: An Effective Algorithm towards Stronger *l*-Diversity. In: Bhowmick, S.S., Küng, J., Wagner, R. (eds.) DEXA 2008. LNCS, vol. 5181, pp. 19–32. Springer, Heidelberg (2008)
9. Xiao, X., Tao, Y.: Anatomy: Simple and effective privacy preservation. In: 32nd International Conference on Very large Data Bases, VLDB 2006, pp. 139–150 (2006)

10. LeFevre, K.R., Dewitt, D.J., Ramakrishnan, R.: Incognito: efficient full-domain K-anonymity. In: International Conference on Management of Data ACM SIGMOD 2005, Baltimore, Maryland (2005)

11. LeFevre, K., Dewitt, D.J., Ramakrishnan, R.: Mondrian Multidimensional K-Anonymity. In: ICDE 2006 (2006)

12. Iyengar, V.S.: Transforming Data to Satisfy Privacy Constrains. In: KDD 2002 (2002)

13. Xu, J., Wang, W., Pei, J., Wang, X., Shi, B., Fu, A.W.-C.: Utility-Based Anonymization Using Local Recoding. In: KDD 2006(2006)

14. UCI. Irvin Machine Learning Repository, http://archive.ics.uci.edu/ml/

15. Tsiafoulis, S.G., Zorkadis, V.C.: A Neural Network Clustering Based Algorithm for Privacy Preserving Data Mining. In: 2010 International Conference on Computational Intelligence and Security, Nanning, Guangxi Zhuang Autonomous Region, China (2010)

16. Bayardo, R.J., Agrawal, R.: Data privacy through optimal k-anonymization. In: 21th ICDE 2005 (2005)

17. Webb, G.I.: Opus: An Effcient Admissible Algorithm for Unordered Search. Journal of Artificial intelligence Research 3, 431–465 (1995)

18. Rymon, R.: Search Through Systematic Set Enumeration (1992)

19. Whitley, D.: The Genitor Algorithm and Selective Pressure: Why rank-based allocation of reproductive trials is best. In: Proceedings of Third International Conference on Genetic Algorithms, 1989, pp. 116–121.

20. Kelly, D.J., Raines, R.A., Grimaila, M.R., Baldwin, R.O., Mullins, B.E.: A Survey of State-of-the Art ion Anonymity Metrics. In: NDA 2008. ACM, Fairfax (2008)

21. Dakshi Agrawal, C.C.A.: On the Design and Quantification of Privacy Preserving Data Mining Algorithms. In: 20th Symposium on Principles of Database Systems Santa Barbara California, USA (May 2001)

22. Evfimievski, A.V., Srikant, R., Gehrke, J.: Limiting privacy breaches in privacy preserving data mining. In: Proceedings of the Twenty-Second ACM SIGMOD-SIGACT-SIGART Symposium on Principles of Database Systems table of Contents, San Diego, California, pp. 211–222 (2003)

23. Sweeney, L.: Achieving k-anonymity privacy protection using generalization and suppression. International Journal on Uncertainty, Fuzziness and Knowledge-based Systems 10(5), 571–588 (2002)

Practical Password Harvesting from Volatile Memory

Stavroula Karayianni and Vasilios Katos

Information Security and Incident Response Unit,
Democritus University of Thrace
skarayianni@gmail.com, vkatos@ee.duth.gr

Abstract. In this paper we challenge the widely accepted approach where a first responder does not capture the RAM of a computer system if found to be powered off at a crime scene. We investigate the presence of confidential data in RAM such as user passwords. Our findings show that even if the computer is switched off but not removed from the mains, the data are preserved. In fact, when a process is terminated but the computer is still operating, the respective data are more likely to be lost. Therefore capturing the memory could be as critical on a switched off system as on a running one.

Keywords: memory forensics, order of volatility, data recovery.

1   Introduction

Forensic analysis of volatile memory is a rapidly developing topic in the recent years [1]. The need to capture and analyse the RAM contents of a suspect PC grows constantly as remote and distributed applications have become popular, and RAM is an important source of evidence [2] containing network traces [3] and unencrypted passwords. However the RAM is captured only when the computer is switched on; in the opposite case the first responder would typically seize the hard disk and other non-volatile media which are further examined according to a dead forensic analysis process.

This paper has two aims. The first aim is to investigate the robustness and reliability of a method of examining RAM data of a system even when turning it off. The second aim is to investigate the feasibility of obtaining sensitive data such as unencrypted passwords from a practical perspective. In order to meet the first aim we introduced two definitions that will assist on structuring and studying the underlying problems.

The paper is structured as follows. In Section 2 the dynamics of seizing volatile memory are presented. In Section 3 the approach for capturing and extracting passwords and cryptographic keys is presented. Section 4 presents the concluding remarks.

2   A Measure of Volatility

The observation that the computer's volatile memory can maintain content for certain seconds even minutes after shut down of power supply, was made first by a team of

H. Jahankhani et al. (Eds.): ICGS3/e-Democracy 2011, LNICST 99, pp. 17–22, 2012.

researchers from the University of Princeton [4]. It was demonstrated that with the use of a bottle of compressed air one could freeze the memory and maintain its contents intact for up to hours. This indicates that confidential data such as cryptographic keys can be exposed.

Flushing memory is an expensive operation and not favoured by operating systems developers. Non-surprisingly, there is no correlation between the operating systems and preservation of RAM contents. The latter depends solely on the hardware and whether the computer system is connected to the mains when switched off.

Definition 1. Complete volatile memory loss is the state of memory where it is not possible to distinguish, for any memory address location, whether the stored value is a result from some past system or user activity.

The above definition refers to the complete "erasure" of the activities in a system – from a volatile memory perspective. Here erasure does not necessarily require that all values are zeroed out; in fact we are interested in the ability to distinguish whether a particular bit stored in memory was part of a particular process activity. Depending on the context of the forensic investigation, the different types of data may have a different weight in terms of forensic value. For example, in malware forensics, the data containing the execution commands of the binary will surely be of some interest since these will be used to extract the malware signature and footprint to be incorporated in an antivirus solution. In contrast, when investigating user activities – say downloading illicit material – the focus would be on the data area of the process. Nonetheless the need to secure the integrity of the data remains, and therefore in a complete volatile memory loss state any data recovered would not be admissible.

However as in most digital forensics cases it suffices to recover portions of data that are capable of proving or refuting a hypothesis therefore even if parts of the memory are valid they may contain the "smoking gun" evidence, or other pieces of data that may support an investigation such as passwords and encryption keys.

Definition 2. Partial volatile memory loss is the state of memory where for $m{>}0$ memory address positions their stored values can be correlated with past system or user activity.

It can be claimed that when $t{=}t_{shutdown}$ (the moment of deactivation of the computer) we have partial memory loss, whereas in time $t{=}t_{shutdown}{+}t_{off}$ with $t_{off}{\rightarrow}\infty$ we have total memory loss. The rate of memory loss depends on the technology of the memory and may also depend upon external conditions (such as temperature). In DDR type RAM there is no memory loss if the computer is switched off but connected to mains. This means that a first responder should enrich the widely accepted procedure of removing and making a bit-stream copy of a hard disk as follows:

Forensic acquisition process
System conditions: Computer is switched off and plugged into mains.

1. Remove power from all hard disks.
2. Connect/replace a DVD/CDROM with a liveCD containing msramdmp or equivalent tool.
3. Connect a forensically prepared USB stick to store the image
4. Power on the PC and configure the BIOS to boot from CD
5. Reset the PC and acquire the image

It is recommended that a liveCD is used instead of a liveUSB as the former is more widespread among systems and therefore it is a safer option.

We performed a memory dump in a very common scenario, where a user accesses facebook, gmail, msn and skype. There were dumps performed straight after closing the application, after 5, 15 and 60 minutes. The results are presented in Fig. 1. The charts depict references to application data over time.

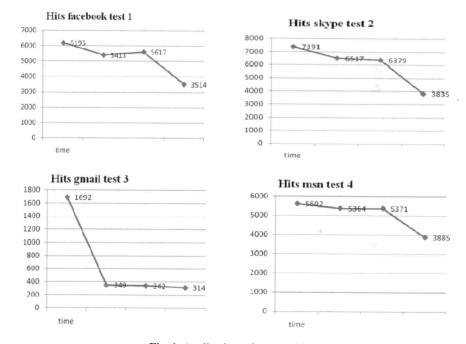

Fig. 1. Application references (hits)

An interesting observation is that the references are not necessarily monotonically decreasing upon the termination of the respective process. This is due to the memory management operations, virtual memory and swapping as implemented by the underlying operating system. Therefore although a user may have terminated a process, the information is not necessarily lost. In fact, in the event that the user shuts down the computer it can be seen that the sooner the computer is shut down (after closing the application in question), the more data are preserved. In addition during a forensic investigation, the population of the hits can be used to offer an estimate as to how long ago a process was terminated. This estimate can be improved by augmenting the proposed approach with other methods establishing the user activity in the system [5].

However, as shown in Fig. 2 the presence of passwords when visiting a web application (in our case Facebook), is less predictable. As expected after 60 minutes of logging out of the application and terminating the browser, the number of password copies drops, but surprisingly there is an increment after 15 minutes of logging out.

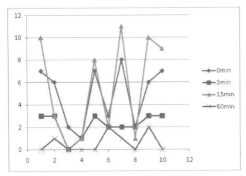

	0m	5m	15m	60m
Mean	4.9	2.2	5.5	0.6
Stdev	2.60	1.03	4.45	0.84

Fig. 2. Password hits and descriptive statistics for a Facebook session

3 Password Discovery

The images described in Section 2 were examined for passwords. It is highlighted that the corresponding applications were terminated prior to performing a memory image dump. This was done in order to cover the case of the computer being switched off or the user terminating the process as in the opposite case – that is when the process is active – all userspace data as well as metadata can be unambiguously identified through memory analysis tools such as the Volatility Framework [6].

To assist the analysis we developed a simple tool that combines strings, egrep and bgrep to search for patterns primarily as regular expressions in a memory dump image. The syntax of the tool is

```
totalrecall.sh <image_file> <pattern_file>
```

where image_file is the memory dump image and pattern_file is the file containing the regular expressions or hex patterns for the strings and binary search respectively. Our findings are summarised and categorised in Table 1.

From the above we can conclude that volatile memory loses data under certain conditions and in a forensic investigation such memory can be a valuable source of evidence.

4 Conclusions and Outlook

Against conventional forensic acquisition recommendations we argue that capturing memory should be performed even when a computer is found to be switched off at a

Table 1. Password states

Application/use case	Encoding	Detection method
Firefox 3	plaintext	Regular expression patterns.
		Gmail signin:
		&Email==[0-9]?{15}[a-z]?{15}%40([a-z]{8}\.)?[a-z]{8}\.com&Passwd==
		Facebook:
		locale=el_GR&email=[0-9]?{15}[a-z]?{15}%40([a-z]{8}\.)?[a-z]{8}\.com&pass=[0-9]?{15}[a-z]?{15}
		Hotmail signin:
		MSPPre=[0-9]?{15}[a-z]?{15}@[a-z]{8}.com|[a-z]?{18}[0-9]?{18}||MSPCID=[a-z]?{18}[0-9]?{18}
Firefox 4	Unicode	Hex patterns of the form:
		00.xx.00.yy.00.xx.00...
MSN	Plaintext in cookie	Regular expression patterns.
		MSPPre=[0-9]?{15}[a-z]?{15}@[a-z]{8}.com|[a-z]?{18}[0-9]?{18}||MSPCID=[a-z]?{18}[0-9]?{18}
Winrar	Plaintext	Indexed strings for dictionary attack

crime scene. This is because memory is not flushed during a system shutdown as this is an expensive and unnecessary operation which is avoided. In addition if the computer is connected to the mains, most of the data are preserved. The position that volatile memory should be considered as an unreliable means of storage when the computing system is switched off is of course valid. However, from a forensic perspective such a coarse consideration is not sufficient. Therefore we have introduced two finer grained definitions of volatile memory loss, offering a more suitable representation of the forensic value of the memory.

Provided that every case is distinct, the primary data gathered in the paper are relatively limited in scope as they were used as a proof of concept to develop the forensic process and submit the recommendation of conducting a memory dump of a switched off computer. Although that it is generally recommended that a memory dump should be performed, it is the first responder's judgment as to whether the memory is examined.

Another well known issue reinstated by this research is the importance of security considerations that need to be adopted by the application developers. Firefox for instance does not protect the sensitive password values. A possible solution could be to erase (zero out) any memory address spaces associated with HTML password type variables. Although these are expected to be protected during transit (through SSL) and they have to be in plaintext in RAM, they can be more ephemeral and be deleted as long as they are not required. Apart from the legitimate needs of a forensic examiner, many organisations have been affected nowadays from advanced persistent threats (APTs) and a malware can trivially perform a RAM dump straight after infecting a computer to speed up the harvesting of passwords.

Lastly, as part of ongoing and applied research a knowledge of different types of RAM chips and motherboard combinations should be developed in order to capture the volatility measurements, as data persistence in memory depends upon the hardware.

References

1. van Baar, R., Alink, W., van Ballegooij, A.: Forensic Memory Analysis: Files. Mapped in Memory. In: Digital Forensic Research Workshop, vol. 5, pp. 52–57 (2008)
2. Gavitt, B.: Forensic analysis of the Windows registry in memory. Digital Investigation 5, 26–32 (2008)
3. Adlestein, F.: Live forensics: diagnosing your system without killing it first. Communications of the ACM 49(2), 63–66 (2006)
4. Halderman, J., Schoen, S., Heninger, N., Clarkson, W., Paul, J., Calandrino, A., Feldman, A., Appelbaum, J., Felte, E.: Lest We Remember: Cold Boot Attacks on Encryption Key. In: 2008 USENIX Security Symposium (2008)
5. Carrier, B., Spafford, E.: Categories of digital investigation analysis techniques based on the computer history model. Digital Investigation 3S, 121–130 (2006)
6. The Volatility Framework: Volatile memory artifact extraction utility framework, https://www.volatilesystems.com/default/volatility

Applied Phon Curve Algorithm for Improved Voice Recognition and Authentication

B.L. Tait

University of Johannesburg, South Africa
bobby@cs.uj.ac.za

Abstract. The ability of a robot, computer or any man made system to understand exactly what a human, and who the human is that said it, is the focus of many research projects. IBM Via voice [1], and efforts in the Microsoft XP operating system, endeavoured on understanding what a person said. We cannot argue the fact that it would be fantastic if a PC can listen, interpret and understand what a human commands. However, this type of effortless, exact voice commanding is still only a feature experienced in futuristic stories like Star Trek. This paper considers a novel approach in improving the current voice recognition and authentication efforts in existing software systems. It does not replace or make any current efforts absolute. In this paper the way that sound essentially works is discussed; Research by Fletcher-Munson [2], [3] on equal loudness is integrated into a new voice recognition proposal, and implemented as a middle tier software algorithm. Considering the suggestions and findings of this paper, will serve as a stepping stone towards allowing man made systems to interact with humans, using voice commands. The application of this algorithm improves the false acceptance rate and false rejection rate of tested voice authentication systems.

Keywords: Voice recognition, Biometrics, Security, Phon Curve, Characteristics of Sound, Fletcher-Munson, Voice authentication.

1   Background

2001: A Space Odyssey is an old movie filmed in 1968 [4]. The central character of this movie is a central command computer known as HAL. The impressive feature of HAL, among many others, is the ability of HAL to seamlessly communicate with the crew on the space ship, using spoken word.

Interacting with a human in this way, today, nearly forty five years later, is still science fiction. Even if you really make a lot of effort to "educate" the software, the system will still often make the odd misinterpretation of what was actually said.

Sound technology, on what all voice recognition and voice authentication approaches are based, is in no way a young technology. The ability to transduce sound into electricity is based on magnetic induction, discovered my Michael Faraday in 1821 [5].

To store sound, analogue methods were first developed, which, among other approaches, physically etch the vibrations from the transducer, into a medium like tin foil, developed by Thomas Edison [6].

H. Jahankhani et al. (Eds.): ICGS3/e-Democracy 2011, LNICST 99, pp. 23–30, 2012.
© Institute for Computer Sciences, Social Informatics and Telecommunications Engineering 2012

Today, sound is digitized using a pulse code modulation (PCM) algorithm, to store or manage sound signals. An IPod is a prime example of a sound device relying on digitized sound.

2   Introduction

This section will briefly consider the building blocks of sound, which is used to identify sounds produced by humans.

2.1   Transduction

A computer system cannot directly interpret a voice commands, it must be digitally presented, for the computer system to work with the sound from this voice.

Thus sound must be changed from sound energy into electrical energy; this is done using a microphone. The first step is to present the sound as electricity (which is analogue in nature). The next step is to convert the analogue electrical signal into a digital representation of the sound. Once in digital format, software algorithms can be applied to process the sound, and analyze the sound. The process of changing sound into electricity is accomplished by two main methods [7], [8]:

Dynamic transduction relies on magnetic induction to generate an analogue electrical representation of a particular sound. A picture of a dynamic microphone is illustrated in figure 1. Essentially sound waves move the diaphragm which is attached to a voice coil, seated on a magnet. The sound waves cause the diaphragm to vibrate, vibrating the voice coil, which, because of the magnet, induces an electric current on the voice coil. This current is then sent to a circuit for further amplification (using a microphone pre-amp).

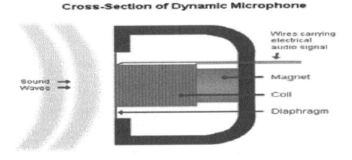

Fig. 1. Cross-Section of dynamic Microphone

Condenser transduction relies of static electricity to transduce sound into an analogue electrical representation of the sound. A picture illustrating the working of a condenser microphone is illustrated in figure 2.

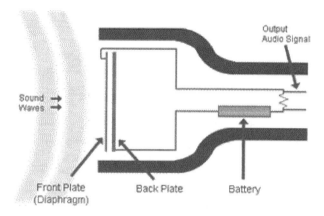

Fig. 2. Condenser transduction

In short the system relies on two plates to be charged with a static electric load. Let's assume that the two plates are charged with a negative static load. If the sound wave are to exert sound pressure on the top, thin plate (in high quality microphones, made of thin gold foil), the negatively loaded plate would move closer to the negatively charged bottom plate, causing electrons to flow through the circuit, thus once again creating an analogues flow of current through the circuit. The transduction is a very important part of the chain of sound production. If the microphone does not effectively convert all the sound signals to electricity, the transduced sound will not be a true representation of the sound that actually occurred. The biometric decision algorithm relies on very specific tolerances, to make the correct decision. If a low quality microphone is used, the false rejection rate is often negatively influenced. If voice recognition is the aim of the system developed, Condenser transduction should be favoured over dynamic transduction. The reasons for this, falls beyond the scope of this paper.

3 Sound Characteristics

Sound characteristics are the fundamental tools used in voice recognition; sound is composed of 3 characteristics [9] – Pitch, Dynamic range, and Timbre. Whenever a human speaks, these 3 characteristics will always be present, in fact for any sound that exists, these 3 characteristics will be present.

3.1 Pitch

As sound is cyclic vibrations, which causes a medium to vibrate, the cycle of each vibration is measured in Hertz (1Hz is one full cycle in one second). A young human ear is sensitive to hearing sound vibrations ranging from 20Hz to 20 KHz. The fundamental sounds that humans produce when speaking is roughly between 120Hz and 7 Khz (take note that there will be a lot more sound content produced by a human, but will be elaborated on, later in the paper). The more accurate the microphone can transduce the sound vibrations emanating from a human, the better the electrical representation will be of the actual sound.

3.2   Dynamic Range

The second characteristic is dynamic range or loudness. A human year can hear a wide dynamic range. The difference between the softest audible sound and the loudest is exponential in nature. If we assume that the dynamic range of two fingers brushing against each other is for e.g. a measure value of 23, then the sound of a rocket being launched should be around 4,700,000,000. In order to address this, Alexander bell devised the decibel [11]. Decibels are designed for talking about numbers of greatly different magnitude, thus huge deviation found in all possible values, such as 23 vs. 4,700,000,000,000. With such vast a difference (deviation) between the numbers, the most difficult problem is getting the number of zeros right. We could use scientific notation, but a comparison between 2.3 X 10 (23) and 4.7 X 10 to the 12th (4,700,000,000,000) is still awkward. In sound the decibel must be presented as a unit of specific measurement, for example decibel SPL (sound pressure level) or decibel Watt, depending on what aspect of the dynamic range was measured.

The decibel of interest in the paper is decibel SPL, which can be calculated using the following formula: 20 Log(Measurement A / Measurement B).

Where the measurement A will be the loudness of an initial sound pressure, and measurement B is the second, altered sound pressure measurement. According to this calculation, the Db SPL of finger brushing against each other will be close to 0 Db SPL (Zero Decibel SPL) [10], and the sound of a launching rocket will be around 140 Db SPL [10]. Normal conversation should be around 60Db SPL [10]. Take note that every 6 Db SPL will sound like a doubling of the SPL on the point of transduction (however, if Db Watt is to be considered, every 3db Watt, will be a doubling of for example current consumed or produced).

3.3   Timbre

The last sound characteristic is known as timbre. Timbre is also referred to as harmonics or overtones. Timbre is determined by its spectrum, which is a specific mix of keynote, overtones, noise, tune behavior, envelope (attack, sustain, decay), as well as the temporal change of the spectrum and the amplitude [11]. As this is the characteristic in sound, mostly responsible for uniqueness, this aspect of sound should enjoy the greatest attention, if voice authentication is to be considered.

Sound is only composed of vibrations (pitch) and loudness (dynamic range). Timbre is also only vibrations, emanating from the source. If we take for example two males, and we ask them to sing a A4 note (440Hz) at the same loudness (let's say 60 db spl), we will agree that the vibrations they both create is around 440Hz, and they both sing the same loudness, but they sound clearly different. Timbre is the reason for this difference. Timbre describes those characteristics of sound which allow the ear to distinguish sounds which have the same pitch and loudness. If any object vibrates in a medium, the object will have a fundamental vibration, but this is not the only vibration which will occur. A human's chest cavity, nose cavity and many other body parts will vibrate and resonate because of the fundamental vibration. The harmonic series is important in objects which produce sounds. The natural frequencies of the string mentioned above form a harmonic series.

A frequency is harmonic if it is an integer multiple of the fundamental frequency. The fundamental is the first harmonic (although it's generally referred to as the fundamental). The second harmonic is two times the frequency of the fundamental; the third harmonics is three times the fundamental, and so on. So with a fundamental of 100 Hz, the second harmonic is 200 Hz, the third is 300 Hz, the fourth is 400 Hz, or if the fundamental frequency is 25Hz, the second harmonic is 50 Hz, the third is 75 Hz, the fourth is 100 Hz etc. Due to harmonics, the frequency range of the human voice can run from 42Hz right up to 30Khz [12]. Often the digitizing process (PCM) will only convert 20hz to 20KHz to digital format.

4   Equal Loudness

Fletcher-Munson [2], [3] conducted research on the way that humans actually hear. They determined that humans hear frequencies differently in relation to other frequencies based on the dynamic range of the frequency. During their research, they tested many humans. Equal-loudness contours were first measured by Fletcher and

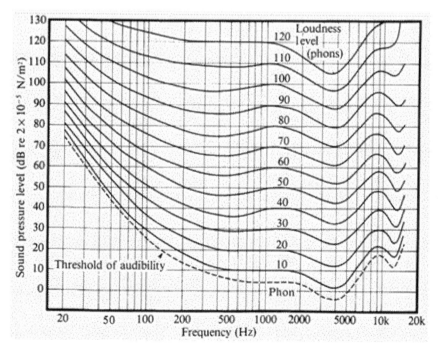

Fig. 3. Phon Curves

Munson using headphones. In their study, listeners were presented with pure tones atvarious frequencies and over 10 dB increments in stimulus intensity. For each frequency and intensity, the listener was also presented with a reference tone at 1000 Hz. The reference tone was adjusted until it was perceived to be of the same loudness as the test tone. Loudness, being a psychological quantity, is difficult to measure, so Fletcher and Munson averaged their results over many test subjects to derive reasonable averages. From this research they produced the Fletcher-Munson curve, illustrated in figure 3. The Fletcher-Munson curve is a measure of sound pressure frequency for which a listener perceives a constant loudness. The unit of measurement for loudness levels is the phon, and by definition two sine waves that have equal phons are equally loud.

Our ears do not perceive all sounds equally at the various frequencies or sound intensities. The sound levels for a particular sound as defined by the level at 1000 Hz will find the same for any given frequency along the curve. This indicates that our ears are less sensitive to low frequency sounds than mid to high frequencies.

The next section of the paper will consider the proposed application of the Fletcher-Munson curves.

5   Applied Phon Curve for Voice Recognition and Authentication

It is clear from the aforementioned sections that there are many factors to be considered when working with sound. During this research, presented in this section, the information presented by the Fletcher-Munson curves are used to improve the ability of software to recognize the person speaking, and to determine what the person said.

5.1   Factors to Note Based on the Fletcher-Munson Curves

Frequency spectrum sensitivity: If sound is transduced by a microphone to electricity, a decent microphone will not perceive any difference between for e.g. a 800hz Sound and a 4.5KHz sound. However, a human will clearly hear frequencies between 2KHz and 6Khz much clearer, and better than the other frequencies found in the audible spectrum.If a computer needs to "listen" the way humans interact, the computer must weight the importance of frequencies.

Bass frequency sensitivity: A second observation if the Fletcher-Munson Curves are considered is the fact that a microphone will not perceive any difference between the intensity of bass frequencies (roughly under 500Hz) and other frequencies.

During a test conducted in this research, it can clearly be demonstrated that if a microphone is supplied with let's say a 40Hz tone, set at 20 db SPL, the human will struggle to hear the test tone, however the microphone will indicate that a 20 db SPL signal is received. On a next test, a test tone of 1 KHz was used, also at 20 db SPL. To the human the 1 KHz tone was clearly audible. In both cases, there was no difference shown by the microphone, as in both cases the microphone register a 20 db SPL signal. However, as indicated by the Fletcher-Munson Curves, if the bass signal produced is of high intensity, the difference between bass and higher frequencies are not as much as in a the case of bass at lower intensities. If the slope on the bass side (20hz to 500hz) of the 20 Phon curve is considered, and compared with the slope of bass side of the 100 Phon curve, the reader will note that the bass side slope from higher intensities (higher Phon curves) are not as steep as in lower intensities (lower phon curves). The human thus struggles to hear low frequencies with low intensity.

6   Software Algorithm Developed

A software algorithm has been developed to apply the insight provided by the Fletcher-Munson curves.

6.1   Frequency Spectrum Sensitivity

The phon curves are used as a weighting system in the algorithm to adapt the system's ability to "hear" the way the human hears. Due to the fact that humans are unconsciously aware of the frequencies which we hear best, humans tend to accentuate the frequencies during speech. Humans tend to use different frequencies based on different situations. If a lady is in distress, she will use higher pitch frequencies to attract attention. Unconsciously we know that higher frequencies are heard well. This ability is programmed into the algorithm, to allow the system to focus on the frequencies for humans of note.

6.2   Bass Frequency Sensitivity

Secondly the algorithm adapts the loudness based on the phon curve detected when a speech signal is received. Thus is a person speaks softly, the system will expect that the bass content will contain less usable info, compared to a situation when speech signal is received on higher intensities.

7   Conclusions

In order to improve current voice recognition and verification systems, the process of converting sound into digital, should consider the way that humans interact with each other using speech.

Sound equipment provides a very clinical approach, and does not have the ability to listen to humans like humans listen to each other. Research done by Fletcher-Munson, paved the way to understand how humans interact with one another using sound, based on how we hear.

By considering two major factors, frequency spectrum sensitivity and bass frequency sensitivity, as interpreted from the phon curve diagrams, a algorithm was developed. This algorithm adapts the sound signal to ensure that the signal being sent for further processing resembles a closer match to the way humans actually communicate and authenticate each other.

The software is installed as a middle layer, between the digitizing software and he voice recognition software. Though the final statistics are still being evaluated, it was abundantly clear that the software managed to recognize spoken words a lot better, compared to the ability of the software excluding the phon curve adaption.

References

1. IBM Via Voice,
   http://www-1.ibm.com/software/pervasive/ embedded_viavoice/
2. Vitz, P.C.: Preference for tones as a function of frequency (hertz) and intensity (decibels). Attention, Perception, & Psychophysics 11(1), 84–88 (1972)
3. Fletcher-Munson Curves,
   http://hyperphysics.phy-astr.gsu.edu/hbase/sound/eqloud.html
4. 2001: A Space Odyssey (1968), http://www.imdb.com/title/tt0062622/
5. Faraday, M.: Science World,
   http://scienceworld.wolfram.com/biography/Faraday.html
6. The Inventions of Thomas Edison, History of the phonograph,
   http://inventors.about.com/library/
   inventors/bledison.htm#phonograph
7. Davis, G., Jones, R.: The Sound Reinforcement Handbook, Yamaha, 2nd edn. (January 1, 1988)
8. Earle, J.: The Microphone Book. From mono to stereo to surround - a guide to microphone design and application, 2nd edn. Focal Press (November 24, 2004)
9. Everest, F.A., Pohlmann, K.: Master Handbook of Acoustics, 5th edn. McGraw-Hill/TAB Electronics (June 22, 2009)
10. Speaks, C.E.: Introduction To Sound: Acoustics for the Hearing and Speech Sciences, Singular, 3rd edn. (March 1, 1999) ISBN-10: 9781565939790
11. Yost, W.A.: Fundamentals of Hearing, An Introduction 5th edn. Emerald Group Publishing Limited (October 2, 2006) ISBN-10: 9780123704733
12. Boulanger, R.: The Csound Book: Perspectives in Software Synthesis, Sound Design, Signal Processing, and Programming. The MIT Press (March 6, 2000)

Tuning the Epidemical Algorithm in Wireless Sensor Networks

Kostis Gerakos[1], Christos Anagnostopoulos[2], and Stathes Hadjiefthymiades[1]

[1] Pervasive Computing Research Group, Department of Informatics and
Telecommunications, University of Athens, Athens, Greece
[2] Department of Informatics, Ionian University, Corfu, Greece
`kostis@dtps.unipi.gr,{bleu,shadj}@di.uoa.gr`

Abstract. We discuss the networking dimension of the Integrated Platform for Autonomic Computing (IPAC). IPAC supports the development and running of fully distributed applications that rely on infrastructureless (ad-hoc) network with multi-hop transmission capabilities. Such environment is typically used for the realization of collaborative context awareness where nodes with sensors "generate" and report context while other nodes receive and "consume" such information (i.e., feed local applications with it). Due to its highly dynamic character this application environment, an efficient solution for the dissemination of information within the network involves the adoption of epidemical algorithms. With the use of such algorithms, a certain node spreads information probabilistically to its neighborhood. Evidently this is a rational approach since the neighborhood changes frequently and nodes are not necessarily in need of the generated contextual stream. IPAC mainly targets embedded devices such as OS-powered sensor motes, smartphones and PDAs. The platform relies on the OSGi framework (a popular middleware for embedded devices) for component deployment, management and execution. We discuss implementation issues focusing on the broad spectrum of IPAC services that were developed in order to facilitate applications. We elaborate on the networking stack that implements epidemical dissemination. We also discuss how such infrastructure has been used to realize applications related to crisis management and environmental protection. We present an adaptive flavor of the epidemical dissemination which expedites delivery by tuning the forwarding probability whenever an alarming situation is detected.

Keywords: wireless sensor networks, dissemination, epidemical algorithm, wildfire, epidemic model, forwarding probability.

1 Introduction

During the last few years advantage of WSN (wireless sensor networks) gave affordable and smart solutions to "real life" problems and situations. IPAC aims at providing all the communication functionality for fully distributed applications including medical monitoring and emergency response applications, monitoring remote or inhospitable habitats, disaster relief networks, crisis management applications, early fire detection in forests, and environmental monitoring.

H. Jahankhani et al. (Eds.): ICGS3/e-Democracy 2011, LNICST 99, pp. 31–37, 2012.
© Institute for Computer Sciences, Social Informatics and Telecommunications Engineering 2012

Following nature's example a good way of disseminating information over WSN are the so called epidemical algorithms and gossip protocols solving the underlying problems that comes with the lack of a secure direct path for the data to be delivered. In this paper we discuss the efficiency in information dissemination of IPAC platform in a emergency case of a wildfire. In such cases multiple factors can be used for understanding the state of fire and predict the spreading so the data to be delivered safely. We use a temperature vs time model behavior as an example to explain the spreading algorithms of IPAC project.

2   Wildfire Behavior

Before further explaining the dissemination of information we must describe the factors that are taken into consideration during the spread of a wildfire into a forest monitored from IPAC sensors. In such cases sensors measuring temperature are preferred from others more sophisticated, like for example heat flux measuring sensors, due of being inexpensive and more reliable.

2.1   General Behavior

According to [1] the temperature course of a wildfire may be divided into three periods:

1.   The growth period.
2.   The fully developed period
3.   The decay period.

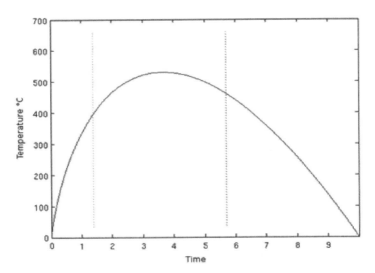

Fig. 1. Temperature produced by a wildfire versus time measured from a constant point. Can be used for emulation of the results that a sensor will receive while measuring absolute values of temperature.

These periods are illustrated in the figure below, where an idealized fire temperature course is shown. During the growth period, heat produced by the burning trees increasing rapidly to high values. After a certain temperature the fully developed period starts and then follows the decay period.

2.2   Wildfire Modeling

According to [5] a relationship between temperature, distance from flame and flame length is the following:

$$I = 300 \cdot L^2 \tag{1}$$

$$Q = 60 \left[1 - exp \left(\frac{-1}{300 \cdot D} \right) \right] \tag{2}$$

where I, L, Q and D denote fire intensity (in kW/m), flame length (in meters), radiation intensity (in kW/m2) and the distance from the flame position (in meters) respectively. Assuming a linear T = a Q relationship (with a=10 as inferred from [3] and [4]) we can establish a temperature distance T = f_L(D) relationship for any given L. On the other hand for large flame height, the authors in [6] have presented a model that estimates the net radiant energy transfer to a fire fighter standing at a specified distance D from a fire of a height L. It is observed that the larger the flame height the larger is the distance from the flame that would result to a specific heat flux (and sensed temperature) value. We can use this work to extract a T = g_L(D) relationship for large flame heights, L > 8m. It is interesting that the two different methods, for small [5] and large [6] flame sizes, produce approximately the same temperature estimates at the cutoff point of L=8m.

3   Adaptive Epidemic Model

In this section we introduce the concept of adjusting parameters of the SIS epidemic model for achieving efficient valid information dissemination in an IPAC WSN. Consider a discrete time domain, i.e., t ∈ N. We consider a IPAC WSN consisting of N + 1 nodes. Each node is indexed by an integer i ∈ N. The node 0 is the source, which generates and transmits data values. The node i = 1, . . . ,N is the (consumer) relay node, which receives, stores and forwards. Nodes disseminate data if they are within the communication range of each other. The source node 0 is equipped with a sensor (for our example a temperature sensor). At each discrete time instance t, the node 0 generates a data value x(t) of a contextual parameter (e.g., temperature data) from an attached sensor and a temporal validity value v(t) ∈ R. The parameter is sampled with frequency z. The υ(t) value indicates the maximum time-horizon that a value x is considered valid, that is, υ(t) = t_E − t. The υ(t) value decreases with time. A υ(t) = 0 indicates that the value x(t) turns obsolete at t. The source forwards the pairs (x(0), υ(0)), (x(1), v(1)), . . .) with a time–varying forwarding probability β(t) ∈ (0, 1]. Any relay node i = 1, . . . ,N, which receives x(t), becomes infected at time t once $\upsilon(t) > 0$ and forwards x(t) to its neighbors with constant forwarding probability $\gamma \in (0, 1]$. Since we have only one source, an infected node, which has recently received (x(t), $\upsilon(t)$), can be re-infected with some received (x(t+1), $\upsilon(t+1)$) at time instance t+1 since $\upsilon(t+1) > \upsilon(t)$, i.e., x(t+1) is more valid data than x(t).

We now discuss the significance of the forwarding probabilities γ for relay nodes and $\beta(t)$ for the source. A high value of γ and $\beta(t)$ leads to (almost) full network coverage (i.e., information diffusion among the nodes) but at the expense of increased energy consumption due to redundant transmissions –receptions of messages. For $\gamma = 1$ we obtain the Flooding scheme. On the other hand, low values of γ and $\beta(t)$ lead to a global ageing of information throughout the network, i.e., the consumer nodes receive (and process) information of lower quality due to the elongation of the time interval $\gamma - t_G$ (reception time-generation time). In addition, the delay of a received piece of information is measured as the time interval between t_G and the reception time at some node in which the information is considered usable. A consumer node relies on the last received piece of data (for further processing by the upper layers) until a new one is received. With a low value of $\beta(t)$ and a low value of γ a newly generated piece of information is received with increased delay. Hence, a random relay node is badly synchronized with the source. A relay node is considered well synchronized with the source if the time interval $(\gamma - t_G)$ is relatively small. On the other hand, synchronization is negatively impacted if the discussed time interval increases. Let us introduce a global error indicator e to clearly indicate the impact of delayed data delivery to consumer nodes. The error indicator captures the timed data value difference between the source and relays. Surely, the e indicator should be kept at low levels and can be adopted as a metric for the assessment of the proposed scheme. Good synchronization leads to a low e value while the opposite holds for poor synchronization.

Evidently, there is a trade-off between data dissemination efficiency and validity. Our idea is to adjust the $\beta(t)$ value on the source prior to injecting information to the WSN according to the data stream(DS) variability experienced there. The DS variability is quantified through the rate of change of the disseminated pieces of information. Intuitively, a DS of high variability has to be disseminated by the source with higher $\beta(t)$ than a DS with low variability. High variability in the DS is manifested through frequent changes in the observed (sampled) quantity.

A high value of γ for the relay nodes safeguards the rapid dissemination of information throughout the network. Distinct values generated by the source (with probability $\beta(t)$) reach the various consumers in the network rapidly. Hence the induced error indicator drops and synchronization improves. A low $\beta(t)$ value increases the inter-arrival time for data readings messages at relay nodes. Received values are not promptly updated and become stale and obsolete. Despite their ageing and expiration, such values can still be exploited by relays, since the DS is relatively static i.e., exhibits low variability. Apart from the discussed $\beta(t)$ tuning, another, closely related parameter (that still qualifies for tuning) is the time-to-live (TTL) of the disseminated data. The maximum temporal validity (TTL) of a sampled piece of information depends on the observed variability of the DS and the relay probability of WSN nodes.

On a high variability DS, the sensed data values have to cover the whole WSN in order all nodes to 'follow' the rate of change of the DS, which is experienced by the source. The proposed adaptive SIS model is entirely data-centric meaning that specific characteristics of the generated DS tune the propagation (dissemination) of information throughout the network.

3.1   The Adaptive Epidemic Model

We use the epidemic model in terms of the adaptive behavior of the source and the forwarding capability of the relay nodes. We assume that the WSN operation starts at t = 0. At that time all the relay nodes are susceptible and the source is infected.

3.2   The Behavior of the Source

Let $x_0(t)$ the temperature that is sensed by the source node 0 at time t. At time $t \geq 0$, the source determines the value for the forwarding probability $\beta(t) \in (0, 1]$ by taking into account the rate of change $\frac{\Delta x_0(t)}{\Delta t}$ of the sensed $x_0(t)$ value(the change of temperature). In addition, the temporal validity value $v(t)$ at time t, i.e., the TTL of the sensed data value $x_0(t)$, depends also on the variability of the temperature and the relay probability of the relay node γ as described later. We introduce the real functions f and g such that

$$\beta(t) = f\left(\frac{\Delta x_0(t)}{\Delta t}\right), f: \mathbb{R} \longrightarrow (0,1] \tag{3}$$

$$v(t) = g(\beta(t), \gamma), g: (0,1] \times (0,1] \to \mathbb{R} \tag{4}$$

The f $(\cdot)$ and g$(\cdot,\cdot)$ functions rely on the nature of the sampled DS $x_0(t)$. The following paragraphs provide details of f $(\cdot)$ functions.

3.3   Adaptive Forwarding Probability

In this section we discuss the characteristics of the f $(\cdot)$ function.

1. The f $(\cdot)$ function produces probability values (forwarding probability $\beta(t)$)
2. The f $(\cdot)$ function is increased in the interval [0, ∞) of the DS variability percentage change $\left(\frac{|\Delta x_0(t)|}{|x_0 t|}\right)$ The higher the percentage change in DS variability gets, the higher the probability of forwarding $x_0(t)$ to the neighbors of the source becomes. In such case the relay node I can reconstruct a DS $x_i(t)$ with high variability assuming a small e value. On the other hand, a DS with low rate of change can be disseminated with lower forwarding probability since the x_0 DS remains quite constant. The reduction in $\beta(t)$ reduces the transmissions for the sake of energy.

3.   The f (·) function should be tunable so as to treat the $\frac{|\Delta x_0(t)|}{|x_0 t|}$ values in a non-uniform way. In other words, the f (·) function should be able to assign varying significance to $\frac{|\Delta x_0(t)|}{|x_0 t|}$ ratio values depending on the application and the actual utility of the transmitted data value. In certain cases, a small change in the DS $\left(\frac{|\Delta x_0(t)|}{|x_0 t|}\right)$ can be regarded as noise and suppressed by the network to preserve energy efficiency while a significant change in the DS would be considered as highly important (e.g., an emergency alarm) and affect the f (·) value accordingly.

We adopt the sigmoid s-shape function (structured as shown below) as it allows the ad hoc, discriminative treatment of the DS changes as discussed above. Specifically,

$$f\left(\frac{\Delta x_0(t)}{\Delta t}\right) = \frac{1}{1 + exp\left(-c\left(\frac{|\Delta x_0(t)|}{\Delta t}\frac{1}{|x_0(t)|} - \omega\right)\right)} \tag{5}$$

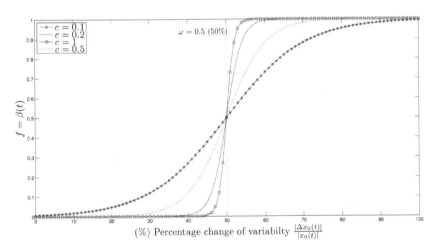

Fig. 2. We observe the different s-shaped graphs for the sigmoid f function versus the percentage change of variability for the different values of constant c. For c = 0.1 the graph approach a linear form.

The c $\in$ [0, 1] and $\omega \in$ (0, ∞) in (5) are the tuning factors of f (·). Without loss of generality, we assume that Δt = 1. The ω parameter is the 'significance threshold', which indicates the percentage change of the variability of the temperature, i.e., $\frac{|\Delta x_0(t)|}{|x_0 t|}$ that yields source forwarding probabilities greater than 0.5. The c parameter is a 'bias factor' that determines the shape of the f (·) function around the ω value. The higher the c the higher the rate of change of f from ω− to ω+ . Evidently, a zero value of c yields a constant f $(\cdot)$ = 0.5 function which is completely independent of $\frac{|\Delta x_0(t)|}{|x_0 t|}$ ($\beta(t)$ = 0.5). In this paper, we deal with a fire-detection application[8] . By inspection of the collected data, we noticed percentage value changes of the DS variability lower than 50%. Hence, we adopt as significance threshold ω = 0.5. In the unlikely case $\frac{|\Delta x_0(t)|}{|x_0 t|}$ > 100% appears in the DS, the $\beta(t)$ = 1 will be adopted as the ceiling value. In addition, we adopt c = 0.1. Such values are aligned with the characteristics points (3) to (5) of f $(\cdot)$ discussed above.

We applied the fire progress details found in studies like [8] and observed the way the $\beta(t)$ parameter fluctuates. Our findings are presented in the following table.

Table 1. Results of $\beta(t)$. Anything above 0.4 alarms the dissemination process.

Condition	$\beta(t)$
Regular Sensor Operation(Ambient Temperature)	0.3-0.4
Alarming Conditions(Possible Fire)	0.4+

4   Conclusions

The proposed scheme satisfies two important requirements for sensor networks in critical safety applications (a) it saves energy throughout regular operation, thus, extending the lifetime of the network and improving dependability and (b) is totally reactive to changes of the sensed environmental parameter, thus, guaranteeing the timely issue of alarms and the required follow-up operations.

References

1. Lie, T.T.: Fire temperature time relations. The SFPE Handbook of Fire Protection Engineering (1988)
2. Manolakos, E.S., Manatakis, D.V., Xanthopoulos, G.: Temperature field modeling and simulation of wireless sensor network behavior during a spreading wildfire. In: 16th European Signal Processing Conference, EUSIPCO (2008)
3. Stroup, D., DeLauter, L., Lee, J., Roadarmel, G.: Fire Test of Men's Suits on Racks. In: Proc. Report of Test FR 4013, p. 25 (2001)
4. Pitts, W., Braun, E., Peacock, R., Mitler, H., Johnsson, E., Reneke, P., Blevins, L.: Temperature Uncertainties for Bare-Bead and Aspirated Thermocouple Measurements in Fire Environments. In: Proc. Annual Conference on Fire Research, pp. 15–16 (1999)
5. Kurt, F.: Prometheus Fire Growth Model: Design and Incorporation of Spotting and Breaching of Fire Break Functionality. In: Post-Fire Research Workshop (2005)
6. Butler, B., Cohen, J.: A Theoretical Model Based on Radiative Heating. Int. J. Wildland Fire 8(2), 73–77 (1998)
7. Boccaletti, S., Latora, V., Moreno, Y., Chavez, M., Hwang, D.: Complex Networks: Structure and Dynamics. Phys. Rep. 424, 175–308 (2006)
8. Zervas, E., Mpimpoudis, A., Anagnostopoulos, C., Sekkas, O., Hadjiefthymiades, S.: Multisensor Data Fusion for Fire Detection. In: Information Fusion, vol. 12(3). Elsevier (2011)

A Robustness Testing Method for Network Security

Yulong Fu and Ousmane Kone

University of Pau and Academy of Bordeaux
yulong.fu@etud.univ-pau.fr, Ousmane.kone@univ-pau.fr

Abstract. In this paper one type of the security problem of DoS (Denial of Service) is studied and transformed to check the robustness of a multiple components system. The network components like attackers, normal clients and the network devices are modeled as implementations of the testing system. And by evaluating the system's robustness, the potential design defects can be detected. The methods on robustness testing of multiple components are studied, and a new model of Glued-IOLTS (Labelled Transition System) is given for defining this kind of multiple and networked system. Then a new approach and algorithm are given for generating the robustness test cases automatically.

1 Introduction

The Denial of Service attack is a normal way of network attacking aiming to crash the network service or make the network resource unavailable. If the system has some potential design defects, it risks to be attacked. As the networking becomes more and more complex and are consisted of different network components, checking defaults are more and more difficult. At the same time, the robustness testing methods consider the problem from the whole system view, and aiming to detect all the possible defects. If we take the system as a multiple components, we can transform this DoS defects checking problem to the problem of robustness testing for a networked and concurrent components.

The concurrent and networked components represent the components which are connected through some kinds of mediums, and communicate with each other to be a concurrent system to achieve some specific functions. While those networked components are generated by different manufactures and implement several network protocols or specifications which are defined by the organisations for standardization like IEEE, ISO...etc. However, different manufactures need their products uniquely and specially, and they will add or extend some functions to their implementations. And because of those expansions and augmentations, the manufactures strongly need to test their products conformance, robustness, and interoperability before they sell them to the market [9]. Related works- In [5] and [1], the authors considered the interoperability testing of two concurrent components, and proposed their C-Methods to describe the concurrent system, then derive the pathes between two components to generate the

H. Jahankhani et al. (Eds.): ICGS3/e-Democracy 2011, LNICST 99, pp. 38–45, 2012.

interoperability test cases. In [8], the authors do well on the robustness testing for the software components, they consider the robustness problems for the closed components by experience. They give a definition of the addition set LSE (language specific error) for "dangerous" input values, and use this "error" set in their "Path generation" to generate their robustness test cases. In [6], the author presents a method to get the extended specification which includes the considered "errors" to present the specification with Robustness. Our work is based on those forward works and go ahead to achieve the problem of robustness testing for the concurrent and networked components.

Our contribution is to extend the IOLTS (Input/Output Labelled Transition System) to give a definition of multiple concurrent and networked components, and then give an approach and algorithm for generating the robustness test cases. We consider black box testing, that is we do note care how the security mechanisms are implemented like in [2], but just whether they are correctly enforced by the network components implementations. This method can be used to design or examine the network protocols including multiple components and different network protocol layer. The method can also be used in the software testing domain.

The following sections are organized as follows: In Section two, we introduce the general testing theories and our testing architecture. In Section three, the formalism based on Labeled Transition System (LTS) is introduced, and our assumptions and approaches are given. In Section four, one case study of concurrent components using RADIUS protocol is given. And the Section five draws our conclusion and future works.

2   Robustness Testing of Concurrent Components

Formal testing methods take the implementations as block-boxes [10], which can be only observed with inputs and outputs. In a specification based testing, a test case is a pair of input and output, which are derived from the specifications, and are executed through the implementation by the tester. The specifications are described as graphs by some kinds of modeling languages like FSM, LTS, etc. The test cases can be taken as traces of the graphs, and the testing methods are trying to see whether the traces of the specifications also exist in the implementations [7]. When running the test case through an implementation, the input sequence of the test case will cause the corresponding output sequence. If the outputs are similar to the pre-defined outputs in the test cases, we say this test case running is successful, and we note "**Pass**" to this test case. Otherwise, the test running is failed, and the test case is marked as "**Fail**" [4].

The concurrent components refer to the networked system which has many local or remote components to work together to finish some functions. Those components are connected through some materials or mediums, and exchange messages and data through them. We considered this concurrent and networked components testing from a simple instance with only two communicated components. The testing architecture is presented in Fig.1. In a concurrent components

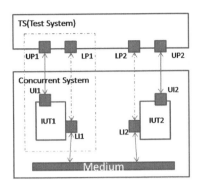

Fig. 1. Test Architecture

testing, each of the *IUT*s (implementation under test) has two kinds of interfaces. The lower interfaces LI_i are the interfaces used for the interaction of the two *IUT*s. These interfaces are only observable but not controllable, which means a lower tester(LT_i) connected to such interfaces can only observe the events but not send stimuli to these interfaces. The upper interfaces UI_i are the interfaces through which the IUT communicates with its environment. They are observable and also controllable by the upper tester(UT_i).

Robustness is the degree to which a system or component can function correctly in the presence of invalid inputs or stressful environmental conditions [3]. Robustness testing concerns the appearance of a behavior which possibly jeopardizes the rest of the system, especially under a wrong input. A system with robustness means it can be executed without crashing, even when it is used inappropriately [6]. We considered the specifications using IOLTS, which emphasize the input and output labels, and then we expand the IOLTS by adding the medium states and transitions into the definition to suit for the requirement of concurrent components.

Labeled Transition System

Labeled transition system is specification formalism studied in the realm of testing, it is used for modeling the behavior of processes, and it serves as a semantic model for various formal specification languages [12].

Definition 1: A labeled transition system is a 4-tuple array $\langle S, L, T, s_0 \rangle$ where

- **S is a countable, non-empty set of states;**
- **L is a countable set of labels;**
- **T is the transition relation, which $T \subseteq S \times (L \cup \{\tau\}) \times S$**
- **s_0 is the initial state.**

The labels in L represent the observable actions which occur inside the system; the states of S are changing just cause of the actions in L. The sign τ denotes the internal and unobservable actions. The definition of T reveals the relations between states in S, for example: $(s_0, a, s_1) \in T$. A trace is a finite sequence of observable actions. The set of all traces over L is denoted by L^* , and ε denotes the empty sequence. If $\sigma_1, \sigma_2 \in L^*$, then $\sigma_1 * \sigma_2$ is the concatenation of σ_1 and σ_2. $|\sigma|$ denotes the length of trace of σ.

Definition 2: An input-output transition system p is a labeled transition system in which the set of actions L is partitioned into input actions L_I and output action $L_U(L_I \cap L_U = \emptyset, L_I \cup L_U = L)$, and for which all input actions are always enabled in any state. If $q \in S$, then $Out(q)$ denotes all the output labels from q, $In(q)$ denotes all the input labels to q, and $Out(S, \sigma)$ denotes the output of S after σ. $ref(q)$ represents the input actions which are not accepted by state q.

3   Our Approach

As we described in Section 2, the concurrent components communicate each other through a common medium using their lower interfaces, and receive the messages from the environments through their upper interfaces(see Fig.1). We separated the states of each component which are directly connected to the common medium into higher_level states, and we use the low_level states to define the common medium.

Definition 3: The states of the concurrent and networked components system have two levels:

- **higher_level state s_i_u connects to the environment or other states of the same component.**
- **lower_level state s_i_l connects to the states of other components**

A common medium is a subset of the lower_level interfaces of the states, which stimulate the messages to other components. We make S_M to denote all the states in the medium, s_i denote some state in $IOLTS_i$, s_j denote some state in $IOLTS_j$ then

$$\{\forall s \in S_M \mid \exists s_i, \ \exists s_j, \ s = s_i\_l, and \ Out(s_i\_l) \cap In(s_j) \neq \emptyset\}$$

With the help of a common medium, we can glue the components together. We connect the medium states and the stimulated component's initial states with the same label as the medium state received(denoted as L_M). Then the different components are glued.

Definition 4
A Glued IOLTS represents a set of IOLTS $\langle S_i, L_i, T_i, s_i\_0 \rangle$ (i=1,n) and a medium M, which is a 4-tuple:
$IOLTS_{glu} = \langle S_{glu}, L_{glu}, T_{glu}, s_{glu}\_0 \rangle$, whith

- $S_{glu} = \langle S_1 \times S_2 \times ... \times S_n \times S_M \rangle$,
- $L_{glu} = \langle L_1 \cup L_2 \cup ... \cup L_n \rangle$,
- $s_{glu}\_0 = \langle s_1\_0, s_2\_0, ..., s_n\_0 \rangle$ is the initial state,
- $T_{glu} \subset S_{glu} \times L_{glu} \times S_{glu}$
  $T_{glu} = \{(s_1, s_2, ...s_i, ...s_m) \xrightarrow{\alpha} (s_1, s_2, ...s'_i, ...s_m) | (s_i, \alpha, s'_i) \in T_i \cup T_M \}$,
  $T_M = \{(s_i\_l, \mu, s_j\_l) | i \neq j, \mu \in Out(s_i\_l) \cap In(s_j\_l)\}$

One example of Glued-IOLTS is presented in Fig.2 of the next Section.

Robustness testing needs to take into account both normal and threatening inputs. In order to obtain all the possible traces in the concurrent and networked components, first we need to extend the specification to include all the possible inputs actions. We use the so called "Meta-graph" [6] to describe the processes of invalid inputs, and use the "Refusal Graph" [12] to describe the inopportune inputs, then join them to one extended Glued IOLTS: S^+_{glu} to describe all the possible pathes.

Here for a better understanding, we use GIB (Graph Invalid inputs Block) to describe the process of dealing with invalid inputs. By adding the elements of invalid and inopportune input actions, the S^+_{glu} includes all possible actions. We say the implementation of concurrent and networked components is robust if it follows the following conditions:

Definition 5
The implementations of a concurrent and networked components system are denoted as $IUTs$, S_{uni} represents the specification of the those implementations, then:

$$IUTs \ Robust \ S_{uni} \equiv_{def} \forall \sigma \in traces(S^+_{glu}) \Rightarrow Out(IUTs, \sigma) \subseteq Out(S^+_{glu}, \sigma)$$

According to this Definition, to check the robustness of the system, we need to see whether any traces in S^+_{glu} can also be found in its implementations.

So the robustness test case can be generated through the following approach:

- Analyze the compositions' specifications to figure out the concurrent system described using Glued IOLTS S_{glu}.
- Calculate the S^+_{glu}
- Calculate all the possible pathes of the S^+_{glu} to generate the test cases.
- Test Cases run on the implementation. If the implementation can pass all the test cases, the implementation is robust. If not, the implementation fail the robustness testing.

We give an algorithm in Listing 1 to calculate the testing cases automatically. We assume the "initial" states are reachable, and we define the "end" states as the states which after them, the system goes back to the "initial" state or stop. The inputs of this algorithm is the Extended Glued_Specification. The pair $\langle stimulate, reponse \rangle$ denotes the actions between different systems, and the function opt() in the algorithm is to calculate the corresponding actions in this pair. The algorithm uses two recursions to trace back the specifications from the "end" states to the "initial" states. The algorithm uses an arraylist "Trace" to record all the passed labels. When the algorithm reach the "initial" state, it uses the function $Check\_glue()$ to detect the actions inputs from the common medium. If it find that the passed traces need the inputs from the medium, then it adds the corresponding medium labels, and continue to trace back to another system. If it can not find the requirements from the passed traces, the algorithm stops this traceback, and continue to the next trace.

Listing 1.1. Algorithm

```
Inputs:  the  states  of  Glued_Specification  S,
          the  labels  of  Glued_Specification  L;
Outputs:  possible  trace  arraylists  trace [m];
int  k,m,n=0;
Arraylist  trace [m] ,  L_sti [k];
//trace [m]  records  the  passed  actions ,  and  m  represents  different  traces.
//L_sti [k]  records  the  actions  in  one  trace  which  will  stimulate  another  systems.
//k  represents  different  traces.
public  main (){
    ArrayList<state>  s_end ;
    For  (int  i=0;i<S. size ();i++){
        if (S. get (i). getStatus (). equals ("end"));
        s_end . add (S. get (i));}
    For  (int  i=0;i<s_end . size ();i++){
        Traceback (s_end [i]);
        For(int  j=0;j<n;j++){
            Check_glue (trace [j]);}
        For(int  j=0;j<n;j++){
            print  trace [j];}}}
public  trace  Traceback (state  s){
    ArrayList L= In(s);// arraylist  L  records  all  the  input  actions  to  state  s
    If  (s  is  initial  state){
        return  trace [m];}
    For(int  i=0;  i<L. size ();  i++){
        trace [m+i]. add (trace [m]);
        m=m+i ;
        n=m;// count  arraylist  trace}
    For(int  i=0;i<L. size ();i++){
        trace [m]. add (L. get (i));
        s=L. get (i). pre_state ;
        Traceback (s);
        m=m−1;}}
public  void  Check_glue (arraylist  trace){
    For(int  i=0;i<trace . size ;i++){
        If  (trace . get (i)  in  L_stiulate ){
            L_sti . add (trace . get (i));}}
    If  L_sti . size ()=0{
        return  trace ;}
    else {
        For(int  i=0;i<L_sti . size ();i++){
            trace . add (opt (L_sti . get (i)));
            Traceback (opt (L_stiulate . get (i)). pre_state );}
        For(i=0;i<m; i++){
            Check_glue (trace [i]);}}}
```

4   Case Study - RADIUS Protocol

RADIUS protocol is a network protocol between three basic components: client, NAS (network access server), and RADIUS server. The three components connected and worked together, to finish the handshaking and AAA (authentication, authorization, and accounting) security processes. This RADIUS system is a concurrent and networked components system, and we need to use our approach to check the robustness of the implementations of the RADIUS protocol.

Analyze the Specification and Construct the Glued_IOLTS

We take the client as one part of the environment, and in the RADIUS protocol, there are two components: NAS and RADIUS server are considered. Fig.2 presents the Glued Specification of the "Authentication" processes between NAS and RADIUS server according to the standard RFC 2865 [11]. The interactions τ of RADIUS server part represent the processes of security checking.

Calculate the S_{glu}^+ and the Possible Traces

By adding the GIB and the refusal graphs at each side of Fig.2 to represent the invalid inputs and the self cycles to represent the inopportune inputs, the S_{glu}^+ can be obtained and presented in Fig.3. In this case study, with the help of the algorithm, we got 17 traces by considering the invalid inputs.

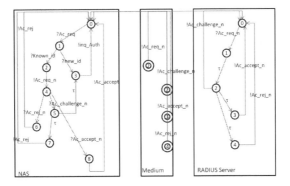

Fig. 2. RADIUS-NAS-Glued-Auth

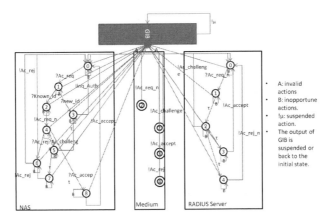

Fig. 3. RADIUS-NAS-Glued-Auth-Plus

Assess the Robustness of the Networked Implementations

After the generations of the test cases, we need to use those test cases to test the implementations. The implementations are tested by checking the outputs with the outputs of the test suites. If the outputs of the implementations are the same as the outputs of the test suites, the implementations are robust. We take the 17th trace of the results: {invalidinput, τ, τ, ?Ac_req_n, !Ac_req_n, ?Known_id, ?Ac_req} as an example. This trace of the RADIUS protocol implies the client(or hacker) sends an access request message(?Ac_req) to the NAS Server to ask for accessing to the protected network, then the NAS Server checks this user's id, and find it is an already known id(Known_id), and send a message {Ac_req_n} with the client's security information to the Radius Server. Then the Radius Server checks the client's encryption method, and find it is supported by the server(the first τ), then it checks the authentication of the client(the second τ), after this, the RADIUS Server receives a undefined message(invalidinput which is maybe an attack), and the system should terminate this session. If after we input this test case to the system, and find it does not terminate the session, then we know there is a potential risk which exists in the system.

5 Conclusion

In this article, we use a formal method to describe the network components and we extend the definition of Labelled Transition System to model the concurrent component systems. Then we give a definition of robustness of concurrent components system, and give our approach to the robustness test design. We also do an experiment to generate the test cases for the RADIUS protocol. We believe by modeling the network system, and checking its robustness, the potential security defects can be detected and then be fixed.

In this work we did not consider extra functional requirements like real-time constraints. For future work, we also plan to investigate the time conditions required in the network behaviour.

References

1. Ansay, T.: Compositional testing of communication systems-tools and case studies. Master's thesis, Concordia University (2008)
2. Boulares, O., Kone, O.: A security control architecture for soap based services. In: International Conference on Emerging Security Information, Systems and Technologies, SECURWARE (2010)
3. Castanet, R., Kone, O., and Zarkouna. Test de robustesse. In: Proc. of SETIT 2003 (Mars 2003)
4. Desmoulin, A., Viho, C.: Interoperability test generation: Formal definitions and algorithm. In: ARIMA-Numero special CARI 2006, pp. 49–63 (2006)
5. Gotzhein, R., and Khendek, F. Compositional testing of communication systems. IFIP International Federation for Information Processing (2006)
6. Khorchef, S. Un Cardre Formel pour le Test de Robustesse des Protocols de Communication. PhD thesis, University of Bordeaux 1 (2007)
7. Lai, R. A survey of communication protocol testing. Systems and Software 62 (2002)
8. Lei, B., Li, X., and Liu, Z. Robustness testing for software components. Science of Computer Programming, 879–897 (2010)
9. Malek, M., and Dibuz, S. Pragmatic method for interoperability test suite derivation. In: The 24th Euromicro Conference, vol. 2, pp. 838–844. IEEE
10. Offutt, J., Liu, S., and Abdurazik, A. Genearting test data from state-based specification. The Journal of Software Testing,Verification and Reliability, 25–53 (2003)
11. Rigney, C., Willens, S., and Rubens, A. Remote authentication dial in user service (radius). Tech. rep., The Internet Society (2000)
12. Tretmans, J. Conformance testing with labelled transition system: Implementation relations and test generation. Computer Networks and ISDN Systems, 49–76 (1996)

Economic Evaluation of Interactive Audio Media for Securing Internet Services

Theodosios Tsiakis[1], Panagiotis Katsaros[2], and Dimitris Gritzalis[3]

[1] Dept. of Marketing, Technological Educational Institute of Thessaloniki, Greece
[2] Dept. of Informatics, Aristotle University of Thessaloniki, Greece
[3] Dept. of Informatics, Athens University of Economics and Business, Greece
tsiakis@mkt.teithe.gr, katsaros@csd.auth.gr, dgrit@aueb.gr

Abstract. Internet Telephony (Voice over Internet Protocol or VoIP) has recently become increasingly popular mainly due to its cost advantages and range of advance services. On the same time, SPam over Internet Telephony (SPIT) referred as unsolicited bulk calls sent via VoIP networks by botnets, is expected to become a serious threat in the near future. Audio CAPTCHA (Completely Automated Public Turing test to tell Computers and Human Apart) mechanism were introduced and employed as a security measure to distinguish automated software agents from human beings. The scope of this paper is to present the security economics frame and to have an in-depth review of the related economic models of SPAM and its analogies with SPIT.

1 Introduction

The evolution of technological innovations for robust Internet Services must not only be efficient enough to solve current security problems at the technical level, but should also incorporate what in [1] is referred as economic implications of a solution's technical design. Today's Internet does not only comprise a series of fast-growing technologies, but it is an entire ecosystem of economic agents with monetary incentives and interdependence [2].

One big challenge is protecting services and resources that are provided through the web from waste or abuse due to the prevalence of malicious software running automated tasks, which is well-known as bot. Bots perform simple tasks that are repeated at a much higher rate than would be possible for a human alone. They usually infect as many vulnerable computers as needed for launching massive attacks against the targeted service or resource. The infected computers is said to form a botnet. In CSI's 2008 Computer Crime and Security Survey, computer security incidents that involved bots were ranked as the second most expensive with an average annual loss of $300,000 for each of the 522 surveyed companies.

The technology used for protecting Internet services and resources is the "Completely Automated Public Turing test to tell Computers and Humans Apart", widely known with the acronym CAPTCHA. A CAPTCHA is a type of challenge-response test trying to ensure that the response to a given challenge is not generated by a computer. It usually involves a server asking the service user to complete a test that is

H. Jahankhani et al. (Eds.): ICGS3/e-Democracy 2011, LNICST 99, pp. 46–53, 2012.

automatically generated and graded, but other computers are supposedly unable to solve. In effect, any user entering a correct solution is presumed to be human. A number of CAPTCHA generation mechanisms have been successfully broken by bots. Also, in [3] it is shown that if someone can employ workers for solving CAPTCHAs with wages no more than 50 cents of dollar for 1000 solved CAPTCHA it is possible to economically break this protection mechanism. The authors claim that this is feasible, since it is a work with no particular skill requirements and therefore is not too difficult to find many willing to do it.

SPHINX is a research project that aims to investigate the use of Interactive Audio Media as a means to lower the costs for provisioning adequate protection for Internet services and resources. SPHINX develops a service that will integrate the use of audio CAPTCHA with appropriate security policies that will allow adjusting the frequency of the resource demanding audio CAPTCHAs to the anticipated needs of a given security problem.

The economic perspective of the technology being developed is a fundamental research component and this article focuses on this particular aspect. In section 2, we place the security economics frame that we consider suitable for evaluating the economic implications of the developed service. In section 3, we provide an in-depth review of the related economic models. The paper concludes with a summary on the current findings and the future research prospects.

2   Economic View

Economics is the social science that studies how people and society decide and choose to allocate their scarce resources among alternative uses and get out the most. It is common to distinguish positive economics that attempts with scientific and objective epexegesis to attribute how economy functions (e.g. imposition of taxes will cause increase in product price), from normative economics that address subjective evaluation methods (deontological – ethical) to admeasure the efficiency of economic plans (e.g. a tax should be enforced in order to ban smoking in public places).

The economic aspect of information considers that dissimilar economic actors have access to different information and so information defines and determines differently economic choices. Economic organizations (especially those of technological sector) develop attitudes that set them in risks and those risks are carried over economy. This diffusion of risk from economic organization to economic organization and from economic sector to economic sector, deregulate economics caused by problems concerned with externalities. Externalities are side effects (external) that arise when actions of a person have effect on the well being of another person. In economics, we are concerned with actions that inhere value. Those in the process of a transaction are translated into expenses associated with an action that do not charge diametrically the relative one with the action people, but some other outside this. Decisions (of production or consumption) that a person will take have direct affect on production or consumption of other persons. Positive externality consist the benefit that people derive from market operation that they do not participate, whereas negative externality is the damage obtained and not recompensed in people that they do not participate in the production or consumption process of a market. Consider creating a college campus in a city. The value of the certain area will increase as it is upgraded and that causes a positive externality. On the contrary, if a city dump is created, then the value of the area will decrease due to the fact that the operation will cause damnification not able to be claimed [4, 5].

Network externalities can cause encirclement by creating a technological pattern that is difficult to replace. They comprise the consequences that a user of a product or service receives from other users that use analogous or compatible products or services. Positive externality is experienced when benefits consist of an ascending function of the number of other users and vice versa negative externality when benefits consist of a descending function of the number of other users. Security is characterized by positive externality. If I take measures at a personal level, I support/invigorate security for others as well as for myself. This discernment broach the subject of free rider problem as one of the classical cases of market imperfection or failure (here the security market). In the frame of this problem, users or private individuals (as individual entities) are not willing to apply security measures or policies, expecting from others to act or relying on others to assure their social welfare. Users partially invest in security as they do not run the real social cost of their actions, which cause negative externality [6, 7]. This application reveals the market failure and necessitates public intervention through regulations [8]. [9] describes the security process in transportation. Security consist positive externality for non users since it is offered to anyone and leaves them with no motive to act collectively, which is the cause of the free rider problem mentioned above. Namely, security is described in terms of marginal social benefits (MSB), payments for services are described as marginal social costs (MSC), while the marginal private benefits (MPB) are also taken into account. The societal optimum occurs where MSB = MSC (for simplicity it has been assumed that marginal social costs are equal to marginal private costs). The equilibrium is established at point F (social optimum) given a quantity Q* and price P*. Point F requires government expenditure to supply the needed quantity of security (Q*- Q), while private sector supplies Q units (Figure 1).

But why there is such a plethora of vulnerabilities? The answer is economic terms is given as follows. Software companies in case are not (economically) motivated to develop secure software and customers are primarily concerned for the price and the special benefits/characteristics. Hereupon, if a software developer is concerned with designing secure software, will have higher production cost and will need a longer period of time to circulate, effectively giving the chance to another developer that might be established and win the market by circulating sooner and faster rich in characteristics products.

Losses from security incidents emerge from inefficient security measures, human errors, frauds, system failures, exogenous factors (economical, technical) etc. Information losses can cause direct economic losses (quantitative determinable) and indirect economic losses (reputation, trust). Economic losses can be classified in several categories such as damage in operational function, computer resources, and human hypostasis.

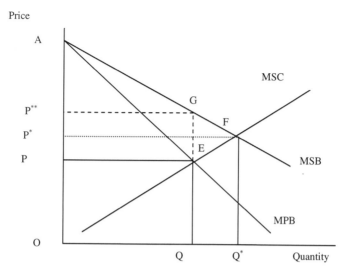

Fig. 1. Economic model of social benefits and costs

Economic analysis is the base of budgeting expenses (investments) in information security. Economic evaluation of security methods is necessary for the rationalization of budgeting/financing security actions. A first group of researchers aim to develop more practical methods to analyze, determine and quantify the optimal level of security investments in terms "what should I implement, what will it cost me and what will I earn"? Economic security metrics are concerned with how efficient a security measure is. Those methods include, Annual Loss Expectancy (ALE), Return On Security Investment (ROSI), Net Present Value, (NPV), Internal Rate of Return (IRR), risk management and focus on economic/managerial evaluation of security investments [10, 11].

The second group is based on classic economic theory, with methods such as efficient market hypothesis. In this theory every stakeholder should try to maximize utility and have orthological expectations in order for optimal investments to emerge, which should be escalated when new information arise.

Investments are divided into two key categories. Firstly in ex ante that aims in determine what firm intends to invest (total expenditure per investment plan). Secondly in ex post that analyze and measure the actual past performance (return achieved) of an investment. The first one consists in deciding whether or not to invest in one security measure or not, as to choose the best alternative solution from the available one. The second one can lead to precise observation and comparison of target. On the other side of security there is insecurity as a formal and not quantitative form of risk. There are several sources of such risk and in economy too. Insecurity causes cost to people and to investors that are risk averse. Economic theory reveals that economic agents who abominate risk prefer economic environment less insecure and are willing to pay insurance to limit risk [12].

3   Economic Modeling

One field for applying SPHINX with economic extensions is fighting Spam over IP Telephony (SPIT). Spamming activity comes from spammers (who create and send spam), but its effects expand far more, concerning Internet Service Providers (ISP), companies and users (receivers of spam), since all of them are stakeholders of this phenomenon [13].

Every economic actor, major companies, tries to achieve the maximum profit by maximizing sells and minimizing costs. Practically, this means raising the price of product – service and lowering expenses such as marketing that should be relatively low. From the moment that spamming has been used as a marketing method it creates benefits rather than cost. Consequently, spam will rise since as we mentioned before forms rational economic choice – behaviour [14]. The spam-based marketing method is also a little bit of paradox, because we all receive disturbing marketing calls/messages but few are those who admit to have taken into consideration those marketing calls and stepped forward to a buying procedure.

At the same time, we observe the enrichment of the content of spam and coinstantaneously maturation of anti-spam/spit tools-methods [15]. The basic problem is indicated in the limited perception we have in three parameters of value proposition of spam: the cost of spam, counterbalance of conversion rate, namely converting visitors/guests into customer and marginal utility (profit) per selling. Furthermore, as [16] suggests according to the subjective Theory of Value "reasonable people are likely to disagree about what constitutes desirable and undesirable content".

[17] mentions that spam makes economic essence, though the negligible percentages of responses that achieves, because it can happen, almost at no cost and that is the reason to be included in internet side effects (Net parasites). The parasitic economics of spam means that cost of sending a message is less for sender than for the other parties implicated in the process, meaning transferring to others the cost than to the sender [18]. While spam has no effect on spammers, for all other postulates a loss of time, disturbance, lost resources (e.g. bandwidth) [19]. How much does spam cost is difficult to quantify in terms of bandwidth, time and nuisance [20].

[21] refers that in order to understand the economics of spam we have to examine two models:

1. There only exists one spammer who has many recipients of his spam
2. A user (of email in his paper of VoIP Services for us) receives spam from many spammers and some other calls for us (emails in the paper)

Spam harmfulness is shown by [22] in three major ways by:

1. degrading user experience
2. containing malicious software that, when is executed, could destroy the computing system
3. transferring and discovering waste a significant amount of network and computing resources

[23] from user side, shows that internet users consider spam "objectionable" due to fact that it induce direct cost (security infrastructure) and indirect cost (information overload). The real financial profit of spam is aiming for the cost of sending spam against anti-spam techniques to be less than the return from the negligible response from recipients [24]. Comparably to e-mail spam SPIT network resources might be ten times more loaded and more obtrusive since the phone will ring with every spam call/message, anytime, disrupting users activity [25]. Companies are also unwilling to outsource their security to outside security providers fearing that they might not execute their services in order to shrink costs and increase their profit. In economics this called as moral hazard problem and depicts the disposition of companies to lower efforts as one part will go to capital [26].

[27] clarifies that many organizations evaluate and predict the economic harm of spam but the numerical data are difficult to compare because they include "different types of spam harm, computation methods and make different assumptions about economic data". He furthermore categories cost as "direct" if it is produced by just occurring and "indirect" if the harm is happening from operations or disoperation that result from spam. [28] also indicates that the existence of Spam directly and indirectly damages the economy. Spam damages production function, decreases labour productivity and the level of the GDP (Gross Domestic Product) [29].

4   Conclusion

Economic measures for solving spam mails are solutions that could be suggested and applied for securing VoIP services, which find application in voice CAPTCHA. Aim should be to find a solution that demands the minimum efforts for changing the way we use Internet services. The basic semblance of solving spam or spit comes from comparing the cost of sending mails with the cost of a telephone call [30]. Since a solution (countermeasure) is defined, the hardest part is to analyze whether benefits overcome costs. If the suggested solution is more likely to cause bigger harm than benefits, then in the possibility of market failure or of choosing not to do anything, this might be the wisest choice. Consequently, Cost Benefit Analysis demands considering the effect of economic motives at the same time with possible no intended results.

Economic literature often formulates concerns of regulating accidents as problems of minimizing cost. Accidents end in harm, economical or physical. Prevention and deterrence of accidents also involves cost. In order to solve the problem we need to minimize the sum of accident cost, prevention cost and also management cost (ex. by applying normative or law). For a CAPTCHA solution the problem is similar. Normative border/matrix and institutional framework/structure must minimize the sum of harm cost that caused from security incidents, costs of preventing incidents and costs of management.

Acknowledgements. This work was performed in the framework of the SPHINX (09SYN-72-419) Project, which is partly funded by the Hellenic General Secretariat for Research and technology.

References

1. Anderson, R.: Why information security is hard: An economic perspective. In Proc. of the 17th Annual Computer Security Applications Conference (ACSAC 2001), USA, pp. 358-365 (2001)
2. Zhao, X., Fang, F., Whinston, A.: An economic mechanism for better Internet security. Decision Support Systems 45(4), 811–821 (2008)
3. Motoyama, M., Levchenko, K., Kanich, C., McCoy, D., Voelker, G., Savage, S.: Re: CAPTCHAs - Understanding CAPTCHA-Solving from an Economic Context. In: Proc. of the USENIX Security Symposium, USA (2010)
4. Lai, F., Wang, J., Hsieh, C., Chen, J.: On network externalities, e-business adoption and information asymmetry. Industrial Management & Data Systems 107(5), 728–746 (2007)
5. Bauer, J., van Eeten, M.: Cybersecurity: Stakeholder incentives, externalities, and policy options. Telecommunications Policy 33, 706–719 (2009)
6. Shetty, N., Schwartz, G., Walrand, J.: Can Competitive Insurers Improve Network Security? In: Acquisti, A., Smith, S.W., Sadeghi, A.-R. (eds.) TRUST 2010. LNCS, vol. 6101, pp. 308–322. Springer, Heidelberg (2010)
7. van Eeten, M., Bauer, J.: The economics of malware: security decisions, incentives and externalities, Directorate for Science, Technology and Industry, Committee for Information, Computer and Communications Policy, DSTI/ICCP/REG, 27, Paris, OECD (2007), http://www.oecd.org/dataoecd/53/17/40722462.pdf
8. Vaknin, S.: The Economics of Spam, http://www.Buzzle.com
9. Prentice, B.: Tangible and intangible benefits of transportation security measures. Journal of Transportation Security 1(1), 3–14 (2008)
10. Ravi, B., Derrick, H., Qing, H.: A System Dynamics Model of Information Security Investments. In: Proc. of the ECIS (2007)
11. Böhme, R., Nowey, T.: Economic Security Metrics. In: Eusgeld, I., Freiling, F.C., Reussner, R. (eds.) Dependability Metrics. LNCS, vol. 4909, pp. 176–187. Springer, Heidelberg (2008)
12. Lelarge, M.: Economics of Malware: Epidemic Risks Model, Network Externalities and Incentives. In: Proc. of the 5th Bi-annual Conference on the Economics of the Software and Internet Industries, France, pp. 1353–1360 (2009)
13. Ridzuan, F., Potdar, V., Talevski, A.: Factors Involved in Estimating Cost of Email Spam. In: Taniar, D., Gervasi, O., Murgante, B., Pardede, E., Apduhan, B.O. (eds.) ICCSA 2010. LNCS, vol. 6017, pp. 383–399. Springer, Heidelberg (2010)
14. Allman, E.: The Economics of Spam. Queue-Distributed Development 1(9), 203–212 (2003)
15. Kanich, C., Kreibich, C., Levchenko, K., Enright, B., Voelker, G., Paxson, V., Savage, S.: Spamalytics: An Empirical Analysis of Spam Marketing Conversion. In: Proc. of the 15th ACM Conference on Computer and Communications Security (CCS), USA, pp. 27–31 (2008)
16. Kimakova, A., Rajabiun, R.: The Dangerous Economics of Spam Control. In: Proc. of the MIT Spam Conference, USA (2008)

17. Leyden, J.: The economics of spam, the register (2003),
    `http://www.theregister.co.uk/2003/11/18/`
    `the_economics_of_spam/`
18. Cobb, S.: The Economics of Spam. Technical Report (2003)
19. Petur, J.: The economics of spam and the context and aftermath of the CAN-SPAM Act of 2003. International Journal of Liability and Scientific Enquiry 2(1), 40–52 (2008)
20. Minto, R.: The economics of spam, Financial Times Tech Blog: Industry analysis (2008),
    `http://blogs.ft.com/techblog/2008/11/the-economics-of-spam`
21. Khong, D.: An economic analysis of SPAM law. Erasmus Law and Economics Review 1(1), 23–45 (2004)
22. Jia, D.: Cost-Effective Spam Detection in P2P File-Sharing Systems. In: Proc. of the 2008 ACM Workshop on Large-Scale Distributed Systems for Information Retrieval (LSDS-IR 2008), USA, pp. 19–26 (2008)
23. Plice, R., Pavlov, O., Melville, N.: Spam and Beyond: An Information-Economic Analysis of Unwanted Commercial Messages. Journal of Organizational Computing and Electronic Commerce 18(4), 278–306 (2008)
24. Chim, H.: To Build a Blocklist Based on the Cost of Spam. In: Deng, X., Ye, Y. (eds.) WINE 2005. LNCS, vol. 3828, pp. 510–519. Springer, Heidelberg (2005)
25. Quinten, V.M., van de Meent, R., Pras, A.: Analysis of Techniques for Protection Against Spam over Internet Telephony. In: Pras, A., van Sinderen, M. (eds.) EUNICE 2007. LNCS, vol. 4606, pp. 70–77. Springer, Heidelberg (2007)
26. Ding, W., Yurcik, W., Yin, X.: Outsourcing Internet Security: Economic Analysis of Incentives for Managed Security Service Providers. In: Deng, X., Ye, Y. (eds.) WINE 2005. LNCS, vol. 3828, pp. 947–958. Springer, Heidelberg (2005)
27. Schryen, G.: Spam and its economic significance. In: Anti-Spam Measures Analysis and Design, pp. 7–27 (2007)
28. Takemura, T., Ebara, H.: Spam Mail Reduces Economic Effects. In: Berntzen, L. (ed.) Proc. of the 2nd International Conference on Digital Society (ICDS), France, pp. 20–24 (2008)
29. Ukai, Y., Takemura, T.: Spam Mails Impede Economic Growth. Rev. Socionetwork Strat. 1, 14–22 (2007)
30. Nakulas, A., Ekonomou, L., Kourtesi, S., Fotis, G., Zoulias, E.: A Review of Techniques to Counter Spam and Spit. In: Mastorakis, N., et al. (eds.) Proc. of the European Computing Conference. LNEE, vol. 27, pp. 501–510. Springer science+Business media, LLC (2009)

On the Evolution of Malware Species

Vasileios Vlachos[1], Christos Ilioudis[2], and Alexandros Papanikolaou[1]

[1] Department of Computer Science and Telecommunications,
Technological Educational Institute of Larissa,
Larissa, GR 411 10, Greece
{vsvlachos,alpapanik}@teilar.gr
[2] Department of Information Technology,
Alexander Technological Educational Institute of Thessaloniki,
P.O. Box 141 GR, 57400 Thessaloniki, Greece
iliou@it.teithe.gr

Abstract. Computer viruses have evolved from funny artifacts which were crafted mostly to annoy inexperienced users to sophisticated tools for industrial espionage, unsolicited bulk email (UBE), piracy and other illicit acts. Despite the steadily increasing number of new malware species, we observe the formation of monophyletic clusters. In this paper, using public available data, we demonstrate the departure of the democratic virus writing model in which even moderate programmers managed to create successful virus strains to an entirely aristocratic ecosystem of highly evolved malcode.

Keywords: malware, computer virus, phylogeny, cybercrime, malware writers.

1 Introduction

Malicious software is one of the most persistent threats to computer users. Earlier types of malcode debuted at the mainframes [1, 2], but a substantial rise could be attributed to the proliferation of home and personal computers [3]. Computer virology was theoretically and experimentally established by Fred Cohen and his supervisor Leonard Adleman [4]. Since then, computer viruses and other parasitic applications have became a common albeit annoyance for most computer users. As a result a multibillion world market for security applications has emerged and soared since then. Europe spent more than 4.6 billion EUR for security applications and services in 2008 [5]. According to antivirus vendors more than 4500 new malware species appear daily [6]. The effective handling of such a large number of threats requires substantial efforts and resources, human as well as computational, in order to provide timely remedies and protective measures. As consequence the absolute number of malware species constantly increases and at the time exceeds 2.6 million threats [6]. The overwhelming majority of the malware is either proof of concept code or flawed malicious programming attempts. Only a small number of viruses and worms manages to propagate in the wild (or in other words to reach and affect normal users), and merely a

H. Jahankhani et al. (Eds.): ICGS3/e-Democracy 2011, LNICST 99, pp. 54–61, 2012.

handful of them had the potential to become epidemics or pandemics. Therefore it is necessary to prioritize the imminent malware threats and devote the appropriate resources accordingly. In this paper we analyze a large data set of the computer viruses and other forms of malcode, that have been seen in the wild and we evaluate the current landscape so as to identify current hot spots that should trigger immediate attention. We believe that through the understanding of malcode evolution, a prioritization of current threats is both viable and beneficial. By extending the well established Darwinian theory, we find that the small percentage of computer viruses which is capable to mutate and adapt to the environment, is responsible for the majority of the security incidents.

The rest of this paper is organized as follows: Section 2 summarizes the related work, Section 3 presents and discusses our findings, whereas Section 4 concludes this paper along with possible future directions.

2 Related Work

A number of analogies between biological and computer viruses have been revealed [4, 7] in the past and more recently [8, 9]. An important outcome of this approach is the realization that the monocultures are particular harmful for the security of the software ecosystem [10–13]. Most of the work, however tackled the evolution of the security mechanisms from the defenders perspective [7, 14–16]. A more aggressive strategy would focus on reconnaissance of the weak points of the malware development process through biological analogies. *Phylogenetics* is the study of the relationships between organisms based on how closely they are related to each other. Researchers have applied similar methodologies to investigate the evolution of software and malware in particular, either using manual methodologies [17] or automated techniques [18–20]. It is reasonable to expect that only successful viruses will have the chance to mutate and eventually to create phylogenetic clusters. Therefore the WildList is better suited to become the basis of an evolutionary study. Though there is no reason to believe that the actual number of computer viruses differs from the estimation of major antivirus vendors, there is a clear difference between the malcode that has been developed for proof of concept purposes, *in vitro* environments and the number of malware strains that can be found *in vivo*. Moreover even if a virus circulates, it is not expected to cause significant damage given the total number of viruses in the wild. In our previous work we examined the factors that contributed to the success or the failure of a worm [8]. In this study we decided to utilize data from the WildList Foundation to capture the malware dynamics that have been seen in the wild. This list is somehow arbitrary as it is based on a limited number of participants, but as we will discuss, we believe that it provides significant advantages over other traditional approaches [21]. Despite the fact that some antivirus vendors [22] and researchers [23] do not agree with the methodology used by the WildList, still in general *"it is considered as an authoritative collection of the widespread malcode and is widely utilized as the test bench for in-the-wild virus testing and certification of anti-virus products by the* ICSA *and Virus Bulletin"* [24].

Various AV vendors provide statistical data about the proliferation of computer malcode, paying more attention to the evolution of the malware codebase and the financial motives of their developers [6]. On the other hand researchers have focused on interviewing malware writers in order to explain their psychosynthesis [25–28]. These findings are important and useful, but have not been updated and correlated with the current trends. Our work shows that the development of malcode is no more a "democratic" activity, in which any individual with moderate skills (for fun, political, religious or other reasons) could develop a new strain of a computer virus and cause significant or widespread damage. Most modern malware incidents are the result of a few number of prominent malcode families which dominate the landscape and are responsible for most annoyances and damages. The rate of which improved versions of the specific families are rolled out predominates most of the malware activity.

3   Discussion

Although the current malware activity can be obtained through various sources, we deliberately choose to work with the WildList because we believe it represents better the observed malcode dynamics. According to their definition *"The list should not be considered a list of 'the most common viruses', however, since no specific provision is made for a commonness factor. This data indicates only 'which' viruses are In-the-Wild, but viruses reported by many (or most) participants are obviously widespread"*. In other words, this list contains the viruses, worms and other types of malicious software that succeeded to propagate sufficiently to be detectable, which clearly excludes proof of concept prototypes, academic examples, or ill engineered malcode artifacts.

The WildList employs an arbitrary naming scheme to identify malware treats which is basically the name most used by different AV scanners or the name given a virus by the person who first reported it. For the purpose of identifying malicious code of the same malware family we analyze the archives of the Wild List Organization from July 1993 till June 2010 and we taxonomize them according to their name. For example during January 2008 we identified several worm strains as members of the W32/Feebs family. This approach which is based on the categorization of the WildList is not as detailed as the manual or automatic inspection of the malcode using "phylogeny model generators (PMGs)" [18] so as to discern their phylogenetic characteristics. Nonetheless we find the method of the WildList Organization sufficient to correctly categorize most of malcode species to malware families. Another issue with the Wild List is the fact that does not provide absolute numbers regarding the malevolent activity of the malware species. Therefore we are not able to know the number of infections so as to categorize the viruses and the worms according to their virulence. As a result a worm with a single entry in the WildLight might have caused more infections than all mutations of a malware family. On the other hand the fact that numerous mutations of a malcode phylogeny managed to propagate to a wide scale so as to be included in the WildList is indicative of its capabilities to exploit a large pool of victims.

In order to proceed with the classification we used a small bash script to download all the monthly archives form the WildList Organization. A Python program stripped all the unnecessary content of the archives and a subsequent Python application identified the malware families and performed analysis on the data. Our applications processed 175 files containing 238474 lines of text which were eventually stripped down to 69820 lines of data.

These data were the basis of the analysis for identifying the current threats in computer virology. The first and most observable trend indicates an important clusterization of the malicious software to a small number of malware families. From Figure 1 we can witness that the percentage of the malcode species that belong to a dominant malware family does not show significant change in respect to the first available data of the year 1993. Though one can observe evident increase for some months after the February of 1997 as well as for the period of the last years (after 2005), the latest measurements show a stabilization of the dominant malicious activity related to the dominant malcode family around 15% of all the viruses, worms, spyware families that were found in the wild each month. Far more important are the findings if we analyze the trends of the three, five or ten most dominant families in conjunction. In that case we can observe that according to the latest data (January 2010) the three most dominant families represent now the 40.81% of all malware species that have been actively circulating compared to a mere 24.04% of the first available data at the July of 1993. The five most dominant families at the same period show a serious increase from 28.85% to 58.77%, where for the ten most dominant malware families we recorded a substantial growth from 38.46% to 77.42%.

The trends depict a significant change of the malware activity. Our interpretations of these findings agree with the work of S. Gordon [25–27], who examined the motivation of malware writers from a psychological perspective and that of S.Savage et al [29], which focused on the economic initiatives that drive the proliferation of computer crimes through the development and the maintenance of botnets. The earliest data (1993) depict a number of different malware strains that managed to propagate sufficiently so as to be included to the WildList. This trend eventually fades out as very few dominant malware families and their respective members represent the vast majority of the viruses that succeed to circulate at large. Therefore it is not as easy for a malicious entity to develop a new virus, worm or spyware as it used to be fifteen years ago. On the contrary one has much better chances to achieve widespread infection using a modified or extended version of a well maintained malware family. Based on the data analysis, an extended view of the malicious software landscape is available in Figure 2. Unfortunately, due to space limitations we had to include only the viruses, worms, spyware and bots that had more than 100 entries in the WildList in total and hence Figure 2 contains only 97 from the 821 malicious applications that were identified in the WildList.

Further analysis of the data indicates that the top ten malware families account for the 37.4% of the 817 total incidents that have been recorded in the WildList, while the top ten malware species are responsible for the 48.5% of all the incidents. In other words ten malware phylogenetic clusters are accountable for half of the cases that formulate the WildList so far. The common characteristic of the top ten entrants is that they have caused widespread problems and are also well known for their ability to mutate rapidly.

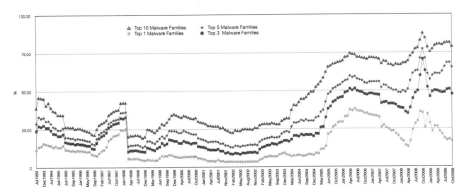

Fig. 1. Percentage of malware incidents attributed to top malcode families

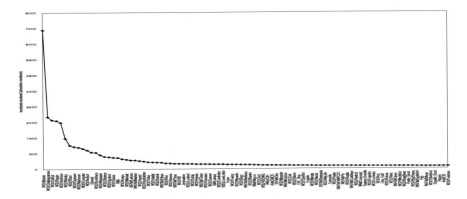

Fig. 2. Dominant Malware in the WildList

The implications of these findings are important as they suggest that most of the viruses, worms, spyware, do not manage to propagate in the wild and remain *in vitro* samples of malicious code. Even the malcode that manages to infect a sufficient number of victims so as to be included in the WildList, either mutates and evolves rapidly, or eventually diminishes and vanishes. Therefore only well written malcode, which offers high degree of upgradability or can be easily mutated, has improved chances to survive in the wild for a sufficient period.

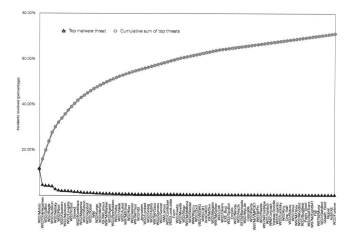

Fig. 3. Top family per month

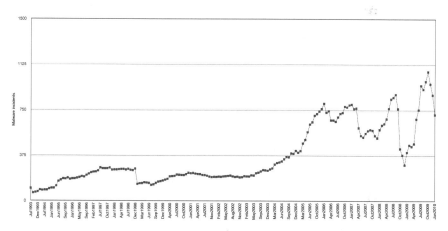

Fig. 4. Number of incidents per month

4 Future Work and Concluding Remarks

Our analysis is targeted to identify the dominant malware phylogenetic clusters and to indicate via statistical means that virus writing has become a professional activity in which amateurs with moderate skills are no more eligible to participate. Of course the available data of the WildList Organization could reveal other significant characteristics of computer virology. Our intention is to work in the future towards the prediction of the imminent threats by implementing econometric models and technical analysis on security data. Specifically, known models such as AR, MA and ARMA could be used to predict future threats depending on past data by finding self-similarities and periodicity.

The latest highly sophisticated malcode of the largest malware families indicates an escalation of the security arms race between malware writers and security researchers. The analysis of the WildList data emphasizes on the fact that malware writing is not any longer a trivial task. Gone are the days when disgruntled teenagers, activists or college dropouts could wreak havoc using simplistic programing tricks and earn their 15 minutes of fame. Competent malware should be able to mutate rapidly so as to propagate sufficiently and overcome the creation of effective signatures and evade other security mechanisms. The available data on the other hand signalize that the spreading of a virus or a worm in a wide scale is far from a trivial task. Therefore from a malware perspective it is better to work on a well maintained malicious code base than to develop new virus strain from scratch. Security professionals might found more promising an approach which prioritizes and concentrates their efforts against the most dominant malware phylogenies rather than trying to neutralize an overwhelming number of threats. For that reason if the available recourses are not adequate, it would be more productive for the research community to focus on the largest malware families, to monitor closely all the related developments and disseminate as fast as possible any findings of this activity. For years malcode developers exploit the monoculture weakness of modern IT in order to perform their vicious acts. By turning our attention to the most common and widely used malcode, we can exploit their tactics for our benefit.

References

1. Ferbrache, D.: A Pathology of Computer Viruses. Springer, NY (1992)
2. Szor, P.: The Art of Computer Virus Research and Defense. Addison-Wesley, Upper Saddle River (2005)
3. Skoudis, E.: Malware: Fighting Malicious Code, 6th edn. Computer Networking and Distributed Systems. Prentice Hall, NJ (2004)
4. Cohen, F.: Computer Viruses: Theory and Experiments. In: Proceedings of the 7th National Security Conference, pp. 240–263 (1984)
5. Anderson, R., Böhme, R., Clayton, R., Moore, T.: Security Economics and the Internal Market. Technical report, European Network and information Security Agency (ENISA) (2008)
6. Turner, D., Blackbird, J., Low, M.K., Adams, T., McKinney, D., Entwisle, S., Wueest, M.L.C., Wood, P., Bleaken, D., Ahmad, G., Kemp, D., Samnani, A.: Symantec Global Internet Security Threat Report. Trends for 2008. Technical report, Symantec (2009)
7. Forrest, S., Hofmeyr, S., Somayaji, A.: Computer Immunology. Communications of the ACM 40(10), 88–96 (1997)
8. Vlachos, V., Spinellis, D., Androutsellis-Theotokis, S.: Biological Aspects of Computer Virology. LNICST, vol. 26, pp. 209–219 (2010)
9. Li, J., Knickerbocker, P.: Functional Similarities Between Computer Worms and Bilogical Pathogens. Computers & Security 26, 338–347 (2007)
10. Geer, D.: Monoculture on the Back of the Envelope. Login 30(6), 6–8 (2005)
11. Goth, G.: Addressing the Monoculture. IEEE Security & Privacy 1(6), 8–10 (2003)

12. Geer, D., Bace, R., Gutmann, P., Metzger, P., Pfleeger, C.P., Quarterman, J.S., Schneier, B.: Cyber Insecurity: The Cost of Monopoly. Technical report, Computer & Communications Industry Association (2003)
13. Geer, D.: The Evolution of Security. ACM Queue, 31–35 (2007)
14. Somayaji, A., Hofmeyr, S., Forrest, S.: Principles of a Computer Immune System. In: Meeting on New Security Paradigms, September 23-26, pp. 75–82. ACM, Langdale (1997)
15. Anagnostakis, K., Greenwald, M., Ioannidis, S., Keromytis, A., Li, D.: A Cooperative Immunization System for an Untrusting Internet. In: Proceedings of the 11th IEEE International Conference on Networks (ICON), pp. 403–408 (2003)
16. Sidiroglou, S., Keromytis, A.: A Network Worm Vaccine Architecture. In: IEEE International Workshops on Enabling Technologies: Infrastructure for Collaborative Enterprises (WETICE), Workshop on Enterprise Security, Linz, Austria (2003)
17. de la Cuadra, F.: The Geneology of Malware. Network Security, 17–20 (2007)
18. Hayes, M., Walenstein, A., Lakhotia, A.: Evaluation of Malware Phylogeny Modelling Systems Using Automated Variant Generation. Journal in Computer Virology 5(4), 335–343 (2009)
19. Karim, M., Walenstein, A., Lakhotia, A., Parida, L.: Malware Phylogeny Using Permutations of Code. Journal in Computer Virology 1(1), 13–23 (2005)
20. Seewald, A.K.: Towards Automating Malware Classification and Characterization. In: Konferenzband der 4. Jahrestagung des Fachbereichs Sicherheit der Gesellschaft für Informatik (German-Language Proceedings), Saarbrücken, pp. 291–302 (2008)
21. Gordon, S.: What is Wild? In: Proceedings of the 20th National Information Systems Security Conference (1997)
22. Bustamante, P.: The Disconnect Between the WildList and Reality. Technical report, PandaLabs (2007)
23. Marx, A., Dessman, F.: The WildList is Dead, Long Live the WildList! In: Virus Bulletin Conference, pp. 136–146 (2007)
24. The WildList Organization International: Wildlist, http://www.wildlist.org/WildList/201001.htm
25. Gordon, S.: Inside the Mind of Dark Avenger. In: Virus News International (1993)
26. Gordon, S.: Generic Virus Writer. In: 4th International Virus Bulletin Conference, Jersey, UK (1994)
27. Gordon, S.: Generic Virus Writer II. In: 6th International Virus Bulletin Conference, Brighton, UK (1996)
28. Gordon, S.: Understanding the adversary. IEEE Security & Privacy 4(5), 67–70 (2006)
29. Kanich, C., Kreibich, C., Levchenko, K., Enright, B., Voelker, G., Paxson, V., Savage, S.: Spamalytics: an empirical analysis of spam marketing conversion. Commun. ACM 52(9), 99–107 (2009)

PINEPULSE: A System to PINpoint and Educate Mobile Phone Users with Low Security

Iosif Androulidakis[1] and Gorazd Kandus[2]

[1] Jožef Stefan International Postgraduate School
Jamova 39, Ljubljana SI-1000, Slovenia
sandro@noc.uoi.gr
[2] Department of Communication Systems, Jožef Stefan Institute
Jamova 39, Ljubljana SI-1000, Slovenia
gorazd.kandus@ijs.si

Abstract. The threats mobile phone users face, are about to increase due to the rapid penetration of advanced smartphone devices and the growing Internet access using them. As such, reinforcing users' security has become a critical imperative. This paper refers to a system that pinpoints and informs mobile phone users that have a low security level, thus helping them protect themselves. The system consists of software-application, installed in mobile phones as well as of software and data bases, installed in the mobile telephony operators' servers. Mobile telephony providers (by adopting this application), as well as manufacturers (by pre-installing it in their phones), could help mitigate the increased security threats effectively protecting the end users.

Keywords: Mobile phones security, User Education, Security Enhancing Application, User Profiling, Behavior Modeling.

1   Introduction

Mobile devices are becoming a critical component of the digital economy, a style statement and useful communication device, a vital part of daily life for billions of people around the world. The threats mobile phone users face, are about to increase due to the rapid penetration of advanced smartphone devices and the growing Internet access using them [1]. Mobile ubiquitous services pose great security challenges [2] while mobile phones are used from both experienced and security savvy users as well as from people that do not pay that much attention to security issues. All of them must be protected from unauthorized third party access to their data and from economic frauds. Since users' alone can't cope with this task, operators and handset manufacturers have to take extra security measures and to educate users.. The best way to deal with the problem, however, is by educating users.

2   Related Work

As previous work has shown [3][4], users exhibit different levels of knowledge in regards to security. A study of mobile users focusing on their awareness and concerns

H. Jahankhani et al. (Eds.): ICGS3/e-Democracy 2011, LNICST 99, pp. 62–66, 2012.

related to security threats, from security vendor McAfee, indicated that more than three quarters of respondents don't have any security at all [5]. In other words, despite of acknowledging the wealth of threats - ranging from phishing scams to viruses - that could impact them (including concerns about losing or having their phone or personal data stolen [6][7][8]), users don't see security strengthening of their phone as a critical concern.

In addition to the above, mobile security is not considered a critical issue by companies. Cell phone security for enterprise devices is seriously lacking, and a little misunderstood as well [9], while the majority of companies do not have a security policy that addresses mobile devices [10]. However, some initiatives are taken in the direction of protecting mobile phones against threats like viruses policies, tools and recruiting technically skilled personnel [11]. In regards to awareness systems, there have been efforts to create a sense of accountability in a world of invisible services that we will be comfortable living in and interacting with [12] as well as mechanisms for managing security and privacy in pervasive computing environments [13] but they still focus mostly in privacy issues and not actual security enhancement through education. In any case there are also significant legal issues as presented in [14].

It is more than clear that the mobile security area is going to be the next battleground since mobile security is an emerging discipline within information security arena and security levels are not high enough [15]. While users are not receiving proper cyber security and training education from schools [16], they are lacking the security awareness and proper etiquette [17]. This presents a vast opportunity for carriers and service providers to play a proactive and strategic role in protecting their subscribers, both through education and also through the security software they deploy across their networks, as is the case presented in this paper. Indeed, thanks to the system described in the following sections, these specific user categories can easily be pinpointed and presented with the right amount of information and dialogs [18] to restore their security level.

3   System's Architecture and Functions

The system consists of an application, installed in mobile phones and software and data bases, installed in mobile operators' main servers. These applications communicate through the mobile telephony network in a ciphered way. The mobile phone installed application (with minor differences in the array of services offered) would be able to function in all kind of devices that have an advanced operating system (e.g. Windows Mobile, Symbian, Android, iOS). A lighter version could also be implemented for older and simple devices using J2ME (Java 2 Micro Edition).

Three main functions are performed by the system. The first function allows pinpointing users, who have a low security level in their mobile phone, for whatever reason. The second function automatically suggests the proper methods, actions and best practices the user has to follow in order to restore security in a higher level. Finally, the third function, allows the encrypted communication and data exchange, between mobile devices and provider's servers.

The device's security level evaluation function can be implemented automatically, manually or with a combination of the two. Using the automatic method, the application transparently examines device's settings and informs the user for those that are in a state possessing security risk. In addition, by addressing questions to the user, the manual method, can check aspects of his behavior that do not reflect directly to the device's settings. Furthermore, the user is asked for his subjective opinion on how secure he feels his mobile is. As it is proven in previous work [14][3][4] users can be grouped in specific security categories, based on demographical and other behavioral elements as well as on the way of using their mobile phones. Results from both the manual and the automatic method are transferred to the applications in the server, where using artificial neural networks and rules, conclusions are extracted for the specific combination of user – mobile phone. Respectively, the answers to proper questions that examine the security practices that users follow, can lead to a security behavioral prediction model of the users. It is also possible to record the hour where changes of security influencing settings take place, as to provide one more element that can help the security model.

The system maintains data bases from studies in large user categories that provide the proper body for the system's training. These data bases are constantly updated with the results and the metrics from the system's operations. Finally, a very important function is the comparison of automated metrics to the user's answers, through which can be determined whether the user actually knows and applies the security measures or not. For this purpose, we use two metrics as awareness and security indicators: The mean actual awareness value (MAAV) and the mean actual security value (MASV), as described in [19]. These two methods, the automatic detection of settings and the conclusions extraction based on user's answers, complete the first stage of evaluating the security level.

At the second stage, the system implements the functionality of informing the user. Examining the current state and user's profile, the application suggests proper methods, actions and best practices the user has to follow in order to restore (if needed) the security in a higher level. If the device allows it and if the user accepts it, device settings can automatically be changed. Depending on the device functionality, instructions are presented to the user, either as a simple text documents or as multimedia material. The user can also configure different graphical user interface and setup elements as customization is a critical issue for software acceptance [20].

For the proper operation of the system, encrypted communication and date exchange between the device's application and the servers of the provider's network takes place. This communication is essential for off-loading the resource intensive neural network classification to the servers, instead of running it in the mobile device. In that way, the mobile device only records settings and the whole process takes place in the servers. Moreover, this communication allows not only the disposal of new multimedia material whenever is available, but also the enrichment of the manual evaluation method with new questions when new scientific data are presented. It can also upgrade the application itself, so that it can examine and locate a greater array of mobile phone's settings that reflect to its security. In any case, the communication takes place in a ciphered way so that interception is not possible.

4   Conclusion

By using this simple to implement system and the powerful data mining and modeling techniques of the underlying scientific principles it is possible to achieve a high security level, minimizing the risk factor attributed to the users. Bad security practices and risky usage are immediately pinpointed. In addition, user profiling and behavior prediction models based on the data gathered allow to further focus security efforts to those users that mostly need them. In any case the educational aspect of the application, using multimedia material improves users' overall security level, leading to greater security feeling and as such increased mobile phone usage.

References

1. comScore M: Metrics: Smarter phones bring security risks: Study (2008)
2. Leung, A., Sheng, Y., Cruickshank, H.: The security challenges for mobile ubiquitous services. Information Security Technical Report 12(3), 162–171 (2007)
3. Androulidakis, I., Kandus, G.: A Survey on Saving Personal Data in the Mobile Phone. Proceedings of Sixth International Conference on Availability, Reliability and Security (ARES 2011), pp. 633–638 (2011)
4. Allam, S.: Model to measure the maturity of smartphone security at software consultancies. Thesis. University of Fort Hare (2009)
5. McAfee: Mobile Security Report 2008 (2008)
6. Trend Micro: Smartphone Users Oblivious to Security. Trend Micro survey (2009)
7. CPP: Mobile phone theft hotspots. CPP survey (2010)
8. ITwire: One-third of Aussies lose mobile phones: survey. ITwire article (2010)
9. ABI Research, Study: Enterprises Need to Address Cell Phone Security (2009)
10. TechRepublic: Survey respondents say companies are lax on mobile security. TechRepublic article (2007)
11. Darkreading: Survey: 54 Percent Of Organizations Plan To Add Smartphone Antivirus This Year. Darkreading article (2010)
12. Langheinrich, M.: A Privacy Awareness System for Ubiquitous Computing Environments. In: Borriello, G., Holmquist, L.E. (eds.) UbiComp 2002. LNCS, vol. 2498, pp. 237–245. Springer, Heidelberg (2002)
13. Cornwell, J., Fette, I., Hsieh, G., Prabaker, M., Rao, J., Tang, K., Vaniea, K., Bauer, L., Cranor, L., Hong, J., McLaren, B., Reiter, M., Sadeh, N.: User-Controllable Security and Privacy for Pervasive Computing. In: Eighth IEEE Workshop on Mobile Computing Systems and Applications, HotMobile 2007 (2007)
14. King, N.J., Jessen, P.W.: Profiling the mobile customer – Privacy concerns when behavioral advertisers target mobile phones. Computer Law & Security Review 26(5), 455–478 (2010)
15. Goode Intelligence: Mobile security the next battleground (2009)
16. National Cyber Security Alliance (NCSA): Schools Lacking Cyber Security and Safety Education (2009)
17. Cable & Wireless: Workers lack mobile phone etiquette (2009)

18. De Keukelaere, F., Yoshihama, S., Trent, S., Zhang, Y., Luo, L., Zurko, M.E.: Adaptive Security Dialogs for Improved Security Behavior of Users. In: Gross, T., Gulliksen, J., Kotzé, P., Oestreicher, L., Palanque, P., Prates, R.O., Winckler, M. (eds.) INTERACT 2009. LNCS, vol. 5726, pp. 510–523. Springer, Heidelberg (2009)
19. Androulidakis, I., Kandus, G.: Feeling Secure vs. Being Secure the Mobile Phone User Case. In: Jahankhani, H., et al. (eds.) ICGS3/e-Democracy 2011. LNICST, vol. 99, pp. 212–219. Springer, Heidelberg (2012)
20. Hakila, J., Chatfield, C.: Personal customization of mobile phones: a case study. In: Proceedings of NordiCHI, pp. 409–412 (2006)

GSi Compliant RAS for Public Private Sector Partnership

Fawzi Fawzi[1,2], Rabih Bashroush[2], and Hamid Jahankhani[2]

[1] Head of IT Developments and Technical Innovations,
London Probation Trust, London, UK
[2] School of Computing IT and Engineering, University of East London, London, UK
{fawzi,rabih,hamid2}@uel.ac.uk

Abstract. With the current trend of moving intelligent services and administration towards the public private partnership, and the security controls that are currently in place, the shareable data modeling initiative has become a controversial issue. Existing applications often rely on isolation or trusted networks for their access control or security, whereas untrusted wide area networks pay little attention to the authenticity, integrity or confidentiality of the data they transport. In this paper, we examine the issues that must be considered when providing network access to an existing probation service environment. We describe how we intend to implement the proposed solution in one probation service application. We describe the architecture that allows remote access to the legacy application, providing it with encrypted communications and strongly authenticated access control but without requiring any modifications to the underlying application.

Keywords: RAS, Secure Mobile Working, Security Standards.

1 Introduction

The public sector model has evolved over the years but it continues to be a reactive model to new legislations and policies. The arching factor of cost versus scalability and robustness has become very visible, and it has established itself as the most significant consideration in any technical design. The traditional Virtual Private Network (VPN) structure has not evolved as fast as technology and the offering of new tools on traditional infrastructures where the essence of these is to protect data and uphold confidentiality. However, the limitation and the disparity between what the private and public sector can offer has exaggerated the need for bridging connectivity over legacy boundaries that are no longer flexible enough to accommodate new advances and developments. This is very much a systematic problem for the public sector in particular where the requirements for personnel to have remote and mobile access to classified data (e.g. at Restricted or IL3 level or higher). The modeling of true, secure mobile working shouldn't be a generic implementation of technology. It needs to ensure acceptance of various managements within a complex structure of partnership adhering to different affiliations' of security

H. Jahankhani et al. (Eds.): ICGS3/e-Democracy 2011, LNICST 99, pp. 67–71, 2012.

standards. To mitigate the risks, the implementation needs to address both technical controls and potential human intervention or malicious intent.

The next section discusses the RAS modeling guidelines. Section 3 then provides an overview of the potential design of the solution. Finally, conclusion and future work is presented in section 4.

2   RAS Modeling Guidelines

In its logical interpretation, the conceptual design of the solution and how it manages security accreditation (certification) [1] is based on the below guidelines:

1. **Protection and Confidentiality:** each traffic flow is protected in accordance with the established requirements. This includes flows between the remote client device and the remote access server, and between the remote access server and internal resources. Protection should be verified by means such as monitoring network traffic or checking traffic logs.
2. **Authentication:** is required and cannot be readily compromised or circumvented. All authentication policies are enforced. Performing robust testing of authentication is important to reduce the risk of attackers accessing protected internal resources.
3. **Applications:** the remote access solution does not interfere with the use of software applications that are permitted to be used through remote access, nor does it disrupt the operation of the remote client devices (for example, a VPN client conflicting with a host-based firewall).
4. **Management:** Administrators can configure and manage the solution effectively and securely. This includes all components, including remote access servers, authentication services, and client software. The ease of deployment and configuration is particularly important, such as having fully automated client configuration versus administrators manually configuring each client. Another concern is the ability of users to alter remote access client settings, which could weaken remote access security. Automating configurations for devices can greatly reduce unintentional errors from users incorrectly configuring settings.
5. **Logging:** the remote access solution logs security events in accordance with the organisation's policies. Some remote access solutions provide more granular logging capabilities than others. An example is logging usage of individual applications versus only connections to particular hosts. So in some cases it may be necessary to rely on the resources used through remote access to perform portions of the logging that the remote access server cannot perform.
6. **Performance:** the solution provides adequate performance during normal and peak usage. It is important to consider not only the performance of the primary remote access components, but also that of intermediate devices, such as routers and firewalls. Performance is particularly important when large software updates are being provided through the remote access solution to the remote client devices. Encrypted traffic often consumes more

processing power than unencrypted traffic, so it may cause bottlenecks. In many cases, the best way to test the performance under load of a prototype is to use simulated traffic generators on a live test network to mimic the actual characteristics of expected traffic as closely as possible. Testing should incorporate a variety of applications that will be used with remote access.

7. **Security:** the remote access implementation itself may contain vulnerabilities and weaknesses that attackers could exploit. High security needs may choose to perform extensive vulnerability assessments against the remote access components. At a minimum, all components should be updated with the latest patches and configured following sound security practices.

8. **Default Settings:** The default values for each remote access setting and alter the settings are reviewed as necessary o support security requirements. The remote access device should be assured to ensure that it does not unexpectedly "fall back" to default settings for interoperability or other reasons.

9. **Acceptance:** the CA "certification authority" will depend on a holistic approach necessary to develop an effective security infrastructure. This is in addition to discussing the individual components and the role they play [2][3].

3   Technical Foundation

The implementation enables the Public/Private partnership to build a RAS offering that meets the requirements for CESG "National Technical Authority for Information Assurance" [8]. The RAS solution will need to meet CESG guidelines for data handling and as such the data classification for the RAS compliance with IL3 level [4][5].

An application database that is hosted within the GSI cloud would be built around application guidelines and would adhere to CESG policy. The database would be migrated into a previously accredited environment and therefore would not be required to follow an additional accreditation submission. The model proposes that the desired solution for Users within the field recording and updating national and protected records would be a 3G enabled device.

This remote device solution will be designed within the following recommendations:

- Hardware must support TPM "Trusted Platform Module" chip technology.
- The Operating System will be Microsoft based.
- The hardware will be encrypted using Windows Bitlocker.
- The Bitlocker entropy will be supplied by Becrypt.
- Backup Entropy will be stored on a secure server within the previously accredited environment.
- USB bitlocker token authentication will be required to log on to the laptop.
- The hardware build will include Cisco VPN client and require client certificates.

- Internet browsing will be by proxy via the secure internet [6].
- 3G dongle for internet connectivity for hardware devices

The figure below shows a user connecting to the complimentary environment via a client/server VPN connection and then being forwarded to the application VLAN within the same environment.

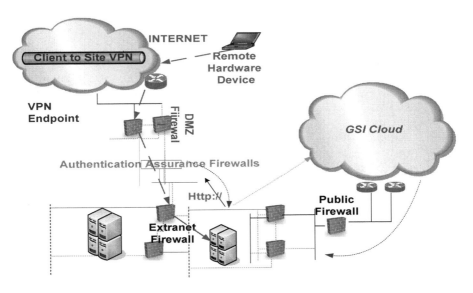

Fig. 1. Proposed solution architecture overview

4   Conclusion

Internet is changing the way public sector activities are conducted. Security compliance of mobile working solutions is the enabling technologies that simplify the management and security of such activities. With the right approach to an accredited implementation, public sector organizations with obligatory responsibility to protect confidentiality can spend less time worrying about security, while focusing on their main activities. For example, confidential documents no longer need to wait for days to be physically shipped. Instead, they can be securely sent through e-mail. Web servers can allow secure access for only designated users, eliminating the need for human intervention. Public sector organization networks including military can securely extend over the Internet, eliminating expensive leased data lines. Future work is geared towards further integration and consolidation of platforms to deliver further efficiencies. In practical terms certifying authorities will be encouraged to come together in a cooperative intervention to deliver an agreed upon security baseline.

References

1. Gerk, E.: Overview of Certification Systems – X.509, CA, PGP and SKIP. Meta-Certificate Group (1998)
2. Andress "Surviving Security" How to Integrate People, Process, and Technology, 2nd edn. Auerbach Publications A CRC Press Company, Boca Raton, London, New York, Washington, D.C.
3. Scambray, J.: Hacking Exposed (April 2, 2001)
4. Burr, W.E.: Public Key Infrastructure Technical Specification. NIST (1997)
5. King, C.: Building a Corporate PKI. INFOSEC Engineering (1999)
6. Warwick, F., Baum, M.: Secure Electronic Commerce – Building Infrastructure for Digital Signatures and Encryption. Prentice Hall (1997)
7. Fraser, R.: Information Governance & Technology Policies - Remote Access Procedure (October 2009)
8. CESG: National Technical Authority for Information Assurance, http://www.cesg.gov.uk/index.shtml

A Probabilistic Key Agreement Scheme for Sensor Networks without Key Predistribution[*]

Vasiliki Liagkou[1,3], Effie Makri[4], Paul Spirakis[1,3], and Yannis Stamatiou[2,3]

[1] University of Patras, Dept. of Computer Engineering, 26500, Rio, Patras, Greece
[2] Mathematics Department, 451 10, Ioannina, Greece
istamat@uoi.gr
[3] Research and Academic Computer Technology Institute, N. Kazantzaki,
University of Patras, 26500, Rio, Patras, Greece
[4] University of the Aegean, Department of Mathematics,
83000, Karlovassi, Samos, Greece

Abstract. The dynamic establishment of shared information (e.g. secret key) between two entities is particularly important in networks with no pre-determined structure such as wireless sensor networks (and in general wireless mobile ad-hoc networks). In such networks, nodes establish and terminate communication sessions dynamically with other nodes which may have never been encountered before, in order to somehow exchange information which will enable them to subsequently communicate in a secure manner. In this paper we give and theoretically analyze a series of protocols that enables two entities that have never encountered each other before to establish a shared piece of information for use as a key in setting up a secure communication session with the aid of a shared key encryption algorithm. These protocols do not require previous pre-distribution of candidate keys or some other piece of information of specialized form except a small seed value, from which the two entities can produce arbitrarily long strings with many similarities.

Keywords: Key agreement, key predistribution, mobile ad-hoc networks.

1 Introduction

Wireless Sensor Networks (WSNs) have some constraints, with regard to battery life, processing, memory and commnication ([1]) capacity, and as such are deemed unsuitable for public crypto-based systems. Thus, symmetric key cryptosystems are more appropriate for these types of networks, but lead to problems with key distribution. These problems are mitigated with key *pre-distribution schemes*, in which candidate keys are distributed to members of the network before the start communication. Many innovative and intuitive key pre-distribution

---

[*] This work was partially supported by the European Union project ABC4Trust (Attribute-based Credentials for Trust) funded within the context of the 7th Research Framework Program (FP7).

H. Jahankhani et al. (Eds.): ICGS3/e-Democracy 2011, LNICST 99, pp. 72–79, 2012.

schemes for WSNs have been proposed for solving the problem of key distribution in sensor networks. On the two ends of the spectrum are key pre-distribution schemes that use a single master key as the encryption key distributed amongst all the nodes, and all pairwise keys, where a unique key exists for every pair of sensors. The former provides the most efficient usage of memory and scales well, but an attack on one node compromises the whole network, whereas the latter provides excellent resilience but does not scale well. In addition, schemes exist which are in essence probabilistic, relying on the fact that any two neighbouring nodes have some probability p of successfully completing key establishment.

Some such schemes (presented in [2–8]) pre-suppose that the sensor nodes have been loaded with some pre-existing information (i.e. the key, or sets of keys) prior to network deployment, except for Liu and Cheng ([9]). They propose a self-configured scheme whereby no prior knowledge is loaded onto the sensor nodes, but shared keys are computed amongst the neighbours.

In this paper, we propose a key agreement scheme whereby network nodes are not pre-loaded with candidate keys, but generate pairs of symmetric keys from two, initially, random bits strings. The initial research conducted ([10]) proposed a protocol that involved the examination of random positions of subsets of size k, and the elimination of a random position if the two bit strings were found to disagree on more than half the examined positions. In that paper, however, the nodes cannot secretly compute the number of differing positions, a problem that is resolved in the present paper using secret circuit computations. In addition, the present protocols do not eliminate differing bits but flips them, depending on the number of bit difference in the examined subset of k bits. This leads to a different stochastic process that called for a different theoretical analysis.

2   The Bit-Similarity Problem

Two entities, say 0 and 1, initially possess an N-bit string, X_N^0 and X_N^1 respectively. The entities' goal is to cooperatively transform their strings so as to increase the percentage of positions at which their strings contain the same bits, which we denote by $X(i)$, with i being the time step of the protocol they execute. Then $X(0)$ is the initial percentage of the positions at which the two strings are the same. Below we provide a randomized protocol in which the two entities examine randomly chosen subsets of their strings in order to see whether they differ in at least half of the places. If they do, one of the entities (in turn) randomly flips a subset of these positions. This process continues up to a certain, predetermined number of steps. The intuition behind this protocol is that when two random substrings of two strings differ in at least half of their positions, then flipping some bits at random in one of the substrings is more likely to increase the percentage of similarities between the strings than to decrease it. In the description of the protocol $X_N^c[S]$ denotes a substring of string X_N^c defined by the position set S. Protocol for user $U_c, c = 0, 1$ Protocol parameters known to both communicating parties: (i) k, l, the subset sizes, (ii) T, the number of protocol execution steps, (iii) the index (bit position) set N, (iv) The circuit

C with which the two entities jointly compute whether there are at least $\lceil k/2 \rceil$ similarities between randomly chosen subsets of their strings.

$i \leftarrow 1$ /* The step counter. */
while $i \leq T$ /* T is a predetermined time step limit.*/
  begin /* while */
    $S \leftarrow$ JOINT_RAND$(k, \{1, \ldots, N\})$/* Shared random set of k positions. See text. */
    same_pos $\leftarrow C(X_N^c[S], X_N^{(c+1 \mod 2)}[S])$ /* A secret computation of number of
                                                          positions with same contents). */
    if (same_pos $\geq \lceil \frac{k}{2} \rceil$ **and** odd$(i+c)$) **then** /* Users 0 and 1 alternate. */
      begin
        $SF \leftarrow$ RAND(l, S) /* Random set of l positions from within S
                                      to be flipped by the user whose turn it is to flip. */
      flip the bits of $X_N^c[SF]$
      end
    SYNCHRONIZE /* Users 0 and 1 wait to reach this point simultaneously */
    $i \leftarrow i+1$
  end/* while */

3   Secret Two-Party Function Computation

During the execution of the protocol, it is necessary for the two communicating parties to see whether they agree on at least half of the positions they have chosen to compare (line 13-14 of the protocol). Thus, the two parties need to perform a computation: compute the number of positions on which the corresponding bits in the two chosen subsets of k bits are the same. This is an instance of an important, general problem in cryptography: *Secure Computation*. More formally, let A and B be two parties with inputs of n_A and n_B bits respectively. The objective is to jointly compute a function $f : \{0,1\}^{n_A} \times \{0,1\}^{n_B} \to \{0,1\}$ on their inputs. The issue, here, is that A and B cannot, simply, exchange their inputs and compute the function since they will learn each other's inputs, something that is not desirable in a secure computation setting. More importantly, even it A and B are willing to share their inputs, they would not allow an eavesdropper to acquire these inputs too. This leads to the problem of *secure function computation*. In our context, we consider the following two Boolean functions:

$$f_r : \{0,1\}^k \times \{0,1\}^k \to \{0,1\} \text{ with } w_A, w_B \in \{0,1\}^k$$

$$\text{and } 0 \leq r \leq k \;:\; f(w_A, w_B) = \begin{cases} 1 & \text{if } X(w_A, w_B) \geq r; \\ 0 & \text{otherwise.} \end{cases}$$

We are interested in $r = \lceil \frac{k}{2} \rceil$.

$$f_X : \{0,1\}^k \times \{0,1\}^k \to \{0,1\}^{\lceil \log_2(k) \rceil} \text{ with } w_A, w_B \in \{0,1\}^k :$$
$$f_X(w_A, w_B) = x, \text{ with } x = X(w_A, w_B) \text{ written in binary.}$$

The function f_X is, strictly, an ordered tuple $(f_X^0, f_X^1, \ldots, f_X^{\lceil \log_2(k) \rceil - 1})$ of $\lceil \log_2(k) \rceil$ 1-bit Boolean functions, where the function f_X^i computes the ith most significant bit of $x = X(w_A, w_B)$ (with $i = 0$ we take the most significant bit and with $i = \lceil \log_2(k) \rceil - 1$ we take the least significant bit). Using techniques from oblivious function computation (see [11] for a survey on these techniques), we can prove that the computation of f_r and f_X can be done with randomized protocols using $O(|C_{f_r}|)$ and $O(|C_{f_X}|)$ communication steps respectively, with C_{f_r} and C_{f_X} being the Boolean circuits that are employed for the computation of f and f_X respectively. Since both f_r and f_X are easily seen to be polynomial time computable Boolean functions, we can construct for their computations circuits of size polynomial in their input sizes, i.e. circuits C_{f_r} and C_{f_X} such that $|C_{f_r}| = O(k^{c_1})$ and $|C_{f_X}| = O(k^{c_2})$, with constants $c_1, c_2 \geq 0$. Since k is considered a fixed constant, we conclude that we can compute f_k and f_X in a constant number of rounds. The number of random bits needed by each step of the randomized protocol is in both cases $O(k)$ and, thus, constant. To sum up, the functions f_r and f_X can, both, be evaluated on two k-bit inputs w_A, w_B held by two parties A, B using a constant number of rounds and a constant number of uniformly random bits. In what follows, we will assume that the communicating parties use the function $f_{\lceil \frac{k}{2} \rceil}$. With regard to the required randomness, we assume that each of the two parties has a true randomness source, i.e. a source of uniformly random bits. Such a randomness source can be easily built into modern devices. This randomness source is necessary in order to implement the randomized oblivious computation protocols for the computation of the function $f_{\lceil \frac{k}{2} \rceil}$. In addition, it will be used in order to produce the randomly chosen positions, are required by Step 6 of the protocol. Since each position can range from 1 up to N (the string size), to form a position index we need to draw $\lceil \log_2(N) \rceil$ random bits. Alternatively, if we allow the two parties to share a small (in relation to N) seed, they can produce the random positions in synchronization and, thus, avoid sending them over the communication channel.

4   Theoretical Analysis of the Protocol

In order to track the density of positions where two strings agree, we will make use of Wormald's theorem (see [12]) to model the probabilistic evolution of the protocol described in Section 2 using a deterministic function which stays provably close to the real evolution of the algorithm. The theorem in [12] essentially states is that if we are confronted with a number of (possibly) interrelated random variables (associated with some random process) such that they satisfy a Lipschitz condition and their expected fluctuation at each time step is known, then the value of these variables can be approximated using the solution of a system of differential equations. Furthermore, the system of differential equations results directly from the expressions for the expected fluctuation of the random variables describing the random process. We will first prove a general lemma that gives the probability of increasing the similarity between two strings through flipping, at random, the contents of a certain number of positions.

Lemma 1. *Let w_1, w_2 be two strings of 0s and 1s of length k. Let also j, $0 \leq j \leq k$, be the number of places in which the two strings differ. Then if l positions of one string are randomly flipped, the probability that s of them are differing positions is the following:* $P_{k,j,l,s} = \frac{\binom{j}{s}\binom{k-j}{l-s}}{\binom{k}{l}}$.

Proof. In the above equation the denominator is the number of all subsets of positions of cardinality l of the k string positions while the numerator is equal to the number of partitions of the l chosen positions such that s of them fall into the j differing positions and the remaining $l - s$ fall into the remaining $k - j$ non-differing positions of the two strings. Thus their ratio gives the desired probability. □

The following lemma, which is easy to prove based on general properties of the binomial coefficients, provides a closed form expression for a sum that will appear later in some probability computations.

Lemma 2. *The following identity holds:* $\sum_{s=0}^{l}(2s - l)\frac{\binom{j}{s}\binom{k-j}{l-s}}{\binom{k}{l}} = \left(\frac{2j}{k} - 1\right)l$.

We will now derive the deterministic differential equation that governs the evolution of the random variable $X(i)$ manipulated by the protocol in Section 2 using Wormald's theorem.

Theorem 1. *The differential equation that results from the application of Wormald's theorem on the quantity $X(i)$ (places of agreement at protocol step i) as it evolves in the agreement protocol is the following:*

$$\mathbf{E}[X(i+1) - X(i)] = \sum_{j=\lceil \frac{k}{2} \rceil}^{k} \sum_{s=0}^{l} [(s - (l - s))P_{k,j,l,s}]P_{n,n-X(i),k,j}.$$

Proof. We will determine the possible values of the difference $X(i+1) - X(i)$ along with the probability of occurrence for each of them. The protocol described in Section 2 flips l positions within the k examined positions, whenever these k positions contain $j \geq \lceil \frac{k}{2} \rceil$ differing positions in the two strings. From the flipped l positions, is s of them ($0 \leq s \leq l$) are disagreement positions, then the two strings will have gained s agreement positions, losing $l - s$. The net total is $s - (l - s)$. The probability that this total occurs, for a specific value of s and a specific value of j is equal to $P_{k,j,l,s}P_{n,n-X(i),k,j}$. Summing up over all possible values of s, j we obtain (in Theorem 1). □

Corollary 1. *The following holds:*

$$\mathbf{E}[X(i+1) - X(i)] = \sum_{j=\lceil \frac{k}{2} \rceil}^{k} l\left(\frac{2j}{k} - 1\right)\frac{\binom{n-X(i)}{j}\binom{X(i)}{k-j}}{\binom{n}{k}}.$$

Proof. The above Equation follows from Theorem 1 using the Equation of Lemma 1 with $k = n, l = k, s = j, n - j = X(i)$, in conjunction with Lemma 2.

Corollary 2. *Using Wormald's Theorem (in [12]), the evolution of the random variable $X(i)$ whose mean fluctuation is given in Corollary 1 can be approximated by the following differential equation:*

$$\frac{dx(t)}{dt} = \sum_{j=\lceil \frac{k}{2} \rceil}^{k} l \left(\frac{2j}{k} - 1 \right) \binom{k}{j} [1 - x(t)]^j x(t)^{k-j}.$$

Proof. By applying the approximation $\binom{N}{k} = \frac{N^k}{k!} \left(1 + O\left(\frac{1}{N}\right)\right)$ of the binomial coefficients which is valid for $k = O(1)$ on the three binomials which appear on the the right-hand side of Equation in Corollary 1, we obtain the following: $\frac{\binom{n-X(i)}{j}\binom{X(i)}{k-j}}{\binom{n}{k}} \simeq \binom{k}{j} \left(1 - \frac{X(i)}{n}\right)^j \left(\frac{X(i)}{n}\right)^{k-j}$. Using Wormald's theorem, we make the correspondence $x(t) = \frac{X(i)}{n}$ and $\frac{dx(t)}{dt} = \mathbf{E}[X(i+1) - X(i)]$, which results in the required differential equation of Corollary 2. □

5 Efficiency of the Protocol

From Corollary 2 we see that the percentage of similar positions, represented by the function $x(t)$, is a monotone increasing function since its first derivative is always positive. In what follows, we will estimate how fast this percentage increases depending on its initial value $x(0)$ as well as the parameters l and k.

Lemma 3. *The solution $x(t)$ to the differential equation given in Corollary 2 is monotone increasing.*

Proof. From the differential equation, we see that the first derivative of the function $x(t)$, which is equal to the right-hand side of the differential equation, is strictly positive, since $0 < x(t) < 1$. Thus, the function $x(t)$ is monotone increasing. □

Lemma 4. *Let $x(t_1)$ be the value of the function $x(t)$ at time instance t_1 and $x(t_2)$ be the value at time instance t_2, $t_1 < t_2$. Let, also, $c(t_1)$ be the absolute value of the point at which the tangent line to the point $(t_1, x(t_1))$ of $x(t_1)$ cuts the t-axis and $c(t_2)$ the corresponding value for t_2. Let, also, $p(x) = \sum_{j=\lceil \frac{k}{2} \rceil}^{k} l \left(\frac{2j}{k} - 1 \right) \binom{k}{j}(1 - x)^j x^{k-j}$. Then, $p(x(t_1)) = \frac{x(t_1)}{c(t_1)+t_1}, p(x(t_2)) = \frac{x(t_2)}{c(t_2)+t_2}$.*

Proof. Let ϵ_1 and ϵ_2 be the two tangent lines to the function $x(t)$ at the points $(t_1, x(t_1))$ and $(t_2, x(t_2))$ respectively, as shown in Figure 1. Due to the monotonicity of $x(t)$, the points at which the two lines intersect with the t-axis are negative. Let $c(t_1)$ and $c(t_2)$ be the absolute values of these two points for lines ϵ_1 and ϵ_2 respectively. Then from the two right angle triangles that are formed we have $\tan(\phi_1) = \frac{x(t_1)}{c(t_1)+t_1}$ and $\tan(\phi_2) = \frac{x(t_2)}{c(t_2)+t_2}$. From the definition of the derivative, $\tan(\phi_1) = \frac{dx(t)}{dt}|_{t_1}$ and $\tan(\phi_2) = \frac{dx(t)}{dt}|_{t_2}$. From the Equations of Corollary 2 and Lemma 4, we have $\frac{dx(t)}{dt} = p(x(t))$ and, thus, the statement of the lemma follows. □

Theorem 2. *Let t' be the time instance at which $x(t') = hx(0)$, with $1 \leq h \leq \frac{1}{x(0)}$. Then, $t_2 \leq \frac{x(0)}{p(hx(0))} \cdot (h - 1)$.*

Proof. We set $t_1 = 0, t_2 = t'$ and $x(t') = hx(0)$ in Lemma 4 and we obtain, the following: $p(x(0)) = \frac{x(0)}{c(0)}, p(hx(0)) = \frac{hx(0)}{c(t')+t'}$. From these equations we obtain

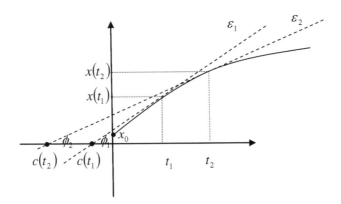

Fig. 1. The two tangent lines for the proof of the Theorem

the following: $\frac{p(x(0))}{p(hx(0))} = \frac{c(t')+t'}{hc(0)}$. Solving for t' we obtain the following: $t' = \frac{hp(x(0))c(0)}{p(hx(0))} - c(t')$.Since $p(x(0))$ is the inclination of the tangent line to $x(t)$ at the point $(0, x(0))$, it holds that $p(x(0)) = \frac{x(0)}{c(0)}$. Thus, t' becomes $\frac{hx(0)}{p(hx(0))} - c(t')$.Since $x(t)$ is monotone increasing, the point at which the tangent to this function cuts the $x(t)$-axis at any point is greater than or equal to $x(0)$ (see Figure 1). Let x_c be this point. Then $p(x(t')) = \frac{x_c}{c(t')}$ or, since $x(t') = hx(0)$, $p(hx(0)) = \frac{x_c}{c(t')}$. Since $x_c \geq x(0)$, $c(t') \geq \frac{x(0)}{p(hx(0))}$. Thus, we obtain $t' \leq \frac{hx(0)}{p(hx(0))} - \frac{x(0)}{p(hx(0))} = \frac{x(0)}{p(hx(0))} \cdot (h-1)$ which is the required. □

Lemma 5. *The following lower bounds hold for the polynomial in the first Equation of Lemma 4: If $x < 1/2$ then $p(x) \geq l[x^k + 1 - 2x]$. If $x \geq 1/2$ then $p(x) \geq \frac{l}{k}(1-x)^k \binom{k}{\lceil \frac{k}{2} \rceil}\lceil \frac{k}{2} \rceil$.*

Proof. In the first Equation of Lemma 4, allowing the sum index to cover all the range from 1 to k reduces the value of the sum since it adds negative terms. Thus $p(x) \geq l\sum_{j=1}^{k} \left(\frac{2j}{k} - 1\right)\binom{k}{j}(1-x)^j x^{k-j}$. Since the sum evaluates to $l[x^k + 1 - 2x]$ the first statement of the lemma follows. If, on the other hand, $x \geq 1/2$, then lower bound given for the first statement of the lemma is not good since it may even become negative. In this case we observe that the term $(1-x)^j x^{k-j}$ is minimized for $j = k$. Setting $j = k$ in the first Equation of Lemma 4, we obtain the second statement of the lemma. □

Corollary 3. *The following bounds hold for the time instance t': (i)If $hx(0) < 1/2$ then $t' \leq \frac{x(0)(h-1)}{l[hx(0))^k+1-2hx(0)]}$.(ii)If $hx(0) \geq 1/2$ then $t' \leq \frac{kx(0)(h-1)}{l[1-hx(0)]^k\binom{k}{\lceil \frac{k}{2} \rceil}\lceil \frac{k}{2} \rceil}$.*

From the first inequality of Corollary 3 we see that the percentage of similarities grows fast, if we start from $x(0)$ aiming at $hx(0)$, with $h \geq 1$ and $hx(0) < 1/2$ is only a very coarse upper bound). If the target is, however, at $hx(0)$ with $x \geq 1/2$ the upper bound is not good as the denominator tends to 0 fast. However, since this denominator is simply the first derivative of $x(t)$ at $hx(0)$, this derivative fast tends to 0 if $hx(0) \geq 1/2$ and, thus, the tangent at this point tends to become parallel to the t-axis. Thus, we have again fast convergence.

6 Conclusions

In this paper we described a series of protocols that can be used in order to increase the percentage of similarities between two strings held by two communicating parties without revealing their values. The propose protocols are, in fact, general and may be used in any situation involving either wireless or conventional networks in which there is no trusted third party or key management authority among the network nodes.

References

1. Carman, D.W., Kruus, P.S., Matt, B.J.: Contstraints and approaches for distributed sensor network security. Technical Report 010, NAI Labs, The Security Research Division Network Associates, Inc. (2000)
2. Eschenauer, L., Gligor, V.: A key-management scheme for distributed sensor networks. In: 9th ACM Conf. Computing and Comm. Security (CCS 2002), pp. 41–47 (2002)
3. Chan, H., Perrig, A., Song, D.: Random key predistribution schemes for sensor networks. In: IEE Symposium of Privacy and Security, pp. 197–213 (2003)
4. Chan, S.-P., Poovendran, R., Sun., M.-T.: A key management scheme in distributed sensor networks using attack probabilities. In: IEEE Global Telecommunications Conference, GLOBECOM (2005)
5. Chan, H., Perrig, A.: Pike: Peer intermediaries for key establishment in sensor networks. In: Proceedings of the IEEE Infocom (2005)
6. Du, W., Deng, J., Han, Y.S., Varshney, P.: A pairwise key pre-distribution scheme for wireless sensor networks. In: 10th ACM Conference on Computer and Communications Security, pp. 42–51. ACM Press (2003)
7. Du, W., Deng, J., Han, Y.S., Chen, S., Varshney, P.: A key management scheme for wireless sensor networks using deployment knowledge. In: IEEE Infocom, pp. 586–597 (2004)
8. Blom, R.: An Optimal Class of Symmetric Key Generation Systems. In: Beth, T., Cot, N., Ingemarsson, I. (eds.) EUROCRYPT 1984. LNCS, vol. 209, pp. 335–338. Springer, Heidelberg (1985)
9. Liu, F., Cheng, X.: A self-configured key establishment scheme for large-scale sensor networks. In: 3rd IEEE International Conference on Mobile Ad-hoc and Sensor Systems (MASS), pp. 447–456 (2006)
10. Makri, E., Stamatiou, Y.: Distributively increasing the percentage of similarities between strings with application to key agreement. In: 5th International Conference on AD-HOC Networks and Wireless, pp. 211–223 (2006)
11. Cramer, R.: Introduction to Secure Computation. In: Damgård, I.B. (ed.) EEF School 1998. LNCS, vol. 1561, pp. 16–42. Springer, Heidelberg (1999)
12. Wormald, N.: The differential equation method for random graph processes and greedy algorithms. Annals of Applied Probability 5, 1217–1235 (1995)

Cryptographic Dysfunctionality-A Survey on User Perceptions of Digital Certificates

Dimitrios Zissis, Dimitrios Lekkas, and Panayiotis Koutsabasis

Department of Product and Systems Design Engineering,
University of the Aegean, Syros Greece
{Dzissis,Dlek,Kgp}@aegean.gr

Abstract. In this paper we identify and define cryptographic dysfunctionality and within this context we perform a study to evaluate user perceptions of public key cryptography concepts. The study makes use of user testing, questionnaires and wrap-up interviews with 121 young, but experienced Internet users during their interactions with selected secure Internet locations. The results show that the vast majority of users are not familiar with fundamental concepts of cryptography, and that they are not capable of efficiently managing digital certificates. This case study serves as first evidence supporting our hypothesis that user interface design is deteriorating cryptographic solutions effectiveness due to usability issues.

Keywords: Public Key Infrastructure, Usability, Security, Digital Certificates.

1 Introduction

In recent years, we have witnessed an explosion in the adoption of social media websites, electronic commerce, electronic banking and cloud solutions. As the popularity of these tools is increasing, stakes are now higher than ever in the field of information and communication security, as profits to be made from scams, extortion, online theft, identity theft have risen analogously. Malware is rapidly on the rise and becoming even more sophisticated. The percentage of computers infected with banking Trojans and password stealers has risen to 17% in 2010 while experiments are now showing a success rate of over 70% for phishing attacks on social networks [1]. While emails containing links to malicious sites continue to increase as a major means of leading new victims to attack sites, sophisticated phishing attacks are now poisoning search engine results with hyperlinks to web pages hosting numerous security risks.

In 2010 we witnessed the most sophisticated malware attack to date, the STUXNET worm [2][3]. STUXNET appeared to target highly sensitive Supervisory Control And Data Acquisition (SCADA) systems, which monitor and control industrial, infrastructure or facility-based processes, and was remarkable for the sophistication of its code and the amount of work involved in its creation. The STUXNET attack, constituted a serious attack on the notion of "trusted software" in information systems [2].

H. Jahankhani et al. (Eds.): ICGS3/e-Democracy 2011, LNICST 99, pp. 80–87, 2012.

Trust is not a new research topic in computer science. The notion of trust in an organization could be defined as the customer's certainty that the organization is capable of providing the required services accurately and infallibly. A certainty which also expresses the customer's faith in its moral integrity, in the soundness of its operation, in the effectiveness of its security mechanisms, in its expertise and in its abidance by all regulations and laws, while at the same time, it also contains the acknowledgment of a minimum risk factor, by the relying party[4]. This trust is represented in the digital world using Digital certificates which are realized by Public Key Cryptography. Digital Certificates are used to establish secure connections to servers, authorize and authenticate users, but also validate software source code origins and guarantee its integrity. A digital certificate presented to an end user, published by a trusted Certification authority, can be defined as the conceptual delegation of this trust from the certificate issuer to the certificate owner. This exact trust was exploited by the STUXNET worm. In addition to exploiting four zero-day vulnerabilities, STUXNET used two valid digital certificates for source code signing, giving it credibility and trusted privileges, thus helping keep the malware undetected for quite a long period of time [3]. These sophisticated attacks, open Pandora's box for information system security as they put in doubt the effectiveness of one of the pillars upon which security in the digital world is built, cryptography and digital signatures.

2   Digital Signatures and Certificates

In 1976, Diffie and Hellman published a pivotal paper in the field of cryptography [5], which introduced a number of pioneer ideas in cryptography, including Public Key Encryption , Digital Signatures, One way functions and Trapdoor functions; the need to preserve the availability, integrity, authenticity and confidentiality of exchanged data and communications had already been identified. Digital signatures and Public key certificates have been perceived as an effective and efficient solution for achieving secure communications and transactions. Public Key cryptography currently realizes the concept of digital signatures; it provides a practical, elegant mechanism for symmetric key agreement. At present numerous Internet Protocols (SSL/TLS, IPsec/IKE, SSH, DNSsec, etc) employ digital certificates and thus public key cryptography to secure online transactions. For years scholars, experts and implementors throughout academia and industry have scrutinized the underlying mathematics and algorithms that enable cryptographic applications. Paradoxically though, 30 years after their inception and in contrast to the rise of information system threats, cryptographic applications have never met with wide public awareness. Even though the usage of PKI's in closed and controlled business environments is quite common, interoperability and usability problems arise when shifting to a broader, open environment [6].

A devastating majority of Internet users, either business or social, seem to lack the basic ability, knowledge or even willingness to effectively use cryptographic applications, in a way that can successfully deter imminent threats. A PKI system trusts its users to validate each other's certificates and effectively protect their private keys. PKI strength can be summarized down to specific end user trust judgments regarding the trustworthiness of certificate issuers and ultimately certificate holders. As no automated mechanism for evaluating and managing the trust relationships exists, to make an effective trust judgment about the validity of a specific public key certificate, an end user is required to evaluate an extensive list of critical parameters, certificate repositories and cross certified authorities[7]. The complexity of this task, dawns on user friendliness and overall usability. When users fail to manage their private keys securely or when they fail to validate each other's public keys rigorously, then authenticity and privacy guarantees weaken and overall security deteriorates. Security software is only defined as usable if the people who are expected to use it [8]:

- are reliably made aware of the security tasks they need to perform;
- are able to figure out how to successfully perform those tasks;
- don't make dangerous errors;
- are sufficiently comfortable with the interface to continue using it.

To achieve secure and authenticated communications, a web server presents its own digital certificate to an end-user in order to prove its identity and to facilitate the establishment of a secure end-to-end session. The end-user is required to:

- Validate the subject on the digital certificate. In this case the subject of the certificate is a domain name, which must match the domain currently visited.
- Validate the signed content of the digital certificate. Typically, the hash value of the certificate's content is signed and the signature is included in the certificate.
- Validate the trustworthiness of the certification path, up to a trusted certification authority
- Check the validity period of the digital certificate (effective and expiration dates)
- Check if the certificate has been revoked
- If executable signed software is implicated, validate the signature of the source code

The above steps are by default performed by the web browser of the end-user and thus it is presumed that the end-user trusts the web-browser program and expects to be properly notified if any of these steps fail. Often these validations require the end user to participate effectively in the process, as is the case if the certification publisher is not pre included in the browsers root certificate repository; thus unknown to the browser or a check fails. At this point overall security is as strong as the end user trust decision. For the user to effectively participate in this process, and for security to adhere to the above definition of usable security, the user is required to have the necessary knowledge and understanding, to evaluate a list of critical parameters, certificate repositories and cross certified authorities. Hence the problem. Realistically only sophisticated users can be expected to meet fully the demands of PKI. Users are unable to effectively make decisions regarding digital certificates in daily transactions due to the lack of informativeness of the user interface and usability issues. Cryptography in its essential form appears to be greatly dysfunctional in every day environments, not due to the inherent complexity of the underlying mathematics, but due to the intricacy of the application interface, lack of informativeness and risk acknowledgment on a user side.

The severity of this vulnerability is critical, as a growing number of sophisticated malware attacks are exploiting end users inability to effectively validate digital certificates. Besides STUXNET, the Zeus Trojan exploited this same vulnerability to steal banking information. Zeus during installation exhibited an expired certificate belonging to Kaspersky's Zbot product, which was designed to remove Zeus [9]. Although this certificate was expired, and contained a different hash value, a plethora of users accepted it as trusted, thus enabling its propagation. Another version of malware exhibited a digital certificate claiming to be published by a trusted CA Avira [10]. When taking a closer look, Microsoft Windows shows a note "A certificate chain processed, but terminated in a root certificate which is not trusted by the trust provider". This message simply means that the certificate has not been created by Avira.

Within this context we define cryptographic dysfunctionality. At present, we identify the problematic dimension of PKI as being a usability and user interface design problem. During application usage, a detachment seems to occur between the application interface, informativeness and operation, which ultimately leads to user exclusion. In this exclusion cryptographic dysfunctionality has its deepest roots.

3   A Study on User Perceptions of Digital Certificates

We identify and define cryptographic dysfunctionality and within this context we perform an investigation, using questionnaires, to evaluate user understanding of cryptographic applications, application informativeness, user friendliness and usability. The results shed light on several aspects of these applications that deter cryptographic functionality in every day transactions. Our case study serves as a test of our hypothesis that user interface design is deteriorating cryptographic solutions effectiveness due to usability issues.

3.1   Goal, Method and Participants

This study's goal was to investigate the extent to which Internet users can (a) understand the most essential concepts of digital certificates, and (b) manage digital certificates effectively during their interactions with a number of selected and familiar web sites. The methods selected for this survey included user testing, questionnaires and wrap-up interviews with students of the department of Product and Systems Design Engineering at the University of the Aegean, Greece. It needs to be noted that all students of the department make daily use of computers for their studies, in various ways, including using email to communicate with academic and administrative staff and using an asynchronous e-learning platform to access electronic content for most of their courses. All participants can be defined as experienced Internet users, if we take into account that they make daily use of the Internet. A total number of 121 users participated in this survey. Users were recruited by an e-mail invitation.

The user testing phase of the study required users to connect to the academic e-mail server and access their accounts using the Mozilla Firefox, Internet Explorer and Opera web browsers, in a step-by-step process. To connect to the server, users were required to establish a secure SSL connection with a server exhibiting a valid digital certificate, which is not included in the Trusted Certification Authority Repository. This process required from the users to bypass the browser warning message to establish a secure connection, and in doing this add the CA to the Trusted Repository. For this, users should review the certificate critical parameters. For each step of the process users were asked about basic aspects of digital certificates and filled in the questionnaire (the questionnaire was available electronically via Google docs). This simple user testing process was followed in order to help users concentrate on the task of establishing an SSL connection, and to allow for a brief search of the issues that they would be enquired about in the questionnaire. At the end of the process, we conducted a number of wrap-up interviews with a selected set of users on the basis of their answers in order to provide some clarifications and interpretations.

The questionnaire comprised of a total of 20 (twenty) questions: the first four (4) were demographic, and the other 16 (sixteen) were about basic concepts of digital certificates and certificate management issues. For three (3) of these questions, users were told where to look for answers: they were also provided with screenshots of browser messages and they were asked whether they could understand their content and purpose.

3.2   Results

A total number of 121 participants took part in this survey; they were all between 18-23 years of age: 18y: 51 users (42%), 19y: 31 users (26%), 20y: 18 (15%), 21y: 7 (6%), 22y: 9 (7%), 23y:5 (4%). All participants are of young age and have considerable experience with using the Internet: 83 users (69%) reported that they have been using the Internet for more than 5 years, 15 users (12%) for more than 10, and 23 users (19%) for less than 5 years. The vast majority of participants make daily use of the Internet (102 (84%), while a total of 81 users (67%) have performed some kind of an electronic transaction, concerning e-commerce (49 users (41%)), e-banking (9 users (7%)), e-government (5 users (4%)) and other (18 users (15%)).

Obviously, users with the above demographic and Internet usage data should be at least aware of basic concepts regarding digital certificates, if not capable of understanding related complex concepts, able to efficiently manage certificates and establish secure connections. User responses raise serious concerns on the effectiveness of many security implementations used in online transactions and shed light on the true nature of the problem. We shall go through the most important answers received and attempt to provide an unbiased interpretation of these.

Users were asked if they have ever established a secure connection to an Internet website in order to protect their online information exchange (Fig. 1). Although 90% of participants had previously stated that they regularly make use of e-commerce and e-banking websites (meaning that they often establish SSL connections), a striking 67 users responded 'no' (56%), 39 users responded 'not sure' (32%), while a poor 12%

answered 'yes'. This answer was a first contradiction to the aforementioned participants' experience of Internet usage, and it is largely due to the fact that the secure connection is quite seamless from the user point of view. However, it need to be noted that even their specific and repeated interaction experience with their web e-mail accounts (during which they are prompted to connect to a 'potentially unsecure location', according to Firefox terminology) has not proved informative enough for the vast majority of users to realize that they are actually establishing secure connections every time they accessed their web e-mail account.

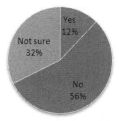

Fig. 1. Have you ever established a secure connection?

Fig. 2. Do you understand what a digital signature is?

An even more surprising set of answers was provided for the following question: "When you connect to a safe Internet location the URL changes to https. Do you understand what this means/does?" The vast majority of users (88%) lack any understanding of the concept of https (66%: 'no'; 22%: 'not sure').

Following this, users were enquired about their basic understanding of digital signatures and their ability to manage these (import, export and delete them), as this is one of the basics tasks users are required to perform in a secure PKI environment. A total of 93% (Fig. 2) responded that they "do not know or understand what a digital certificate is" (67%: 'no', 26%: 'not sure'). In the following question, answers revealed that an 85% of all respondents lacked the necessary knowledge to effectively manage digital signatures, this includes deleting a comprised Certification Authority from the trusted rooted certificate repository. When enquired about their understanding of SSL, 93% responded that they were unable to understand this, 3%: were 'not sure', and a small 4% responded 'yes'. These answers reveal that there is an astonishing majority of young experienced Internet users that are not aware of the most basic terms and concepts of secure online transactions.

Alarmingly when users were asked if they had ever viewed a digital certificate to validate it, only 2 % responded positively [2 responded positively (2%); 111 responded negatively (91%) and 8 responded not sure (7%)] (Fig. 3). As a PKI strength can be summarized down to specific end user trust judgments, regarding the trustworthiness of certificate issuers, after reviewing the validity of a specific public key certificate, an extensive list of critical parameters, certificate repositories and cross certified authorities, an end-user inability to participate effectively diminishes the solutions overall effectiveness. What is even more striking is that a total 60% of users, responded that they were able to bypass the browser warning message and accept the digital certificate, thus visiting the website that had previously been deemed "unsecure" [32 users responded that they were able to bypass the message (26%), 41 that they believed they knew how to (34%) and 48 that they were unable to (40%)]. This was done without reviewing the certificate parameters.

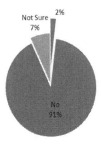
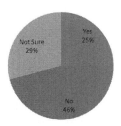

Fig. 3. Have you ever reviewed/validated a digital certificate?

Fig. 4. Do you know how to bypass such a warning message?

At this point we can state that the data clearly points towards users being unable to effectively perform in this situation. These questions were made while users were required to interact with the web site and check out related Firefox messages and pages. However, a very small number of users responded satisfactorily, which certainly rings a bell. Despite the fact that there has been over a decade since the first studies on the usability of cryptographic user interfaces (with most influential that of Whytten & Tygar [8]), it seems that current web-based user interfaces are still not 'passing the message' to online users.

In the following questions we enquired about users understanding of the messages presented to them when visiting a web server exhibiting a certificate issued by a RootCA not included in the Trusted Certificate Repository. A user's knowledgeful participation in this process is vital, as if a user accepts a certificate from an untrusted publisher, the user could be a victim of a plethora of malicious attacks, including password and information stealing, enabling malicious code execution etc. When visiting a website that exhibits a certificate not trusted by the Firefox browser, a message is presented to warn the user, such the following one, "This Connection is Untrusted- You have asked Firefox to connect securely to (domain name), but we can't confirm that your connection is secure". On many occasions trustworthy websites use certificates that are not included in the Trusted Root Certificate Repository. When enquired about this only 16% responded to understanding the nature of such a message.

Following this users were asked if they understood the message "The certificate is not trusted because the issuer certificate is not trusted". An overall of 93% does not seem to understand the nature of such a message (7% responded yes, 63% Responded No, 30% responded not sure). When users were asked if they understood what "This certificate is untrusted because it is self-signed" means, only 3% appears to understand. While most users do not understand the nature of these messages 60% knows how to override such a message and visit an untrusted site.

Acknowledging the issue the Extended Validation Certificates have been issued. EV Certificates use color-coding of the Web browser's address bar to signal secure connections. The browser navigation window turns green to indicate an authentically validated site with an EV Certificate, full security, and encryption in place, and turns red when it encounters an untrustworthy site. When enquired about these, only 39% responded to have ever noticed the coloring [47 responded had noticed the coloring (39%), 63 had not (52%) and 11 were not sure (9%)], while a total of 98% had no idea as to what the purpose of this coloring was [3 responded positively (2%), 106 negatively(88%) and 12 were unsure(10%)].

4   Summary and Conclusion

Overall, the collected data indicates that users are unable to effectively complete specific tasks that are required from an end-user to establish secure communications in the context of PKI environments. In view of these tasks, while users are required to validate the domain name, expiration date on the digital certificate or check if a certificate has been revoked, 98% of responders (from a group that is considered above average) have never viewed a digital certificate or are not sure how to view one. Even in the case that one of these checks fails, 92% of responders does not know how to manage (delete) certificates. While users are required to validate the trustworthiness of the certification authority, 93% of responders do not understand what a certification authority is but most dangerously 54% does know how to get past a warning security message and add an exception to a specific certificate. The exponential rise of risks in the digital world demands a redesign of applications interface that manage, use and interact with digital certificates, as the problematic dimension in a PKI environment, appears to be a usability problem.

References

1. APWG: Phishing Activity Trends Report 2nd Quarter 2010 (2010)
2. Matrosov, A., Rodionov, E., Harley, D., Malcho, J.: Stuxnet Under the Microscope. ESET Technical Report (2011)
3. Kaspersky Lab: Kaspersky Lab provides its insights on Stuxnet worm. Kaspersky Lab Technical Repost (2010), http://www.kaspersky.com/news?id=207576183
4. Lekkas, D.: Establishing and managing trust within the Public Key Infrastructure. Computer Communications 26(16), 1815–1825 (2003)
5. Diffie, W., Hellman, M.E.: New Directions in Cryptography. IEEE Trans. on Info. Theory IT-22, 644–654 (1976)
6. Massimiliano, P., Smith, S.: Finding the PKI needles in the Internet haystack. Journal of Computer Security 18(3) (2010); The 2007 European PKI Workshop: Theory and Practice (EuroPKI 2007)
7. Davis, D.: Compliance Defects in Public-Key Cryptography. In: Proc. 6th Usenix Security Symp., San Jose, CA, pp. 171–178 (1996)
8. Whitten, A., Tygar, D.: Why Johnny can't encrypt: A usability evaluation of PGP 5.0. In: Proceedings of the 8th USENIX Security Symposium, pp. 169–183 (1999)
9. Kirk, J.: Zeus malware used pilfered digital certificate. In: Computer World (2010)
10. Wegele, T.: Malware signed with fake Avira Certificate. Computer Security News & Articles (2011)

Towards Colored Petri Net Modeling
of Expanded C-TMAC

Apostolos K. Provatidis, Christos K. Georgiadis, and Ioannis K. Mavridis

University of Macedonia, Department of Applied Informatics,
Egnatia 156, 540 06 Thessaloniki, Greece
{Provatidis,geor,mavridis}@uom.gr

Abstract. Today advancements in information technology have led to multi-user information systems of high complexity, where users can group, collaborate and share resources. The variety of such systems include a wide range of applications such as collaborative document sharing and editing, social networks, work flow management systems, mobile location based applications etc. As those systems continue to evolve, additional requirements arise which need to be met, such as context inclusion in access control decision making and security policies that support grouping, collaboration and sharing. To address this need, we are working on expanding C-TMAC, a security model that intrinsically supports grouping, collaboration and context awareness. In this perspective, we utilize the mathematical modeling language of Colored Petri Nets, along with the CPNtools, in order to represent and analyze the basic components of C-TMAC model.

Keywords: Security, Access Control, C-TMAC, RBAC, Colored Petri Nets, CPNtools, Formal Modeling and Analysis.

1   Introduction

A multi-user, information and resource sharing environment is bound to the conflict of the competing goals of collaboration and security, as ease of access is not easily paired to the availability, confidentiality, and integrity requirements of a solid security policy. In addition, the inclusion of context in these systems means that information of high sensitivity is processed which needs to be very carefully controlled. The particular need of controlling the information flow between individuals in such systems, demands for a security model that can effectively address these combined requirements.

Besides the classical access control approaches, like Mandatory Access Control (MAC), Discretionary Access Control (DAC) and Role based Access Control (RBAC), the Context-Based Team Access Control (C-TMAC) model was first introduced in [1]. C-TMAC is an extension of the highly established RBAC [2]. The purpose of this paper is to formally represent and analyze the basic components of the C-TMAC model, in order to identify its strengths and shortcomings. Working on this direction, we aim at expanding C-TMAC by enriching its intrinsic support of

H. Jahankhani et al. (Eds.): ICGS3/e-Democracy 2011, LNICST 99, pp. 88–95, 2012.
© Institute for Computer Sciences, Social Informatics and Telecommunications Engineering 2012

grouping collaboration and context awareness. In order to represent and analyze the C-TMAC model we utilize the strong mathematical modeling language of Colored Petri Nets (CPNs) that permit future analysis and verification processes.

The rest of the paper is organized as follows: the fundamental notions and notations used throughout the paper are presented in Section 2, which includes a brief presentation of the C-TMAC model. Moreover, the mathematical language chosen for modeling C-TMAC and the specific tool suite CPNtools for editing, simulating, and analyzing Colored Petri nets are briefly discussed. Section 3 contains related research that has been developed in two directions: exploiting of the context concept in RBAC-based access control approaches and utilizing formal analysis and verification methods for access control requirements addressing purposes. The developed Colored Petri Net of the expanded C-TMAC, is presented in Section 4. Section 5 concludes this paper and outlines future research directions.

2   Background

2.1   C-TMAC

The need for Users being able to collaborate in Teams and the notion of access rights associated to Teams was recognized early in the development of access control models. In RBAC [2] [3] models, Users belonging to the same Role can be defined as a group, but there are limitations in collaboration of users assigned to different Roles. Thomas in [4] proposed the Team Based Access Control (TMAC) model in which he explores the team-based nature of access and work in collaborative settings by defining two aspects of the collaboration context, user context and object context and the ability to apply this context to decisions concerning permission activation.

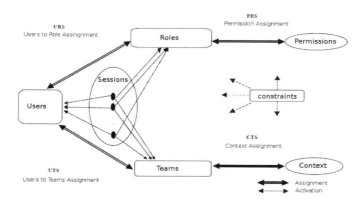

Fig. 1. The C-TMAC model

With the introduction of the C-TMAC model [1], the original TMAC was extended in two key directions: a framework to integrate TMAC concepts with RBAC and the use of other contextual information besides what is currently used in the user context and object context in TMAC such as time, place, etc. Context is integrated as an entity in the model schema (Fig 1). A further expansion of C-TMAC is discussed in Section 4.

2.2   Colored Petri Nets and CPNtools

A Petri Net or Place – Transition Net, is a graphical tool used for the description and analysis of concurrent processes which arise in systems with many components, first proposed by Carl Adam Petri in 1962. The classical Petri net is a directed bipartite graph with two node types: rectangular shapes which denote Places (or Conditions or States) and round shapes which denote Transitions. They are interconnected by directed arcs. Only connections between different types of nodes are allowed. At any given time a place can contain zero or more Tokens, drawn as black dots. Tokens indicate the present state-of affairs and can be moved by the occurrence of transitions.

An extension of Petri Nets was introduced by Jensen [5], named Colored Petri Nets (CPNs), allowing tokens to be associated with colors. CPNs are an extension of Petri Nets with more expressive power. In a standard Petri net, tokens are indistinguishable. In a CPN, every token has a value (color).

In order to be able to practically make use of CPN graphical tool we need the aid of computer tools supporting the creation and manipulation of models. CPNtools is a tool suite for editing, simulation, and state space or performance analysis of CPN models. CPNtools suite provides a graphical representation of the CPN model, which is easy to edit, and capable of running extensive simulations.

3   Related Work

Several research efforts have addressed the issue of context inclusion in RBAC based models such as the TRBAC model [6] that allows temporal constraints on role enabling and disabling. The GTRBAC model [7] is a more generalized version of the Temporal RBAC model that supports various temporal constraints on User-Role assignment, Role activation, Role-Permission assignment, Role hierarchy and Separation of Duty. Covington et al. [8] define context information as environmental Roles, which are used to perform context-dependent tasks, and are activated based on environment conditions at the time of request. In a different approach [9], context based constraints are associated with activation of Role permissions. In [10] a programming framework for building context aware applications is presented, providing mechanisms for specifying and enforcing context-based access control requirements.

Also in a more collaborative approach, Liscano and Wang [11] extends the dRBAC model [12], by applying context information conditions into delegations and propose a temporary Session Role, which Users can use to delegate a set of their permissions, in order to enable access to each other's resources. Collaborations in Teams, was also explored in [13]. In addition, Tolone et al. in [14] provide an examination of access control models as applied to collaboration, pointing out the benefits and the weaknesses of these models. In their work the C-TMAC model promisingly addresses the criteria the models are examined against, but as they state: "is not yet been fully developed, and it is not clear how to incorporate the team concept into a general RBAC framework".

As context inclusion and collaboration support in the security model of multi-user environments is an ongoing research area, we contribute to the need for the C-TMAC model to be further investigated and explored. In order to accomplish that, a formal verification method is required: our decision to relay on CPNs is consistent with several other researchers' efforts that explored RBAC based models using the same method.

Specifically Shafiq et al. in [15] proposed a Petri-Net based framework for the verification of correctness of event-driven RBAC policies. Rakkay and Boucheneb in [16] use CPNs and CPNtools to provide a general CPN model that shape most access control aspects with respect to RBAC policy requirements, also using CPN reachability analysis to check whether the access control requirements have been sufficiently addressed. Timed CPNs are used in [17] to model temporal constraints and analyze the TRBAC model [6]. Furthermore, Generalized Temporal RBAC (GTRBAC) model [7] is analyzed in [18] with the aid of timed automata.

To the best of our knowledge, no attempt has been made yet to represent and analyze TMAC or C-TMAC using CPNs or any other formal verification method.

4   Modeling C-TMAC

Over the last decade there were many important advancements concerning RBAC based models, as illustrated in the previous sections. In order to expand the C-TMAC model, we adopt the event based realization of RBAC specified in GTRBAC [7]. GTRBAC distinguishes between different states of a Role, namely *assigned, enabled* and *active*.

If a User is authorized to use a Role then this Role is *assigned* to the User. The *enabled* state indicates that Users who are authorized to use a Role at the time of the request may activate the Role and subsequently the *disabled* state indicates that the Role cannot be used in any User Session (due to constraints). A role in the *active* state implies that there is at least one User who has activated the Role.

According to previous CPNs of RBAC based models [15, 16], the constraints related to state transitions of Roles that are taken into account are:

- Cardinality constraints
- Role hierarchy constraints
- Separation of Duty constraints

In the C-TMAC model, both Roles and Teams are assigned to Users (see figure 1). The use of Teams as an intermediary to enable Users obtain context is similar to the use of Roles as an intermediary to enable Users obtain Permissions. Context entity includes information regarding the required data objects for a specific activity, as well as contextual information such as locations or time intervals, and can be expressed in terms of ranges of values.

For the detailed representation of the C-TMAC, we isolate in this work two important aspects of the model: the User-Role-Session aspect and the User-Team-Session aspect.

In the User-Role-Session aspect of C-TMAC the User obtains the sum of Permissions of the Roles he activates within a Session (we call them Session-Roles Permissions). The event based RBAC CPN model presented in [16] can be sufficiently used for the User-Role-Session aspect of the C-TMAC.

In the User-Team-Session aspect of C-TMAC, the User obtains the sum of Context of all Teams he participates in a Session (we call it Session-Team Context). Besides context, the User also obtains a combination of permissions of the Roles participating in those Teams (combination responds to Aggregation, Maximum/Minimum or Current Team Structure, see [1]), which we call Team-Roles Permissions. Following the event based approach, we define states for the Teams as well, which in accordance to these of Roles are: *assigned*, *enabled* and *active*. The CPN representation of the User-Team-Session aspect of the event based C-TMAC model is shown in figure 2.

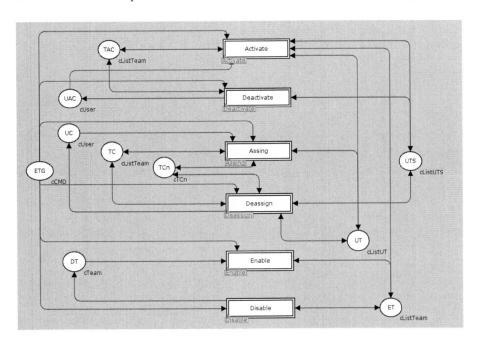

Fig. 2. CPN representation of the User-Team-Session aspect of the event based C-TMAC model

The specification of this CPN is similar to the previously mentioned User-Role-Session CPN. Due to space limitations we state some key elements and differences:

- Color declarations are changed to include Teams instead of Roles (figure 3).
- Role Cardinality (RC), Role Activation Cardinality (RAC), Enabled Roles (ER), Disabled Roles (DR), User Role Assignment/Authorization (UR) and

User Role Session Activation (URS) places are replaced with Team Cardinality (TC), Team Activation Cardinality (TAC), Enabled Teams (ET), Disabled Teams (DT), User Team Assignment/Authorization (UR) and User Team Session Activation (UTS) places respectively.
- There are no hierarchy constraints. Instead we have Teams that are in conflict with each other and cannot be assigned to the same User, thus Role hierarchy (RH) place is replaced with Team Conflict (TCn) place.
- Guard functions and tokens are changed accordingly.

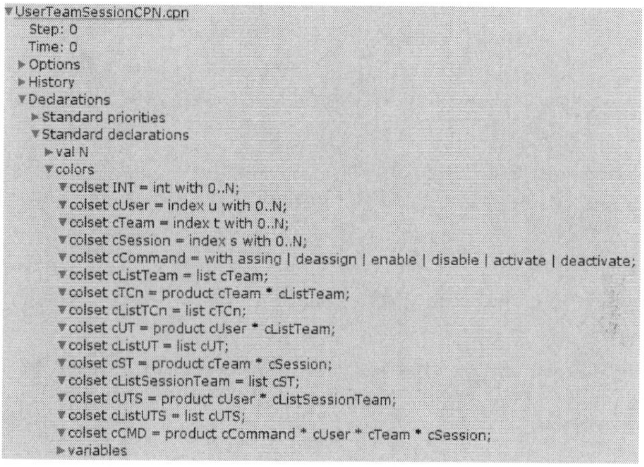

Fig. 3. Color declarations of User-Team-Session CPN

The constraints related to state transitions of Teams, which are defined and taken into account in this CPN, are:

- Cardinality Constraints
- Team Cardinality (TC): The number of authorized Users for any Team does not exceed the authorization cardinality of that Team.
- User Cardinality (UC): The number of Teams authorized for any User does not exceed the maximum number of Teams the User is entitled to acquire.
- User Activation Cardinality (UAC): The number of Teams activated by any User does not exceed the maximum number of Teams the User is entitled to activate at any time
- Team Activation Cardinality (TAC): The number of Users who have activated a Team in their Sessions does not exceed the Team activation cardinality.
- Separation of duty Constraints
- Any two Teams assigned to the same User are not in conflict with each other

The two aspects of the C-TMAC jointly provide the final Permission set of the User: the Context-based Permissions, which are produced by the combination of Session-Roles Permissions and Team-Roles Permissions, filtered by Session-Team Context.

This CPN can be used for security policy verification regarding the participation of Users to Teams within Sessions. In combination with the corresponding CPN of the User-Role-Session aspect, they form a framework for security policy verification of C-TMAC systems.

5   Conclusions

In this paper an expanded C-TMAC model is presented, which combines notions of GTRBAC with grouping and context awareness. Using CPNs to represent the expanded C-TMAC aids to the clarification of the model, and makes the incorporation of the Team concept into a general RBAC framework clearer. Several Team related constraints could now be defined and illustrated along with the process of User participation to Teams within a Session in the corresponding CPN. For the CPN produced, an effort has been made to be as much identical to the one illustrating Roles constraints and User activation of Roles within a Session, as possible. This significantly reduces the complexity of the C-TMAC formal verification using CPNs.

Furthermore, adopting the event based approach of GTRBAC and integrating it to Teams as well as Roles results into an expanded version of C-TMAC and aids to the definition of Team Constraints. Temporal constrains in a context aware model are certainly a direction worth of closer examination in future research. An extensive version of this paper can include the full specification, simulations and reachability analysis of the CPNs for security policies verification of C-TMAC systems. Also, more Team related constrains can be defined, tailored to specific case studies.

Among the various applications of C-TMAC, defining a fine grained framework of Teams (groups) formation and user-permission assignment on them based on context, can aid to today's struggle of fine-tuning user permissions on the emerging social networks and the privacy concerns that they have surfaced.

C-TMAC can be particularly effective on emergency information systems, where the group of people corresponding to the emergency must obtain elevated permissions in accordance to the context of the emergency event.

References

1. Georgiadis, C.K., Mavridis, I., Pangalos, G., Thomas, R.K.: Flexible Team-Based Access Control Using Contexts. In: Proceedings of the Sixth ACM Symposium on Access Control Models and Technologies, Chantilly, Virginia, USA (2001)
2. Sandhu, R.S., Coyne, E.J., Feinstein, H.L., Youman, C.E.: Role-based access control models. Computer 29(2), 38–47 (1996)
3. Ferraiolo, D.F., Sandhu, R., Gavrila, S., Kuhn, D.R., Chandramouli, R.: Proposed NIST standard for role-based access control. ACM Trans. Inf. Syst. Secur. 4(3), 224–274 (2001)
4. Thomas, R.K.: Team-Based Access Control (TMAC): A Primitive for Applying Role-Based Access Controls in Collaborative Environments. In: Proceedings of the Second ACM Workshop on Role-based Access Control, Fairfax, VAUSA, pp. 13–19 (1997)
5. Jensen, K.: Coloured Petri Nets. Basic Concepts, Analysis Methods and Practical Use. Three Volumes (1997)

6. Bertino, E., Bonatti, P.A., Ferrari, E.: TRBAC: A temporal role based access control model. ACM Transactions on Information and System Security 4(3), 191–223 (2001)

7. Joshi, J.B.D., Bertino, E., Latif, U., Ghafoor, A.: A generalized temporal role based access control model. IEEE Transactions on Knowledge and Data Engineering 17(1), 4–23 (2005)

8. Covington, M.J., Long, W., Srinivasan, S., Dey, A.K., Ahamad, M., Abowd, G.D.: Securing Context-Aware Applications Using Environment Roles. In: SACMAT 2001: Proceedings of the Sixth ACM Symposium on Access Control Models and Technologies, pp. 10–20 (2001)

9. Neumann, G., Strembeck, M.: An Approach to Engineer and Enforce Context Constraints in an RBAC Environment. In: SACMAT 2003: Proceedings of the Eighth ACM Symposium on Access Control Models and Technologies, pp. 65–79 (2003)

10. Kulkarni, D., Tripathi, A.: Context-aware role-based access control in pervasive computing systems. In: SACMAT, pp. 113–122 (2008)

11. Liscano, R., Wang, K.: A SIP-based Architecture model for Contextual Coalition Access Control for Ubiquitous Computing. In: Proceedings of the Second Annual Conference on Mobile and Ubiquitous Systems (MobiQuitous 2005). IEEE Computer Society Press (2005)

12. Freudenthal, E., Pesin, T., Port, L., Keenan, E.: dRBAC: Distributed Role-based Access Control for Dynamic Coalition Environments. In: 22nd International Conference on Distributed Computing Systems (ICDCS 2002), pp. 411–420. IEEE ((2002)

13. Alotaiby, F.T., Chen, J.X.: A Model for Team-based Access Control (TMAC 2004). In: Proceedings of the International Conference on Information Technology: Coding and Computing (ITCC 2004), vol. 2, p. 450. IEEE Computer Society, Washington, DC (2004)

14. Tolone, W., Ahn, G., Pai, T., Hong, S.: Access control in collaborative systems. ACM Comput. Surv. 37(1), 29–41 (2005)

15. Shafiq, B., Masood, A., Joshi, J., Ghafoor, A.: A role-based access control policy verification framework for real-time systems. In: WORDS 2005: Proceedings of the 10th IEEE International Workshop on Object-Oriented Real-Time Dependable Systems, pp. 13–20. IEEE Computer Society, Washington (2005)

16. Rakkay, H., Boucheneb, H.: Security Analysis of Role Based Access Control Models Using Colored Petri Nets and CPNtools. In: Gavrilova, M.L., Tan, C.J.K., Moreno, E.D. (eds.) Transactions on Computational Science IV. LNCS, vol. 5430, pp. 149–176. Springer, Heidelberg (2009)

17. Kadloul, L., Djouani, K., Tfaili, W.: Using Timed Colored Petri Nets and CPN-tool to Model and Verify TRBAC Security Policies. In: Fourth International Workshop on Verification and Evaluation of Computer and Communication Systems, VECoS 2010 (2010)

18. Mondal, S., Sural, S., Atluri, V.: Towards formal security analysis of GTRBAC using timed automata. In: Proceedings of the 14th ACM Symposium on Access Control Models and Technologies (SACMAT 2009), pp. 33–42. ACM, NY (2009)

Leveraging the e-passport PKI to Achieve Interoperable Security for e-government Cross Border Services

Dimitrios Lekkas and Dimitrios Zissis

Department of Product and Systems Design Engineering
University of the Aegean, Syros, Greece
{Dlek,Dzissis}@aegean.gr

Abstract. Public Key Infrastructure is identified as the essential architecture upon which security and trust are built, in order to provide authentication, identity verification, encryption and non-repudiation in electronic transactions. Cross border availability of e-government services requires such a security infrastructure to provide a horizontal level of service across all implicated entities. This paper identifies the unique characteristics of a necessary interoperable security infrastructure and towards this goal explores the restrictions of current authentication approaches. Following this, the ability of the electronic passport PKI solution to extend and meet the demands of an interoperable cross border e-id solution is explored, as the requirements of such an authentication mechanism correlate to the characteristics of the deployed e-passport infrastructure. Finally, this paper proposes leveraging the e-passport infrastructure, to build a secure cross border authentication mechanism.

Keywords: Public Key Infrastructure (PKI), e-passport, e-ID, identification, authentication, e-government, e-voting.

1   Introduction

Countries and states globally, realizing the benefits that Information and Communication Technologies can offer, by increasing the effectiveness, efficiency, interactiveness, decentralization, transparency, and accountability of delivered services have proceeded in implementing electronic governments. These implementations have been guided by a number of initiatives and policies which set the target goals and required development frameworks. Today the field has reached a stage of relative maturity, due to the intense scrutiny that has occurred over recent years, and a change of focus is taking place. Current initiatives are moving away from offering solutions in an asymmetrical method and are building towards electronic governments with strong synergy between them, while achieving high citizen participation, promoting knowledge sharing and achieving economies of scale.

Towards this goal, the Lisbon Treaty introduces a whole new dimension of participatory democracy alongside that of representative democracy on which the European Union is founded [1]. The Lisbon Treaty, enables one million citizens who are nationals of a significant number of Member States to call directly on the

H. Jahankhani et al. (Eds.): ICGS3/e-Democracy 2011, LNICST 99, pp. 96–103, 2012.
© Institute for Computer Sciences, Social Informatics and Telecommunications Engineering 2012

European Commission to bring forward an initiative of interest to them in an area of EU competence"[1]. This provision provides an opportunity to bring the Union closer to its citizens and to foster greater cross-border debate about EU policy issues, by bringing citizens from a range of countries together in supporting one specific issue.

The guiding principles for the implementation of the citizen initiative in the Lisbon Treaty are as follows; [1],

— The conditions should ensure that citizen initiatives are representative of a Union interest, whilst ensuring that the instruments remain easy to use.
— The procedures should be simple and user-friendly, whilst preventing fraud or abuse of the system and they should not impose unnecessary administrative burdens on Member States.

Given the importance of these new provisions of the Treaty for citizens, civil society and stakeholders across the EU, and considering the complexity of some of the issues to be addressed, the Commission launched a broad public consultation with the adoption of a "GreenPaper" on 11 November 2009. Respondents broadly supported the idea of having a common set of procedural requirements for the collection and verification of statements of support, so as to ensure a uniform process across the EU and to avoid organizers having to comply with different rules in each Member State. The possibility of online "signing" was called for unanimously, since it would greatly facilitate the collection of signatures [2]. However, in order to ensure that statements of support collected online are as genuine as those collected in paper format, the proposal requires that online collection systems should have adequate security features in place, and that the Member States should certify the conformity of such systems with those security requirements, without prejudice to the responsibility of the organizers for the protection of personal data [2].

Although the vision of using digital certificates for the verification and authentication of e-government services deployed across Europe, appears to be commonsense, the inherent perplexities and complexities of the task at hand, are soon evident. Digitally signing a document is a process we have become accustomed to, as it provides for the electronic representation of the traditional signing process. Digital signatures are used to preserve the basic security characteristics of digital documents, such as integrity and authenticity, while acting as the principal verification method of the signer's intended meaning, as expressed in the respective document. The creation of a digital signature cannot be denied as an action (non-repudiation), since it can be algorithmically proven, using cryptographic techniques. But the process of evaluating a digital signatures authenticity relies upon a horizontal support infrastructure that guarantees the uniqueness and originality of the signature, while correlating it to a specific individual (the signer). Cross-border digital signing requires an infrastructure that can provide this service uniformly across borders and services, that at present is not in existence. Today, the e-government services themselves are rarely, or not easily, available across borders. Europe currently needs better administrative cooperation to develop and deploy cross-border public online services, including practical e-Identification and e-Authentication solutions [3].

It is vital, that all present and future plans and implementations for electronic democracy build upon the principles identified in these initiatives, which include

- Targeting enhancing participation in electronic democracy [2]
- Providing better services delivered over fewer resources, by optimizing the use of available resources and instruments [4]
- Targeting overcoming economic, social and environmental challenges [4]
- Promoting cross border interoperability of services [3]
- Promoting cross border collaboration and scalability [3]
- Encouraging the exchange of best practices between Member States[3]
- Are designed as part of a horizontal security service, so as to ensure uniform conditions of access to e-government services across member states [2]

These principles suggest a design framework for architects, implementers, researchers and stakeholders with recommendations that can assist in decisions regarding deployment choices but also assist in understanding the ambiguities, complexities and requirements of planning, designing and deploying such Information Systems.

2   Electronic Identification and Authentication

High risk threshold applications, such as electronic government services, services dealing with highly sensitive information, require strong multifactor authentication to ensure protection of data and communications. This need is addressed by electronic IDentification (e-ID) systems. An e-ID infrastructure is understood as an Authentication Framework that enables individuals to access various e-services offered by government and non-governmental entities, using a single dedicated identity profile and making use of multi-factor authentication techniques. In terms of STORK project "Electronic Identity" is defined as "a collection of identity attributes in an electronic form" [6]. These attributes are combined with smart card technology, digital signatures and a user's "knowledge" of a pin number to generate multifactor authentication. The development of e-ID infrastructures varies considerably across Europe. From 2000 onwards, a number of countries have implemented e-ID card projects, with Italy and Finland being the early adopters (2000 and 2003, respectively), Austria and Belgium followed in 2004, the Netherlands and Sweden in 2005, Portugal in 2007, Germany and Poland are currently starting their e-ID card rollout, while a large number of countries are planning deployment[7].

Public Key cryptography realizes the concept of digital signatures; it provides a practical, elegant mechanism for symmetric key agreement; and in combination with smart card technology currently enables the strongest available authentication of involved entities and secure communications. A Public Key Infrastructure (PKI) is a set of hardware, software, people, policies, and procedures needed to create, manage, distribute, use, store, and revoke digital certificates. A PKI infrastructure is comprised of several working units, which can be easily correlated to the required services an e-Id infrastructure is required to provide. PKI deployments often include a Certification Authority and a Registration Authority. The CAs role is to certify the key pair/identity binding, by digitally signing a data structure that contains some representation of the identity and a corresponding public key. This data structure is called a digital certificate. The concept of National PKI is conceived by a large number of governments, as the de facto infrastructure onto which policies, technology and security can be built upon, in order to provide authentication, identity verification, encryption and non-repudiation in electronic services [7].

It is safe to say that across Europe, all countries are not only at different stages of maturity with regards to deployment of e-id infrastructures and respective PKI's, but also lack a common set of implementation mechanisms [8]. While at a national level the schemes might operate as initially designed, attempting to use e-ID cards to address cross-border function's, has proved to be nearly impossible as these systems are highly interoperable; at a smart card communication level, data access protocols, data definition, algorithms and at a PKI level[4][8]. Identifying the problem, a series of European Union initiatives and frameworks have been issued. Notable examples include the Secure Identity Across Borders Linked (STORK) for Electronic Identities (e-ID), the eID Interoperability for PEGS project and the Pan European Public Procurement Office (PEPPOL) for public procurement [9]. While these initiatives can be considered as steps into the correct direction, unfortunately they are mostly lacking to capture some vital requirements, such as enabling in-card el-gamal signature to achieve scalability such as e-voting etc [10].

Achieving interoperability of e-ids at a PKI trust level is crucial as the electronic services for identification, authentication and signature creation purposes are based on public key procedures. The validation of these processes requires a level of trust above the end user. This trust requires cross border cooperation, between the Certification Authorities of National PKI's. This certainly requires a common understanding of all identity management issues (legal, technical, organizational). End user certificates, which are stored on the card and link user specific data (unique identifiers, etc.), with the corresponding public keys, are signed with the PKI's root certificate (or an intermediate certificate, which in turn is signed by the root certificate). If this cross border cooperation is not achieved, it is not possible to effectively validate a citizen's signature, or authentication request successfully[4]. Unfortunately in current implementations the notion of trust is not clearly identified and either the researchers do not address it or it is considered as de facto granted.

The deployment of a large Public Key Infrastructure, that shall effectively and proficiently escalate into a pan-European Electronic Identification Infrastructure, covering all needs of security for e-Government, is a highly complex task. Such an infrastructure is itself required to be highly-interoperable, scalable and efficient. Overall, an authentication mechanism, achieving cross border interoperability is required to fulfill a number of requirements,

—Technology compatibility (Common Data formats-Semantics; Communication Protocol Compatibility; Algorithm usage compatibility; Card compatibility-Reader Compatibility)
—Policy Compatibility (Registration procedures and requirements(identity proofing etc); Operational Requirements
—Security Schema Compatibility(Common understanding of security risk assessment analysis; Common definition of risk assessment criteria, typically combined with a consideration of potential damage in case of incidents; these should be the basis for determining security requirements, i.e. Authentication Assurance Levels)
—Legal Compatibility (Privacy & Data Protection legal framework; Legal Data Signature Validity)

—PKI Compatibility (Trust relationships must be established between issuing authorities; Deployment architecture compatibility)
—Directories must be complex free and achieve high compatibly
—Infrastructure must be able to achieve high scalability to respond to dynamics of user population

3   Leveraging e-Passport Infrastructure

While the research community has been involved in time consuming recursive debates on how to implement a globally acceptable and trusted Public Key Infrastructure, it seems that the e-passports PKI currently deployed in several countries provides a potentially friendly environment for achieving the necessary global trust. Electronic passports, or e-passports, are being issued and inspected across the globe in accordance with International Civil Aviation Organization (ICAO) standards for Machine Readable Travel Documents (MRTD). Every e-Passport has an embedded electronic chip that contains the holder's personal information and photo found in the passport. To achieve interoperability a common understanding between participants on data structures and communications was required. This was achieved in MRTD, as all MRTDs follow a standardized layout to facilitate reading of data on a global basis by both eye readable and machine readable means. In order to increase confidence in the MRTD scheme, the ePassport chip is digitally signed to prevent unauthorized alteration and ensure authenticity. In order to verify a digital signature, border and other authorities need to access the ePassport's public key. As electronic passports are designed to be of maximum use in facilitating international travel, successfully validating these documents at inspection points is critical. That is why it is crucial to share the public keys as widely as possible [11]. The aim of this process is to link the passports validity and authenticity back to the issuing authority.

To achieve this, a web of trust is set up between implicated parties. The inspecting entity accepts the e-passport as valid, because it trusts the authenticity of the signing respective authority. Basically, a chain of electronic certificates and signatures is created with one end securely anchored in the authority of the issuing state and the other end securely stored in the respective chip [12]. The validity of these documents is checked by comparing the validity of the implicated certificates, usually at the top of the chain, with the certificate of the country's issuing authority. This validation, requires that the inspection entity has access to the certificate of the respective country, to validate against it, otherwise this process is broken.

The most important advantage currently offered by the e-passport infrastructure is the established worldwide trust; the e-passport PKI offers a global multilateral framework to verify the entire chain of certificates issued by each country. This is achieved either with country cross certification, or by using the ICAO Public Key Directory (PKD). Technically, a trust relationship is established when a Country decides to trust the root certificate (the certificate of the CSCA) of another Country. This de-facto trust infrastructure overcomes the basic drawback of the most commercial or closed-groups PKIs. It is critical that e-id infrastructure's leverage this global trust framework, as it provides the required platform for global interoperability at a PKI level. In addition, leveraging the e-passport infrastructure achieves economies of scale and knowledge, according to the requirements set by recent initiatives, (as identified in previous section).

A strategic decision for the current implementation of e-passports, is the lack of citizen certificates, in order to facilitate a fast-track implementation and to avoid the complexity of managing client certificates and keys. The X.509 digital certificates, which are issued for the ICAO PKI implementation, are currently restricted only to the authorities issuing the passports (i.e. the hierarchy of Country Signing CA and the subordinate Document Signing CA). Although the e-passport does not contain an X.509.v3 certificate and it is not designed for everyday Internet transactions, it exhibits all-but-one of the characteristics of a typical PKI-enabled smart card, containing a private key and the relevant digital certificate.

The e-passport member states PKIs, follow the standard architecture proposed by ICAO and are deployed in a hierarchical architecture. A hierarchical architecture has been proven under real-world conditions to scale smoothly from hundreds to millions of users [13]; thus achieving the demanded scalability requirement. Trust operates in a hierarchical manner, starting at the country's highest certification authority. At the top of the hierarchy is the Country Signing Certificate Authority, which is responsible for issuing certificates for the subordinate Document Signer Certificate Authority and for cross certification with other national CSCA. The Document Signing CA signs the passport's data, including a public key (Active Authentication key) stored in each passport. Leveraging existing software, procedures and policies, we propose deploying a subordinate CA, the Identification Signing Certification Authority (ISCA), which can be deployed with minimal complexity and cost, and shall be delegated with the authority of issuing end user X509 certificates. This ISCA is deployed as a subordinate CA to CSCA inheriting cross country trust relationships. This enables certificates issued by the ISCA, to be automatically trusted by any other state or country that has been cross certified or has joined the ICAO PKD.

Extending the e-passport infrastructure can address a plethora of previously identified requirements, while adding value to the overall security of e-government. The deployment of the e-passport infrastructure enabled the development of policies and procedures that guarantee strict citizen identification and registration required for a secure e-id infrastructure. These procedures include designing processes such as secure registration, deployments, contingency and recovery planning, and many more. These procedures easily correlate to the required procedures for safe issuance of secure e-ids as they share a common security profile. Leveraging the e-passport infrastructure provides a plethora of additional benefits. Since the ID cards are accepted as travel documents within Schengen States, their profile is required to be in conformity with many ICAO specifications, common to the e-passport [14]. The global e-passports implementation seems to be an attractive PKI establishment, since:

—The passport as a digital identity is issued by governmental authorities, under very strict and reliable identification and issuance procedures for the citizens; due to the standardization of most of this process, member states are interoperable at policy procedures.

—The e-passports and electronic identity documents have common security profiles.

—The technology used throughout the world is compatible and, thus, interoperable. Due to the standardization of the PKI infrastructure it is highly interoperable and scalable, as common deployment models have been adopted across member states.

—High security procedures and operational models were defined during the deployment of e-passports, including the creation of high security facilities for the issuance of e-passports and for the protection of related data. The e-passport requirements are identical to the requirements of an e-id infrastructure at this level.

—A worldwide Web-of-Trust is established through a reliable and secure exchange of countries self-signed certificates.

—The member states legal framework has been addressed to be compatible with the e-passports; thus providing compatibility for e-id cards (registration requirements, policy, digital signatures , etc)

—The e-passport member states PKIs, follow the standards proposed by ICAO and are deployed in a hierarchical architecture.

Many enterprises currently operate independent directories based on closed propriety protocols. As the number of applications and utilities relying on these directories are increasing, current practices are becoming inefficient. In numerous occasions, electronic communications between unknown entities are staggered due to the lack of authenticity. There is a trust deficit in electronically presented credentials. Relying on information provided by a trusted directory would increase trust in all communication between member entities. The homogenous availability of a trusted directory, easily accessible and highly available overcomes this requirement, enabling stronger and safer e-commerce as it guarantees the validity of credentials of implicated parties. But also on a citizen's side, interaction with web services can be verifiable, as directories contain lists of information of natural but also legal entities. Validating an e-services certificate would thus increase the integrity of communications.

4   Conclusion

Currently, initiatives globally, and specifically in Europe, are targeting at increasing the interoperability and scalability of their services as they are aiming at providing cross border service delivery to their citizens. There is a growing need that stronger authentication mechanisms are implemented and in this direction e-id solutions based on PKI and smartcard technology are explored. A crucial element of e-ID infrastructures is achieving interoperability and scalability at PKI level. An e-ID infrastructure is as strong and as effective as the authentication services ability to correlate an entity's provided credentials with an entity's valid credentials. The validation of these processes requires a level of trust above the end user. Current PKI deployments lack the ability to address cross border cooperation, as differences exist either at a policy or functional level, arising serious limitations on cross border availability of these services.

In this paper we explore the e-passport PKI deployment, as it provides a potentially friendly environment upon which the necessary global trust is built. The e-passport infrastructure provides a successfully deployed architecture in many countries and states, which exhibits a plethora of required characteristics, which efficiently correlate to the requirements of an e-id infrastructure. At present, the e-passport infrastructure has established a worldwide trust net, offering a global multilateral framework to verify the entire chain of certificates issued by each country. We propose leveraging the existing infrastructure and processes by deploying the Identification Signing Certification Authority as a subordinate to the CSCA, inheriting the global web of trust relationships. The ISCA is delegated with the responsibility of issuing member states natural or legal entities certificates, either in hard or soft format, leveraging the existing infrastructures abilities and knowledge. The e-passport PKI infrastructure can be extended, with minimum complexity and cost to meet the additional demands of an interoperable e-id infrastructure. The proposed architecture provides a common interoperable security platform, while achieving economies of scale and knowledge.

References

1. SEC (2010) 370. Proposal for a Regulation Of The European Parliament And Of The Council on the citizens' initiative. Brussels (2010)
2. COM (2010) 119. Outcome of the public consultation on the Green Paper on a European Citizens Initiative. Brussels (2010)
3. EU Ministerial Declaration on e-Government. Malmö, Sweden (2009)
4. MEMO/10/681. Digital Agenda: eGovernment Action Plan –"what would it do for me?" Brussels (2010)
5. Zefferer, T.: (AT-TUG). STORK Work Item 3.3.5 Smartcard eID Comparison (2010)
6. Gutierrez, A., Piñuela, A.: STORK Glossary and Acronyms (2009)
7. Patsos, D., Ciechanowicz, C., Piper, F.: The status of National PKIs – A European overview. Information Security Technical Report 15(1), 13–20 (2010)
8. Arora, S.: National e-ID card schemes: A European overview. Information Security Technical Report 13(2), 46–53 (2008), doi:10.1016/j.istr.2008.08.002
9. IDABC. Study eID Interoperability for PEGS, Analysis & assessment report (2009)
10. Meister, G., Huhnlein, D., Eichholz, J., Araujo, R.: eVoting with the European Citizen Card. In: BIOSIG 2008, pp. 67–78 (2008), Retrieved from,
    http://www.ecsec.de/pub/ECC-voting.pdf
11. ICAO. Overview- The ICAO Public Key Directory (2009)
12. Hartmann, M., Körting, S., & Käthler, O.: A Primer on the ICAO Public Key Directory. Retrieved from,
    http://www.securitydocumentworld.com/client_files/
    hjp_pkd_promotion-paper_v1_5_20090520.pdf
13. HHS-IRM-2000-0011, HHS IRM Policy for Public Key Infrastructure (PKI); Certification Authority (CA) (2009)
14. Eurosmart. Position Paper European Citizen Card: One Pillar of Interoperable eID Success (2008), Retrieved from,
    https://www.eid-stork.eu/dmdocuments/public/
    ecc-position-paper-final.pdf

Genre-Based Information Hiding

Russell Ogilvie and George R.S. Weir[*]

Department of Computer & Information Sciences
University of Strathclyde
Glasgow G1 1XH
{rogilvie,george.weir}@cis.strath.ac.uk

Abstract. While data encryption is an effective means of keeping data private it does not conceal the presence of 'hidden' information, rather it serves as an indicator that such data is present. Concealing information and hiding the fact that information is hidden are both desirable traits of a confidential data exchange, especially if that exchange takes place across a public network such as the Internet. In the present paper, we describe an approach to textual steganography in which data is not only hidden, in virtue of its encoding, but the presence of hidden data is also concealed, through use of human-readable carrier texts. Information transmitted in this fashion remains confidential and its confidential nature is also concealed. The approach detailed addresses several shortcomings in previous work in this area. Specifically, we achieve a high rate of accuracy in message decoding and also produce carrier texts which are both coherent and plausible as human-readable plain text messages. These desirable features of textual steganography are accomplished through a system of sentence mapping and a genre-based approach to carrier text selection that produces contextually related content in the carrier messages.

Keywords: Textual steganography, genre, data hiding.

1   Introduction

The major attraction of steganography is not the goal of concealing data, since this can be achieved very effectively with current encryption techniques, but, more specifically, the goal of concealing the presence of concealed data [1]. Although such information hiding is often addressed through use of media data files as the 'carrier' for concealed data [2], there is an alternative but underdeveloped approach that seeks to conceal data within plain text. Such textual steganography is appealing but problematic when compared to transmission via image or audio carrier files. The major issues facing textual steganography are twofold:

(i)   Provide an encoding mechanism that is sufficiently flexible to conceal any required message;

(ii)   Create carrier texts that are plausible as 'ordinary' texts;

---

[*] Corresponding author.

H. Jahankhani et al. (Eds.): ICGS3/e-Democracy 2011, LNICST 99, pp. 104–111, 2012.

The first criterion relates to the successful encoding and decoding of messages while the second relates to the successful concealment of hidden data. In the following, we describe several approaches that have been used previously as a basis for textual steganography before proposing an alternative technique that we have developed, based upon sentence mapping and genre-specific carrier texts.

2   Strategies for Textual Steganography

Concealing data in text requires that aspects of the text serve as markers or codes for the concealed data. This parallels the use of altered pixel brightness or colour values in images as the 'codes' for concealed data. In the textual realm we may distinguish two varieties or strategies for steganography: presentational and linguistic. The presentational approach is simpler and uses variations in features such as inter-word or inter-line spacing to represent the hidden data. This is similar in concept to image steganography since it relies upon visual aspects in the carrier presentation that will be 'inconsequential' to the human observer but discernible through appropriate software analysis. Linguistic approaches tend to be more ambitious in their selection of coding strategy and rely upon changes to the textual content as a basis for conveying the hidden message.

2.1   Presentational Strategies

Presentational strategies for textual steganography include the use of features such as inter-word spacing; tabs and spaces; and line shifting. These approaches are outlined below.

Inter-Word Spacing
Delina [3] describes the technique of generating a cover text depending on the length of the secret message and altering the number of spaces between the words in the carrier text. One space between a word and the next word indicated a 0 and two spaces indicated a 1. The advantage of this method is that additional spaces in documents are fairly common especially if text justification or text centering is used. Thereby, this feature is unlikely to rouse suspicion. When a small font is used for document presentation a human cannot easily tell the difference between one space and two spaces. So it is likely that the presence of a secret message will not be discerned. However, a potential down side to this approach is that to convey a single character will generally require eight bits, meaning that eight inter-word spaces would be required to represent one character. This constraint means that only short hidden messages can be transmitted, unless the carrier text is very long.

A similar approach, termed 'word shifting', is described by Kim et. al. [4]. Arguably, this form of shifting may be less easy for a human to detect because horizontal shifting of words is common in newspapers, magazines and other documents to fill up lines of text and achieve text justification [5].

Tabs and Spaces

This variation on the use of inter-word spacing was developed by Mansor et. al [6]. Their program (SNOW) takes the secret message and a carrier text as input and uses an algorithm to add extra spaces and tabs to the end of some or all of the lines in the carrier text. A tab is always added first to indicate the start of the concealed message and then sequences of spaces and tabs are added to make up the secret message. The extra spaces and tabs cannot normally be seen by readers so will not arouse suspicion to a human who has a glance at it as the original carrier text is preserved. One drawback of this technique is that extra spaces and tabs may be detectable if the carrier text was viewed in a text editor. This may arouse suspicion that confidential data is hidden within.

Line Shifting

Textual steganography by means of 'line shifting' conceals data through small vertical adjustments (e.g., 1/300th of an inch) to the lines of text in the carrier message [7]. The receiving system detects these changes in vertical alignment and reconstitutes the hidden message accordingly. As with other presentational approaches, there is some risk that a human reader may notice slight variations in the alignment of the lines of text in a carrier message [8]. Furthermore, while this technique could be used in formatted electronic documents, it is best suited to printed texts [9]. Recovering the hidden information may be problematic in cases where the carrier text has been edited or retyped.

2.2   Linguistic Strategies

While presentational approaches can successfully conceal data and may do so in ways that are not noticed by the average human reader, they are primarily limited by their dependence upon preservation of document format and layout. This makes them better suited to document-based data hiding than 'live' transmission systems. In contrast, linguistic approaches to textual steganography adopt strategies that depend upon changes to the meaning of the carrier message. Unlike presentational approaches, linguistic techniques require a mechanism that changes words or word combinations as a basis for concealing the data. Linguistic strategies for textual steganography include the use of features such as word spelling, synonyms and phrase structures. These approaches are outlined below.

Changing Word Spelling

In this approach, data is concealed by changing the spelling of specific words in a piece of text, for example, British and US spelling [10]. A database (the resource) is created which holds lists of words which have different spellings in the British and US and the encoding program searches through the carrier text to find words which have different British and US spellings. The system changes words in the carrier text so that a US word denotes a 0 and a UK word denotes a 1 so that data can be hidden in the carrier text. At the receiver end the same database of words is used to search through the document in order to build up a sequence of 0 and 1s and thereby extract the hidden message. A potential downside to this approach is its sparsity of encoding. Only a small amount of data can be hidden in the carrier text because a whole word indicates only a single binary digit. Despite this limitation, this method would be very difficult to detect unless a human reader notices the mixture of American spelling and British spelling.

Synonym Replacement

An attempt to use synonym replacement as the mechanism for concealing data in carrier texts was developed by Morran & Weir [11]. This required the use of part-of-speech tagging on the secret text and the carrier text in order to identify suitable terms for synonym replacement, with the aim of maintaining the meaning and sense of the carrier text. Thereby, the private message may be concealed in the cover text with a key used to identify which words have been changed and, therefore, which words conceal parts of the hidden message. In order to eliminate the risk of significant changes in meaning, this approach also adopted word-sense disambiguation. Despite the sophistication of this approach, the resultant carrier texts were not always grammatical and meaningful.

Phrase Structures

Chapman et. al. [12] used part-of-speech analysis in order to identify specific phrasal forms in the carrier texts that could be replaced as a means of concealing data. This was implemented as a system called NICETEXT but, as with Morran and Weir's synonym replacement approach, NICETEXT was impaired by the limitations of part-of-speech tagging and suffered from occasional grammatical anomalies in the carrier texts [1].

3   Genre-Based Textual Steganography

With a view to addressing the main requirements of textual steganography, viz., providing a flexible encoding mechanism and creating carrier texts that are plausible as 'ordinary' texts, we combined two aspects in our prototype system. The first aspect is the use of a word to sentence mapping as a means of converting secret text to carrier text. This employed a database with a large set of words and an associated database of sentences. Words in the secret text are mapped algorithmically to specific sentences and the carrier text is a compilation of the successive sentences. This approach ensures that each sentence in the carrier text is grammatically well formed. The second aspect in our steganography system addresses the need for coherence across sentences. This is addressed through use of datasets of genre-specific sentences.

In principle, there might be any number of discrete genre-specific sentence datasets. Our prototype system presently operates with two sentence databases. The first of these is composed of sentences drawn from a corpus of computer science literature while the second is composed of sentences drawn from the Brown corpus. Before creating a carrier text from a specific secret text, the user chooses one or other genre database. Each word of the secret text is then mapped to a sentence from the selected genre dataset. The choice of genre is also conveyed as a concealed data item in the carrier text, thereby ensuring that the decoding process operates with the appropriate sentence dataset.

In the process of formulating the carrier text, each word of the secret text is located in the word dataset. For any word not already present in the dataset, the system adopts the 'new word' procedure. In this case, the new word is added to the sender-side database and then broken down into individual characters. The word dataset also contains a set of individual characters each of which can map to an item in the sentence dataset. This permits newly encountered words to be concealed and included within the carrier text. At the receiving side, new words are identified by an in-text code, decoded from the sentences in the carrier text and automatically added to the receiver-side database.

3.1   Example Codings

In the following examples, we show the secret message followed by the carrier texts from the Computer Science (CS) genre and then the Brown Corpus (Brown) genre.

Secret text 1: *I like watching films in the evening.*

CS Carrier text: *The stat_formula() interface allows derived instrumentation to be declared, creating a metric that is a function of other counters. SimpleScalar's software architecture has been improved and modularized, making the code easier to understand and modify. For tracers in real-world environments, however, especially on backbone networks where network traffic is very high, more memory will likely be needed. In GOMS terms, there must exist a method with operators to execute the command. An open distribution model has potential drawbacks, however. Direct user support creates by far the largest demand. The growth in the number of homes with always-on, high-speed broadband Internet connections has enabled hackers to spread bots widely and quickly, according to David Perry, global director of education for antivirus-software vendor Trend Micro.*

Brown carrier text: *It was marked by controversy, anonymous midnight phone calls and veiled threats of violence. The United States, State Department officials explain, now is mainly interested in setting up an international inspection system which will prevent Laos from being used as a base for Communist attacks on neighboring Thailand and South Viet Nam. Everybody has a different idea on the ethics and morals of driving away neighbors, when and if. This resulted in revisions of the King James Bible in 1881-85 as the English Revised Version and in 1901 as the American Standard Version. Kansas, regarded as tops in the nation in its treatment of the mentally ill, spends $9 per day per patient. And after several correspondents went into Pathet Lao territory and exposed the huge build-up, administration spokesmen acclaimed them for performing a great service and laid the matter before the Southeast Asia Treaty Organization. Of the millions who have served time in concentration camps in Siberia as political prisoners of the Soviet state, few emerge in the West to tell about it. Some 30 spectators remained in the court during the day and were on hand to hear the verdict read.*

Secret text 2: *The queen has gone to roost.*

CS carrier text: *One is that all DR(i, k)s are distributed evenly in a given range. Both evaluations followed the same layout and question structuring. In contrast to other bots, Bobax's primary purpose is to send spam. Problems in the representation of meaning in information retrieval. Naturally, this reflects on the accuracy of the relevance decision. Expected Output: +word +word +word Actual Output: As expected Pass/Fail: Pass. Most web pages you find today are written in HTML (HyperText Markup Language).*

Brown carrier text: *Research projects as soon as possible on the causes and prevention of dependency and illegitimacy. Mr and Mrs Stevens and the bride's other uncles and aunts, the Rush C Butlers, the Homer E Robertsons, and the David Q Porters, will give the bridal dinner tonight in the Stevenses' home. We (the Chicago Association of Commerce and Industry) expect to establish closer relations with nations and their cultural activities, and it will be easy as a member of the fair staff to bring in acts, explains Mrs Geraghty. Led fight on teamsters Gladden has been an outspoken critic of the present city administration and led his union's battle against the teamsters, which began organizing city firemen in 1959. The city is not adequately compensated for the services covered by the fees, he said. Families go out to the edge of the terraces to sit on carpets around a samovar. Those three other great activities of the Persians, the bath, the teahouse, and the zur khaneh (the latter a kind of club in which a leader and a group of men in an octagonal pit move through a rite of calisthenics, dance, chanted poetry, and music), do not take place in buildings to which entrance tickets are sold, but some of them occupy splendid examples of Persian domestic architecture : long, domed, chalk-white rooms with daises of turquoise tile, their end walls cut through to the orchards and the sky by open arches.*

3.2   Issues

While every tested example of encoded text has been successfully decoded, there remain some issues with the current prototype that we aim to address in future work. In the first place, the word-to-sentence mapping results in considerable expansion from the secret message size to the carrier text size. This is an inherent consequence of the mapping of individual words to sentences but can be reduced through more careful selection of sentences for the genre datasets. Specifically, we aim to prioritize shorter sentences in order to reduce the data inflation effect.

A second issue concerns the coherence of the resultant carrier texts. Although there is a high degree of coherence in the resultant sentences, there are indications that 'noise' in the sentence datasets can detrimentally impact upon the carrier text by introducing partial sentences (e.g., computer science article titles). This signifies a need to carefully filter the content of the sentence datasets in order to ensure their sentential integrity.

4   Conclusion

The aim of this work was to establish an effective means of concealing and conveying hidden messages in plain text such that the presence of such messages would not be discernible in the carrier texts. In evaluating the encoding and decoding process, 40 different secret texts of differing lengths and compositions were tested with the system. The results showed that 100% of the secret texts fed in to the system were recovered successfully. While such testing cannot guarantee that all possible carrier text will be decoded correctly, it lends plausibility to the system's effectiveness and shows that it is able to cope with a wide range of different secret texts.

As indicated above, the plausibility of carrier texts produced by the current prototype is high but occasionally leaves room for improvement. Overall, we are led to conclude that this approach achieves the two major issues facing textual steganography:

(i)   Provide an encoding mechanism that is sufficiently flexible to conceal any required message;

(ii)   Create carrier texts that are plausible as 'ordinary' texts.

The system on the whole does produce plausible carrier texts containing sentences which belong to the same genre and are grammatically and syntactically correct.

References

1. Weir, G.R.S., Morran, M.: Hiding the Hidden Message: Approaches to Textual Steganography. International Journal of Electronic Security and Digital Forensics 3(3), 223–233 (2010)
2. Marwaha, P.: Visual Cryptographic Steganography in Images. In: Proceedings of the 2010 Second International Conference on Computing, Communication and Networking Technologies (ICCCNT 2010), pp. 1–6 (2010)
3. Delina, B.: Information Hiding: A New Approach in Text Steganography. In: Proceedings of the International Conference on Applied Computer and Applied Computational Science, World Scientific and Engineering Academy and Society (WSEAS 2008), pp. 689–695 (2008)
4. Kim, Y., Moon, K., Oh, I.: A Text Watermarking Algorithm based on Word Classification and Inter-word Space Statistics. In: Proceedings of the Seventh International Conference on Document Analysis and Recognition (ICDAR 2003), pp. 775–779 (2003)
5. Shirali-Shahreza, M.: A New Synonym Text Steganography. In: Proceedings of the 2008 International Conference on Intelligent Information Hiding and Multimedia Signal Processing, pp. 1524–1526 (2008)
6. Mansor, S., Din, R., Samsudin, A.: Analysis of Natural Language Steganography. International Journal of Computer Science and Security (IJCSS) CSC Journals 3(2), 113–125 (2010)
7. Alattar, A., Alattar, O.: Watermarking Electronic Text Documents Containing Justified Paragraphs and Irregular Line Spacing. In: Proceedings of SPIE, Security, Steganography, and Watermarking of Multimedia Contents VI, vol. 5306, pp. 685–695 (2004)

8. Whitiak, D.: The Art of Steganography. SANS Institute, as part of GIAC Practical Repository, GSEC Practical (v.1.4b) (2003)

9. Shirali-Shahreza, M.: Text Steganography in SMS. In: Proceedings of the 2007 International Conference on Convergence Information Technology, November 21-23, pp. 2260–2265 (2008)

10. Shirali-Shahreza, M.: Text Steganography by Changing Words Spelling. In: 10th International Conference on Advanced Communication Technology (ICACT 2008), pp. 1912–1913 (2008)

11. Morran, M., Weir, G.: An Approach to Textual Steganography. Global Security, Safety, and Sustainability: Communications in Computer and Information Science 92, 48–54 (2010)

12. Chapman, M., Davida, G.: Hiding the Hidden: A Software System for Concealing Ciphertext as Innocuous Text. In: Han, Y., Quing, S. (eds.) ICICS 1997. LNCS, vol. 1334, pp. 333–345. Springer, Heidelberg (1997)

In the Hacker's Eye:
The Neurophysiology of a Computer Hacker

Wael Khalifa[1], Kenneth Revett[2], and Abdel-Badeeh Salem[1]

[1] Faculty of Computer and Information Science
Ain Shams University
Abbassia
Cairo, Egypt
{wael.khalifa,absalem}@asunet.shams.edu.eg
[2] Faculty of Informatics and Computer Science
British University in Egypt
El Sherouk City
Egypt
ken.revett@bue.edu.eg

Abstract. This paper presents data from a preliminary investigation on the neurophysiological changes that occur when a person attempts to crack a password. A password cracking scenario was provided to a small cohort of university students and while they were attempting to crack into the password, their EEG was recorded. The results indicate that the overall frontal lobe power (at electrode position F7) was significantly different during cracking as opposed to typing alone. Further, the principal visual area (O1 and O2 electrodes) electrodes displayed much more variability in the cracking scenario than in the transcriptional typing scenario. Further, the anterior frontal electrodes displayed much higher activation than in the transcriptional typing task. These results suggest that using EEG recording alone, a unique signature can be acquired in real-time which provides significant and suggestive evidence that the user is not merely typing – that they may be trying to crack into the system.

Keywords: affective computing, biometrics, electroencephalography, heart rate variability, neurophysiological computing, password hacking.

1   Introduction

This pilot study had two principal aims: 1) to investigate the effect of typing on the EEG and 2) to investigate whether a person attempting to hack into a computer system by on-line password cracking could be identified using standard electroencephalography (EEG) technology. The password cracking scenario was implemented using subjects that manually (as opposed to an automated character generating approach) attempted to guess a user's password while sitting at the host machine. This approach requires the user to type entries and as such, there are two elements involved in this process that are relevant here: i) the actual typing process and ii) and the hacking process. The assumption utilised in this study is that is that by

H. Jahankhani et al. (Eds.): ICGS3/e-Democracy 2011, LNICST 99, pp. 112–119, 2012.

subtracting out the typing element during keyboard entry based password cracking, we would be left with the 'cracking' aspects of this behavior. It is interesting to note that the literature is sparse on the effects of typing on the EEG – i.e. that those aspects of cognition involved in typing have not yet been elucidated based on published literature. A side effect of this paper is to provide some basic data on brain activation patterns that occur during transcriptional typing. Subjects are asked to perform keyboard entry of a small corpus of text (approximately 300 words) prior to the hacking scenario. The subjects were asked to type the corpus with no time limit – which was completed in approximately 10 minutes (range 7 +/- 2 minutes). The subjects were told that they did not have to worry about correctness – though the typing errors were on the order of 10%, indicating that the subjects were consciously attempting to correctly enter the corpus text.

Transcriptional typing also entails reading the text while typing, typically using an interleaving approach where text is read and stored in a 'mental buffer' – short term memory and the typed. Professional typists will be able to type without looking – and hence they can read the text continuously while typing, thereby producing very fast typing rates (60+ wpm). The subjects were university students and hence not professionally trained typist. They deployed a 'read-store-type' loop during the typing process and produced typing speeds of approximately 30 wpm. The critical issue with respect to the transcriptional typing task is to control for the reading sub-task which is implicit in transcriptional typing. We asked subjects to read a small corpus of text prior to typing corpus of the same length (but different) text. The goal here is to try to identify those activation patterns associated with reading and subtract these patterns from the transcriptional task. In theory, this would leave only those activities associated with typing, which in turn would be removed from the hacking scenario, yielding activity patterns associated with hacking per se.

2   Methods

It is for obvious reasons difficult to acquire physiological recordings while a person is attempting to hack into a computer system. In this investigation, we asked volunteers (right-handed male university students, aged 20-22) to attempt to crack a password system while we acquired their EEG using the Emotiv headset system. The subjects volunteered (three in this pilot) for this study without full knowledge of the actual purpose of the study, though they were told they would be attempting to hack into a computer system. Subjects were asked to sit in a quiet room with normal lighting. The subjects were then fitted with the Emotiv headset after assuming a comfortable position in an armchair placed in front of a laptop computer. Further, we deployed both ECG (3-lead) and a blood pulse volume electrode (placed on the left ear lobe) in order to acquire information regarding heart rate variability. We used the Vilistus system for the ECG and BVP recordings [1],

The experiment started once all of the electrodes (EEG, ECG, and BVP) were positioned and the recording signal was stable. The subjects were asked to relax as much as possible all subjects indicated that the recording equipment was not uncomfortable and did not obstruct their hand motion during typing in any way. The experiment protocol used in this study is depicted in Table 1. The experiment consisted of four contiguous phases as depicted in table 1. Note all phases of this experiment were carried out using a standard 102-keyboard integrated into a laptop. All subjects were filmed during the experiment and all software deployed (the Evotiv TestBench and the Vilistus (v 1.2.38 professional)) and video recording were synchronized to a common clock for subsequent data processing and analysis.

Table 1. Experimental protocol used in this study. Note that the text corpus read in stages 1 and 3 was the same, and different from the corpus deployed in the transcriptional typing task.

Read silently (2 minutes)	Transcriptional Typing (10 minutes)	Reading silently (2 minutes)	Login test (0.5 minutes)	Hacking (5 minutes)

After reading the page of text (stage I), the subjects were asked to type in a page of text containing approximately 300 words. This text contained very generic information about how to hack into computer systems, extracted from a website. Upon completion of this task, the subjects were asked to read another page of text (which was different from the original page they read) silently (stage III). Once this task was completed, the subjects were then provided with the account hacking scenario. This scenario attempted to reproduce the hacking process as much as possible. The subjects were told that they had to try to hack a 10 character password in 5 minutes. Note the hints were presented before the experiment began and were not displayed during the hacking scenario. As the subject correctly 'hacked' elements of the password (which were all lower case letters and digits), they were displayed as asterisks '*' in there correct position on the screen. At the end of the 1st minute, a timer was positioned on the screen in the upper right hand corner of the screen (in the default color black). After the 2-minute mark, the timer digits color was changed to RED and the size of the image box which contained the numerical digits of the time in a standard stopwatch timer countdown format was enlarged so it was more conspicuous. The presentation of the time was meant to induce stress in the subjects during the hacking process. At the end of the 2-minute mark, 50% of the characters correctly 'hacked' were displayed (half + 1 if the number of hacked entries was odd). At the end of the next minute, 50% of the remaining correctly hacked characters were revealed, and at the last minute, all characters were displayed in addition to any newly discovered elements until the test terminated. This test phase of the experiment terminated when either the password has been cracked or the timer has expired. The subjects were then de-briefed and thanked for their participation.

Once the test was completed, the data was saved and analysed off-line using EEGLab (v 9.0.4.6) for the Emotiv EEG data and Matlab (v7.0.6.324, R2008a) scripts were used for analyzing the heart rate variability data acquired from the ECG and BVP electrodes [2,3]. The EEG data was obtained using the emotive headset, which contains 14 dry electrodes and 2 mastoid reference electrodes (adhering to the 10-20 electrode system). In order to reduce motion artefacts, subjects were requested to sit as still as possible, with elbows placed firmly on the arms of the chair. The subjects were asked to type on a standard laptop style 102-keyboard which was positioned at a level and distance deemed to be comfortable for each subject. The EEG was recorded and event markers were generated whenever excessive subject movement was noted. A digital recording of the experiment was also acquired to provide additional criteria for motion artefact detection to enhance the quality of the data. In addition, the BVP and ECG were utilised to assist in motion artefact, detection, and the video recording assisted in eye blink detection and synchronization as well. Briefly, the EEG data was collected at 128 Hz with mastoid referencing in EDF (European Data Format) format, which can be directly imported into EEGLab (which runs within Matlab). A channel location file was generated which corresponded to the electrode layout for the Emotiv headset, and care was taken to ensure that the electrodes were positioned at the same positions across all subjects. The first processing stage requires that markers are placed in the data indicating the start, termination point, and the phase boundaries. All recording components were synchronised to a digital clock and audio data was also deployed in order to indicate boundary points. Eyeblinks can be an effective means of placing timer marks in the data – they can be caught on camera as well and serve as useful and frequent time event markers. Timing (event markers) were placed in the datasets (note all recoding modalities were acquired at the same sampling rate of 128 Hz) for subsequent analysis. In the next phase, data cleansing was required in the form of artefact removal. The data was first examined for gross artefact detection manually – any sections of the recording that contained significant artefacts were rejected. All rejected segments were removed from the data and the 'cleansed' data was utilised for further processing.

The heart rate variability (HRV) was also deployed in order to provide additional information about typing and the 'hacker' tasks. Data for HRV analysis was acquired using both 3-lead electrocardiogram (ECG) and blood volume pulse (BVP) monitoring was performed using a photoplethysmograph (PPG) placed on the left earlobe. All data acquired form HRV determination was band passed filtered (1-50 Hz) prior to further processing.

The data was epoched according to experimental phase in the same fashion as the EEG data, and artefact removal and band pass filtering (0.1-40 Hz) was performed. Any missing elements were filled in with baseline values to maintain temporal correlation with the EEG dataset. The BVP serves as a separate measure of heart rate which recorded the changes in the volume of the underlying vasculature when the heart beats. It is generally considered less susceptible to noise then the ECG and tends to produce more stable data then the ECG. The level of physiological data that can be extracted using BVP is more limited then the ECG in general, as it does not provide cardiac physiology details. It was deployed in this study to determine how well it correlated with the ECG in terms of capturing HRV data. The key advantage to BVP is the simple method used to obtain the data – a simple clip on the ear lobe is typically deployed and could be integrated into a headphone that are currently employed in many mobile phones and portable listening devices.

The EEG analysis focused on a subtraction method, whereby data from phase II – the typing phases was analysed with respect to phase I – the reading phase. Any differences in the recordings between these 2 phases would represent the difference between the tasks – namely the EEG correlates of typing. Likewise, the hacking phase (phase IV) data was subtracted from the subtracted phase II data – the typing phase, in order to reveal changes associated with the hacking component. Since this is a preliminary study, aimed at producing an appropriate design methodology, not all possible outcomes were examined. The results from this analysis are presented in the next section.

The HRV was measured using a method which determines the distance between the peaks of each heart beat. The peak of the QRS wave is sought for all heart beats, and the time between peaks is measured (variation in beat-to-beat interval). Variations in beat-to-beat intervals is recorded and used to access the physiological stress the subject may be experiencing [4,5]. The experiment of induced hacking was designed to simulate the expected stress levels associated with a time based task and it is reasonable therefore to assume that the subject will experience stress. The deployment of ECG and BVP was designed to determine whether or not this assumption held in our experimental paradigm.

3   Results

The principal result obtained from this experiment was that the subject did feel that they were under physical stress during the hacking scenario. This result is predicated on changes in HRV which was recorded throughout the experiment. The results in table 2 depict the average HRV within each of the four phases of the experiment across all three subjects.

Table 2. Heart rate variability presented as the average across all subjects for each experimental phase. HRV was measures as the coefficient of variation (CV) for the last 100 heart beats in each phase.

Phase I	Phase II	Phase III	Phase IV
0.3%	1.1%	0.5%	3.8%

The HRV was significantly larger ($p < 0.001$) for the phase IV subjects, and this held true across all subjects. The same trend held for the BVP measurements, which indicates a variation on the heart rate of the subject. Further, the subjects self reported that they felt under stress when trying to hack the password. Further confirmation was obtained by analyzing the video recording of the subjects, which captured the subjects' actions throughout the experiment. All subjects appeared agitated, displaying a variety of facial grimaces and general heightened arousal during the hacking phase relative to the reading and typing phases.

The EEG results indicated significant changes in the power spectrum during various stages of the experiment, which varied across electrodes. The difference between the transcriptional typing and reading phases suggested that the F3 electrode and both occipital electrodes (O1 and O2) especially displayed a high level of activation during transcriptional typing relative to reading alone. The alpha frequency band (8-12 Hz) power was raised significantly relative to the reading alone scenario, with other bands appearing roughly equal in power. The second reading task was not significantly different from the initial reading task (Phase III v Phase I), though there was a non-significant change in the delta band (1-4 Hz) power spectrum in the occipital field electrodes (O1 and O2). The hacking scenario produced the most significant changes of all phases. The power spectrum for the more frontally position electrodes (F3 and AF3) were strongly *elevated* relative to the transcriptional typing phase of the experiment in the alpha band. In addition, there was *reduced* activation of the occipital electrodes (O1 and O2) relative to the transcriptional typing task (across all frequency bands). Thus a pattern emerged which was consistent across all subjects: hacking yielded a reduced occipital power spectrum across all frequency bands, and yielded elevated activity pattern in the frontal electrodes (F3 and AF3) in the alpha band relative to transcriptional typing and reading.

Table 3. Summary of the changes in spectral power across all major frequency bands for each of the experimental phases. The results are the grand averages across all subjects. These results are for the frontal electrode (F3 and AF3). Note that there are also changes in the occipital electrodes (O1 and O2), as indicated in the text. Note the reading task was assumed to be the control for this experiment.

Phase I	Phase II	Phase III	Phase IV
Delta - 1.0	Delta - 1.1	Delta - 1.0	Delta -1.3
Theta – 1.0	Theta – 1.2	Theta - 1.2	Theta - 1.5
Alpha –1.0	Alpha – 2.6	Alpha - 1.2	Alpha – 4.2
Beta – 1.0	Beta – 1.4	Beta -1.1	Beta - 1.2

4   Conclusion

This study had two principal objectives in mind: 1) to record the EEG from subjects while engaged in typing and 2) to determine how the EEG changes when a person is attempting to hack into a computer system by password guessing. The experimental paradigm was designed to incorporate controls for both pure transcriptional typing and the password hacking task. The transcriptional typing component entailed a dictation protocol, where the subjects were asked to type what they were reading in real time. Further, the typing of text was used as a control for the hacking component, which also involves typing. Typing is a very common motor task that involves a series of steps: reading the text, hand positioning, and the actual typing movements. Which parts of the brain are engaged during this task has not been clearly presented in the literature to date (though see [6,7]). The first stage of this study was designed to acquire quantitative data to determine which part(s) of the brain is/are correlated with typing as determined from EEG recordings. The results presented in this study indicate that there are particular regions of the brain that become activated during transcriptional typing (see [8]). The EEG headset contained 14 electrodes (excluding two mastoid references), as such it could certainly be the case that other regions of the brain could yield additional changes that were not recorded in this experiment because of a small electrode set. This can be examined by using a much larger electrode array (we are planning to use a high resolution 128 BioSemi system in the near future to examine this issue in detail).

5   Discussion

The actual hacking scenario did produce a change in the overall power spectrum that was reproducible across all subjects. The pattern was based on relative changes in power across frequency bands, a common measure that reflects the brain activity within a given frequency band. The pattern that emerged in this study was that transcriptional typing produces a unique pattern relative to a passive reading task. This is a novel result and will be explored more fully using a quantitative EEG electrode setup. Furthermore, this study produced results indicating that the actual process of password hacking yields a characteristic signature when examined using EEG, ECG, and PPG. The ECG and PPG results provide information on the stress level of the individual – the heart rate variability is a significant indicator of stress level – and PPG is typically deployed to record physical exertion level – though it is suggested by this study that it can also be used to measure mental exertion as well. The two measures provided *physiological* evidence that password hacking per se can induce a mental exertion which causes changes in HRV and heart rate generally [9,10,11]. The EEG data suggests that there is a unique brain activation pattern associated with password hacking that can be recorded using a small electrode helmet such as that available in the Emotiv headset. These results suggest that a profile of a hacker can be deduced readily – based on the physiological responses engendered by the hacking process. Whether these results would hold true for a 'professional' hacker is a point that requires further investigation. The subjects deployed in this study were Nubian hackers and these results may simply reflect their lack of expertise in this task!

Acknowledgement. We would like to thank the students from the British University in Egypt, Faculty of Informatics and Computer Science for their kind participation.

References

1. Vilistus: http://www.vilistus.com/products.shtml
2. EEGLAB: http://sccn.ucsd.edu/eeglab/
3. Emotiv: http://www.emotiv.com/
4. Palaniappan, R., Krishnan, S.M.: Identifying individuals using ECG beats. In: Proceedings of the International Conference on Signal Processing and Communications (SPCOM 2004), Bangalore, India, pp. 569–572 (2004)
5. Revett, K., Deravi, F., Sirlantzis, K.: Biosignals for User Authentication - Towards Cognitive Biometrics? In: EST 2010, International Conference on Emerging Security Technologies, University of Kent, Canterbury, September 6-8, pp. 71–76 (2010)
6. Coan, J.A., Allen, J.J.B.: Frontal EEG asymmetry as a moderator and mediator of emotion. Biological Psychology 67, 7–49 (2004)
7. Riera, A., Soria-Frisch, A., Caparrini, M., Grau, C., Rufini, G.: Unobtrusive Biometric based on electroencephalogram analysis. EURASIP Journal on Advances in Signal Processing, 1–8 (2008)

8. Palaniappan, R., Revett, K.: Thought Based PIN Generation Using Single Channel EEG Biometric. International Journal of Cognitive Biometrics (in press)

9. Jönsson, P.: Respiratory sinus arrhythmia as a function of state anxiety in healthy individuals. International Journal of Psychophysiology 63, 48–54 (2007)

10. Luay, M., Revett, K.: On the applicability of heart rate for affective gaming. In: WSEAS Special Session on Knowledge Engineering for Decision Support Systems, the CSCC Multiconference, Corfu Island, Greece, July 15-17, pp. 267–272 (2011)

11. Cacioppo, J.T., Bernston, G.G., Larsen, J.T., Poehlmann, K.M., Ito, T.A.: The psychophysiology of emotion. In: Lewis, M., Haviland-Jones, J.M. (eds.) Handbook of Emotions, 2nd edn., pp. 173–191. The Guilford Press, New York (2004)

Untangling Public Service Usage for Agribusinesses with Dialogic E-government

Sotiris Karetsos, Maria Ntaliani, Constantina Costopoulou,
and Alexander B. Sideridis

Informatics Laboratory, Agricultural University of Athens, 75 Iera Odos str,
11855 Athens, Greece
{karetsos,ntaliani,tina,as}@aua.gr

Abstract. E-government has raised many expectations to public administration employees, businesses and citizens, regarding the simplification of their transactions. Nonetheless, in practice the provision of electronic services is followed by much complexity in the way they are used. A common phenomenon is the confusion of businesses on various issues connected with public service use, such as which public service to use to cover their needs, whether they are eligible to do so, and which agency they should address to. Therefore, the paper tries to address such issues by presenting a dialogic information service for helping agribusinesses' employees to find easily appropriate public services for their business needs and using them without having to search relevant legislation or various public agency Web sites. The proposed service comprises a new extension of the pilot system Agroportal, and has been based on the methods and tools of a European project.

Keywords: Electronic government, portal technology, agribusinesses.

1 Introduction

Electronic government (e-government) is continuously changing the way that businesses, citizens and governments transact, and the way that public services are governed and delivered. Governments, in order to promote citizens and businesses participation, deliver various types of services through their Web sites like e-mails to contact government officials, surveys assessing citizens' opinion about service delivery, forums for citizens to raise opinions on different issues, like policies, environment, etc. [1]. Towards this direction, the i2010 Action Plan focused on the development of such enabling conditions. There is no doubt that these initiatives have created the conditions for the development of e-government in the entire European Union (EU).

However, delivering such services through government Web sites is not enough. Although e-government has raised many expectations towards the simplification of public service transactions, in practice the provision of electronic services is followed by much complexity in the way they are used. A common phenomenon is the confusion of businesses and citizens on various issues connected with public service

H. Jahankhani et al. (Eds.): ICGS3/e-Democracy 2011, LNICST 99, pp. 120–125, 2012.

use, such as which public service to use to cover their needs, whether they are eligible to do so, and which agency they should address to.

Being that the case, it is usual that a business applies for a service merely because another one has done so. Also, businesses tend to use services that provide subsidies even though they are not aware about their requirements or their final output. For example, recently at the Centre for Genetic Improvement of Animals located in central Greece, more than 500 applications have been submitted by livestock farmers in order to enlist their farms in pedigree books. The investigation of these applications required scheduling approximately 60 on the spot inspections at the livestock farms by 8 public servants. Obviously, the administrative, economic and time costs for livestock farmers and the public agency were considerable. However, only 8% of the applications corresponded to actual needs, while the rest of them did not fulfill the relevant criteria.

The aim of this paper is twofold: firstly to present the progress of e-government in Europe and especially in Greece and secondly to implement a dialogic information service for helping agribusinesses' employees to find easily appropriate public services for their business needs and using them without having to search relevant legislation or various public agency Web sites. Therefore, the structure of the paper is as follows: the following section provides an overview of the e-government status in Greece with reference to the agribusiness sector. The third section presents the Agroportal system and provides a structured dialogue that helps agribusinesses among others, to find out whether they are eligible for a specific public service. The fourth section concludes the work and provides directions for future research.

2   Electronic Government in Greece

The i2010 e-government Action Plan was designed aiming at modernizing public services and making them more efficient and more targeted to the needs of different population groups. To do this, it has proposed a series of priorities and a roadmap to accelerate the deployment of e-government in the EU. The measurement of progress is based on 20 basic services (12 for citizen and 8 for businesses). EU shows a continuous progress according to the full online availability indicator. The overall EU measure has risen to 71% in 2009 from 59% in 2007. According to the sophistication indicator EU stands at 83%, compared with 76% in 2007. However, the report indicates that the difference across countries is still significant [2].

Greece is taking on the challenge to enable a step change in its Information Society performance. It is prioritizing its investment in information technologies to become more competitive. Greece's recent efforts have led to 83% e-government usage among businesses, compared to 68% of the EU average. However, e-government use by citizens has stalled and online availability remains below the EU average (10% compared to 28% of the EU average). The households and businesses with broadband connection are 31% and 74%, compared to 60% and 81% of the corresponding EU averages. Also, Greece and Ireland are the only EU countries that do not have a national electronic procurement platform or portal. These scores put Greece in the bottom of EU countries scale for the two core indicators, namely availability and sophistication [2]. Moreover, Greece recognizes the need for enhancement of the population as well as for ease of access for rural areas and has announced the "Rural Broadband project". This project will provide broadband Internet connections for more 820.000 people living in rural areas.

As far as the agricultural sector is concerned, a close investigation reveals that the e-government progress that the Greek Ministry of Agriculture (MoA) succeeded the last seven years (2005-2011) is insufficient. The platform of the main Web site has not been updated and may be characterized as rather outdated in terms of look and feel, usability and technologies used. It mainly provides information and news at its first (home) page and only in Greek language. The English language version is very poor, not updated for many years and several links are broken.

However, the MoA has announced the implementation of six electronic services, namely: permissions for distribution of fertilizers, agro-environmental plans, announcements for trading perishable agricultural products, permissions for production and trade of propagule, permissions for organic agriculture. Currently, five of them are at analysis or design phase and only one is marked as completed (analysis and design phase, not the implementation phase). Moreover, the MoA supervises agencies that have developed independent portals or Web sites that offer mainly information. A notable exception is the Greek Agricultural Payment Agency (OPEKEPE in Greek) by offering adequate number of electronic services for farmers and agribusinesses, such as the following: integrated system of business unified application, electronic economic supports, agricultural consultants, electronic cotton management, tobacco reconstruction system and distribution control of animals and meat.

3   An Innovative Dialogic Informative Service

Agroportal system (http://meli.aua.gr/agroportal) is an e-government portal that has been implemented under the research project "Pythagoras: A pilot system for electronic agricultural services", which has been funded by the European Union (75%) and the Greek Ministry of Education (25%). Agroportal aims at supporting agribusinesses in transacting with Greek agricultural governmental agencies [3].

The necessity for deploying Agroportal has been evinced by thorough research (of literature, the Internet, and questionnaires), showing that the provided e-government services for agribusinesses are insufficient in terms of variety and content. The Web sites providing them are not linked and not updated for many years. The ways of accessing them are inflexible, neglecting a major preference trend of agribusinesses towards mobile phones. An agribusiness can access the Agroportal through a PC with connection to the Internet in order to access information and governmental services, as well as send and receive Short Message Service (SMS) messages to a mobile phone in order to request information or apply for a public service. Agroportal provides the following types of services [4] [5]:

- **Information services:** providing information on agricultural fields, statistics, characteristics of agricultural products, cultivation techniques and bibliography; news for events, conferences, new regulation and other; useful links; frequently asked questions; and weather forecast.
- **E-government services (electronic government to business-G2B):** providing information about completing a process (e.g. acquiring a certificate); form/application download; and electronic submission of forms.
- **M-government services (mobile G2B):** providing information via SMS messages for: agricultural products and their cultivation; epidemic alerts for the outbreak of an epidemic and proposing measures for confrontation; weather alerts for extreme conditions; legislation news for the issuing or abolition of related law; administrative information for deadlines (e.g. submission of applications); market information for traders, wholesalers, processors (e.g. price tendencies, demand forecasting and trends); chat among agribusinesses.
- **Value-added Services:** enabling the communication between agribusinesses and government agencies through synchronous communication methods (e.g. real-time chat), as well as asynchronous communication methods (e.g. email, forum, private messages).

The Agroportal system has been extended with new services for the informative stage of a public service, namely information that a business should know before executing a particular public service (e.g. its eligibility to perform a service; the public agencies that are responsible for it; and what kind of documents should adduce so as to apply for the service) [6]. These new services are described as follows:

- **Dialogic Informative e-Services:** providing a structured dialogue that helps agribusinesses among others, to find out whether they are eligible for a specific public service or not; and if eligible to personalize the public service related information according to their profile and their specific needs.

The importance of such services lays on the facilitation of businesses in finding information for the "informational phase" of public services, namely for information that a business should know before executing a particular public service. Such information concerns the business's eligibility to perform a service, the public authorities that are responsible for it or what kind of documents the business should adduce so as to apply for it. This information is determined by laws and regulations that in many cases are very complex, regularly change and cause errors of ignorance, confusion or misinterpretation. This complexity constrains business dexterity and induces imparity, since it limits the effectiveness of government's incentives for businesses, creates a barrier for applying to development frameworks and is a potential source of fiscal corruption across public agencies. On the other hand, the provided dialogic services "decode" laws and regulations into simple dialogues that are highly descriptive, explicit and accurate. Therefore, they drive e-democracy by increasing the efficiency of G2B services and enabling business' participation in them.

The service model of the dialogic informative e-services has been based on relevant work undertaken in the context of the "Rural Inclusion" project (www. rural-inclusion.eu). Currently, the dialogue (Fig. 1 in Greek) concerning the "Issuance of permit of agricultural truck" service has been implemented. Instead of searching regulation, visiting or calling a public agency for finding information on eligibility of use and how to apply, a farmer can just answer a series of simple questions, such as: "Is farming your main occupation?", and "Are you registered in an agricultural cooperation?". The service can be used via the following URL: http://meli.aua.gr/agroportal/process/process_q1.htm.

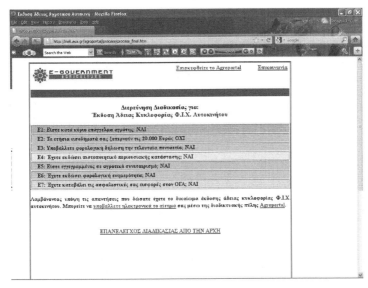

Fig. 1. Agroportal dialogue for the service "Issuance of permit of agricultural truck"

Agroportal is a pilot system and currently it is operated by the Informatics Laboratory of the Agricultural University of Athens. For the modelling of the e-government services that the Agroportal system provides the Business Process Modelling Notation (BPMN) has been used. BPMN is a standard for business process modelling, and provides a graphical notation for specifying business processes. The objective of BPMN is to support business process management for both technical and business users. The Agroportal implementation is based on Internet technology, uses open source software, requires minimal investment and provides a cheap way of carrying out a set of G2B transactions.

4   Conclusions

Following the successful implementation of the Agroportal, a new extension of the system has been deployed for untangling the public service usage by agribusinesses. More specifically, dialogic e-services for the informative stage of a public service help businesses in finding out whether they are eligible for a specific public service and if eligible details on applying for a service are given. The efficiency of G2B services is increased and business' participation in them is enabled by resolving law complexity of public services through simple dialogues.

Future work regards the evaluation of the proposed service by agribusinesses so as to receive useful feedback on how to proceed to the application of other dialogic e-government services. Also, much effort will be put on providing similar dialogic services for mobile devices so as to harmonize more public service provision with the agribusinesses' preferences.

Acknowledgments. Part of this paper has been supported by the European Commission, and the project No 238900 "Rural-Inclusion: e-Government Lowering Administrative Burdens for Rural Businesses" of the ICT Policy Support Programme.

References

1. Rodriguez, R., Estevez, E., Giulianelli, D., Vera, P.: Assessing e-Governance Maturity through Municipal Websites Measurement Framework and Survey Results. In: 6th Workshop on Software Engineering, Argentinean Computer Science Conference (2009)
2. European Commission Directorate General for Information Society and Media: Smarter, Faster, Better eGovernment. 8th eGovernment Benchmark,
   http://ec.europa.eu/information_society/eeurope/
   i2010/docs/benchmarking/egov_benchmark_2009.pdf
3. Ntaliani, M., Karetsos, S., Costopoulou, C., Harizanis, P., Kaloudis, S., Passam, H.: Supporting Agricultural E-governance. In: 2nd Conference of The Scientific Council for Information Society on Electronic Democracy Information Society and Citizen's Rights, pp. 143–151 (2006)
4. Ntaliani, M., Karetsos, S., Costopoulou, C.: Implementing E-government Services for Agriculture: the Case of Greece. In: Isaias, P., McPherson, M., Bannister, F. (eds.) e-Society 2006, pp. 243–249 (2006)
5. Chatzinotas, S., Ntaliani, M., Karetsos, S., Costopoulou, C.: Securing M-government Services: the Case of Agroportal. In: Kushchu, I., Broucki, C., Fitzpatrick, G. (eds.) 2nd European mGovernment Conference, pp. 61–70 (2006)
6. Ntaliani, M., Costopoulou, M., Luccini, M., Sideridis, A.: Collaborative Training for Agricultural Public Authorities for Innovative Provision of Information and Services. In: EFITA/WCCA 2011, pp. 195–203 (2011)

On the Deployment of Artificial Immune Systems for Biometrics

Ruben Krishnamurthy[1], Kenneth Revett[2], and Hossein Jahankhani[1]

[1] University of East London
School of Computing & Technology
University Way
Beckton
London E15 2RD
ruben.krishnamurthy@gmail.com
h.jahankhani@uel.ac.uk
[2] Faculty of Informatics and Computer Science
British University in Egypt
El Sherouk City
Egypt
Ken.revett@bue.edu.eg

Abstract. Artificial immune systems (AIS) are a computational metaphor based on biological implementations of immune systems. Natural immune systems are capable of performing computation based on several properties that they possess. Immune systems are capable of adapting to new stimuli – they respond appropriately to novel stimuli, and they can remember previous encounters with stimuli. The processes which natural immune systems utilise are a combination of cellular and humoral responses – which act independently and in concert to perform stimulus identification and eradication, with minimal impact on the host. This provides an overview of artificial immune systems – which attempt to implement the basic functionality of natural systems. The basic properties and their interrelations are described in this paper – which is a prelude to their application in the context of biometrics. It will be demonstrated that the AIS approach is both a natural and potentially very effective approach to providing biometric security within a range of modalities.

Keywords: artificial immune systems, biometrics, computer security, distributed systems, natural computation.

1   Introduction

Artificial Immune System (AIS) is a new branch of computer science which uses the natural immune system as a metaphor for solving computational problems. AIS detect unusual/suspicious or rare events by using the ideology of the Immune system. AIS can be used for various applications namely Machine Learning (ML), Computer Security, Fault detection, behaviour of robots and for Novelty detection. A Pathogen is any agent could be virus, bacterium that may cause trouble. The Immune System is our primary defence against pathogens and it consists of nonspecific and specific

H. Jahankhani et al. (Eds.): ICGS3/e-Democracy 2011, LNICST 99, pp. 126–130, 2012.

defences. Non Specific Defences are the body's first line against any disease. Their normal function is to guard against all infections regardless of their cause. Specific Defences are attempts generated by the body to defend itself against certain pathogens.

2   Role of Immune Systems

One of the main role of the Immune System is to protect our bodies from infection and operating via two non specific lines of defence barriers and general attack namely and later via specific line of defence which entails the primary immune response whose role is to launch a response to invading pathogens and the secondary immune response whose role is to remember the past encounter which leads to a faster response the second time the same attack happens. The body's most important nonspecific defence is the skin, unbroken skin provides a continuous layer that protects the whole body. The sweat and oil glands at the surface of the skin produces a salty and acidic environment that kills the bacteria and other microorganisms. An infection occurs when a small portion of the skin is normally broken or scrapped off.

2.1   Second Line of Defence

When pathogens do get past the skin and mucous membranes and enter the body, the second line of defence takes an active role, triggered by the process of injury to tissues in the body. These injured cells release a protein called Histamine which then starts a process called the Inflammatory Response. Histamine normally increases the blood flow to the injured area and hence increases the permeability of the surrounding capillaries hence resulting in fluids and White Blood Cells (WBC's) leaking into tissues nearby from the blood vessels. Phagocytes engulf and destroy the Pathogens. If after all these lines of defence a pathogen is still able to get past the body's non specific defences, the Immune System (IS) would then react with specific defences that attack the disease causing agent and this is called the Immune Response (IR). An Antigen is known as a substance that triggers the specific defences of the Immune System. An Antigen is also a substance that the WBC identifies as not belonging to the body.

3   Algorithms

3.1   Negative Selection Algorithm

Forrest et al in [1] proposed an algorithm which is based on the biological negative selection principle. The algorithm is developed to detect anomalies in a set of strings which could be changed in the checksum and length which is done by using malicious codes or programs like a virus. A procedure called censoring is done first where the protected string is split into substrings which then form a collection S of Self (Substrings). The next step is to generate random strings R0. These randomly generated strings which match self are then eliminated and those which do not match any strings of S become a member of the detection collection called R – repertoire. Once this repertoire is produced, the monitoring phase is then started whereby the match is done continuously from S against those in R. The effect of negative selection is to make a two-class problem a one-class problem. When the randomly generated pool of antibodies are culled (when they match the host antigens too strongly), only those antibodies with minimal reactivity will remain for subsequent maturation. If the mature antibodies respond to an unseen antigen, then one can as assume that the antigen was not from the host [2]. This antigen should then be considered for removal if this occurred in the context of a classic human immune system.

3.2   Clonal Selection Algorithm

This algorithm is modelled on the B-Cell mechanism. Naive B-Cells circulate in the blood and the lymphatic organs. Once the receptors of such a B-Cell match to an antigen, they proliferate quickly and they also change to attain a better matching value. Those B-Cells which have attained better matching proliferate again and again hence producing the best matching B-Cells. The induced changes are implemented as mutations, which serve to enhance the population of responding cells to the antigen. The rate of mutation within the immune system is much higher than the normal cellular mutation rate – this provides the search and sensitivity features of an adaptive immune system [3].

3.3   Immune Genetic Algorithm

This algorithm is based on a search technique mainly used in computing to determine approximate or true solutions, and also for optimization and search problems. A typical Genetic Algoritm first requires a genetic representation of the solution domain and secondly a fitness function for evaluating the solution domain. This standard representation is done via a bit array. The fitness function is dependent on the problem and measures the quality of the represented solution. Once both the genetic and fitness functions are defined, the Genetic Algorithm then initializes a population of solutions randomly then improving it thorough repetitive application of mutations, crossovers and selector operators. One main draw back with this algorithm was that it was not very good in local searches and is good with global search [4]. To overcome this problem Chun et al [5] proposed a new algorithm, which was based on the genetic algorithm whereby the antigen and the antibody are the objective functions and the solution and the affinity between an antibody and the antigen is the solution fitness. This method mainly improves the selection operator to produce a very good global search.

4   Applications

4.1   System Security

One of the most common application areas for AIS is in the deployment of intrusion detection systems (IDS). An intruder is an entity which attempts to acquire computing resources without proper authorisation. There are two basic forms of intrusion detection: signature and anomaly detection. The former deploys a 'typical' template for an intruder – the format is acquired through a supervised training approach in which hackers are asked to attempt to hack into the system. In anomaly detection, any behaviour which deviates from typical behaviour is flagged as a possible intrusion. Anomaly detection is more likely to lead to large false positives, while a signature based approach tends to lead to increased false acceptance rates. Both types of IDS can be implemented using an AIS based approach. The antigen is the series of system calls that a user process generates during interaction with the host system. The antibodies are deployed to recognise 'typical' system calls. Those that are not recognised could be considered suspicious and further action must be undertaken to determine if this is a real threat [6].

In addition to intrusion detection, AIS have been deployed to detect viruses and worms [7]. Kephart deployed integrity monitors (based loosely on a minimalist AIS system) along with activity monitors to detect a variety of known viruses and worms. Forrest and colleagues have used AIS systems to detect changes in system executables using a similar approach [8]. Any change to system files is detected by exposing a set of antibodies to the typical suite of executables located on the computer system. Any change in the executable that would alter the contents of the programme would be flagged as an attack and appropriate action would be taken to preserve the integrity of the file system.

4.2   Fault Detection

This is used to detect malfunctions in a network or in a single system. The Negative Selection Algorithm is common here too. Bradley and Tyrell [9] created a hardware immune system that runs in real time to monitor continuously a machine for errors. They used the Negative Selection Algorithm to differentiate between normal and abnormal system operations. This system provides a unique solution to autonomous monitoring the state of a physical plant. The plant is examined and a feature set is extracted which depicts parameters and their values that are indicative of tolerated operation levels. If the parameter values fall outside of the expected operational range, an immune response is generated which signals an alert to the system monitor.

4.3   Data Mining

Data mining is the process of searching large volumes of data automatically for patterns using tools such as clustering or rule mining. J.Timmis and T.Knight [10] came up with an immunological approach to data mining which uses the clonal selection and called their Algorithm AINE (Artificial Immune Network). AINE uses a network of B-cells. AINE has been used in a variety of machine learning and pattern recognition tasks, typically in a hybrid approach. Tasks such as automated image analysis, spectra recognition, and function optimisation generally have all been met with varying degrees of success using AIS alone or in conjunction with other machine learning approaches (the AINE is such a hybrid approach).

5   Conclusion

This brief survey of the components of an AIS demonstrate that it has all of the hallmarks of a computational framework that is capable of an adaptive response to a variety of novel stimuli. It provides this capability without any prior learning - the system is designed *de novo* to respond differentially to self and non-self. In the context of biometrics, the self is the authorised person and the non-self is everyone else. The ability to make this discrimination without being trained for both cases is a distinct advantage the AIS approach has over more traditional approaches such as supervised neural networks. Further, the basis of the immune system is very consistent – and would leave one to believe that this approach is a natural one for biometrics – in more ways than one! This paper describes essential features of the human artificial immune system and some notion of how the biological metaphor is naturally suitable for use in a variety of computer security applications. To date, virtually all research efforts in AIS in the context of computer security have focused on their deployment as an automated intrusion detection system. The authors believe that this is just the beginning – that AIS can be deployed in more classical biometrics such as keystroke dynamics, signature verification – essentially any form of biometrics would serve as a useful application domain. This is the basis of our future work in this field.

References

1. Forrest, S., Perelson, A.S., Allen, L., Cherukuri, R.: Self-nonself discrimination in a computer. In: SP 1994: Proceedings of the 1994 IEEE Symposium on Security and Privacy, pp. 202–212. IEEE Computer Society, Washington, DC (1994)
2. Ebner, M.m, Breunig, H-G., Albert, J.: On the use of negative selection in an artificial immune system. In: GECCO 2002 Proceedings of the Genetic and Evolutionary Computation, pp. 957–964. Morgan Kaufmann (2002)
3. Hofmeyr, S.A., Forrest, S.: Architecture for an artificial immune system. Evolutionary Computation 7(1), 45–68 (2000)
4. Wang, L., Jiao, L.: The immune genetic algorithm and its convergence. In: Fourth International Signal Processing Proceedings, pp. 1347–1350 (1998)
5. Chun, J., Kim, M., Jung, H., Hong, S.: Shape optimization of electromagnetic devices using immune algorithm. IEEE Transactions on Magnetics 33(2), 1876–1879 (1997)
6. Kim, J., Bentley, P.J., Aickelin, U., Greensmith, J., Tedesco, G., Twycross, J.: Immune System Approaches to Intrusion Detection – A Review. In: Nicosia, G., Cutello, V., Bentley, P.J., Timmis, J. (eds.) ICARIS 2004. LNCS, vol. 3239, pp. 316–329. Springer, Heidelberg (2004)
7. Kephart, J.O.: A biologically inspired immune system for computers. In: Brooks, R.A., Maes, P. (eds.) Artificial Life IV: Proc. of the 4th Int. Workshop on the Synthesis and Simulation of Living Systems, pp. 130–139. MIT Press
8. Hofmeyr, S.A., Forrest, S.: Immunity by design: an artificial immune system. In: Proc. of the Genetic and Evolutionary Computation Conference, pp. 1289–1296. Morgan Kaufmann
9. Bradley, D., Tyrrell, A.: A hardware immune system for benchmark state machine error detection. In: Proceedings of the 2002 Congress on Evolutionary Computing, vol. 1, pp. 813–818 (2002)
10. Knight, T., Timmis, J.: Aine: An immunological approach to data mining. In: ICDM 2001: Proceedings of the 2001 IEEE International Conference on Data Mining, pp. 297–304. IEEE Computer Society, Washington, DC (2001)

A Prediction Model for Criminal Levels Specialized in Brazilian Cities

Marcelo Damasceno de Melo[1,2], Jerffeson Teixeira[2], and Gustavo Campos[2]

[1] IFRN - Campus Macau, R. das Margaridas, 350, Macau-RN, Brazil
http://www.ifrn.edu.br
[2] Universidade Estadual do Ceará, Av. Paranjana, 1700, Fortaleza-CE, Brazil
{marcelodamasceno,jeff,gustavo}@larces.uece.br
http://www.uece.br

Abstract. The increase in violence around the world is becoming a major problem, causing severe damages to society: material, social and physical ones. The Government needs effective tools to fight against crime, and therefore, some tools are necessary to assist in the prevention of further crimes, in the allocation of its resources and visualization of geographic areas with high crime concentrations.

This paper proposes a model of data mining, predicting criminal levels in urban geographic areas. The model was proposed to work using Brazilian data, specifically criminal and socio-economic ones. This work shows the approach proposed to face the problems of this social phenomenon, as a unified process to build a system which can able to help decision managers to fight and prevent crime.

To validate the proposed procedure it was used as a case study. Using the crime and socioeconomic data of the Metropolitan Region of Fortaleza - Brazil (RMF). The case study proved that the process is useful and effective in building a predictor of criminal levels. The model achieves 70% of accuracy using an innovative method and heterogeneous data sets.

Keywords: Prediction Model, Criminal Levels, Data Mining Model, Brazilian Crime, Predicting Crime.

1 Introduction

The increase in violence in recent years has been the object of study of many researchers. Governments and society in general have problems with the inconvenience caused by this phenomenon (violence). Each year, governments spent millions of dollars combating the violence, providing equipment, training and purchasing tools to assist the police work.

Each crime can raise a lot of data, such as: date, time and place of the crime, *modus operandi*, crime type and socio-economic status of the victim. This type of data may facilitate the use of data mining tools such as prediction. Such data are important because they provide a computer system able to predict

H. Jahankhani et al. (Eds.): ICGS3/e-Democracy 2011, LNICST 99, pp. 131–138, 2012.
© Institute for Computer Sciences, Social Informatics and Telecommunications Engineering 2012

the occurrence of crimes and even listing all the variables that affect the event (crime).

The crime prediction is often used for predicting future places where crime will occur [1,2,3]. Several theories develop activities within the study of criminal behavior, like: routine activities, *hot spot* [4] and crime ecology.

Data mining is one of the steps in a process of discovering patterns embedded in the data [5]. Data mining has been important because it is a powerful tool to extract valuable information found in a database. There are applications in some areas such as fraud detection, lifting profile, marketing and monitoring.

Our work is a proposal of a prediction model using criminal and socio-economic data. The model deals with all steps to build a system to predict criminal levels using criminal and socio-economic data. Criminal data are information about date, local and informations about the crime and socio-economic data are information about economic and social variables in a city, like salary or number of schools. We define the criminal levels as a measure of danger in a certain demographic region. One of the most interesting aspects of our work is the use of socio-economic aspects, because these factors have great relevance in the crime occurence and were not taken into account in several studies.

2   Prediction

Every corporation plan their day-to-day actions based on data generated in their actions. Data collected must illustrate their experiences and demonstrate the rights and wrongs committed daily. Quantitative forecasting models basically use historical data to detect patterns and estimate them in the future. Thus, the acquisition of tools of this kind should be seen as an organizational gap, add support for the decisions made by managers.

The act of predicting can be defined as obtaining an accurate answer on a question that should happen in the future, based on the past. The future shall be understood as a scenario or a situation never experienced by a corporation or something you want to pursue. Thus, the predictions must be conducted in completely independent variables based on data from past and present stored in databases and experience of managers and other professionals involved.

A process that determines the steps to build a prediction systems must be followed because it facilitates the development of the adjustments and the resolution of problems arising in the implementation of a forecasting technique [6]. One of the purposes of this work is to develop a model based on a process for developing a prediction application to criminal levels, using machine learning algorithms, which can be applied to any Brazilian city.

3   Prediction Model

The process of Knowledge Discovery in Databases (KDD) is not a simple task [7]. The information obtained from the application of this process is not just coming from the direct application of learning algorithms, but also the understanding of the business, collecting, cleaning and processing of data, post-processing and visualization of knowledge.

The approach proposed in this paper serves as a guide to conduct crime level prediction in a Brazilian city, with little adjustment for application in any cities. The prediction process must use social, economic and criminal data, because crime is a phenomenon that can be explained using these characteristics. The definition of these data was based on characteristics of the crime phenomenon observed in the literature. The process will address traditional and new tasks such as task-specific prediction of crimes using Brazilian data.

The definition of a specialized model for the problem of crime prediction makes the resolution of the problem easier to achieve using data mining. The model will deal clearly and objectively with all the steps in order to provide convenience and security in the results.

The Figure 1 shows the steps that must be executed. Each step must be executed in order that it appears. There are single and double connections between steps. Single connections mean there is just a way of execution, without return; and double connections mean there is a way to return to the previous step. After the Evaluation task, there are two connections, one to the Distribution step and another one to Bussiness Understanding. It means if the evaluation is bad, there is a way to restart all the process. Thus, the process allows a way to fix some problems that were not view previously. If the evaluation is good, the process guide to the Divulgation task. All the steps shown in the Figure 1 were implemented in the predictive model.

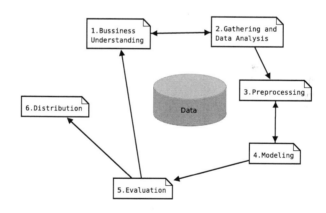

Fig. 1. Steps of the prediction model

Each model step below is described from the characteristics experienced in the case study using the proposed model. The case study used socio-economic and crime data of the Metropolitan Region of Fortaleza (MRF). MRF is a big region with 13 cities and more than 2 milions citizens.

3.1 Bussiness Understanding

This step performs an understanding of crime in the city that will be used in the study. It must consider criminal, social, demographic and economic characteristics. It is essential to raise small details like date, time, location and type of crime committed. Besides raising data on crimes committed, it is important to collect social data for the region such as population density, illiteracy, rates of life quality, sport and culture, numbers of people distinguished by sex and age.

In addition to understanding the criminal, social and economic issues, it is necessary to define the technical objectives to be achieved. As the proposed model is focused on predicting criminal levels, it was decided to use five criminal levels calculated from the number of crimes committed grouped by criminal and social/economic variables. The levels are very low, low, medium, high and very high. Thus, the predictive method will consist of five models that will say what level a given region belongs. Each model will be specialized in predicting a certain criminal level.

Besides defining the data that must be used and the data mining goal that the analyst must achieve, this step has a task that guides what minimum accuracy must be get to the project has to be accept. We suggest that the true rate must be defined by a crime specialist at the demographic region that is being studied. This work was not supported by a crime specialist, so we accept a true rate superior than 50%.

3.2 Gathering and Data Analysis

This step will deal with how to obtain and how to analyse the data. As it was said before, we suggest that the model uses crime and socio-economic data. Below is described how we obtained the data used in our case study.

The data crime used in the case study were obtained through the Department of Public Safety and Social Defense of the State of Ceará(SSPDS-CE). The information refers to crimes committed between 2007 and 2008. The available data contain information about time, location, type and subtype of the crime.

The socio-economic data obtained are related to the Census occurred in 2000 conducted by the Brazilian Institute of Geography and Statistics (IBGE). The data contain all the variables studied in the Census grouped by geographic areas known as Data Expansion Areas (DEA). Several districts may belong to the same DEA, because the definition of so large a DEA is dependent on population variables. So the extension of the DEA depends on the number of citizens for example.

3.3 Preprocessing

It was necessary to integrate criminal and socio-economic databases to become only a table that contained all the collected data. To integrate the databases was used the attribute DEA, originally belonging to socio-economic database. The transformation performed in the crime data creates a DEA attribute too. After the integration is completed, the dataset has 69 socio-economic and criminal attributes.

As it was decided in the bussiness understading step, our prediction model will be composed of 5 models, each one will predict a specific criminal level. Thus, it must divide the database (flat table) into five subdivisions, setting each example to their criminal level.

The regions with the lowest amount of crime received the very low crime level using all the criminal, social and economic variables.

The very high level was determined for the regions with the highest crime numbers using all the variables previously cited. The intermediate levels (low, medium and high levels) were calculated using a scale. The minimum (min) and maximum (max) value of this scale is lowest and the highest crime numbers respectively. Each step (s) at a scale was determined by ($max - min/5$).

Thus, 5 different sets are generated, each one representing each level. Each dataset has the same number of instances and attributes of the original set.

To improve the accuracy and running time it is needed an attribute selection. We suggest the use of the Ranker search method using the Information Gain as a measure of evaluation [5]. The attribute selection was applied and it selected the 15 best attributes of each dataset, according to the evaluation measure used. Different attributes were extracted for each dataset, thus, it was necessary to standardize the attributes that would be used. It was chosen the seven best attributes of each execution of the selection algorithm. Now each dataset only has 35 attributes, seven attributes selected from each dataset.

The set of attributes selected by the selection algorithm does not contain attributes so important as the city, day, month and year of crime occurrence. As the temporal attributes are important for understanding the criminal dynamics, it was decided to build a new dataset containing the attributes selected by the selection algorithm plus the temporal attributes excluded. So we have two predictive models, one constructed with the selected attributes and another one with the selected attributes plus the excluded ones.

3.4   Modeling

Several machine learning algorithms were tested, but the Neural Networks were chosen [5] due to the results achieved and the constraints imposed by the data. For each data set, a network was trained, where the network will be used to predict the crime level of a certain region in a near future. We have two predictive models, composed of five Neural Networks each. Remember, the first model was trained using the first set of attributes and the second on using the same attributes of the first set plus the temporal attributes excluded by the selection algorithm.

3.5   Evaluation

With the use of trained neural networks it was obtained an accuracy (hit rate) over 70% and mean error and mean square error of at most 0.36 and 0.47, respectively. As it was defined at the bussiness understanding step, the accuracy must be at least 50%, so the 70% of accuracy was a good result.

3.6   Distribution

It was utilized plots to show the predictions. After a question is put on the system, the system outputs a plot showing its answer. The plot has two lines to represent the prediction and the model confidence. The model confidence was calculated using the neuron activation values of the exit layer of neural net. The black line shows the predicion made by each model. When the value is 1, it means that region has the level represented in the abscissa, and 0 otherwise. The grey line determines how much of confidence each model has in its prediction.

Thus, the plot displayed in Figure 2 shows that the predictors that represents high and very high levels say that instance belongs to their levels with 65% and 60% of confidence respectively. All other models deny the participation of the instance in their levels.

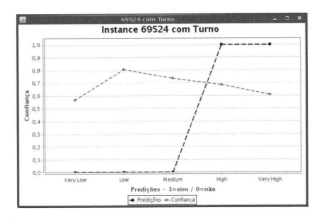

Fig. 2. Prediction of a negative instance of medium level belongs to the second data set

The chart in Figure 3 shows that all models predict the instance as negative. The question was made for the first model, the model trained with the first data group, the group with 36 attributes. A greater confidence for the prediction was made by the model that predicts the high level and the smallest on for the model that predicts the very low level. The prediction was not so wrong, it was wrong for the class, but its confidence in asserting such prediction for the very low level was low. Thus, we can conclude that region may have very low criminal level. We will use the second model to ensure the prediction made by the first model.

The figure 4 displays the prediction using the same question used in the previous example, but now using the attributes of the second group of data. Like the previous result, all models predict the instance as negative for the criminal

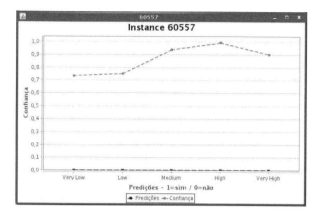

Fig. 3. Prediction of a first data set instance with positive very low level

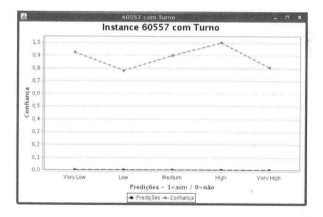

Fig. 4. Prediction of a second data set instance with positive very low level

level that it represents. The lower confidence in the statement was made by the model that predicts the low level and the highest value was for the model that predicts the instances with high level. Unfortunately the second model showed a high confidence in denying the very low level, however denying the low level with low confidence. From the results of the two predictors we can conclude that the criminal level of the region is on the threshold between low and very low, based on the result of the first and second models. Thus, it can predict a trend in the growing of crime, from the very low level to low level. Besides predicting the criminal level, our model can show trends of growth or decline in violence.

Like the case before, there are cases in which the predictors have undecided results or low confidence in their results, for this, it is used the other model to support the results of the first executed model. Thus, a system uses two different predictive models, in which the analyst can use them to support their decisions.

4   Conclusion and Further Works

The model defined is made as a tool for help decisions makers using predictions. Its predictions were based on criminal levels using data from Brazilian geographic areas. Besides being possible to implement it in any city in Brazil, because the necessary data can be collected locally through its security secretary and IBGE. Our model may be extended for other cities for differents countries just doing few adjustments. We believed that the socioeconomic characteristics of a region influence local crime, this hypothesis is proven in our case study. Any industry can use our intelligence model to build an agile and reliable system to predict criminal levels.

For the case study it was used the Fortaleza Metropolitan Region. We got an accuracy better than 70% and a distinct method of analyzing the result. Using two models to reinforce the results obtained by the predictors.

As a future work, we will apply the built model using the latest data. Besides the evaluation, we suggest the use of a map system GIS for easier viewing of results. New learning algorithms can be used and may provide superior results to those found using Neural Networks.

References

1. Mitchell, M., Brown, D., Conklin, J.: A Crime Forecasting Tool for the Web-Based Crime Analysis Toolkit. In: IEEE Systems and Information Engineering Design Symposium, SIEDS 2007, pp. 1–5 (2007)
2. Henderson, M., Wolfers, J., Zitzewitz, E.: Predicting Crime. Arizona Law Review 52, 15–173 (2010)
3. Mohler, G., Short, M., Brantingham, P., Schoenberg, F., Tita, G.: Self-exciting Point Process Modeling of Crime. Journal of the American Statistical Association 106(493), 100–108 (2011)
4. Furtado, V., Ayres, L., de Oliveira, M., Vasconcelos, E., Caminha, C., D'Orleans, J., Belchior, M.: Collective Intelligence in Law Enforcement - The WikiCrimes System. Information Sciences 180, 4–17 (2009)
5. Witten, I.H., Frank, E.: Data Mining: Pratical Machine Learning Tools and Techniques, 2nd edn., Diane Cerra. The Morgan Kaufmann Series in Data Management Systems (2005)
6. Mahmoud, E., DeRoeck, R., Brown, R., Rice, G.: Bridging the Gap between Theory and Practice in Forecasting. International Journal of Forecasting 8, 251–267 (1992)
7. Fayyad, U., Piatetsky-Shapiro, G., Smyth, P.: The KDD Process for Extracting Useful Knowledge from Volumes of Data. Communications of the ACM 39, 27–34 (1996)

MASSIF: A Promising Solution to Enhance Olympic Games IT Security

Elsa Prieto[1], Rodrigo Diaz[1], Luigi Romano[2], Roland Rieke[3],
and Mohammed Achemlal[4]

[1] Atos Research and Innovation (ARI), Atos Origin
{elsa.prieto,rodrigo.diaz}@atosresearch.eu
[2] Consorzio Interuniversitario Nazionale per l'Informatica (CINI)
{lrom}@uniparthenope.it
[3] Fraunhofer - Institut für Sichere (SIT)
{roland.rieke}@sit.fraunhofer.de
[4] Orange - France Telecom SA
{mohammed.achemlal}@orange-ftgroup.com

Abstract. Nowadays, Olympic Games have become one of the most profitable global media events, becoming at the same way more and more attractive target from the terrorist perspective due to their media diffusion and international dimension. Critical for the success of such a highly visible event is protecting and securing the business and the supporting cyber-infrastructure enabling it. In this context, the MASSIF project aims to provide a new generation SIEM framework for service infrastructures supporting intelligent, scalable, and multi-level/multi-domain security event processing and predictive security monitoring.

Keywords: Information Security Management, Security Event Management, Systems Safety, Data Security, Software Protection, Secure Architecture Design.

1 Introduction

Recent terrorist attacks across the world indicated that terrorists continue to target crowded places and show how vulnerable high profile venues and events can be used to perpetrate such incidents for maximum impact across the globe.

Terrorism attacks can adopt many forms, not just a physical attack on life and limb. It can include interference with vital information or communication systems, causing disruption and economic damage. For this reason, in addition to the physical security of the event venues, the cyber-security of the IT event infrastructure should be protected in the same way.

Nowadays, Olympic Games have become one of the most profitable global media events. From the terrorist perspective, Olympics can be seen as one of the most attractive events to commit actions due to their media diffusion, international dimension and symbolic representation. As a consequence of this, security has become a top focus and budget priority. Surpassing all before it in size and scope,

H. Jahankhani et al. (Eds.): ICGS3/e-Democracy 2011, LNICST 99, pp. 139–147, 2012.
© Institute for Computer Sciences, Social Informatics and Telecommunications Engineering 2012

security at the Vancouver Olympic Games of 2010 cost an estimated USD $1 billion and included a 15,000-person force of Canadian military, Vancouver police, U.S. security forces, and private contractors to guard the city by air, land, and sea[1]. Vancouver marked a transition into an unparalleled era of Olympic security in terms of cross-national cooperation, planning, and spending. The scope, however, was limited—the majority of funds and efforts aimed to maintain calm during the two-week event and did not address longer-term security concerns.

As the Worldwide IT Partner for the Olympic Games and Top sponsor, Atos Origin integrates, manages and secures the vast IT system that relays results, events and athlete information to spectators and media around the world. The Atos Origin contract with the International Olympic Committee (IOC) is the world's largest sports related IT contract and was recently extended to cover the Sochi Olympic Winter Games in 2014 in Russia and the Rio Olympic Summer Games in 2016 in Brazil. The major challenge is to create an IT solution for each Olympic Games that allows the capture and reporting of every moment of the action and brings it to the world via television and the Internet. Critical for the success of such a highly visible event is protecting and securing the business and the supporting cyber-infrastructure enabling it and naturally, security is a top priority.

With innovation as the cornerstone of its business and strategy, Atos Origin is coordinating the European research project MASSIF (MAnagement of Security information and events in Service Infrastructures, http://www.massif-project.eu/). The MASSIF Consortium consists of 12 project partners from 6 different European countries (France, Germany, Italy, Portugal, Russia, Spain) and South Africa including three different groups of business roles: scenario providers (Atos Origin, Epsilon, France Telecom and T-Systems), scientific partners (Fraunhofer SIT, Institut Telecom, SPIIRAS, C.I.N.I., Universidad Politécnica de Madrid and Universidade de Lisboa) and SIEM developers (Alienvault and 6cure). This paper addresses the challenges that arise in the cyber-security of Olympic Games and how the results of the MASSIF project can help to improve it.

The paper is structured as follows: Section 2 provides an overview of the existing IT infrastructure while Section 3 includes the challenges addressed by the MASSIF project. Section 4 gives an overview of the related work. Finally, Section 5 concludes this paper and provides pointers for future work.

2   Olympic Games IT Infrastructure

Olympic Games are getting more and more huge events, numbers in this context are gigantic. For instance, in the Beijing games 10.708 athletes were competing, 5.600 written press & photographers were accredited, 12.000 rights holding broadcaster staff, 70.000 volunteers, more than 60 competition and non-competition venues (http://en.beijing2008.cn/media/usefulinfo/).

The Olympic Games, must successfully issue and activate more than 200,000 accreditations for Games that comprise around 300 events representing over 4,500 hours of live competition. Live commentator services are delivered for around 20 sports. More than 15 million information pages are viewed, with peaks of 1 million pages viewed on specific days. Over 3Gb of live results are provided in around 800,000 messages to the Olympic website, broadcasters and sports federations.

The complex, massive IT infrastructure of the Olympic Games is deployed by large teams of people into different environments every other year. Such a major task could potentially pose significant risks, but these can be offset through preserving and sharing the knowledge gained from previous Games.

The Olympic Games have 3 core systems that support the operations of the Games. These systems are summarised below:

Core Games System (CGS). CGS is a set of applications for assisting in the capture and management of data about people who will be attending the Games events and the staff supporting them. Among others, this includes Accreditation and Workforce management (including Volunteers).

Information Diffusion System (INFO). INFO comprises of a set of applications that retrieve and distribute information related to, and supporting, of the Games. The information is provided by different sources e.g. Results system, interfaces with CGS, Weather provider etc. The information is processed and distributed to internal clients e.g. broadcasters, journalists, and other members of the Olympic and Paralympics Families. IT is also sent to external clients e.g. World News Press Agencies (WNPA), sports federations and governing bodies, and Internet Service Providers (ISPs).

Results Systems, are grouped into two sets of systems:

Timing & Scoring Systems (T&S) capture real-time data during the competition. Through electronic feeds to other systems, this data is made available for use on the scoreboard, in TV graphics and other related outputs, by OVR.

On Venue Results Systems (OVR) running at each of the competition venues receives both data from T&S and manually entered data to calculate results of each Olympic event. OVR Systems then distribute the results to INFO.

Concerning the security of the IT infrastructure, for the Beijing 2008 Olympic Games, more than 12 million IT security events were collected and filtered events each day to detect any potential security risk for the Olympic Games IT systems. From these, less than 100 were identified as real issues. All were resolved, with no impact at all on the Olympic Games (http://www.atosorigin.com/olympic_games).

For an event of this magnitude, deadlines are not negotiable, when world-class athletes are ready to compete for gold after years of rigorous training and qualification and viewers are anxious to enjoy such a show, there are no second chances. System disruption or failure is not acceptable. In this context, the main challenge of the SIEM infrastructure in Olympic Games is to protect the games IT infrastructure from any undesired and/or uncontrolled phenomena which can impact any part of the result chain and associated services.

3   Security Management Challenges

Security Information Event Management (SIEM) solutions have become the backbone of the all Service Security systems. They collect data on events from different security elements, such as sensors, firewalls, routers or servers, analyze the data, and provide a suitable response to threats and attacks based on predefined security rules and policies. Despite the existence of highly regarded commercial products, their technical capabilities show a number of constraints in terms of scalability, resilience and interoperability.

The MASSIF project aims at achieving a significant advance in the area of SIEMs by integrating and relating events from different system layers and various domains into one more comprehensive view of security-aware processes and by increasing the scalability of the underlying event processing technology. The main challenge that MASSIF will face is to bring its enhancements and extensions into the business layer with a minimum impact on the end-user operation.

A further goal of the MASSIF project is to integrate these results in two existing Open Source SIEM solutions, namely OSSIM (http://alienvault.com/community) and Prelude (http://www.prelude-technologies.com/) and to apply them to four industrial scenarios, including the Olympic Games IT infrastructure.

Aligned with the security needs of these scenarios, MASSIF challenges can be arranged according to the following dimensions:

3.1   Collection

The data gathering must have the ability to deal with a large number of highly heterogeneous data feeds. The capabilities of the SIEM will be improved by the integration of new types of security tools/probes. This implies that the parsing/processing logic (and code) should be as much as possible decoupled from the specific characteristics of the data format and related technologies. Additionally, the parsing logic and related languages must allow effective processing of virtually any type of security relevant event in cyber-environment, including, in the future, possible extensions to capture and process security events from physical security equipment.

Moreover, the volume of events to be collected and processed per unit of time can occasionally increase resulting in load peaks. The data collection layer should be able to handle such peaks and to propagate relevant events to the SIEM core platform without loss of information.

These concepts are implemented in MASSIF by the Generic Event Translation (GET) framework. The GET framework relies on grammar-based parsing [2], [3] and compiler-compiler technology to implement effective processing of security-relevant events. The main components of the Generic Event Translation Framework are represented in Fig.1. A brief description of each component is provided in the following:

Generic Event Translation (GET) Manager. This component is responsible for the activation of all the modules which belong to the Generic Event Translation framework. In particular, it is in charge of the generation of new Adaptable Parser modules, as new grammars are added to the system.

Event Dispatcher. This component connects each source of sensor events to the appropriate GET Access Point (GAP), in order to provide it with an Adaptable Parser which is capable of processing the specific event format.

GET Access Point (GAP). It is responsible for orchestrating the translation process of the GET. It is in charge of extracting the content of source messages in the source specific format, using the event parsing capabilities of the Adaptable Parsers and requesting the final conversion to the MASSIF Event Format by the MASSIF Event Manager (MEM).

Format-Specific Grammars. These contain semantic description of the different event formats that are used for the creation of the Adaptable Parsers.

Adaptable Parsers. These components provide the parsing capabilities for the different types of events used in MASSIF. They allow for extraction of the relevant information for the event to be inserted in the MASSIF Event Format.

MASSIF Event Manager (MEM). It translates the event content, extracted by the Adaptable Parser to the MASSIF Event Format, thus allowing the event to be sent to the reliable event bus. It also attaches to each MASSIF Event a timestamp, which is made available by the synchronized time source of the Resilient Architecture.

Sender Agent. It is the component that finally sends MASSIF-formatted events to the reliable event bus.

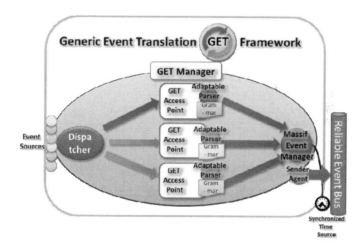

Fig. 1. Generic Event Translation main components

3.2   Processing

The core of MASSIF is an event processing engine capable of handling high input rates and of optimizing the amount of resources based on the actual load [4]. In other words, the system should monitor both input loads and vital parameters, such as CPU utilization, in order to adjust the amount of resources, i.e., provision more resources during peak load times and decommission them during valley load periods. The system must process input data at high rate and provide meaningful results with soft real-time requirements. The engine should be able to aggregate, abstract and correlate heterogeneous events from multiple sources at different levels of the system stack.

3.3   Correlation

MASSIF targets at correlation capabilities across layers of security events, from network and security devices as well as from the service infrastructure such as correlation of physical and logical event sources. The engine should be shipped with a set of predefined correlation rules to identify well-known attacks. However, it should also support easy and intuitive creation of user-defined rules.

3.4   Resilience

Special emphasis will be placed on providing a highly resilient architecture against attacks, concurrent component failures, and unpredictable network operation conditions. The event flows should be protected, from the collection points through their distribution, processing and archival. The designed mechanisms should offer flexible and incremental solutions for node resilience, providing for seamless deployment of necessary functions and protocols. These mechanisms should take into consideration particular aspects of the infrastructure, such as edge-side and core-side node implementations.

3.5   Timeliness

The infrastructure should provide for (near) real-time collection, transmission and processing of events, and ensure the corresponding reliable and timeliness generation of alarms and countermeasures when needed.

3.6   Sensitive Information

MASSIF features for forensic support will satisfy the following requirements:

Data Authenticity. Security event data contents, as well as additional/added information related to data origin and destination, must be the reliably stored.

Fault and Intrusion-Tolerant Stable Storage. The stable storage system on which data for forensic use will be persisted must be tolerant both to faults and to intrusions.

Least Persistence Principle. With respect to sensitive data, only information which is actually needed should be persisted to stable storage (most of the data should be processed in real-time and thrown away).

Privacy of Forensic Records. Forensic evidence related to security breaches will be made available only to authorized parties.

4   Related Work

The research in MASSIF combines aspects of process monitoring, simulation, and analysis as well as trustworthiness and scalability of the complex event processing architecture itself. Relevant contributions from these broad areas are:

Attack Modelling, Simulation and Risk Evaluation. The technology most relevant to the modelling and simulation methods to be developed for MASSIF is commonly called attack-graph analysis, an approach presented by Phillips and Swiler [5] in. Two participants of the MASSIF team namely Fraunhofer SIT and SPIIRAS are actively researching in that area [6], [7].

Predictive Security Analysis. The predictive security analysis in MASSIF will use the method given in [8] to analyse the security requirements. Based on this, the attack models together with the SIEM's information about the current attack state and the process models together with the SIEM's information about the current process state can be used to derive a near future view of possible upcoming security problems [9]. This information can now be used in an ontology-driven approach to select appropriate countermeasures [10].

SIEM Scalability and Trustworthiness. Complex Event Processing (CEP) is a promising technology to improve current SIEM systems. It allows processing of large amounts of streaming data in real time and provides information abstraction and correlation, similarly to SIEM correlation engines. MASSIF will develop new parallel distributed CEP technology that overcomes scalability limitations due to single node bottlenecks or high distribution overhead [4]. The trustworthiness of the SIEM architecture will be improved by utilising secure digital chains of evidence [11].

5   Conclusions and Outlook

The MASSIF project is still at an early stage. However, the challenges that the project aims to achieve will provide a significant advance in the area of Security Information and Event Management (SIEM) by integrating and relating events from different system layers and various domains into one more comprehensive view of security-aware processes and by increasing the scalability of the underlying event processing technology. To address the challenges the MASSIF partners plan to develop a novel SIEM system with the following solutions and implied research and development needs.

In order to enable a highly scalable security situation assessment, the MASSIF event engine will provide a flexible language to express filtering, transformation, abstraction, aggregation, intra-layer and cross-layer correlation as well as storage of security events. The event engine will be able to process with the same language both the real-time event flow as well as stored events for forensic analysis. Additionally, specific collectors to translate from the external languages into the event engine language will be provided.

Ideally, the MASSIF system should be able to analyze upcoming security threats and violations in order to trigger remediation actions even before the occurrence of possible security incidences. Therefore, new process and attack analysis and simulation techniques will be developed in order to be able to relate events dynamically from different execution levels, define specific level abstractions, evaluate them with respect to security issues and during runtime interpret them in context of specific security properties. Novel adaptive response technologies will enable anticipatory impact analysis, decision support and support impact mitigation by adaptive configuration of countermeasures such as policies.

Due to the highly distributed and heterogeneous nature of the various components, and the hostile and unpredictable operational environment, it becomes a challenge to design an integrated solution for the protection of the SIEM framework itself. Therefore, the MASSIF system will be based on a resilient, trust-enabling architecture with trusted collection of security-relevant data from highly heterogeneous trusted networked devices in order to ensure unforgeability of stored security events and to support criminal/civil prosecution of attackers.

Acknowledgements. The work in this paper has been sponsored by the EC Framework Programme as part of the ICT MASSIF project (grant agreement no. 257644).

References

1. McRoskey, S.R.: Security and the Olympic Games Making Rio an Example. Yale Journal of International Affairs (2010)
2. Turmo, J., Ageno, A., Catala, N.: Adaptive Information Extraction. ACM Computing Surveys 38(2) (2006)
3. Campanile, F., Cilardo, A., Coppolino, L., Romano, L.: Adaptable Parsing of Real-Time Data Streams. In: Proc. of The Fifteen Euromicro Conference on Parallel, Distributed and Network-based Processing (PDP 2007), Naples, Italy, February 7-9, pp. 412–418. IEEE Computer Society Press, Los Alamitos (2007)
4. Gulisano, V., Jimenez-Peris, R., Patiño-Martínez, M., Valduriez, P.: A Large Scale Data Streaming System. In: 30th IEEE Int. Conf. on Distributed Systems (ICDCS), Genoa, Italy (2010)
5. Cynthia, A.P., Swiler, L.P.: A graph-based system for network-vulnerability analysis. In: NSPW 1998, Proceedings of the 1998 Workshop on New Security Paradigms, pp. 71–79. ACM Press (1998)
6. Rieke, R.: Abstraction-based analysis of known and unknown vulnerabilities of critical information infrastructures. International Journal of System of Systems Engineering (IJSSE) 1, 59–77 (2008)
7. Kotenko, I., Stepashkin, M., Doynikova, E.: Security Analysis of Computer-aided Systems taking into account Social Engineering Attacks. In: 19th Euromicro International Conference on Parallel, Distributed and network-based Processing (PDP 2011), Ayia Napa, Cyprus (2011)

8. Fuchs, A., Rieke, R.: Identification of Security Requirements in Systems of Systems by Functional Security Analysis. In: Casimiro, A., de Lemos, R., Gacek, C. (eds.) Architecting Dependable Systems VII. LNCS, vol. 6420, pp. 74–96. Springer, Heidelberg (2010)

9. Rieke, R., Stoynova, Z.: Predictive Security Analysis for Event-Driven Processes. In: Kotenko, I., Skormin, V. (eds.) MMM-ACNS 2010. LNCS, vol. 6258, pp. 321–328. Springer, Heidelberg (2010)

10. Cuppens-Boulahia, N., Cuppens, F., Lopez, J., Vasquez, E., Guerra, J., Debar, H.: An ontology-based approach to react to network attacks. International Journal of Information and Computer Security 3, 280–305 (2009)

11. Kuntze, N., Rudolph, C.: Secure digital chains of evidence. In: Sixth International Workshop on Systematic Approaches to Digital Forensic Engineering (SADFE) 2011, Oakland, USA (2011)

An Ontology-Based Model for SIEM Environments

Gustavo Gonzalez Granadillo, Yosra Ben Mustapha, Nabil Hachem, and Herve Debar

Telecom Sudparis, SAMOVAR UMR 5157
9 rue Charles Fourier, 91011 EVRY, France
{G.Granadillo,Y.Mustapha,N.Hachem,H.Debar}@it-sudparis.eu

Abstract. The management of security events, from the analysis of attacks and risk to the selection of appropriate countermeasures, has become a major concern for security analysts and IT administrators. Furthermore, network and system devices are designed to be heterogeneous, with different characteristics and functionalities that increase the difficulty of these tasks. This paper introduces an ontology-driven approach to address the aforementioned problems. The proposed model takes into account the two main aspects of this field, the information that is manipulated by SIEM environments and the operations that are applied to this information, in order to reach the desired goals. We present a case study on Botnets to illustrate the utilization of our model.

Keywords: SIEM, Ontology, Data Model.

1 Introduction

A Security Information and Event Management (SIEM) system[1] is an integrated, information security oriented platform offering the following services:

- Log management (log collection, storage, organization and retrieval)
- IT regulatory compliance (audit, validation or violation identification)
- Event correlation (normalization, fusion, verification, analysis)
- Active response (decision analysis, counter-measure response, prioritization)
- Endpoint security (monitoring, updating, configuration)

SIEM platforms need to acquire high volumes of information from heterogeneous sources and manipulate them on the fly. SIEM deployments thus focus on writing ad-hoc collectors and translators to acquire information and normalize it, and on writing correlation rules to manipulate the normalized information. This operational focus leads SIEM implementers to operate on information syntax rather than semantic, and to use feature-poor operations (counts, and sequences) in their correlation languages.

This paper addresses the previous issues by proposing a system solution for modeling SIEM-related data structures and operations to ensure interoperability. It abstracts the most important concepts from pre-existing formats (i.e.,

H. Jahankhani et al. (Eds.): ICGS3/e-Democracy 2011, LNICST 99, pp. 148–155, 2012.

IDMEF[RFC4765], IODEF[RFC5070], Syslog[RFC5424], M4D4[2], ...), to focus on information *semantics* and define a clean formal model for reasoning and modeling purposes. This preserves the capability of interacting with these formats while relaxing operational limitations that would artificially alter the data model. We thus specify an abstract model and will implement translations (on an as needed basis, using for example XSLT transformations) to push the concepts developed to operational environments at a later stage.

The proposed solution provides a general framework that formally models SIEM information and operations. It is developed using Protégé-OWL 4.1 beta platform, which incorporates the advantages and characteristics of the OWL2 language [3] into a flexible architecture. The remainder of the paper is structured as follows: section 2 briefly describes ontologies and the relevant state of the art; section 3 describes our Security Information Model; section 4 presents a use case of the proposed model; finally, some conclusions and future work are given in section 5.

2   Ontology

An Ontology can be seen as a mechanism to define the knowledge associated to a specific subject in a way that it can be interpreted by machines and shared by scientists and researchers. Some authors [4], [5] agree on the fact that Ontologies allow the reuse of knowledge from a specific domain, separate domain knowledge from operational knowledge and make inferences on the data. Furthermore, they can be used to find the right data at the right time while dealing with several information models; it is possible to use them in real environments (a use case is provided in section 4); and they enable the extensibility of attack and signature languages to be used among heterogeneous systems.

2.1   Elements

Ontologies are generally composed of instances, classes and properties. Instances are representations of individuals or objects in the domain of interest (e.g. Botnet, Network, Probe, etc). Classes generally group two or more instances according to common characteristics (e.g. the class Attack has Botnet, Phishing and Trojan horse as instances). Properties are used to describe features and/or attributes to link instances (e.g. directed_to, results_in, etc). They are shared by classes in order to give to the inheriting class (subclass) a more restrictive definition than the one provided by the ascendant class (superclass).

2.2   Related Work

Ontologies have been used in many disciplines such as: artificial intelligence, semantic web, systems engineering, biomedical informatics, information architecture, network security, and many others. Lopez et al. in [4], propose, for instance, the use of Ontologies to share alerts among SIM systems. As a result the Ontology enables a mapping from the format message to the corresponding ontology instances, making possible the translation of the information contained on each message into an instance of alert.

Similarly, Cuppens et al. in [6], propose an Ontology framework to react to network attacks by using format languages such as IDMEF and OrBAC. As a consequence, it is possible to know which context rules are to be active as a reaction for a given attack. Other authors [7], introduce the use of Ontologies to detect and counteract to computer attacks, which enables the system to send suitable alarms so that appropriate reactions are implemented. Furthermore, Razzaq et al.[8] present an Ontology solution against web application attacks. As a result, violation of rules is efficiently undertaken, information retrieval is well performed and malicious inputs are correlated intelligently.

It is important to mention that some concepts and relationships from the aforementioned ontologies have been considered in the development of our information model. However, we designed a novel ontology-basis model that introduces more elaborated relations among concepts and that can be implemented as an abstraction of several format languages.

3   Proposed Security Information Model

Our solution provides an ontological model composed of two concepts: the *Information Class*, which models all the necessary information regarding the system and network configuration, as well as the security logs and events; and the *Operation Class*, which models treatments that are needed to propose the security policies and countermeasures. The distinction between these two classes makes the SIEM efficient and more consistent.

The Operation and Information classes are primarily related by an *Analysis* property that consists of requesting convenient data to ensure its functionalities. The instantiated individual within the Operation class will eventually update or modify the available information throughout the *Decision* property.

3.1   Information Class Model

In our Ontology, the information class is composed of two subclasses: the *configuration class*, which includes all the system and network information (such as protocols, machines, services, users and operating system); and the *security class*, which includes all the information regarding events, vulnerabilities, signatures, impact and security policies (figure 1).

The *event class* models abnormal or suspicious situations that need to be analysed by a security device since it can be considered as an attack or as an unusual activity performed by an authorised user. Its definition and classification is essential for the appropriate performance of the SIEM model, which eliminates ambiguities and misinterpretation of the processed data.

The *impact class* denotes the cost that a response action may have over a detected intrusion. It is modeled as TimeImpact and MonetaryImpact. The *policy class* defines all the information related to the security polices used to mitigate the effects of an intrusion. It includes the *expectation class*, which conveys to the impact report the actions that the sender may request, such as: doing nothing; contacting source, target or sender; blocking port, network or host; etc.

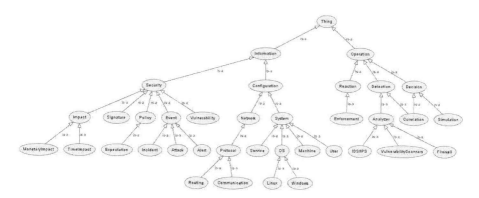

Fig. 1. Information Class Model

The *configuration class* has two subclasses: the network and system classes, which define a topology and a cartography model respectively, as proposed in [2]. The *network class* mainly focuses on the protocols (e.g., routing information protocols), necessary for the correlation process to calculate the path followed by a packet in the monitored domain. The *system class* describes a system involved in an event and it is categorized according to the role it played in the incident through the category attribute.

Some instances of our proposed Ontology may have multiple inheritances, meaning that one instance can inherit properties from more than one class. As a matter of fact, system or network instances (a server configuration, a network protocol, etc), which inherit all the properties from the configuration class, can also inherit properties from the vulnerability class, which is defined in the security information concept.

3.2   Operation Class Model

SIEM operations are generally composed of several activities and processes such as: detection, decision, and reaction (see figure 1).

Detection: This operation includes the subclass Analyzers, (i.e., IDS, vulnerability scanners, firewall, sensors, and other security devices), which generate a huge amount of heterogeneous events. Processing these events directly would be too complex and inefficient. Thus, an alert correlation engine, which essentially provides a higher level view of the occurring intrusion, will be important to explore.

Decision: This class contains two subclasses: *correlation* and *simulation*, whose primary goal consists on providing system support for a global view of network attacks by analyzing raw alerts in a simulated environment. As a result, the countermeasure impact is evaluated in terms of money, user/root access, damage, attack efficiency, etc., and an *impact report* is generated. This report can be a support for security administrators to evaluate and guarantee the respectfulness of security policies and to design or implement the counter-measures to react against defined attacks.

Reaction: This operation consists of an enforcement point that transforms on the first phase the selected countermeasures by the correlator and the evaluator from a high to a low specification level. In the second phase, this process enforces the configurations and rules on the different system and network components. These countermeasures include not only access control policies (i.e. blocking a user), but also management actions (i.e. taking down server, changing sensor configurations).

Table 1 summarizes the inputs, outputs, and goals of the different modules.

Table 1. Operation functions

Operations	Input	Output	Goals
Detection	Events related information	Events from heterogeneous sources	Efficient attack detection
Decision	Correlated data and countermeasures	Countermeasure costs and impact report	Optimal countermeasure decisions
Reaction	Countermeasures and information	Configurations and rules	Rules and configurations enforcement based on countermeasure decisions

4   Case Study

The first part of this section provides a general model for SIEM operations, while in the second section we explain the procedure to detect Botnet attacks and the actions to be taken as counter-measures.

4.1   General Model of SIEM Operations

We can model the SIEM utilization by using the following expressions, where all the elements that take place in the process are expressed between curly brackets ({}); the arrow ($\rightarrow$) represents the definition of the global process; the addition process, expressed by the plus (+) symbol, refers to the activities that need to be performed in order to combine the different set of elements; and the equal symbol (=) denotes the resulting product of the process.

$$\mathbf{A} \rightarrow \{\mathbf{Config}\} + \{\mathbf{Information}\} = \{\mathbf{Events}_{(1..n)}\} \tag{1}$$

An analyzer (A) take a combination of a set of predefined system configuration parameters plus the information received, which generates, as a result, one or many events for a particular incident.

$$\mathbf{R/SIEM} \rightarrow \{\mathbf{Config}_{(t)}\} + \{\mathbf{Events, Policies}\} = \{\mathbf{Config}_{(t+1)}\} \qquad (2)$$

Similarly, a Reaction process (R) in a SIEM environment can be modeled as the addition of a system configuration at time t and the detection of an event or policy, which in turn produces a new configuration at time t+1.

$$\mathbf{C/SIEM} \rightarrow \{\mathbf{Alerts}_{(1..n)}\} + \{\mathbf{Config}_{(t)}\} = \{\mathbf{Policy}_{(1..n)}\} \qquad (3)$$

The Correlation Process (C) in a SIEM environment takes into account one or more alerts along with the configuration information of the system at time t. As a result, one or many security policies can be generated.

The following equation can be proposed as a model to evaluate the impact of an attack:

$$\mathbf{Min}_i \rightarrow \{\mathbf{Config}_{(i, usage)}\} = \{\mathbf{Cost}\} \qquad (4)$$

By dynamically evaluating attack impacts, the same attack is considered to have different impacts (i), depending on the pre-established system configuration and usage. All the resulting impacts are then quantified, meaning that their corresponding cost is calculated, the minimum (Min) of which is then proposed as the best security policy.

4.2   Botnet Use Case

Botnet attack life cycle generally consists of three main phases: Spreading/Infection, Control, Usage [9].

Infection: During the Spreading/Infection phase, analyzers including HIDS (ex: antivirus, vulnerabilities scanners) and NIDS (ex Snort) generate events when detecting or suspecting any malicious actions. this is modeled in the following equation, where the system and network configuration are instances of the configuration class; and signature, vulnerabilities and rule sets (polices) are instances of the security class.

$$\mathbf{A}_{Antivirus} \rightarrow \quad \{\mathbf{SystemConfig}\} + \{\mathbf{Signature}\} = \{\mathbf{Events}\} \qquad (5)$$
$$\mathbf{A}_{V.Scanner} \rightarrow \quad \{\mathbf{SystemConfig}\} + \{\mathbf{Vulnerabilities}\} = \{\mathbf{Events}\}$$
$$\mathbf{A}_{Snort} \rightarrow \{\mathbf{NetworkConfig} + \mathbf{Traffic}\} + \{\mathbf{Rulesets}\} = \{\mathbf{Events}\}$$

Control: Through the control phase, masters might use different ways to control their distributed bots. Analyzers on the network and system level might generate different events that might be useful for the detection of a Botnet attack and its corresponding C&C covert channel. These analyzers include Filters, Routers, Firewalls, Port scanners and others.

$$\mathbf{A_{portscanner}} \rightarrow \{\mathbf{SystemConfig, Connections}\} + \{\mathbf{Portsets}\} = \{\mathbf{Events}\} \quad (6)$$
$$\mathbf{A_{Netfilters}} \rightarrow \quad \{\mathbf{NetworkConfig, Traffic}\} + \{\mathbf{Rulesets}\} = \{\mathbf{Events}\}$$

Usage: The same case in the usage phase; Bots perform different services which can be categorized in DDoS attacks, Spamming and Spreading malwares, espionage and hosting malicious activities. Each category can be identified by different Analyzers.

$$\mathbf{A_{spamfilters}} \rightarrow \{\mathbf{NetworkConfig, Traffic}\} + \{\mathbf{Rulesets}\} = \{\mathbf{Events}\} \quad (7)$$
$$\mathbf{A_{DDoS}} \rightarrow \{\mathbf{NetworkConfig, Traffic}\} + \{\mathbf{Rulesets}\} = \{\mathbf{Events}\}$$

These analyzers might be able to take actions by themselves as for the firewall and the spam filtering situation.

$$\mathbf{R/SIEM_{firewall}} \rightarrow \{\mathbf{Config_{(t)}}\}_{IPopened} + \{\mathbf{Alert}\} = \{\mathbf{Config_{(t+1)}}\}_{blockIP} \quad (8)$$

Detection-Decision: These systems taken separately, cannot detect attacks or incidents in which networks and systems are involved, nor distinguish false positives and negatives. In order to detect this false rates and attacks, a correlation phase is needed to filter and aggregate the events (alerts, logs...) received from different analyzers. These events are then associated in the alert fusion process during the correlation. This phase will send countermeasures to the reactor or suggest different countermeasures (e.g. participation in taking down C&C server, blocking traffic, blocking port ...) to the simulation phase depending on the countermeasure's clarity and attack's severity.

$$\mathbf{C/SIEM} \rightarrow \{\mathbf{Events}\}_{Antiviruses,Snort,DDoS,...} + \{\mathbf{Network, SystemConfig}\} \quad (9)$$
$$= \{\mathbf{Policies}\}_{TakingdownC\&Cserver,Blockingtraffic,Port,Website...}$$

The Simulation phase studies the impact of these countermeasures (policies). By collaboration with the correlation process, they can decide which actions to be taken and forward the best security policy(s) to the reactor (ex: Blocking access to a specific website, cleaning hosts).

$$\mathbf{Min} \rightarrow \{\mathbf{Config_{Takedownserver,Blockwebsite...}usage}\} = \{\mathbf{Cost}\} \quad (10)$$

Reaction: When the reaction process receives these countermeasures, it applies them on the system and network using different configurations and rules depending on the predefined configurations (Environment) and the corresponding data models. In this case, the reaction can be: blocking a website on the DNS server, forwarding the info to other network domains (in cooperative detection scenario) and cleaning the infected hosts.

$$\mathbf{R/SIEM} \rightarrow \{\mathbf{Config_{(t)}}\}_{WebsiteOpened} + \{\mathbf{Policies}\}_{BlockWebsite} \quad (11)$$
$$= \{\mathbf{Config_{(t+1)}}\}_{BlockingWebsite,BlockingDNSServer...}$$

5   Conclusions and Future Works

In this document we have proposed a first attempt to define a global unified security information model to share information from heterogeneous sources in a SIEM infrastructure. Our proposal uses Ontologies as a shared vocabulary between elements and classes, which can ensure interoperability among the system components (i.e. services, machines, and users) and constant processes.

We defined two main classes: the information and operation classes, as well as the derived subclasses and the relationships among them. The information class describes the configuration and security information related to the different system and network devices; and the Operation class describes three main processes: Detection, Decision and Reaction, necessary to enable the detection of upcoming security threats and trigger appropriate mitigation actions.

An example on the applicability of the proposed model over a Botnet attack is provided at the end of the document, showing the functionality of the main operations that integrate the defined security information model. Future work will concentrate on the implementation of this architecture and the analysis of the obtained results.

Acknowledgements. The work in this paper has been sponsored by the EC Framework Programme as part of the ICT MASSIF project (grant no. 257644).

References

1. Miller, D., Harris, S., Harper, A., Van Dyke, S., Blask, C.: Security Information and Event Management (SIEM) Implementation. Mc Graw Hill (2010)
2. Morin, B., Me, L., Debar, H., Ducasse, M.: M4D4: A Logical Framework to Support Alert Correlation in Intrusion Detection. Information Fusion Internationale (2008)
3. Web Ontology Working Group: M4D4: OWL 2 Web Ontology Language, http://www.w3.org/TR/owl2-overview/
4. Lopez, J., Villagra, V., Holdago, P., De Frutos, E., Sanz, I.: A semantic web approach to share alerts among. Security Information Management Systems (2010)
5. Undercoffer, J., Joshi, A., Pinkston, J.: M4D4: Modeling Computer Attacks: An Ontology for Intrusion Detection. In: 6th International Symposium on Recent Advances in Intrusion Detection, pp. 113–135. Springer (2003)
6. Cuppens-Boulahia, N., Cuppens, F., Lopez, J., Vasquez, E., Guerra, J., Debar, H.: An ontology-based approach to react to network attacks. International Journal of Information and Computer Security 3, 280–305 (2009)
7. Abdoli, F., Kahani, M.: Ontology-based Distributed Intrusion Detection System. In: Proceedings of the 14th International CSI Computer Conference, pp. 65–70. IEEE (2009)
8. Razzaq, A., Hur, A., Ahmed, H., Haider, N.: Ontology based Application Level Intrusion Detection System by using Bayesian Filter (2009)
9. Hachem, N., Ben Mustapha, Y., Gonzalez Granadillo, G., Debar, H.: Botnets: lifecycle and taxonomy. In: 6th Conference on Network Architecture and Information Systems Security, IEEE (2011)

Analyzing the Economic Impacts of Security Breaches Due to Outsourcing

Dimitrios Koumaridis, Emmanouil Stiakakis, and Christos K. Georgiadis

University of Macedonia, Department of Applied Informatics,
Egnatia 156, 54006 Thessaloniki, Greece
{koumaridis,stiakakis,geor}@uom.gr

Abstract. In our study, we present four different approaches on the subject that are connected more or less to each other, giving more attention on outsourcing security issues. A case study for the use of outsourced services is also presented using empirical data from an insurance company. This work concludes with an overview of our research, its limitations and by giving some research questions for future work.

Keywords: security economics, outsourcing, security breach.

1   Introduction

The aim of this work is to identify and examine some of the major approaches in the area of security economics. More specifically, four different approaches are examined. We start by presenting them in the section of theoretical background and then we mostly emphasize on the one dealing with the outsourcing policy of companies. These four approaches are connected to each other since they deal with the same subject but from a different point of view.

The first approach is a research by Wang [1] about the effects that disclosures have in business economics, regarding security policies and cases of security breakdowns. The second approach by Ioannidis et al. [2] presents the "conflict" between system administrators and system users about confidentiality and availability. The authors also present the endless effort of the administrators to exploit their budgets properly in order to raise their effectiveness. The third approach on the subject of security economics comes from Anderson [3] and is more behavioral rather than technical, as security is a combination of technology and policy over the proper usage of it. It deals mainly with differences in sentiments upon information security. The fourth approach deals with the rising development of the third partner services in many businesses and the problems occurring from the adoption of this outsourcing policy. It is of great importance that a company gives the opportunity to another company to process crucial and sometimes top secret data. The last approach is the main topic of our work. We conclude with a case study concerning a Greek insurance company about the usage of outsourced services and their impacts.

H. Jahankhani et al. (Eds.): ICGS3/e-Democracy 2011, LNICST 99, pp. 156–163, 2012.

2   Theoretical Background – Literature Review

For a non-experienced observer, the aforementioned approaches are not connected to each other; however, there are certain similarities among them. These similarities will be understood once the following presentation of the approaches has been completed.

2.1   The Effects of Information Disclosures in Business Economics

Business nowadays relies heavily on information technology to perform daily operations. Because of this increasing reliance on information technology, information security related incidents could result in a tremendous impact on a firm's operation and significant financial losses [1]. In order to address the issues and better manage information security risks, researchers and managers have strived to better understand and assess information security risks.

Some firms announce risks related to information security publicly. There are two competing motivations from the literature why firms disclose risk factors. On the one hand, the disclosure of risk factors may contribute to the reduction of the uncertainty that investors have regarding the firm's performance [4]. On the other hand, a firm may disclose risk factors in order to reduce its future litigation costs associated with adverse events [5]. In the information security context, any motivation may be valid. Some firms are inclined to disclose to indicate preparedness, which corresponds to the first motivation, whereas other firms disclose in order to head off lawsuits, which is the second motivation.

Wang [1], through his research, tries to further examine investors' reactions to security breaches. Investors' reactions provide explanations to managers and researchers about what leads to the price and volume reactions to security incidents. When there is no disclosure cost, full disclosure exists because investors believe that non-disclosing companies have the worst possible information. However, if disclosure costs or uncertainty exist, companies will disclose only when the benefits exceed the costs. Disclosure may also be used to reduce ex post legal and reputation costs from bad news or when the firm faces earnings disappointments. General market participants can actually adjust their investment decisions regarding breach announcements given the sophisticated investors' reactions. A trading strategy is performed to demonstrate profitable short-term investment opportunities given the information asymmetry among investors. There is a strong association between the textual contents of the news articles about security breach reports, and both the stock price and trading volume reactions to breach announcements. The results suggest that general breach announcements lead to different assessments of the impact of security incidents. However, specific news articles and those about confidential information result in a more consistent negative belief of the impact of security incidents on a firm's future performance. By taking advantage of the different perceptions among investors, it is shown that, on average, one can make about 300% annual profit around the breach announcement date.

2.2   Cost vs. Performance

In our second research approach, we focus on the relation between cost and performance [2]. Information security and network integrity are issues of the utmost importance to both users and managers [6]. The cost of security breaches and fraud is considerable and such issues constitute growing concerns for policy makers, in addition to the legitimate concerns of the specialist technological community of experts. As the importance of networks increases for all individuals who act as both providers and consumers of information, the integrity of such systems is crucial to their welfare. In the presence of threats to the system, agents must decide the amount of resources required to maintain the system at an acceptable operational state.

Gordon and Loeb in [7] adopt an optimizing framework for the economics of information security, which provides an extensive list of references that address technological issues in information security and point out the distinct lack of rigorous economic analysis of the problem of resource allocation in information security. They adopt a static optimization model where IT managers calculate the optimal ratio of investment in information security to the value of the expected loss under different assumptions regarding the stochastic process that generates the security threats. Within the framework of the model, they conclude that a risk-neutral firm should spend on information security just below 37% of the value of the expected loss that will occur in the event of breach.

The model relies on rather restrictive assumptions and has prompted lively debate regarding the "optimal" ratio of investment in information security. What is of interest is that, the relationship between investment in information security and vulnerability is not always a monotonic function. Other researchers [8-9] are postulating an alternative functional form of vulnerability, showing that the ratio cannot be supported and introduce the notion of the existence of a level of expenditure of information security that removes all threats, as an additional parameter, thus completely securing the information. Under this specification, the "optimal" ratio can vary according to the value of this parameter. The authors give examples where optimal investment ranges between 50% and 100% of the value of information that is protected.

2.3   The Human Factor

The third approach is more theoretical, with a subject that deeply has to do with the human factor and more specifically the human attitude. Anderson [3], one of the pioneers in the field, deals with information security putting forward a contrary view rather than a technical one: information insecurity is at least as much due to perverse incentives. Many of the problems can be explained more clearly and convincingly using the "language" of microeconomics: network externalities, asymmetric information, moral hazard, adverse selection, liability dumping, and the tragedy of the commons.

A characteristic example about the human factor and mainly the human behavior is given in [10], concerning fraud against auto teller machines. In a survey, it was found that patterns of fraud depended on who was liable for them. In the USA, if a customer disputed a transaction, the onus was on the bank to prove that the customer was mistaken or lying, and this gave US banks a motive to protect their systems properly. But in Great Britain, Norway, and the Netherlands, the burden of proof lies on the customer: the bank is right unless the customer could prove it wrong. Since this was almost impossible, the banks in these countries became careless. Eventually, epidemics of fraud demolished their complacency. US banks, meanwhile, suffered much less fraud; although they actually spent less money on security than their European counterparts, they spent it more effectively.

2.4   Outsourcing

Analyzing the last approach (outsourcing), we can understand that it is really tight with the first approach, because the disclosure of such a strategic decision usually affects an enterprise positively or negatively. Positively, because such a decision reduces the fixed costs of the enterprise by giving the effectuation of services somewhere else to a third partner; on the other hand, it gives the expression that the enterprise doesn't have strict security over the third partner which is generally a genuine assumption. Usually third partners that outsource services to others are secured enough, but it is not the same thing as to have every service and equipment within your own responsibility. That is why enterprises should always be really careful about their partners and keep checking their performance of the services they provide to them. A difficulty from a third partner, even a small failure that will last only an hour, sometimes has dramatic effects to the enterprise, because it will possibly stop its usual operation and when something stops functioning usually means losing money. It is even worse to lose reputation in the market since the enterprise has to fight hard to regain it. A disclosure of such an event will affect both partners, the seller and the buyer, but the buyer can always buy from another provider. A low-quality service provider will not sustain competition for a long time.

3   Analyzing Outsourcing-Related Security Issues

Zhou and Johnson [11] are among the researchers that work on the problem of security breaches due to outsourcing. There have been several recent efforts to develop a common reference for rating the information risk posed by partners. They developed a simple analytical model to examine the impact of such information security ratings on service providers, customers, and social welfare.

In this, so-called, Software as a Service (SaaS) model, business applications are provided on demand as a service to customers. SaaS allows firms to reduce many fixed costs associated with the required internal IT infrastructure, application deployment, testing, maintenance, and patch management. It also lowers cost through competition. While these different forms of outsourcing provide enterprise customers with both flexibility and cost benefits, the use of external service providers handling sensitive business data introduces new security risks [12]. Many widely publicized security breaches have been the consequences of a partner failure. Sometimes these failures stem from neglect or under-investment in security. In other cases, the security challenges arise from the nature of the service provider's business model. Providers, who frequently enhance their service offerings in response to evolving customer demand, introduce the possibility of new security bugs with every additional feature. Traditional methods in software assurance, with significant code testing, can be time consuming, slowing the vendor's ability to compete and tempting them to cut corners.

There have been recently several efforts to develop a common risk rating. The idea behind such ratings is to reduce the burden for both enterprise customers and service providers by creating a single risk rating that can be efficiently used by many sides (rather than each firm individually assessing each of their vendors) [13]. While it is tempting to directly equate information security rating with ratings of financial instruments, security ratings are quite different from credit ratings (which measure the default probability for a debt issuer). A good credit rating generally enables the debt issuer to raise money from the financial market at a lower cost [14]. However, a good security rating does not necessarily benefit a high-security service provider because the security rating may have subtle impacts on the competition among service providers, their incentives to improve security levels, and their prices charged to customers.

Zhou and Johnson, through their research, have tried to answer some demanding questions, as for example, if risk ratings always benefit the high-security service provider (or hurt the low-security service provider). If not, how does the risk rating affect different service providers under different market conditions? Another of their concerns is whether risk ratings always benefit the most demanding customers who desire highly secured business partners? And lastly, does risk rating increase social welfare? Some very interesting results have been found: while it is commonly believed that information security rating benefits high-security service providers (and conversely hurts low-security providers), they found that, surprisingly, information security ratings can hurt or benefit both types of service providers, depending on the market conditions. This occurs when the absence of a security rating softens competition allowing the low-security service provider to appear identical to the high-security service provider. In that case, the low-security provider is able to charge a higher price than otherwise and the high-security service provider is able to avoid providing a positive net surplus to the high-type customer to guarantee that the customer does not choose the low-security provider. Therefore, it is possible that the information security rating can intensify competition and hurt both service providers. On the other hand, in some cases, information security ratings can benefit both service providers. Since ratings clearly reveal the security of providers, such information helps service providers to differentiate themselves, and thus can benefit both.

While the literature [15] shows that improved information always benefits the high-type customer, the model shows that information security ratings can hurt the high-type customer. This is because their model captures competition between heterogeneous providers while prior researchers assumed homogeneous providers where profit is competed away. They found that information security ratings have subtle effects on the competition. When the rating is provided, it may reduce the low-security service provider's incentives to invest in security. This reduces the quality of the alternative choice for the high-type customer. Thus, the high-security service provider will not need to provide a large net surplus to lure the high-type customer. This explains why the high-type customer can be hurt by an information security rating of providers. Although the information security rating has subtle effects on service providers and customers respectively, it always increases the social welfare. The policy implication is that information security ratings should be encouraged by social planners.

4   A Case Study of an Insurance Company

It is always useful to present data from the daily operation of a company. We present the case study of the company Infotrust SA. This is an insurance brokerage company located in Thessaloniki, Greece, with two other branches in Athens and Rhodes. Its functions are between the functions of insurance advisors and those of insurance companies. However, there is the need for this company for electronic communication and data handling. The company separates the two functions; it keeps the clients' personal data within its own infrastructure, within its own servers, but it outsources its CRM (Customer Relationship Management) system to another company using Software as a Service.

A personal interview was conducted with the company's IT administrator. The questions used in this interview and the answers given (as "yes" or "no" to the answer, for brevity's sake) are presented in Table 1.

Table 1. Questions used in the personal interview with Infotrust's IT administrator

	QUESTION	YES	NO
1)	Is the outsourcing decision irreversible?		✔
2)	Are you able to operate the new system?	✔	
3)	Does the system lack in integration?	✔	
4)	Is there excessive dependence on outsourcer?	✔	
5)	Does the outsourcer lack in experience?		✔
6)	Does the outsourcer comply with the contract?	✔	
7)	Are there any hidden costs?		✔
8)	Is there any unclear cost to benefit relationship?		✔
9)	Are the data secured? (confidentiality)	✔	
10)	Any specialized equipment needed for the operation of the CRM?		✔
11)	Would it be possible to have the same level of services from within the IT department with the same cost?		✔
12)	Are clients personal data involved in the systems transactions or kept within the premises of the company?		✔
13)	Are you satisfied from the everyday support from the outsourcer? (debugging, development, etc.)	✔	
14)	Any loss of expert staff because of outsourcing?	✔	

We can combine the given answers with the following data. The number of company's employees is 40, so forty licenses (e-mails) are needed, at least. Each license costs 30 € per month so there is a cost for the company just from the usage of the CRM around 1200€ per month and almost 15000€ per year. But if one puts it against the cost of a fully manned IT department with a number of employees and much equipment, it is better, of course, to outsource those services.

One major issue for this kind of services is whether a contract exists between the company and the outsourcer about when the services are not fulfilling what the outsourcing company wants to receive. In this occasion, such a contract exists and states that the service is available 24 hours per day / 7 days per week. When problems occur, the outsourcer should reply to the notice within 4 hours and fix it, give a solution within 48 hours.

5   Discussion

As we noticed there are connections between the four different approaches because information security encompasses technology, economics, and human behavior; hence, it is not an one-dimensional topic. It can be viewed from many aspects. That is why problems about information security are not unilateral and can be solved only through cooperation of people in all the different fields just mentioned. It would be useful to set some research questions for the readers that could help them continue their own work on the subject.

We have just passed the first decade of activity on this subject and still, especially in developing countries, information security is not a real concern or it is in the hands of IT managers without a real security policy from the administrations. Another question that supplements the first one is whether enterprises are aware of the real dangers that accompany the handling of information, especially in areas when laws about information handling and information security are getting really tough.

Given the continuing increase in IT outsourcing adoption from the enterprises, a final question is whether the related dangers will increase or the enterprises will understand those dangers and take measures to face them.

6   Conclusion

Businesses only recently started to be involved in security economic issues by applying certain policies concerning their data. Firms without a formal information security policy will be less competitive, because security of the business data and also its clients will not be at the highest level available. Without a security policy, there will not be a proper training for the staff and a proper usage of the investments for information security. An ideal investment arises when there is a good usage of it and a good security policy and does not exclusively depend on the volume of it. That is why we mentioned the example of US Banks with smaller budgets having better results in information security than the European ones.

Particularly for the third partners and the enterprises that outsource their activities, some interesting findings can be summarized. There is a tremendous increase in that field that is going to continue furthermore in the near future. It is important to have an IT department but without having a single person as IT staff in this department. The right selection of the third partner is the most important process when the time comes to outsource IT to an enterprise. The right selection of which part of the IT department is going to be outsourced is also a serious issue. And all that for what price, because in terms of economics, everything in business has a price.

References

1. Wang, T.W.: Essays on Information Security from an Economic Perspective. Center for Education and Research Information Assurance and Security Purdue University. Technical report (2009)
2. Ioannidis, C.: Investments and Trade-offs in the Economics of Information Security. School of Management, University of Bath, Hewlett-Packard Laboratories Bristol UK (2009)
3. Anderson, R.: Why Information Security is Hard: An Economic Perspective. University of Cambridge Computer Laboratory (2001)
4. Jorgensen, B.N., Kirschenheiter, M.T.: Discretionary Risk Disclosures. The Accounting Review 78(2), 449–469 (2003)
5. Skinner, D.J.: Why Firms Voluntarily Disclose Bad News. Journal of Accounting Research 32(1), 38–60 (1994)
6. Anderson, R., Böhme, R., Clayton, R., Moore, T.: Security Economics and the Internal Market. Report to the European Network and Information Security Agency, ENISA (2007)
7. Gordon, L.A., Loeb, M.P.: The Economics of Information Security Investment. ACM Transactions on Information and Systems Security 5(4), 438–457 (2002)
8. Hausken, K.: Returns to Information Security Investment: The Effect of Alternative Information Security Breach Functions on Optimal Investment and Sensitivity to Vulnerability. Information Systems Frontiers 8(5), 338–349 (2006)
9. Willemson, J.: On the Gordon & Loeb Model for Information Security Investment. In: The Fifth Workshop on the Economics of Information Security WEIS, Cambridge, UK (2006)
10. Anderson, R.J.: Why Cryptosystems Fail. Communications of the ACM 37(11), 32–40 (1994)
11. Zhou, Z.Z., Johnson, M.E.: The Impact of Information Security Ratings on Vendor Competition. Center for Digital Strategies, Tuck School of Business Dartmouth College (2009)
12. Macura, I., Johnson, E.: Information Risk and the Evolution of the Security Rating Industry. Working paper, Tuck School of Business Dartmouth College (2009)
13. Kark, K.: Can Moody's Solve Your Third Party Assessment Problem?, http://blogs.forrester.com/srm/2008/05/can-moodys-solv.html
14. Kliger, D., Sarig, O.: The Information Value of Bond Ratings. The Journal of Finance 55(6), 2879–2902 (2000)
15. Shapiro, C.: Investment, Moral Hazard, and Occupational Licensing. The Review of Economic Studies 53(5), 843–862 (1986)

Study of the Perception on the Portuguese Citizen Card and Electronic Signature

Isabel Cerqueira, Vítor J. Sá, and Sérgio Tenreiro de Magalhães

FaCiS, Universidade Católica Portuguesa, Campus Camões, 4710-362 Braga, Portugal
isabel.cerqueira@cm-vilaverde.pt,
{vitor.sa,stmagalhaes}@braga.ucp.pt

Abstract. This article presents an analysis of the adoption the Citizen Card in Portugal based on a survey, in which 601 citizens participated. The survey focused on the knowledge of the card and of its features, as well as in the digital signature capabilities. First the survey population was informed about the concept of the Citizen Card, its applicability, and the technological mechanisms associated with their use. We extracted a set of conclusions, which may be useful to countries seeking to implement this type of technology/procedures.

Keywords: Citizen Card, Digital Signature, Digital Citizenship.

1 Introduction

The Portuguese Citizen Card has been recently created and implemented. It allows, not only the citizens authentication, but also the digital signature of documents, with legal value. Therefore, an assessment of the existing knowledge on this issue is critical, as well as an assessment of the users acceptance of this technology, that includes fingerprint authentication of the user in association with the possession of the card.

This paper will start by describing the Citizen Card, the technological and political context of deployment and the associated costs. This paper will also make a small presentation of the implemented digital signature process, clarifying the concept and the used technologies. The results of an inquiry made to 601 Portuguese citizens are then presented and, finally, the results are discussed.

2 The Citizen Card

2.1 Context Information

The Citizen Card is a unique identification card, in the sense that it substitutes most of the previous existing identification cards: Health System Card, Identity Card, Fiscal Identification Card, Social Security Card and Electoral Identification Card. The card can be used both for physical and electronic recognition. Physically, the card is a classic Smart Card, presenting:

H. Jahankhani et al. (Eds.): ICGS3/e-Democracy 2011, LNICST 99, pp. 164–170, 2012.

— In the front:
  o The user's picture (in black and white);
  o Name
  o Surname
  o Gender
  o Height
  o Nationality
  o Date of Birth
  o Civil Identification Number
  o Expiration date
  o Chip (responsible for the electronics functionalities and for storing the digital certificates and other protected information)
  o Optical reading field
— In the back:
  o Father and mother names
  o Fiscal Identification Number
  o Social Identification Number
  o Health System Identification Number.

The Citizen Card expires after five years and can be exchanged in the 6 months period prior to expiring or when the information that it contains changes.

The Citizen Card is the result of the technological project of modernization of the public administration, created by the XVII Constitutional Govern. The Citizen Card is a pillar of the modernization strategy, aiming to simplify, aggregate, and de-materialize the processes in a secure environment. The system is supposed to provide [1]:

— Better accessibility to the public services and, therefore, better services provided;
— Administrative processes and procedures simplification.
— Guaranties in the citizens' recognition process.
— Services Integration.

2.2 Technologies

The Citizen Card, being an electronic card it is, obviously, a result of the new Information and Communication Technologies and requires hardware and software in order to be fully used. For the citizen to be digitally identified by a public service it is required that the service is equipped with a digital card reader. At the present time there are four types of reader:

— Simple reader: it consists on an external reader, without *Pinpad* (a pad for the insertion of a Personal Identification Number), connecting to a computer through a Universal Serial Bus (USB).
— Reader for telephonic authentication: it is a reader with *Pinpad* that generates a one-time use password, from the data existing in the card.

- Combined reader: aggregating both the simple reader capabilities (reading information for later use) with the capability of the telephonic reader (generation of the password).
- Accessibility reader: reader with special features, designed for the visually impaired.

For the readers to work, the hosting system must have installed an application specifically developed for the integration of the Citizen Card. This application is available for download at http://www.cartaodecidadao.pt. This application will allow the user to visualize the information stored in the card, accordingly to the authorizations previously provided by the citizen, and interconnect with other applications developed in this scope, also allowing registering digital certificates for authentication and signature of documents and electronic actions.

2.2.1   Digital Signature

The digital signature of a document is similar do the handwritten signature, in the sense that it associates an author to the document in such a way that it can be verified by a third party. The Digital Signature consists of a binary sequence that is always unique for each signed document [2]. The digital signature aims to assure to origin and authenticity of the document, while assuring the integrity (it is very unlikely for two sets to originate the same sequence) and the authenticity of the document (once the public key of the issuer is associated to its owner's identity through the digital certificate that is signed by a known certifying entity). It is also prevented the repudiation of the document by the signer, once there is an unique association between the public and the private key and this is known only by its owner.

The public key is the verifier of the corresponding pair, the private key, used to sign the document. Despite being a pair, one cannot be obtained through the other, as long as they have been well constructed. The role played by the certifying entities is crucial for the security of the entire process, once it is necessary to be sure that the public key is in fact from who it is claimed.

2.2.2   Digital Certificates

The digital certificates are public documents, cryptographically secured, controlled by the certifying entities. It is the certifying entity responsibility to establish and assure the identity of those possessing certificates belonging to the infrastructure, protect the access to the information, define certificate creation policies and update revocation lists [3]. These documents can have, typically they do, a limited lifetime which can be controlled by a non-changeable expiry date or by a revocation certificate. A revocation certificate is a document, issued by a certification entity, stating that a given public key belongs to some entity and that it is not valid after a certain date.

For a digital certificate to be considered as qualified it has to be issued by a credentialed certifying entity. If so, digitally signed documents have, under the Portuguese law, the same value of a manually signed document.

Popular certificates are those that are issued by the users, like:

- X-509
- SPKI (Simple Public Key Infrastructure)
- PGP (Pretty Good Privacy)

3   The New Portuguese Citizen Card

To better understand the context in which the Citizen Card is implemented in Portugal, it is necessary to analyze other countries existing similar projects. Germany, Spain, Estonia, Austria, Italy, Belgium and Portugal share the same adopted principles in the implementation of the national identification card, sharing a common methodology and scope [4].

The modernization of the public services processes and methods was a challenge considered to be crucial for the sustainability of State, as it is now, both in Portugal and in Spain. The transformations there were seen as necessary, made it mandatory for those countries to deploy means of digital authentication with legal value. Therefore, the adoption of an electronic identification card, usable across the several State services, comes as natural.

3.1   Advantages of the Citizen Card

All Portuguese citizens will be required to have an electronic Citizen Card. But the transition can be done because the old identification card (a paper card with some of the citizen's information and photograph) has expired, because some of the information that it contains has changed (like the address or the marital status), or because the citizen recognizes the advantages of the new card and decides to claim one and use it.

The advantages of this new card, according to the Portuguese State are:

- Reduction from five cards to one.
- Possibility to authenticate and digitally sign in the dematerialized processes of the public services, using the Internet (increase in productivity and efficiency for both the services and the users).
- Increase in security.
- Increase in the harmonization between different countries public services.
- Better public services.

4   Perception Survey

4.1   Methodology

In order to study the perception on the Citizen Card of the Portuguese citizens a survey was prepared and 601 citizens from the Portuguese mainland answered to it. The citizens were contacted through telephone and the survey was also available on the Internet. This mix of telephone and Internet answers tries to overcome the problems inherent to the traditional methods, as the type of persons that has a non-VoIP telephone at home gets more and more specific in Portugal. On the other hand, Portugal has a wide cover of Internet and most of the citizens use it.

The questions in the survey were:

1. Do you know the Citizen Card? (binary answer)
2. Do you have a Citizen Card? (binary answer)
3. What is the difference between the Portuguese Identity Card and the Portuguese Citizen Card? (textual answer)
4. Do you know what the Digital Signature is? (binary answer)
5. Do you know how to digitally sign a document? (binary answer)
6. Have you ever used the Digital Signature? (binary answer)
7. Do you find the Digital Signature safer than the manuscript signature? (binary answer)

The survey also collected some data on the citizen, like occupation, age, gender and the region where the citizen lives (divided in North, Lisbon, Center, Alentejo and Algarve). The answers were then balanced accordingly to the real distribution of the Portuguese population in order to compensate social factors that could affect the perception on the Citizen Card (for instance, Alentejo is a region where the communist party prevails, so the political view of the government actions, including the Citizen Card, can be very different from the views in other regions). The answers were also balanced in order to have the relative weight of the answers of women and man could be the same as the relative weight of women and man in the Portuguese Population.

The survey was done between the 14th December 2010 and the 7th January 2011. 601 citizens answered the survey. 61.7% were female and 38.3% were male.

4.2   Results

4.2.1   Question 1: "Do You Know the Citizen Card?"

Almost 95% of the inquired citizens have some kind of knowledge on the Citizen Card (Figure 1), what is a reflex of the Government´s capability to disseminate this information and, therefore, disseminate the importance of adopting the Citizen Card.

The obtained results have an error margin of 1.7% at a 95% confidence level.

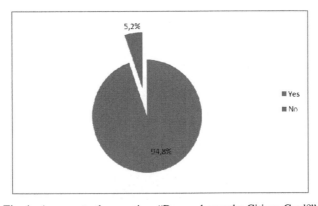

5,2%

■ Yes
■ No

94,8%

Fig. 1. Answers to the question: "Do you know the Citizen Card?"

4.2.2   Question 2: "Do You Have a Citizen Car?"

Almost 60% of the answers are from citizens that already have adopted the Portuguese Citizen Card (Figure 2). Some of them have adopted it because of the advantages associated with it, but many probably did so because the old identification card has expired, because their marital status has changed, or for any other reason that made the adoption mandatory. Looking back on the study, it would have been interesting to question the motivations for the adoption. The obtained results have an error margin of 3.9% at a 95% confidence level.

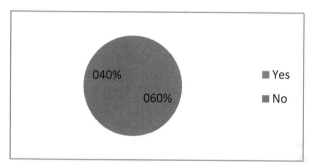

Fig. 2. Answers to the question: "Do you have a Citizen Card?"

4.2.3   Question 3: "What Is the Difference between the Portuguese Identity Card and the Portuguese Citizen Card?"

This was an open question that aimed to bring some light on another underlying question: if the citizens know what the citizen card is. The large majority of the inquired citizens knew that the new card substitutes several of the old cards, but only a few mention the electronic capabilities of the Citizen Card.

4.2.4   Questions 4 to 7, Relative to the Digital Signature

The results on the remaining questions allow some qualitative conclusions, but limited quantitative, once the telephone operators have detected a semantic problem on these questions. When the citizen requests a Citizen Card he has to sign in a digital pad and for many citizens this is the digital signature. Therefore, the authors were asking about one thing and many of the citizens were answering about another. This problem does not affect those saying that they do not know what the digital signature and therefore we can conclude, from the obtained answers and with a 95% confidence level, that:

— At least 36.51% of the citizens do not know what the digital signature is.
— At least 53.15% of the citizens have never used the digital signature.
— At least 69.31% of the citizens do not know how to digitally sign a document.
— At least 39.79% of the citizens do not find the digital process of signing (whatever that means) safer than the traditional process and, therefore, will probably consider the Citizen Card as no more than the aggregation of the several old ones.

5   Conclusions

This study has proven that the concept of an electronic enabled unified identification card has reached a considerable part of the Portuguese Population. Despite this, the number of citizens that know that the card substitutes several old identification cards is considerably larger than those that know that it has electronic capabilities. This might be a consequence of the fact that the adoption of the card is mandatory, when the old identification card expires or when a citizen changes address or changes is marital status, combined with a use limited to non-electronic environments in those people not familiar with Information and Communication Technologies.

The Portuguese Government will need to better promote the electronic capabilities and their advantages if it plans to use the Portuguese Citizen Card to transform the Portuguese Public Services.

References

1. UMIC: Prova de Conceito do Cartão de Cidadão. Agência para a Sociedade do Conhecimento. Ministério da Educação e Ciência, Portugal (2006)
2. Guedes, N.F.: Implementação de Solução de Assinaturas Digitais. Master Thesis, Instituto Superior Técnico, Lisboa (2008)
3. Magalhães, P.S.: Estudo de viabilidade da utilização de tecnologias biométricas comportamentais na autenticação do cidadão. DoctoralThesis, Universidade do Minho, Guimarães (2008)
4. ENISA: Privacy Features of European eID Card Specifications. Position Paper, European Network and information Security Agency (2009)

Securing Transportation-Critical Infrastructures: Trends and Perspectives

Marianthi Theoharidou, Miltiadis Kandias, and Dimitris Gritzalis

Information Security and Critical Infrastructure Protection Research Laboratory
Dept. of Informatics, Athens University of Economics and Business
76 Patission Ave., Athens, GR-10434, Greece
{mtheohar,kandiasm,dgrit}@aueb.gr

Abstract. Critical infrastructure Protection (CIP) includes ensuring the resilience of transportation infrastructures. This sector is considered vital worldwide due to its economic importance and due to the various interdependencies with other infrastructures and sectors. This paper aims at examining the current state in national policies and in research regarding the protection of transport infrastructures. It examines methods to model interdependencies and to assess risk suitable for transport CIP. It recommends future steps for research in this sector.

Keywords: Critical Infrastructure, Transport, Interdependencies, Risk.

1 Introduction

Transportation is a key economic sector; it facilitates the movement of people, food, water, medicines, fuel, and other commodities. It faces multiple threats, ranging from accidents, failures or human errors to malevolent actions, namely sabotage, insider threats or terrorist attacks. Examples of the latter are the events in New York and Washington (2001), Madrid (2004), and London (2005). The common element of these incidents is the use of components of the transport infrastructure [1]. In several cases, transportation components were used as the main means for the attack; in other cases, they were used as the target, which included cyber attacks, too. Potential threats include the disruption of a meganode in the transportation network, the use of a transport component as an attack method and the release of a biological agent at a major passenger facility (rail station, ferry terminal, hub airport) [2]. The increasing need of protecting transport infrastructures is recognized by most countries; all of them name the transportation sector among their critical sectors [1]. Assessing risk in critical infrastructures requires a different approach than in traditional information systems, mainly due to high complexity, multiple interdependencies, and the need for managing an heterogeneous infrastructure network [3].

Critical Infrastructures (CI) refer to an 'asset, system or part, which is essential for the maintenance of vital societal functions, health, safety, security, economic or social well-being of people, and the disruption or destruction of which would have a significant impact as a result of the failure to maintain

H. Jahankhani et al. (Eds.): ICGS3/e-Democracy 2011, LNICST 99, pp. 171–178, 2012.

those functions' [4]. Transport CIs fall into six main categories [2]: *Aviation, Maritime, Mass Transit, Highway, Freight Rail,* and *Pipeline.* Each type has its own characteristics, operates independently within both regulated and non-regulated environments, and yet is highly interdependent to other CIs.

In this paper, we examine the current state, regarding transport Critical Infrastructure Protection (CIP). In Section 2, we first review national initiatives and policies, regarding the assessment of transport risk. In Section 3, we identify interdependency types, and we review the literature regarding modeling and assessing interdependencies between transport infrastructures. Finally, we present conclusions and indicate future research steps.

2   National Initiatives and Policies

In order to examine the state of CIP in the Transportation sector, we first have to look into national and international strategic plans and guidelines. The US Transportation Security Administration is responsible for the sector-specific protection plan regarding transportation security [2]. It describes a generic systems-based risk management approach. The main goal of the method is to counter terrorism, enhance resilience, and facilitate the cost-effective security for transportation. It offers explicit guidelines on identification of assets, systems, networks and functions, risk assessment, development, and implementation of security programs, coupled with suggestions on security evaluation. The proposed method, under the prism of physical, human and cyber factors, defines six phases: (a) setting security goals, (b) identification of assets, systems, networks and functions, (c) risk assessment, (d) prioritization, (e) implementation of protective programs, and (f) measurement of effectiveness.

The US Government Accountability Office (GAO) conducted an assessment of transportation security [5],[6]. In general, GAO attempts to spot weak points in method and implementation and propose appropriate improvements. Their findings are quite interesting when compared to the actual plan of the DHS, especially to those who are interested in developing, implementing or evaluating a risk assessment method that deals with transportation. Regarding the security of the rail system, GAO has published an assessment of the actions taken by TSA to enhance mass transit and rail security [5].

Sandia National Laboratories also conduct research on transportation of hazardous material. The field of interest is safety of nuclear weapons stockpiling, energy and infrastructure assurance, nonproliferation of weapons of mass destruction, and enhancing the safety of CIs. They have developed RADTRAN [7],[8], an ad hoc international standard for transportation risk assessment for radioactive materials. RADTRAN combines parameters, such as user-determined demographic, routing, transportation, packaging, and other intelligence such as materials, meteorological, and health physics data, in order to calculate expected radiological consequences of incident-free radioactive materials transportation and associated accident risks. An implementation of the method is provided

(RADCAT[1]); it focuses on highway and rail transportation of radioactive material and on accident dose risk due to radiation exposure.

The Transportation Risk Assessment Working Group's handbook [9] aims to increase the efficiency and effectiveness of transportation risk assessments prepared pursuant to the National Environmental Policy Act (NEPA). Chronologically, it is the first attempt to propose a method to assess the risk of radioactive material transportation. The quantitative base of the method is RADTRAN [7],[8] and RISKIND [10], which contribute in computing cargo and vehicle related risk. The method specializes on accident risk and consequence risk.

In Europe, the Polish 'Management of Health and Environmental Hazards' (MANHAZ) Center focuses on the protection of human health, welfare and environment. It has published a quantitative transportation risk assessment method, which deals mainly with road and rail transportation of hazardous substances [11]. The proposed approach includes the assessment of transportation risk and environmental and land use safety factors, capability of the existing network and cumulative traffic implications, economic distribution considerations and operators' requirements for practical economics.

UK's Department of Transport has published guidance on how to implement a transportation assessment [12]. It includes general guidelines and useful tables to support the process of assessment, mainly in the urban environment. Although a specific method is not proposed therein, advice, suggestions, and guidelines over transportation assessment are provided. Similar guides on transportation assessment are also followed in Scotland [13] and in Northern Ireland [14].

Except for general directives on CIP [4], the European Commission is active in the area of transportation security and safety research. The Research and Innovation in Transportation Committee[2] funds research programs for aeronautics, rail, water, road, and multimodal transportation, though no official method or standard was found published. The STARTRANS[3] project aims to develop a comprehensive Transportation Security Risk Assessment Framework in interconnected, interdependent and heterogeneous transport networks. Also the Safety@Sea[4] project specializes in maritime transportation security. It deals mainly with risk assessment and management, coastal management and routing and safe seaways assurance in the North Sea, as well as with creating a maritime rescue coordination center in order to increase safety awareness.

Based on the above, it appears that only the US policy suggests a specific method on transportation CIs. The resulting method is system-based and calculates the risk as the function of threat, vulnerability, and impact. A lot of research focuses on material transportation [9],[11] and, in particular, radioactive [7],[8]. Most governments have adopted appropriate plans to strengthen both security and safety of transportation, with a strong emphasis on accidents, in particular when these affect people and the environment. It also appears that

---

[1] http://radtran.sandia.gov/
[2] http://ec.europa.eu/research/transport/
[3] http://www.startrans-project.eu/
[4] http://www.safetyatsea.se/

the regulations remain domain-based, even within the transport sector, and do not reflect the dependencies between transport CIs or to other sectors.

3   Interdependencies and Cascading Failures

One of the main characteristics of CIs in general is the multiplicity of interdependencies between them and their respective sectors. This is vital when one refers to transport CIs, as they are prerequisite for various other CIs [2]. For example, the Energy Sector relies on coal, crude oil, petroleum products, and natural gas to be transported by ship, barge, pipeline, rail, or truck. The Banking and Finance and the Government Sectors also rely on mass transit systems in large urban areas for employees to access the workplace. The ICT Sector co-locates much of its networking equipment (routers, fiber optic cable, etc.) along existing transportation routes (rail lines, highway tunnels, and bridges), the destruction of which may impact service availability in wide geographic areas. On the other hand, the Transport sector relies on the Energy Sector for fuel [15], or on the ICT Sector for the transmission of information necessary for the efficient operation of the transportation network. Beyond these obvious examples, cascading effects may also occur, due to changes in individual behavior during a crisis, like the work of [16], which studies the effect of a failure in Transportation sector and how it affects various wireless networks (ICT Sector).

3.1   Types of Dependencies and Disruptions

Dependencies [15],[17] can be: (1) *Physical* (a CI depends upon the output(s) of the other CI), (2) *Cyber/Informational* (a CI depends on information transmitted through the other CI), (3) *Geographic* (a CI depends on an environmental event on another CI), (4) *Logical* (a CI depends upon another CI via a non-physical, cyber, or geographic connection) and (5) *Social* (a CI is affected by the spreading of disorder to another CI related to human activities).

Interdependencies may fall into these non-mutually exclusive types, but one should not assume the complete availability or unavailability of a CI, as these may be available on different levels of quality [18]. Examples of quality degradation may include *quantity* (of power), *speed* (of transport or communication services), *reliability* (of information), *pressure* (of gas), *purity* (of water), etc. Also, multiple factors should be taken into consideration, such as state operations, social influence, political consequences and technological implications.

Rinaldi et al. classify interdependence-related disruptions or outages as *cascading, escalating,* or *common cause* [15]. A cascading failure occurs when a disruption in one CI causes the failure of a component and a subsequent disruption on a second CI. An escalating failure occurs when an existing disruption in one CI exacerbates an independent disruption of a second CI, generally in the form of increasing the severity or the time for recovery or restoration of the second failure. A common cause failure occurs when two or more CIs are disrupted at the same time: components within each CI fail because of a common cause.

3.2   Review of Dependency Risk Assessment

Generic risk assessment methods for CIs have been initially reviewed in [3]. The main observation is that such approaches assess risk in terms of threat, vulnerability and impact, with a high emphasis on the societal impact of a CI failure or disruption. However, they fail to model and assess the risk caused by interdependencies, which have been proven crucial in transport CIP in the past [1]. Any modeling and simulation attempt faces several challenges, namely data accessibility, model development, and model validation. In the case of CI interdependency, such a task is further complicated by the detailed and disparate cross sector analysis which is required [19]. The lack of reliable real-time data makes the identification of interdependency related failures even worse [20].

Related work in identifying and modeling dependencies includes the use of sector-specific methods, e.g. gas lines, electric grid or ICT, or more general methods that are applicable in various types of CIs. Interdependency models fall into six broad categories: (a) Aggregate Supply and Demand Tools, (b) Dynamic Simulations, (c) Agent-Based Models, (d) Physics-Based Models, (e) Population Mobility Models and (f) Leontief Input-Output Models [21].

Dependencies also vary according to the level of analysis selected. Different aproaches have been used to examine dependencies under a microscopic or macroscopic view. One approach [22] focuses on CI components (microscopic view), and demonstrates several types of multi-dependency structures for both linear and particularly cyclical dependencies among multiple infrastructure types. It also considers unbuffered and buffered types of resources. Another approach [23] focuses on the component level as well and models/simulates two types of vulnerability: (a) structural and (b) functional. It calculates the interdependent effect and the effect of interdependence strength. It includes examples on power grid and gas pipeline models. Other models examine dependencies between different CIs [18], within the same or different sectors of a country [24]. A method to map interdependencies with a workflow enabling the characterization of coupled networks and the emerging effects related to their level of interdependency is presented by [25]. This work aims at mapping the interdependency between electrical and related communication nodes.

Several methods that are proposed for evaluating risk in interdependent CIs, apply Leontief's Inoperability Input-Output model (IIM), which calculates economic loss due to unavailability on different CI sectors based on their interdependencies [24],[26],[27],[28]. The same model is also applied by [29], so as to include elements of business continuity and the cost to recover from an event.

Theoharidou et al. assess risk in three layers: (a) infrastructure level, (b) sector level, and (c) national/intra-sector level [3],[30],[31]. They identify first-order dependencies and provide a method for evaluating societal risk between CIs and sectors. These interdependencies can form risk graphs in order to identify multiple order interdependencies and assess risk on chained events. A similar approach is adopted on [32]. It follows six steps: (1) Identify the initiating event, (2) Identify interdependencies and Perform qualitative analysis, (3) Perform semi-quantitative assessment of the scenario, (4) Perform detailed quantitative analysis of interdependencies (optional), (5) Evaluate risk and measures to reduce interdependencies, and (6) Perform Cost/benefit analysis(optional).

Approaches for assessing dependencies and risk in transport CIs can be also found; they follow similar approaches as the above. For example, [33] uses a Petri Net analysis procedure to estimate indirect losses in networks of critical transport infrastructures. The rest of the literature focuses on the risk assessment of hazardous materials (i.e. [7],[8],[9],[11],[34]).

4   Conclusions

In this paper we reviewed the current state-of-the-art in transportation CIP. One of the main characteristics of this sector is the multiple types of infrastructures within itself. These types vary both technologically and in terms of regulation, standards, and best practices. They also face different kinds of threats and vulnerabilities. Applying a universal method for these infrastructures should take into account multiple characteristics and should be combined with existing specific methods, which mainly focus on accidents and environmental security. Cross-sectoral regulation and standardization is particularly difficult, as it can only be initiated by international or national organizations and bodies.

Current approaches usually focus on a specific subsector and fail to assess the risk introduced by interdependencies. There are several recent approaches focusing on assessing risk of interdependencies, but they only focus on specific and isolated parts of the problem. Identifying and mapping societal interdependencies or identifying potential cascading effects is a really challenging aspect in terms of discovery, mapping, and validation of dependencies [19]. This requires cross-sector and cross-border collaboration.

The static nature of risk assessment models is another issue; models serve as a snapshot of a transport CI. Transport CIs are dynamic systems, a parameter which is reflected on risk as well. Most approaches also fail to connect the risk assessement process to spatial information [34]. Novel approaches for dynamic, real-time risk assessment could contribute significantly towards such a direction.

Since transport CIs are vast networks, they also share a significant -in number and variable- user-base. In highly critical systems, this factor introduces threats, thus assessing risk on a per-user basis could contribute significantly in mitigating the really important insider threat. Such a variable and vast user-base can be also used during the risk assessment process. Using collaborative technologies, in order to ensure more accurate and detailed data collection, could also be a promising future research step.

Acknowledgments. This work was supported in part by the S-Port (09SYN-72-650) project, which is funded by the Hellenic General Secretariat for Research & Technology, under the *Synergasia* Programme.

References

1. Brunner, E., Suter, M.: International CIIP Handbook 2008/2009: An Inventory of 25 National and 7 International Critical Infrastructure Protection Policies. Center for Security Studies, ETH Zurich, Switzerland (2008)
2. Transportation Security Administration: Critical Infrastructure and Key Resources Sector-Specific Plan as input to the National Infrastructure Protection Plan. Dept. of Homeland Security, USA (2007)
3. Theoharidou, M., Kotzanikolaou, P., Gritzalis, D.: Risk-based criticality analysis. In: Palmer, C., Shenoi, S. (eds.) 3rd IFIP Int. Conf. on Critical Infrastructure Protection (CIP 2009), pp. 35–49. Springer, USA (2009)
4. European Council: Directive 2008/114/EC on the identification and designation of European critical infrastructures and the assessment of the need to improve their protection. Official Journal L345, pp. 75–82 (2008)
5. Government Accountability Office: Key Actions Have Been Taken to Enhance Mass Transit and Passenger Rail Security, but Opportunities Exist to Strengthen Federal Strategy and Programs. Committee on Homeland Security, USA (2009)
6. Government Accountability Office: Comprehensive Risk Assessments and Stronger Internal Controls Needed to Help Inform TSA Resource Allocation. Committee on Homeland Security, USA (2009)
7. Neuhauser, K., Kanipe, F.: RADTRAN 5, User Guide. SAND2000-1257, Sandia National Laboratories, USA (2000)
8. Neuhauser, K., Kanipe, F.: RADTRAN 5, Technical Manual. SAND2000-1256, Sandia National Laboratories, USA (2000)
9. U.S. Department of Energy, Resource Handbook on DOE Transportation Risk Assessment. Report DOE/EM/NTP/HB-01, National Transportation Program, Office of Environmental Management, USA (2002)
10. Yuan, Y., Chen, S., LePoire, D., Rothman, R.: RISKIND-A Computer Program for Calculating Radiological Consequences and Health Risks from Transportation of Spent Nuclear Fuel. Energy Science and Technology Software Center, USA (1993)
11. Borysiewicz, M.: Transportation Risk Assessment. Report IAE B-54/2006, Institute of Atomic Energy, Poland (2006)
12. Department of Transport: Guidance on Transport Assessment, UK (2007)
13. Scottish Executive: Transport Assessment and Implementation: A Guide, UK (2005)
14. Department for Regional Development: Transport Assessment: Guidelines for Development Proposals in Northern Ireland, UK (2006)
15. Rinaldi, S., Peerenboom, J., Kelly, T.: Identifying, Understanding and Analyzing Critical Infrastructure Interdependencies. IEEE Control Systems Magazine 21(6), 11–25 (2001)
16. Barrett, C., Beckman, R., Channakeshava, K., Huang, F., Kumar, V., Marathe, A., Marathe, M., Pei, G.: Cascading failures in multiple infrastructures: From transportation to communication network. In: 5th Int. Conf. on Critical Infrastructure (CRIS), pp. 1–8 (2010)
17. De Porcellinis, S., Oliva, G., Panzieri, S., Setola, R.: A Holistic-Reductionistic Approach for Modeling Interdependencies. In: Palmer, C., Shenoi, S. (eds.) 3rd IFIP Int. Conf. on Critical Infrastructure Protection (CIP 2009), pp. 215–227. Springer, USA (2009)
18. Nieuwenhuijs, A., Luiijf, E., Klaver, M.: Modeling dependencies in critical infrastructures. In: Goetz, E., Shenoi, S. (eds.) Critical Infrastructure Protection. IFIP, vol. 253, pp. 205–214 (2008)

19. Pedersona, P., Dudenhoeffer, D., Hartley, S., Permann, M.: Critical Infrastructure Interdependency Modeling: A Survey of U.S. and International Research. INL/EXT-06-11464, Idaho National Laboratory, USA (2006)
20. Andersson, G., Donalek, P., Farmer, R., Hatziargyriou, N., Kamwa, I., Kundur, P., Martins, N., Paserba, J., Pourbeik, P., Sanchez-Gasca, J., Schulz, R., Stankovic, A., Taylor, C., Vittal, V.: Causes of the 2003 major grid blackouts in North America and Europe and recommended means to improve system dynamic performance. IEEE Trans. on Power Systems 20(4), 1922–1928 (2005)
21. Rinaldi, S.: Modeling and simulating critical infrastructures and their interdependencies. In: 37th Hawaii Int. Conf. on System Sciences, vol. 2. IEEE, USA (2004)
22. Svedsen, N., Wolthunsen, S.: Connectivity models of interdependency in mixed-type critical infrastructure networks. Information Security Technical Report 1, 44–55 (2007)
23. Min, O., Liu, H., Zi-Jun, M., Ming-Hui, Y., Fei, Q.: A methodological approach to analyze vulnerability of interdependent infrastructures. Simulation Modeling Practice and Theory 17, 817–828 (2009)
24. Aung, Z., Watanabe, K.: A framework for modeling Interdependencies in Japan's Critical Infrastructures. In: Palmer, C., Shenoi, S. (eds.) 3rd IFIP Int. Conf. on Critical Infrastructure Protection (CIP 2009), pp. 243–257. Springer, USA (2009)
25. Rosato, V., Issacharoff, L., Tiriticco, F., Meloni, S., De Porcellinis, S., Setola, S.: Modeling interdependent infrastructures using interacting dynamical models. Int. J. Critical Infrastructures 4(1/2), 63–79 (2008)
26. Santos, J., Haimes, Y.: Modeling the demand reduction input-output inoperability due to terrorism of interconnected infrastructures. Risk Analysis 24(6), 1437–1451 (2004)
27. Haimes, Y., Santos, J., Crowther, K., Henry, M., Lian, C., Yan, Z.: Risk Analysis in Interdependent Infrastructures. Critical Infrastructure Protection 253, 297–310 (2007)
28. Setola, R., De Porcellinis, S., Sforna, M.: Critical infrastructure dependency assessment using the input-output inoperability model. Int. J. Critical Infrastructure Protection 2(4), 170–178 (2009)
29. Crowther, K.: Decentralized risk management for strategic preparedness of critical infrastructure through decomposition of the inoperability input-output model. Int. J. Critical Infrastructure Protection 1, 53–67 (2008)
30. Theoharidou, M., Kotzanikolaou, P., Gritzalis, D.: A multi-layer criticality assessment methodology based on interdependencies. Computers & Security 29(6), 643–658 (2010)
31. Theoharidou, M., Kotzanikolaou, P., Gritzalis, D.: Risk Assessment Methodology for Interdependent Critical Infrastructures. International Journal of Risk Assessment and Management (Special Issue on Risk Analysis of Critical Infrastructures) 15(2/3), 159–177 (2011)
32. Utne, I.B., Hokstad, P., Vatn, J.: A method for risk modeling of interdependencies in critical infrastructures. Reliability Engineering & System Safety 96(6), 671–678 (2011); ESREL 2009 Special Issue
33. Di Febbraro, A., Sacco, N.: A Petri Nets approach for the interdependence analysis of Critical Infrastructures in transportation networks. In: 12th World Conference on Transport Research, Portugal (2010)
34. Gheorghe, A., Birchmeier, J., Vamanub, D., Papazoglou, I., Kroge, W.: Comprehensive risk assessment for rail transportation of dangerous goods: a validated platform for decision support. Reliability Engineering & System Safety 88, 247–272 (2005)

E-Government in Greece: Serving State's Economic Needs – Respecting the Fundamental Right to Data Protection

Zoe Kardasiadou, Evi Chatziliasi, and Konstantinos Limniotis

Hellenic Data Protection Authority,
Kifisias 1-3, 11523, Athens, Greece
{kardasiadou,exatziliasi,klimniotis}@dpa.gr

Abstract. Due to the recent economic crisis Greece is facing, the government has developed several initiatives using information and communication technologies (ICT) in order to foster the economic growth, enhance trust and transparency in the operation of public administration, streamline the public expenditure and combat corruption and tax evasion. Such initiatives include: a) the "transparency project", b) the electronic prescription, c) the publication of tax data on the internet, d) the use of a tax card and finally e) the eGovernment Law. As data protection is a fundamental right according to Greek and EU law, this paper aims at analyzing whether such initiatives pass the proportionality test and may justify "legitimate" restrictions of the aforementioned right and which particular data security and other measures may alleviate the restrictions occurred.

Keywords: e-Government, personal data protection.

1 Introduction

E-government services are being characterized as a "guiding vision towards modern administration and democracy" [1]. Notably, the appropriate use of ICT technologies for interactions with the public sector results in several benefits, including transparency, openness, convenience, revenue growth and cost reductions. On this direction, the European Commission launched in 2010 the Europe 2020 Strategy[1] which sets objectives for the growth of the European Union by 2020, including better exploitation of ICT in order to foster innovation, economic growth and progress.

In light of the recent financial crisis which exceeds the Greek borders, it becomes evident that the aforementioned goal is of major importance. Moreover, in this highly evolving environment, reconciling public interests and fundamental rights, such as the right to data protection, is crucial. As it is explicitly pointed out in the Digital Agenda (one of the seven pillars of the Europe 2020 Strategy), the right to privacy and the

---

[1] The Europe 2020 strategy was proposed by the Commission on 3 March 2010 [COM/2010/2020] and adopted by the European Council on 26 March 2010.

H. Jahankhani et al. (Eds.): ICGS3/e-Democracy 2011, LNICST 99, pp. 179–185, 2012.

protection of personal data are fundamental rights which should be effectively enforced using the widest range of means: from the wide application of the principle of "Privacy by Design" in the relevant ICT technologies to dissuasive sanctions, wherever necessary.

The Greek government in the era of economic crisis but also as an addressee of the Europe 2020 Strategy is developing several initiatives based on ICT, aiming at fostering economic growth and transparency, increasing accountability, strengthening control mechanisms and a tax compliance culture, and streamlining public expenditure.

This paper studies e-government services in Greece and how these affect the right to data protection. The question whether they pass the proportionality test is addressed, mainly based on the relevant Opinions of the Hellenic Data Protection Authority (HDPA)[2]. More precisely, the paper is organized as follows: Section 2 discusses the legitimate limitations of fundamental rights. Recent ICT initiatives in Greece are studied in Section 3, where relating data protection issues are highlighted. Concluding remarks are given in Section 4.

2   Limitations of Fundamental Rights in the CJEU Case Law

Given that the operation of e-government services may impose limitations on the exercise of the fundamental right to the protection of personal data[3] the relevant case law of the Court of Justice of the European Union should be considered. Accordingly, limitations imposed on fundamental rights should be provided for by law, meet objectives of general interest recognised by the European Union (e.g. transparency and accountability regarding the use of public funds) or the need to protect the rights and freedoms of others and be subject to the principle of proportionality in the sense that they are necessary in order to meet the aforementioned objectives.

A prominent example of how to strike the proper balance between legitimate public interests and the right to the protection of personal data is the recent decision of the Court of Justice regarding the publication on a website of identifying (personal) information relating to the beneficiaries of agricultural funds within the Common Agricultural Policy (CAP) of the EU[4]. In this case the Court first accepted that such a publication is provided for by law and is appropriate to enhance transparency, which constitutes a legitimate interest as being established in the EU Treaties (it enables citizens to participate in the decision making process, guarantees that the administration enjoys greater legitimacy and is more effective and more accountable to the citizen in a democratic system). It continued that the right to data protection is not an absolute right,

---

[2] The Hellenic Data Protection Authority, established by the Data Protection Law 2472/1997, is a constitutionally entrenched independent authority (art. 9A of the Hellenic Constitution).

[3] The right to the protection of personal data is laid down in article 8 of the European Convention on Human Rights and more explicitly in article 8 of the Charter of Fundamental Rights of the European Union. The Charter has binding legal effect, equal to the Treaties, after the entry into force of the Lisbon Treaty.

[4] See Court of Justice of the EU, joined cases C-92/09, C-93/09 Volker und Markus Schecke GbR / Hartmut Eifert vs Land Hessen.

but must be considered in relation to its function in the society. Having said that, the Court found that the lack of any criteria for publishing personal data (e.g. the periods for which the beneficiaries received aid, the frequency, nature and amount of aid received) exceeds the limits imposed by the proportionality principle and renders the processing illegal.

From the aforementioned decision it can be concluded that the proportionality principle shall be respected in a way that at least the core of the fundamental right in question is not affected. To achieve this, differentiating criteria as well as data security measures shall be established. Otherwise the endeavour may be rendered illegal. In the following section this rule will be applied to some eGov initiatives in Greece.

3   E-Government Initiatives in Greece

3.1   The Transparency Project

The transparency project (Law 3861/2010) is aiming at enhancing the accountability of the public administration. To this end, it provides for the publication on the Internet of all legislative and a series of categories of administrative acts, including the appointment of civil servants, the issuance of building permits and public expenses. In addition, easy search capability for documents is supported by using keywords and/or thematic meta-data. The uploaded documents (.pdf format) are digitally signed and automatically provided with a unique number.

The HDPA has been consulted prior to the adoption of the law and issued the Opinion 1/2010[5] on the draft law, imposing restrictions in the publication:

1. Sensitive data should not be uploaded unless the HDPA issues a prior permit. As a response to this, the Law 3861/2010 excluded sensitive data from its scope.
2. Further use of the published data shall be allowed only for the purpose of free access to public information and not for other purposes, such as commercial ones. To this end, the central web site http://et.diavgeia.gov.gr/ of the transparency project states explicitly, in its "Terms of Use", that illegal processing (by third parties) is prohibited; however, it is not further explained which purpose is considered legal.
3. Appropriate technical measures should be adopted, to avoid unlawful processing of personal data (e.g. creation of individuals "profiles"). After the initiation of the project, the HPDA specified several measures towards this direction. These include: i) measures to prohibit the processing by external search engines (since transparency may be adequately served via the dedicated web sites of the authorities), such as appropriate lock of uploaded .pdf files, as well as the use of the Robots Exclusion Protocol, b) measures to prevent massive downloads, such as usage of appropriate challenge/response tools (e.g. Captcha) and c) proper administration of tracking cookies with the use of friendly techniques for opt-out

---

[5] All the Opinions referred in this paper are available (in Greek) at the HDPA's site http://www.dpa.gr

instead of forcing users to change their browser settings. Up to the cookies the aforementioned measures are not yet implemented[6].

4. A time limitation for the publication should be in place; such a limitation is not in conflict with the need for transparency, since each file's meta-data may be available for longer in order to facilitate citizens' requests for access directly to the competent authorities. This condition is not yet implemented.

As a result, the project still lacks of some essential safeguards for an efficient protection of personal data.

3.2   The Electronic Prescription

Law 3892/2010 provides for an integrated electronic prescription system which shall support the effective control of insurance funds' expenditures, amongst others by limiting unnecessary prescriptions. The system is currently focusing on some insurance funds in the process of completing the pilot site.

The HDPA has been prior consulted and issued a permit approving the data processing upon specific conditions, namely:

1. A single entity (i.e. the General Secretariat for Social Security) should be appointed as data controller in terms of the Data Protection Act to ensure legal responsibility.
2. Authentication of the system's users should be put in place.
3. The access to data should be in accordance to the need-to-know principle (where the cases of the data controller, social insurance organisations, pharmacists and doctors are treated separately). Doctors' access to patient information produced by others is subject to patients' prior consent.
4. Any access should be logged.
5. Data should be kept for 20 years from the last treatment.
6. The HDPA shall be consulted prior to the issuance of the ministerial decision concerning the procedure and the technical requirements for the registration and the identification of the system's users.

3.3   Publication of Taxpayers' Data on the Internet

Towards combating tax evasion and enhancing compliance, the Ministry of Economy suggested as an exception to tax secrecy, the publication on the Internet of the annual income and the tax due by the taxpayers. Accordingly, a) access is limited to identified users, b) searches may be performed by specific criteria, that is the unique tax number or address and part of the name or business name, c) a limitation on the number of requests (up to 20 retrievals per month) will be in place, d) storage of data in editable form shall not be enabled.

---

[6] A new web site http://yperdiavgeia.gr/, maintained in the meanwhile by a computer expert, provides for more powerful searches due to the lack of the aforementioned measures.

The HDPA with the Opinion 1/2011 ruled that the aforementioned processing of personal data is not compliant with the proportionality principle, since there is no evidence that such publication is really necessary to combat tax evasion. On the contrary, one shall first consider the improvement of control mechanisms and powers of the competent authorities.

3.4   Tax Card

According to the Greek taxation law receipts for the purchase of goods or services may be deducted up to a certain amount from the taxable income and are also used for the establishment of the minimum of income, exempted from taxation. The Ministry of Economy introduced an optional system for the collection of such data, based on a magnetic card and the existing bank payment infrastructure (POS) at the suppliers' site. The system has a double purpose: it enables the automatic storage of the necessary data in the IT system of the Ministry while at the same time is used for the control of issuance of receipts by the suppliers. The data are transferred in real time through the banks to the tax authority without revealing purchasers'/taxpayers' identity. The supplier's name, the amount paid, and the unique identifier of the card are only transferred. After the data are received by the tax authority, this may link the information to a specific taxpayer on the basis of card's unique identifier. By the end of the calendar year the total amount spent by each taxpayer is calculated for the taxation, whereas the taxpayer may access at any time the information related to him/her via a secure web service.

The HDPA in the Opinion 4/2010 stressed that there was no sufficient legal basis for the processing of personal data in this system. Even if the use of the card should be optional, i.e. upon consent of the taxpayer, this shall be provided for by law. The HDPA also raised the concern that, although banks receive anonymous data, there is a possibility to identify data subjects if a credit card is used for the said payment. Thus there is the risk to create "consumer profiles". In our opinion, there is also the risk of creating suppliers' profiles, especially regarding their revenues. In addition, the HDPA pointed out that there is no need, even for the tax authority, to identify the taxpayers in real time, but at the end of the calendar year. In order to address these risks, the HDPA suggested the use of two different infrastructures to meet the two different purposes (a smart card for the taxpayers for the first purpose/connection of suppliers' cash registers with the system of the tax authority for the second purpose). Nevertheless, the tax card shall be introduced in October 2011 without implementing HDPA's remarks.

3.5   The eGovernment Law

Recently, the eGovernment Law 3979/2011 was adopted. The main objectives of this law are described as following: a) provide for the right of citizens and businesses to communicate with the public sector via ICT, b) user friendly services also for disabled people, c) reinforcement of trust between citizens, businesses and the public sector.

The law addresses several key issues, such as the protection of personal data, the identification/authentication of users, the validity of electronic documents and the shared use of telecommunication systems, computational resources, ICT infrastructure and data amongst public sector bodies (which may understood as the first attempt to introduce cloud computing and grids). In order to fully deploy legal effects however the law provides for the prior adoption of 24 implementing acts!

Regarding personal data protection, the law explicitly establishes the privacy-by-design and the data minimisation principle, the conduct of privacy impact assessments and the appointment of a Data Protection Officer in each public body. Moreover, it states that that the right to access should be exercised upon users' authentication and appropriate security measures. The future use of one's personal data is allowed only on the basis of consent. As a remark, these high-level principles need to be further specified in order to effectively enhance personal data protection.

Development of a Greek e-ID Card. The eGov Law 3979/2011 constitutes a first step towards the e-ID card. In this context, electronic identification and authentication schemes are prerequisites for proving one's identity, whereas electronic signature schemes are also necessary to create legally binding documents; hence, these three levels of protection (which have been also pointed out in the seminal paper [2]), constitute the main building block for any e-ID card.

Despite though the common underlying goals, a strong diversity exists regarding the adopted design approaches for the e-ID cards within the European Union; more precisely, while security of online public services is the primary aim, privacy seems to be a rather implicit goal [3]. Indeed, linkage of personal data for profiling purposes is not adequately treated in the current e-ID solutions - exceptions being Austria and Germany, which have taken some important steps towards unlinkability and selective disclosure [4]. The linkability problem mainly stems from unique identifiers, although decentralized data storage as well as context separation are also important factors to resolve this threat [3].

We subsequently briefly describe the Austrian case [5] which, according to some relevant publications (e.g. [6]), seems to have influenced the greek legislator. All individuals are registered in one of the national registers, whereas a unique 12-digit identifier (PIN) is assigned to each individual. PIN though is not used for identification and is not even stored in the card; instead, a unique source personal identification number (sourcePIN), derived by strong encryption from the citizen's PIN, is stored in the e-ID card (as a separate XML-based data structure, containing the individual's public key which is associated with a certificate). The sourcePIN Register Authority is the Data Protection Commission. Moreover, each public service provider is assigned a specific sector's code and a personal sector-specific identifier (ssPIN) is generated by applying a one-way hash function to the sPIN and the sector code; for each sector, identification is based on ssPIN, stored by the public service provider. Hence, an individual (with a unique sPIN) has a different ssPIN per service, whereas it is not possible, from a given ssPIN to derive either the sPIN or other ssPIN.

In the Greek case, many important questions need still to be answered: for instance, the law does not specify how the level of required security is determined, as well as whether identifiers are stored by the public entities. Moreover, although there is a reference for "per-service" generation of identifiers and credentials, it is not clear whether unlinkability (to ensure that a user may make multiple uses of services without others being able to link these uses together) is a design objective. From the perspective of the fundamental right to personal data protection unique identifiers, although technically convenient, should be avoided since they violate unlinkability and the principles of data minimization and purpose limitation.

4   Conclusions

Current economic crisis put at risk fundamental rights, especially because economic constraints may influence the criteria for striking the right balance, i.e. when applying the proportionality test. The boundaries of the margin of appreciation are set where the balance of public interests, such as transparency, accountability, combating tax evasion etc. on the one side, and the right to personal data protection on the other side, renders the latter invalid. A win-win situation may benefit the most through the serious consideration of privacy by design measures and an early consultation with the Data Protection Authorities.

References

1. Wimmer, M., Traunmuller, R.: Trends in electronic government: Managing distributed knowledge. In: Database and Expert System Applications, pp. 340–345 (2000)
2. Fiat, A., Shamir, A.: How to Prove Yourself: Practical Solutions to Identification and Signature Problems. In: Odlyzko, A.M. (ed.) CRYPTO 1986. LNCS, vol. 263, pp. 186–194. Springer, Heidelberg (1987)
3. Strauß, S.: The Limits of Control – (Governmental) Identity Management from a Privacy Perspective. In: Fischer-Hübner, S., Duquenoy, P., Hansen, M., Leenes, R., Zhang, G. (eds.) Privacy and Identity Management for Life. IFIP AICT, vol. 352, pp. 206–218. Springer, Heidelberg (2011)
4. Naumann, I., Hobgen, G., et al.: Privacy features of European eID card specifications. In: European Network and Information Society Agency, ENISA (2009)
5. Aichholzer, G., Strauß, S.: The Austrian case: multi-card concept and the relationship between citizen ID and social security cards. In: Identity in the Information Society. LNCS, vol. 3, pp. 65–85. Springer, Heidelberg (2010)
6. Drogkaris, P., Geneiatakis, D., Gritzalis, S., Lambrinoudakis, C., Mitrou, L.: Towards an Enhanced Authentication Framework for eGovernment Services: The Greek case. In: EGOV 2008 7th Int. Conf. on Electronic Government, pp. 189–196 (2008)

Cryptanalysis and Enhancement of a Secure Group Ownership Transfer Protocol for RFID Tags

Hoda Jannati and Abolfazl Falahati

Department of Electrical Engineering (DCCS Lab)
Iran University of Science and Technology, Tehran
{hodajannati,afalahati}@iust.ac.ir

Abstract. Ownership transfer and grouping proof protocols are the two most important requirements for RFID tag in various applications such as pharmaceutical distribution and manufacturing. In 2010, Zuo integrated these two requirements and introduced a protocol for RFID tag group ownership transfer (GOT), i.e., transferring the ownership of a group of tags in one session. However, this paper shows that Zuo's protocol is vulnerable to de-synchronization attack and tag impersonating in the presence of cheating old owner. This paper also proposes solutions to fix the security flaws of Zuo's GOT protocol.

Keywords: de-synchronization attack, grouping proof, ownership transfer, RFID tags.

1 Introduction

Too much attention has recently been given to RFID systems because of the ease of its deployment over a wide range of applications. In fact, RFID systems have become very popular and concrete tools in various applications such as identifying, target tracking, sense ambient conditions of tagged objects, guarding patient safety and etc.; indeed there is an enormous growing for such system implementations [1]. Due to these so many advantages, a large number of research scientists have begun to improve RFID systems recently [2–4].

With the rapid development of RFID tags, different kinds of security requirements have been revealed within RFID communication network. In many applications, tag ownership transfer and grouping proofs with tag privacy, mutual authentication as well as data confidentiality are considered as the most critical requirements [5].

Furthermore, in many applications, an RFID tag may change its owner a number of times during its life cycle. Thus all information associated with the tag must be passed from the old owner to the new owner. Hence, in the secure tag ownership transfer protocol, the new owner privacy, the old owner privacy and the authorization recovery must be well satisfied [6–9].

Moreover, in 2004, Juels proposed a different concept which was called yoking proof or grouping proof [10]. According to his concept, a pair or group of RFID

H. Jahankhani et al. (Eds.): ICGS3/e-Democracy 2011, LNICST 99, pp. 186–193, 2012.

tags can generate a proof which certifies the same reading device to scan the tags simultaneously [11, 12]. Recently, the grouping proof protocol has been adopted to improve inpatient safety and can indeed avoid death due to medication related errors [13].

However, it is possible to transfer the ownership of a group of RFID tags one by one but it is inefficient and time consuming, and cannot ensure the simultaneous presence of multiple tags. In order to solve this problem, Zuo integrated ownership transfer and grouping proof protocols and introduced RFID tag group ownership transfer (GOT) protocol, i.e., transferring the ownership of a group of tags in one session [14].

However, this paper shows the Zuo's protocol has some security weaknesses in the presence of cheating old reader. Zuo's protocol is vulnerable to de-synchronization attack. Under such attacks, a valid tag is identified as an illegal tag. Also, under certain circumstances, an attacker can obtain the secret key of the tags and impersonate them. These weaknesses are of importance here for further improvements.

Organization. The remainder of this paper is organized as follows: in Section 2, Zuo's group ownership transfer protocol is reviewed. Weaknesses of Zuo's protocol are discussed in Section 3. In Section 4, our improved protocol is described. Finally, we summarize our research in Section 5.

2   A Review of Zuo's Group Ownership Transfer (GOT) Protocol

Zuo proposed the Group Ownership Transfer (GOT) protocol in [14]. He assumed that there are n tags in the group whose ownership is to be transferred from the current owner to a new owner. For simplicity he illustrated his protocol with two tags, but the protocol can be extended to any number of tags.

There are three phases in Zuo's protocol: RFID tags identification phase, group ownership transfer phase and verification phase. In this section, we describe Zuo's GOT protocol. In order to describe Zuo's protocol, we will use the following notations:

- $S_{current}$: the server of the current owner,
- $R_{current}$: the reader of $S_{current}$,
- S_{new} : the server of the new owner,
- TS : the trusted server in the system,
- T_i : i^{th} tag,
- ID_i : the identification of T_i,
- $f(k, m)$: pseudorandom function taking seed k and message m,
- $E_k(m)$: message m encrypted with key k using standard cryptographic function, i.e., AES,
- k_{s1} : l-bits secret shared between $S_{current}$ and TS,
- k_{s2} : l-bits secret shared between S_{new} and TS,

- k_i : l-bits secret shared between T_i and owner,
- k_{group} : l-bits secret shared among the members of a group,
- s_i : l-bits secret shared between T_i and TS,
- k_{ss} : l-bits secret shared between $S_{current}$ and S_{new},
- N_R : a random nonce generated by $S_{current}$,
- N_T : a random nonce generated by TS,
- $H(\cdot)$: a secure one-way hash function,
- $\|$: the operation of concatenation,
- $\oplus$: the operation of Exclusive-OR (XOR),
- $\{,\}$: a set of elements.

- **RFID Tags Identification Phase:**

  1. S_{new} submits a ownership transfer request and its credentials with an identification G_{id} to $S_{current}$ for ownership transfer over a group of tags.

  2. $S_{current}$ evaluates the ownership transfer request, S_{new}'s credentials and condition of ownership. If the based business transaction is authorized, the ownership transfer request will be honored. Then, $R_{current}$ scans the tags in its field and collects their IDs. Next, $S_{current}$ confirms that all the tags in the group are present and sends an acknowledgement message ACK to S_{new} which includes IDs of the tags in the group.

- **Group Ownership Transfer Phase:**

  1. For $1 \leq i \leq 2$: S_{new} chooses a new secret key k_{i-new} to be shared with tag T_i and a new group key $k_{group-new}$ to be shared among the members of the group. Then, S_{new} randomly chooses k_{i-mask} and $k_{group-mask}$ and compute $M_{1,i}$ according to (1).

  $$M_{1,i} = \{ID_i\|(k_{i-new} \oplus k_{i-mask})\|(k_{group-new} \oplus k_{group-mask}) \atop \|E_{k_{s2}}(k_{i-mask})\|E_{k_{s2}}(k_{group-mask})\} \quad (1)$$

  After that, S_{new} sends $E_{k_{ss}}(M_{1,1})$, $E_{k_{ss}}(M_{1,2})$ and G_{id} to $S_{current}$.

  2. For $1 \leq i \leq 2$: $S_{current}$ checks ID_i in message $M_{1,i}$. If so, $S_{current}$ constructs $M_{2,i}$ according to (2).

  $$M_{2,i} = \{ID_{snew}\|ID_{scurrent}\|ID_i\|E_{k_{s2}}(k_{i-mask})\|E_{k_{s2}}(k_{group-mask})\} \quad (2)$$

  Then, $S_{current}$ sends $E_{k_{s1}}(M_{2,1})$ and $E_{k_{s1}}(M_{2,2})$ to TS.

  3. TS randomly chooses N_T. Then, For $1 \leq i \leq 2$: TS checks ID_{snew}, $ID_{scurrent}$ and ID_i in message $M_{2,i}$. If so, TS applies k_{s2} to retrieve k_{i-mask} and $k_{group-mask}$ by performing the decryption function on

$E_{k_{s2}}(k_{i-mask})$ and $E_{k_{s2}}(k_{group-mask})$ respectively. Then, TS constructs $M_{3,i}$ according to (3).

$$M_{3,i} = \{ID_i\|(f(s_i, N_T) \oplus k_{i-mask})\|(f(s_i, N_T) \oplus k_{group-mask})\} \quad (3)$$

Finally, TS Sends $E_{k_{s1}}(M_{3,1})$, $E_{k_{s1}}(M_{3,2})$ and N_T to $S_{current}$.

4. $S_{current}$ randomly chooses N_R and transfers all necessary information to $R_{current}$ in a secure way, so that $R_{current}$ can interact with each tag in the group.

5. For $1 \leq i \leq 2$: $R_{current}$ constructs $M_{4,i}$ according to (4),

$$M_{4,i} = \{(f(s_i, N_T) \oplus k_{i-mask}), \; C_{1,i} \; , (f(s_i, N_T) \oplus k_{group-mask}), \; C_{2,i}, \\ (k_{i-new} \oplus k_{i-mask}), \; C_{3,i} \; , (k_{group-new} \oplus k_{group-mask}), \; C_{4,i}\} \tag{4}$$

where $C_{j,i}$ is a credential on j -th message, i.e., the credential on $f(s_i, N_T) \oplus k_{i-mask}$ is computed as $C_{1,i} : \{N_{1,i} = f(k_i, N_R) \oplus f(s_i, N_T) \oplus k_{i-mask}$ and $N_{2,i} = H((f(s_i, N_T) \oplus k_{i-mask} \oplus N_R)\|k_i)\}$.

Then, $R_{current}$ sends $M_{4,1}$ and N_R to T_1 and also, $M_{4,2}$ and N_R to T_2.

6. T_1 verifies the credentials in $M_{4,1}$. If so, T_1 constructs $M_6 = f(k_{group}, N_R\|c)$ and $M_7 = f(k_1, N_R \oplus c)$, where c represents a counter set by T_1. Then, T_1 sends M_6, M_7 and c to $R_{current}$.

7. $R_{current}$ sends M_6 and c to T_2.

8. T_2 verifies M_6. If so, T_2 knows that it is interacting with a tag in the same group. Then, it performs the following operations to update its new keys:

   - Apply s_2 to retrieve k_{2-mask} and $k_{group-mask}$ by performing XOR operations on $f(s_2, N_T)$ and the received messages $f(s_2, N_T) \oplus k_{2-mask}$ and $f(s_2, N_T) \oplus k_{group-mask}$ in message $M_{4,2}$ respectively.

   - Apply k_{2-mask} and $k_{group-mask}$ to retrieve the new secret key k_{2-new} and the new group key $k_{group-new}$ by performing XOR operations on k_{2-mask} and $k_{group-mask}$ and the received messages $(k_{2-new} \oplus k_{2-mask})$ and $(k_{group-new} \oplus k_{group-mask})$ in message $M_{4,2}$ respectively.

Then, T_2 computes $M_8 = \{f(k_{2-new}, N_R\|c)\|f(k_2, N_R \oplus c)\}$ and $M_9 = f(k_{group-new}, N_R \oplus c)$ and sends M_8 and M_9 to $R_{current}$.

9. $R_{current}$ sends M_9 to T_1.

10. T_1 performs the following operations to update its new keys in a similar way with T_2. Then, T_1 verifies M_9. If so, T_1 knows that it is interacting with a tag in the same group and computes M_{10} according to (5) and sends it to $R_{current}$. Finally, T_1 updates $c = c + 1$.

$$M_{10} = \{f(k_{1-new}, N_R\|c)\|f(k_{group-new}, N_R \oplus c)\} \tag{5}$$

11. $R_{current}$ constructs a group ownership transfer proof message $M_{11} = \{f(k_{1-new}, N_R\|c)\|f(k_{group-new}, N_R \oplus c)\|f(k_{2-new}, N_R\|c)\}$. Then it is forwarded to S_{new} for verification.

– **Verification Phase:**

At this stage, S_{new} verifies M_{11}. It is supposed that all the tags in the group have already updated their secret keys as set by the new owner. Then, as the final step of a complete group ownership transfer process, S_{new} conducts a challenge response process using a grouping-proof protocol or using a tag-reader authentication protocol.

3   Weaknesses of Zuo's GOT Protocol

Unfortunately Zuo's GOT Protocol described above is completely insecure in the presence of cheating old owner. In this section, we propose several attacks to Zuo's protocol.

– *De-synchronization attack:*
   In this attack we assume that the protocol has been performed till step 4 in group ownership transfer phase. So, $S_{current}$ knows messages $M_{1,1}$ and $M_{1,2}$, therefore it knows:

$$k_{1-new} \oplus k_{1-mask} \tag{6}$$

$$k_{2-new} \oplus k_{2-mask} \tag{7}$$

$$k_{group-new} \oplus k_{group-mask} \tag{8}$$

Also, $S_{current}$ knows messages $M_{3,1}$ and $M_{3,2}$, therefore it knows:

$$f(s_1, N_T) \oplus k_{1-mask} \tag{9}$$

$$f(s_2, N_T) \oplus k_{2-mask} \tag{10}$$

$$f(s_1, N_T) \oplus k_{group-mask} \tag{11}$$

$$f(s_2, N_T) \oplus k_{group-mask} \tag{12}$$

By performing XOR operations on (6) and (9), $S_{current}$ obtains:

$$f(s_1, N_T) \oplus k_{1-new} \tag{13}$$

By performing XOR operations on (7) and (10), $S_{current}$ obtains:

$$f(s_2, N_T) \oplus k_{2-new} \tag{14}$$

By performing XOR operations on (11) and (13), $S_{current}$ obtains:

$$k_{group-mask} \oplus k_{1-new} \tag{15}$$

By performing XOR operations on (12) and (14), $S_{current}$ obtains:

$$k_{group-mask} \oplus k_{2-new} \tag{16}$$

And also, by performing XOR operations on (15) and (16), $S_{current}$ obtains:

$$k_{1-new} \oplus k_{2-new} \tag{17}$$

Now in step 5 in group ownership transfer phase, $R_{current}$ sends $f(s_1, N_T) \oplus k_{1-new}$ and $(k_{1-new} \oplus k_{2-new})$ instead of $f(s_1, N_T) \oplus k_{1-mask}$ and $(k_{1-new} \oplus k_{1-mask})$ in message $M_{4,1}$ to T_1. Also, $R_{current}$ sends $f(s_2, N_T) \oplus k_{2-new}$ and $(k_{1-new} \oplus k_{2-new})$ instead of $f(s_2, N_T) \oplus k_{2-mask}$ and $(k_{2-new} \oplus k_{2-mask})$ in message $M_{4,2}$ to T_2.

Therefore, in step 8 in group ownership transfer phase, T_2 retrieves k_{1-new} and in step 10 in group ownership transfer phase, T_1 retrieves k_{2-new} instead of their new secret keys. But, the new owner stores k_{1-new} for the new secret key of T_1 and k_{2-new} for the new secret key of T_2 in its data base. Such an attack on a tag causes loss of synchronization between the tag and the new owner. Later, when tags want to use their keys, the reader identifies tags as illegal tags. Note that, in verification phase, $R_{current}$ must change messages sent on behalf of the new owner to tags.

– *Obtain the secret key of the tag:*
   When there is a group of tags, the members of the group have a group key which is common among the members of the group but they do not access the secret key of each other. From (17), it is known that new secret keys of the tags relate to each other. It is a serious problem. Because, $S_{current}$ can obtain $k_{1-new} \oplus k_{2-new}$ and T_1 knows k_{1-new}. So, if $S_{current}$ and T_1 conspire, they can obtain the secret key of T_2, i.e., k_{2-new}. Therefore, $S_{current}$ and T_1 can impersonate T_2.
   Also, this attack can be performed on the T_1 too similar to T_2. If $S_{current}$ and T_2 conspire, they can obtain the secret key of T_1, i.e., k_{1-new}. Therefore, $S_{current}$ and T_2 can impersonate T_1.

4   The Improved Zuo's GOT Protocol

Some vulnerabilities of GOT protocol that have been employed through the above attacks are as the random number N_T used in $f(s_i, N_T) \oplus k_{group-mask}$

is the same as that used in $f(s_i, N_T) \oplus k_{i-mask}$. Also, the ID of tags has no impact on the computation of M_8, M_9 and M_{10}.

In this section, we improve GOT protocol to overcome against described attacks. In fact, the only changes of the GOT protocol are described in this section are summarized as follows:

- In step 3 in group ownership transfer phase, TS must randomly choose two numbers N_{T1} and N_{T2} and compute $M_{3,i} = \{ID_i \parallel (f(s_i, N_{T1}) \oplus k_{i-mask}) \parallel (f(s_i, N_{T2}) \oplus k_{group-mask})\}$ and send N_{T1} and N_{T2} to $S_{current}$ along with $E_{k_{s1}}(M_{3,1})$ and $E_{k_{s1}}(M_{3,2})$.

- In step 5 in group ownership transfer phase, $R_{current}$ must construct $M_{4,i}$ in form of $M_{4,i} = \{f(s_i, N_{T1}) \oplus k_{i-mask}, C_{1,i}, f(s_i, N_{T2}) \oplus k_{group-mask}, C_{2,i}, (k_{i-new} \oplus k_{i-mask}), C_{3,i}, (k_{group-new} \oplus k_{group-mask}), C_{4,i}\}$.

- In step 8 in group ownership transfer phase, T_2 must compute M_8 and M_9 in the form of $M_8 = \{f(k_{2-new}, N_R \parallel c \parallel ID_2) \parallel f(k_2, N_R \oplus c)\}$ and $M_9 = f(k_{group-new}, N_R \oplus c \oplus ID_2)$ respectively.

- In step 10 in group ownership transfer phase, T_1 must compute M_{10} in form of $M_{10} = \{f(k_{1-new}, N_R \parallel c \parallel ID_1) \parallel f(k_{group-new}, N_R \oplus c \oplus ID_1)\}$.

These modifications strengthen the security of GOT protocol against the mentioned weaknesses.

5   Conclusion

In 2010, Zuo integrated two important requirements for RFID tags (tag ownership transfer and grouping proof protocols) and introduced a protocol for RFID tag group ownership transfer (GOT). In this paper, it is shown that Zuo's protocol has some security weaknesses in the presence of cheating old owner. Zuo's protocol suffers from de-synchronization attack and tag impersonating. Under these kinds of attacks, a valid tag is identified as an illegal tag. Also, under certain circumstances, an attacker can obtain the secret key of the tags. Here, we improved Zuo's GOT protocol to overcome such weaknesses.

References

1. Finkelzeller, K.: The RFID Handbook, 2nd edn. John Wiley-Sons (2003)
2. Han, D., Kwon, D.: Vulnerability of an RFID Authentication Protocol Conforming to EPC Class 1 Generation 2 Standards. Computer Standards and Interfaces 31(4) (2009)
3. Rizomiliotis, P., Rekleitis, E., Gritzalis, S.: Security Analysis of the Song-Mitchell Authentication Protocol for Low-cost RFID Tags. IEEE Communications Letters 13(4) (2009)

4. Jannati, H., Falahati, A.: Cryptanalysis and Enhancement of two Low Cost RFID Authentication Protocols. International Journal of UbiComp (IJU) 3(1), 1–9 (2012)
5. Fouladgar, S., Afifi, H.: A Simple Privacy Protecting Scheme Enabling Delegation and Ownership Transfer for RFID Tags. Journal of Communications 2(6), 6–13 (2007)
6. Chen, C.-L., Chen, Y.-Y., Huang, Y.-C., Liu, C.-S., Lin, C.-I., Shih, T.-F.: Anti-Counterfeit Ownership Transfer Protocol for Low Cost RFID System. WSEAS Transactions on Computers 7(8), 1149–1158 (2008)
7. Kapoor, G., Piramuthu, S.: Vulnerabilities in Some Recently Proposed RFID Ownership Transfer Protocols. IEEE Communications Letters 14(3), 260–262 (2010)
8. Alaraj, A.-M.: Ownership Transfer Protocol. In: IEEE International Conference for Internet Technology and Secured Transactions (ICITST 2010), pp. 1–6 (2010)
9. Li, T., Jin, Z., Pang, C.: Secured Ownership Transfer Scheme for Low-Cost RFID Tags. In: IEEE International Conference on Intelligent Networks and Intelligent Systems (ICINIS 2010), pp. 584–587 (2010)
10. Juels, A.: Yoking proofs for RFID Tags. In: Second IEEE Annual Conference on Pervasive Computing and Communications Workshops, Washington, DC, USA, pp. 138–143 (2004)
11. Chien, H.-Y., Liu, S.-B.: Tree-based RFID yoking proof. In: IEEE International Conference on Networks Security, Wireless Communications and Trusted Computing (NSWCTC 2009), pp. 550–553 (2009)
12. Lopez, P.-P., Orfila, A., Castro, J.-C.-H., van der Lubbe, J.-C.-A.: Flaws on RFID Grouping-Proofs, Guidelines for Future Sound Protocols. Journal of Network and Computer Applications 34(3) (2011)
13. Yu, Y.-C., Hou, T.-W., Chiang, T.-C.: Low Cost RFID Real Lightweight Binding Proof Protocol for Medication Errors and Patient Safety. Journal of Medical Systems (2010), doi:10.1007/s10916-010-9546-4
14. Zuo, Y.: Changing Hands Together: A Secure Group Ownership Transfer Protocol for RFID Tags. In: The 43rd IEEE Hawaii International Conference on System Sciences (HICSS 2010), Honolulu, HI, pp. 1–10 (2010)

Paving the Way for a Transformational Public Administration

Ioannis Savvas[1], Nick Bassiliades[2], Elias Pimenidis[3], and Alexander B. Sideridis[1]

[1] Informatics Laboratory, Agricultural University of Athens, 75 Iera Odos str.,
Athens 11855, Greece
[2] Aristotle University of Thessaloniki,
[3] University of East London
{jsav,as}@aua.gr, nbassili@csd.auth.gr, e.pimenidis@uel.ac.uk

Abstract. Transformational government as a newborn scientific field seeks for implementation through integration of its components. As a contribution to this end this work impresses a Public Administration's operation ontology modeling and an algorithm for tracing malfunctions and changing the case. PA is considered as a production unit and any administrative act as the output of its processes. This output creates effects and consequences which are to be met stakeholders' goals in order to balance socioeconomic problems.

Keywords: Transformational government, PA ontology modeling, Service transformation algorithm, stakeholder goals.

1 Transforming Government

Transformational Government (t-gov) uses technology to improve public service provision, just like e-government does. However it goes beyond the use of technology; it is more oriented to managerial aspects. It focuses on new governance and organizational structures, the redesign of business processes, and the creation of a facilitating infrastructure that is flexible enough to support these changes at low cost [1].

The ultimate aim is to make a government demand driven as of stakeholders needs, accountable and transparent, innovative, efficient and effective, agile and flexible, providing multi channel services, automating back office operations such that more resources can be released to deliver 'frontline' services [2].

Transforming government has to do with the consistent improvement of processes, meaning the automation of some tasks, the removal of the redundant ones and the creation of new, simpler ones. This is a continuous and iterative process bearing certain restrictions due to the nature of PA and its operational needs. As such, research directions require investigating the change process and resulting structures.

Transformational Government Annual Report identifies three distinctive themes integral to t-Government [3]. These include, Customer-Centric Services; Shared Services and Professionalism (leadership, social entrepreneurship, performance driven management). Most of them are e-government challenges too. The new is the need of

H. Jahankhani et al. (Eds.): ICGS3/e-Democracy 2011, LNICST 99, pp. 194–203, 2012.

governments to have radical changes in core processes across their organizational boundaries or beyond the traditional organizational borders to cross-organizational business processes to realize t-government [4]. This may requires new governance structures.

Decision makers in Government will need models of Governance that fulfil transformational objectives. Modelling is an essential ingredient of most transformation processes, as it aims at abstracting from reality only its essential and relevant elements [5, 6].

2   Modeling Public Administration's Operation

Public Administration (PA) aims at achieving goals like development, prosperity, equity, transparency, justice, freedom, democracy. To achieve these goals PA provides certain *services.* In order to provide services PA issues administrative acts. The issuing of acts is the core activity of PA; it is always a State activity and concerns e-government.

In modeling PA an approach through ontology was adopted. This model addresses the operation of PA at a top level reusable mode. The ontology of Greek PA procedures [7], represents which types of *documents* are produced by which PA *units* and how these documents *flow* among these units. The ontology consists of two parts. The first part represents, in OWL, the Greek PA *structure* (i.e. administrative units and their hierarchical relationships) and *documents*, which are either used by these units as a legal framework or they are produced by them. Thus, documents are further divided in Judicial/legislative and Administrative/citizen. In the second part, the *procedures* are represented in OWL-S service models. The ontology is updated continuously as new laws, administrative regulations and procedures are issued.

On the "structural aspect" of the ontology, all agents (actors) of the administrative universe of discourse are included, namely the three independent authorities (judicial, administrative and legislative), as well as citizens and businesses. In this work we consider in detail only the structure of the administrative authority. Moreover, the PA document type hierarchy is distinguished in four major classes:

Administrative documents, i.e. documents produced by PA, which can be either *informative*, i.e. they do not have actual impact on the real world but they just inform a citizen or an administrative unit about something, or *acts*, i.e. the decisions have an impact for citizens or business (e.g. an approval for funding). Administrative documents also play the role of *products* of PA procedures.

The PA procedures ontology is represented as an extension to OWL-S (Fig. 1). The key concepts of the ontology are procedures, full procedures, and tasks. Full procedures (or total procedures, as called later in the revised ontology) are composed by one or more procedures and procedures are composed by one or more tasks. Every procedure (and task) has a name which declares or indicates its objectives. The language used to depict this objective might not be strictly administrative. Thus, each procedure has a name, title and a short description providing the possibility to citizens and inexperienced civil servants to understand its aim. The title of an administrative act is used as a title for the procedure that produces this act.

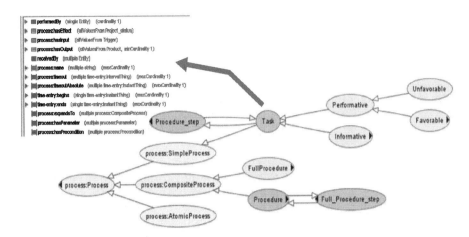

Fig. 1. The public administration procedure ontology as an extension of OWL-S

Tasks are atomic activities that cannot be further cut down to smaller ones, performed by a single administration unit. Every task has as input any kind of text, namely administrative, legal, etc. The output of the task is the document that it produces.

Procedure is defined as each integrated part (or step) of a *full procedure* (service).

In this work PA procedures whose products address to the organization's external environment are regarded. This environment includes citizens/businesses, other public organizations and public servants acting as citizens.

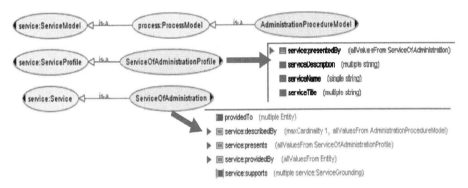

Fig. 2. Specializations of OWL-S Service, Service Profile and Service Model

Full procedure is defined as a number of procedures intertwined. A full procedure may reflect to the provision of a service to one or several entities (property *providedTo*). Fig. 2 shows the specializations of the OWL-S service, service profile and service process model classes. Procedures may be sequential or in an acyclic graph. In this ontology, the control constructs of OWL-S are adopted. Some examples of procedures that can be represented using this ontology are:

- Hierarchical control that is anticipated by a law.
- Hierarchical control that is performed due to objections/appeals.
- Communication between public organizations due to joint responsibilities for the expression of agreement in order for a project to accomplish.
- Sequential procedures that lead to the provision of a service.

2.1   Extensions / Adaptations of the Generic Object / Process Models

The initial generic PA procedures modeling ontology of [7] did not always cover all use cases. Therefore, some (but not many) adaptations have been performed to this generic modeling framework. These adaptations were general enough, in order to be applicable to the use cases already developed using the generic framework.(e.g. The human resource management use case).

A significant development in the (revised) generic object/process model is the modeling of the performative task. More specifically, the new ontology contains two types of administrative documents that harmonize with the products' role produced by the performative procedure found in Public Administration: [8]

Act: It includes all the acts that can be produced by the Public Administration's procedures.

Announcement of Act: It includes only the acts that are announcements of decisions either to another PA unit or to individuals. Announcements, although sound like informative tasks only, because they just deliver information to the interested parties, we consider them as performatives, because according to the Greek Law, the enforcement of an act begins only after its announcement; therefore, the announcement of an act has effects on the real world (fig. 3).

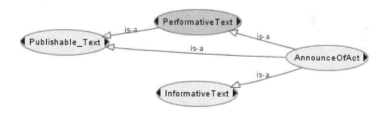

Fig. 3. The document (product) types involved in the Public Administration

In the revised PA procedure modeling framework, every task that produces an act or an announcement of act is considered to be a performative task. The rest of the tasks are considered as informative ones. Thus, a *procedure* consists of:

- One or more informative tasks
- Exactly one performative task (Act or Announce of Act)

A *total procedure* consists of at least one or more (simpler) procedures; therefore, a total procedure is usually composed of:

- One or more informative tasks,
- One or more performative tasks, one for each (simple) procedure,
- One announcement of act, usually in the last (simple) procedure of the process.

Note that a task is considered performative for a PA unit only when the act is carried out by this public organization. That means that the same task could be performative for one PA unit and informative for another depending on the point of view.

3   Performance Driven Management of PA

Performance Measurement is a process that uses and produces information about performance. The use of this information is what is called performance management. Performance measurement is an organizational process that yields performance information. Boucaert and Peters [9] consider performance information truly important for the internal management of an organization. Yet, performance measurement goes beyond public sector reform. It is found in recurring activities in public management and public policy [10]. Performance measurement is based on indicators and concepts of effectiveness and efficiency.

To assess the transformational needs of the whole of a PO's operation and every single process, one can start from the effectiveness part. Effectiveness is the measure of achieving goals that are not necessary financial. They could be goals regarding democracy, equality, etc. and in contemporary theories they should reflect stakeholders' needs.

Step 1. *The effectiveness part.* The ratios of output over effect (Output/Effect) and effect over consequence (Effect/Consequence) are the two effectiveness measures.

(i) **Effect/Consequence**. The ideal situation is to identify consequences of the administrative action with goals/objectives as set by politicians. These objectives are measurable interpretations of the abstract goals of the stakeholders. Effect is the service. The ratio is expressed as actual over prospective, meaning that the service achieves or not the goal that the government and the politicians had set. A problem with this ratio reflects for example policy objectives setting and law making problems.

(ii) **Output/Effect.** This is act/service. It refers to the number of the acts that actually provide the requested service (note that service is also the denial of a request). It concerns number of acts that are invalid due to objections or appeals, number of acts that provide service to persons that are not entitled for that and number of acts that provide the service to people who are beneficiaries of a better similar service. Such problems call for changes to the quality of acts (structural and typical matters, matters of interpretation of the legal framework and discretion margins of public servants, matters of dissemination of information.)

Step 2. *The efficiency part.* The ratio of input over output (Input/ Output) expresses the measure of efficiency. Acts as outputs need three types of inputs: information, communication and expression as resources. All three are tested versus two variables, time and cost.

3.1   An Application Profile

A metadata application profile for keeping information for the overall and sectional performance of a public organization or service was created. The application profile follows the rationale for the operation of PA, which is already organized in the ontology mentioned, while is formulated by elements and sub-elements existing in international and national well established standards. Some of the variables taken under consideration for this application profile are mentioned below:

(Objections + Appeals) sustained, Time for composing an act, Time for issuing an act, Time for Information provided to potential users of the service in addition to what already provided by laws, sites etc., Time for Additional information asked after submitting the application and the documents, Information which other POs provide for the issuing of the act (in relation to law preconditions, law-article-paragraph), Waiting time for this Information, Positive acts/decisions, Information asked by citizens/businesses (in relation to law preconditions), Negative acts/decisions, Waiting time for Information asked by citizen and businesses.

In addition many other variables were used to lead to the exact definition of the problem and the suggestion of the suitable service. For example there were used: Objections sustained for typical or non typical reasons, type of communication, cost of communications, number of phone calls, cost of connection, use of e mails, cost of personnel, number of employees, wages, person hours for seeking for legal framework, person hours for interpreting legal framework, number of phone calls asking information about the service, number of applications for the service, number of applications redirected to the suitable PO, kind of data stored - kind of information asked - information asked by citizens and given by a PO in relation to law preconditions etc.

3.2   PASTA

In order to improve PA's performance an algorithm named PASTA (Public Administration Service Transformation Algorithm) is proposed [11]. This algorithm is a useful tool for decision making in PA. It provides a necessary solution in identifying malfunctions and proposing services to remedy public service failings. Furthermore, the use of PASTA increases the accuracy of the final specifications of functional requirements of e-government systems that should be introduced. It defines the services that are required and what is required from each service. It primarily addresses the conceptual level creating all the necessary plug-ins for the contextual and the logical level according to the Integrated Architecture Framework (IAF) proposed by CapGemini [12]. The conceptual level addresses the "what" aspect of architectural design. This algorithm extends and validates a stepwise approach that was proposed in [13].

In formulating PASTA three main initial assumptions were made:

- Objectives set by politicians are qualitatively related to consequences
- Setting of Thresholds has been done correctly. If not, PASTA can make suggestions using percentages or probabilities.

- There has been, in advance, a setting of accepted limits in consequences, effects, outputs, inputs. In that sense, production of more acts, effects and consequences than predicted is not a problem, since they are achieved by the scheduled inputs. This is simply a best practice and a motive to executives to rethink efficiency matters.

The PASTA rationale is explained further in [11]. Another critical issue is the one of the spotting of redundant tasks. This is made possible through the connection of the information asked (law prerequisite) from a PO or a citizen/business with laws number - article number – paragraph number. If there is the same reference to two different information sources then duplication might occur.

PASTA's service proposals/suggestions were validated against PA experts' suggestions and the resulting proposals of a big Greek project studying the reorganization of certain PA's processes/ services. The validation proved that PASTA is capable of being used in service reorganization projects by utilizing it to suggest very useful services and override experts' proposals. It can also provide suggestions on effectiveness, which are seldom provided by other methodologies, and hardly ever by experts.

4   Related Work

Related work concerns various aspects of the problem we address, namely use of semantic web technologies, like metadata, ontologies, web services, etc., for e-government and PA knowledge, performance measurement and algorithms. PA ontology modeling is a fast evolving field as ontologies are considered critical knowledge infrastructure to address semantic interoperability problems. They provide the necessary basis for further development of SW and SWS eGovernment applications. Due to the fast development of SW and SWS technologies and the research interest in applying such technologies in PA, we expect to see in the next few years a substantial growth on demand for reusable and scalable PA domain models and ontologies.

Currently there are several research efforts that try to address interoperability/integration issues in eGovernment in all three EIF dimensions. The UK e-GIF (e-Government Interoperability Framework) [14] model focuses on 4 perspectives: interconnectivity, data integration, e-services access, and content management. In [15–17] a survey of existing e-Government interoperability initiatives and enterprise architectures in the EU and USA is presented. In [18] a classification of semantic conflicts in database systems is given. Park and Ram in [19] also give a description of semantic interoperability conflicts regardless of the application domain, while in [20] the resolution of these conflicts is proposed using an ontology. The Semantic Interoperability Community of Practice (SICoP) [21] has identified the semantic conflict types in information systems and has recognized the importance of Semantic Web (SW) technologies in this area. In [22], model-driven initiatives and efforts to achieve eGovernment interoperability are reviewed and compared.

In the context of the research regarding the performance of an organization Gartner proposed the Gartner's Government Performance Framework (GPF) [23] as a tool to assess the value IT can add in a public sector context. GPF groups activities for a public sector organization in three layers [24], Political Management, Service Supply Management and Support Services. The overall perspective has not been focused to provide a top level domain model for the governance system, and this becomes apparent by the way these layers are further decomposed into Aggregates and further more into Primes. Furthermore the Gartner framework does not focus on certain aspects of PA's operation like the back office operations.

5   Stakeholders' Needs (Extensions and Future Work)

In [25], PA's stakeholders were identified and their strategic relationships in the socioeconomic environment, national and supranational were defined. Stakeholders were defined on both sides of public service provision, supply and demand.

The demand side includes citizens (also as employees) and businesses. Judicial power (administrative courts) and Legislative power can also be classified here. Parliament receives PA services in law making process and it is interested in the application of the laws it provides. Courts are control mechanisms regarding public service provision. They are interested in the application of their decisions concerning administrative acts and they support administrative processes providing jurisprudence.

The supply side includes the indivisible of governance. Government national and supranational (EU case). When we are referring to a certain service though, final provision is being made from one Public Organization (PO). The demand side then might includes other POs too.

Especially for the case study of the Greek PA a first set of stakeholder requirements has been presented. In this case, stakeholders are not only national but supranational as well, as Greece is part of the E.U. Stakeholders belong to the direct and the indirect environment of PA and have been defined as: Government, the EU, citizens/businesses, public organizations, public servants, the Law courts and country's Parliament.

To incorporate stakeholders' goals/needs to the whole of a PO's function and every single process, one can start from the effectiveness part, as mentioned above in the performance driven management section.

The above PA ontology is supplemented by goal taxonomy. The taxonomy is not yet fully fledged. It provides goal decomposition based on technology and administrative resources.

6   Discussion and Conclusions

This paper constitutes an overview of the authors' efforts for modeling and transforming PA's operation.

At first a methodological approach to the ontology modeling of PA is presented. It follows a certain rationale of its operation and regards administrative act as the output of every non material service provided by the PA. There are many efforts for modeling PA's operations using ontologies. This certain approach is differentiated as to the use of administrative act as the core object.

Performance measurement is a research field with mass production of efforts over the last decades. The work presented here follows the rationale of an input-output model which results from a "Flemish perspective" expressed by van Dooren's work [10], which in turn was based on Pollitt and Bouckaert [26]. Based on this input output model administrative act is set as output, service as effect, and as consequence of an administrative operation, the long term effect of which is going to be aligned with the aggregation of goals of the stakeholders as set by politicians.

GFP is the most widespread framework for assessing performance in PA. Our approach considers PA as a production unit and uses an algorithm to trace malfunctions and suggest remedies.

In order to exploit the whole benefit of the proposed method the existence of technological infrastructures is a fundamental prerequisite. At this certain moment the Greek PA is under a strong reformative initiative (Kallikratis). This could be the right momentum for the application of transformational efforts in the operation of PA.

Acknowledgments. Ioannis Savvas is a Phd candidate whose research is supported and funded by the Greek State Foundation (IKY).

References

1. Irani, Z., Sahraoui, S., Ozkan, S., Ghoneim, A., Elliman, T.: T-Government for Benefit Realisation. In: Proceedings of European and Mediterranean Conference on Information Systems (2007)
2. Janssen, M., Shu, W.S.: Transformational Government: Basics and Key Issues. In: Proceedings of ICEGOV 2008 (2008)
3. Cabinet Office. Transformational Government 2006 Annual Report (2007)
4. Weerakkody, V., Dhillon, G.: Moving from EGovernment to T-Government: A Study of Process Reengineering Challenges in a UK Local Authority Perspective. International Journal of Electronic Government Research 4, 1–16 (2008)
5. Janssen, M.: Designing Electronic Intermediaries. An agent-based approach for designing interorganizational coordination mechanisms. Delft University of Technology, Doctoral Dissertation. Delft, The Netherlands (2001)
6. Janssen, M., Sol, H.G.: Evaluating the role of intermediaries in the electronic value chain. Internet Research- Electronic Networking Applications and Policy 10, 406–417 (2000)
7. Savvas, I., Bassiliades, N.: A Process-Oriented Ontology-Based Knowledge Management System for Facilitating Operational Procedures in Public Administration. Expert Systems with Applications 36(3-1), 4467–4478 (2009)
8. Savvas, I., Bassiliades, N., Kravari, K., Meditskos, G.: An Ontological Business Process Modeling Approach for Public Administration: The Case of Human Resource Management Handbook of Research on E-Business Standards and Protocols: Documents, Data and Advanced Web Technolgies book to be published by IGI Global (2012)
9. Bouckaert, G., Peters, B.G.: Performance Measurement and Management. The Achilles' Heel in administrative modernization. Public Performance and Management Review 25(4), 359–362 (2002)

10. Van Dooren W.: Performance Measurement in the Flemish Public Sector: A Supply and Demand Approach. PhD dissertation, Faculteit Sociale. Wetenschappen - Onderzoekseenheid: Instituut voor de Overheid [IO], K.U. Leuven (2006)
11. Savvas, I., Bassiliades, N., Pimenidis, E., Sideridis, A.: A Public Administration Service Transformation Algorithm (under review)
12. Capgemini: Architecture and the Integrated Architecture Framework (2006), retrieved from,
    http://www.capgemini.com/resources/thought_leadership/
    architecture_and_the_integrated_architecture_framework/
13. Savvas, I., Pimenidis, E., Sideridis, A.: Using egov systems to remedy public service failings: in search of a "transformation" algorithm. In: Proceedings of eGovernment Workshop 2008, Brunel University, West London (2008)
14. UK CabinetOffice: e-Government Interoperability Framework, Version 6.1 (2005),
    http://www.govtalk.gov.uk/schemasstandards/
    egif_document.asp?docnum=949
15. Guijarro, L.: Semantic interoperability in eGovernment initiatives. Computer Standards & Interfaces (2007), doi:10.1016/j.csi
16. Guijarro, L.: Interoperability frameworks and enterprise architectures in e-government initiatives in Europe and the United States. Government Information Quarterly 24(1), 89–101 (2007)
17. Guijarro, L.: Analysis of the Interoperability Frameworks in e-government Initiatives. In: Traunmüller, R. (ed.) EGOV 2004. LNCS, vol. 3183, pp. 36–39. Springer, Heidelberg (2004)
18. Naiman, C.E., Ouksel, A.M.: A classification of semantic conflicts in heterogeneous database systems. Journal of Organizational Computing 5(2), 167–193 (1995)
19. Park, J., Ram, S.: Information systems interoperability: what lies beneath? ACM Transactions on Information Systems 22(4), 595–632 (2004)
20. Ram, S., Park, J.: Semantic Conflict Resolution Ontology (SCROL): an ontology for detecting and resolving data and schema-level semantic conflicts. IEEE Transactions on Knowledge and Data Engineering 16(2), 189–202 (2004)
21. SICoP : Introducing semantic technologies and the vision of the semantic web, version 5.4, Semantic Interoperability Community of Practice, White Paper Series Module 1 (2005)
22. Peristeras, V., Tarabanis, K., Goudos, S.K.: Model-driven eGovernment interoperability: A review of the state of the art. Computer Standards & Interfaces 31, 613–628 (2009)
23. Gartner: Gartner Business Performance Framework v1.0 (2003),
    http://www.gartnerg2.com/fw/fwbpf.asp
24. Gartner: New performance framework measures public value of IT, Research Note (2003)
25. Savvas, I., Pimenidis, E., Sideridis, A.: Proposing a high-level requirements mapping framework, for testing implementation compatibility in e-government projects. In: Proceedings of ECEG. The 7th European Conference of e-Government, Den Haag, The Netherlands, June 21-22, pp. 459–468 (2007)
26. Pollit, C., Bouckaert, G.: Public Management Reform. A Comparative Analysis. Oxford University Press, Oxford (2004)

Cybercrime: The Case of Obfuscated Malware

Mamoun Alazab[1], Sitalakshmi Venkatraman[1], Paul Watters[1],
Moutaz Alazab[2], and Ammar Alazab[2]

[1] Internet Commerce Security Laboratory
School of Science, Information Technology and Engineering
University of Ballarat, Australia
{m.alazab,s.venkatraman,p.watters}@ballarat.edu.au
[2] School of Information Technology
Deakin University, Australia
{malazab,aalazab}@deakin.edu.au

Abstract. Cybercrime has rapidly developed in recent years and malware is one of the major security threats in computer which have been in existence from the very early days. There is a lack of understanding of such malware threats and what mechanisms can be used in implementing security prevention as well as to detect the threat. The main contribution of this paper is a step towards addressing this by investigating the different techniques adopted by obfuscated malware as they are growingly widespread and increasingly sophisticated with zero-day exploits. In particular, by adopting certain effective detection methods our investigations show how cybercriminals make use of file system vulnerabilities to inject hidden malware into the system. The paper also describes the recent trends of Zeus botnets and the importance of anomaly detection to be employed in addressing the new Zeus generation of malware.

Keywords: Cybercrime, Obfuscation, Malware, Intrusion Detection.

1 Introduction

In the context of crime-ware, malicious code is the most valuable resource to perform unauthorized access by cybercriminals [1]. Malicious software (Malware) attackers are taking advantage of our increased reliance on digital systems, available digital resources, and increased connectivity and activity through Internet. On one hand, technology advancements have resulted in home computers featuring 1 Terabyte (TB) of storage that are now available for purchase. On the other hand, sophistication in malware offers a new class of criminal activity that has created new challenges for law and forensic examiners [2]. Current threats [3] posed to organizations by cybercrimes continue to aggressively hunt and develop new techniques to steal money and credential information.

A review of the history of malware and anti-malware reports [2] [3] [4] and predictions [5] show a continuous growth thriven in sophistication over the years, and traditional malware detections appear insufficient to tackle increasingly sophisticated malware. Therefore, the detection of malware is not only of interest

H. Jahankhani et al. (Eds.): ICGS3/e-Democracy 2011, LNICST 99, pp. 204–211, 2012.
© Institute for Computer Sciences, Social Informatics and Telecommunications Engineering 2012

to researchers but is also a major concern to the general public. Malwares are designed to perform illegal activities being designed more for financial gains, leading to a huge impact against individuals, organisations and business assets. Recent trends in malware for such malicious and illegal purposes indicate increasing complexity and are evolving rapidly as systems provide more opportunities for more automated activities of late. Hence, the damages caused by malware to individuals and businesses have dramatically increased in 2010 [3], [5].

In this paper we perform investigations on the obfuscated techniques used in the malicious code, and illustrate with recent trends in exploits that use file system vulnerabilities including Zeus botnets.

The remainder of this paper is organized as follows. In Section 2, we discuss the malicious code growth in the wild. We describe the recent trends in cybercrime attacks in Section 3. We discuss and investigate the recent obfuscation techniques that are used in malicious code, in Section 4. We also discuss new threats, in particular feature the Zeus as a case study. Finally, Section 5 provides a summary.

2   Malicious Code Growth

The current situation is that known malware can be recognized by all the popular anti-malware engines. Malware detection usually occurs in an online system and the anti-virus (AV) software forms the primary tool for the defense against malware. However, cybercriminals continually develop new techniques for creating malware that cannot be detected leading to what is known as a 'zero-day-attack'. In other words, once new malicious code is released, the detection engines will have to update their signatures in order to detect and combat the new malicious code. Though the quality of such malware detectors is improving in their techniques from virus signature-based detection towards heuristic-based detection, the malware cybercriminals are one step ahead [1] of the AV engines and anti-forensic methods adopted. The present malware detection systems usually rely on existing malware signatures with limited heuristics and are unable to detect those malware that can hide itself during the scanning process in online systems [8].

In general, countermeasures such as AV engines must perform 3 main tasks to provide protection to systems: Scanning, Detection, and Removal. As shown in the *equation* below a Malware detector MD is defined as a function to determine if an executable program (file) is malicious or benign MD: p ? malicious, benign. Modern and traditional anti-malwares scan the files in a system for a byte sequence or malware signature(s) that are stored in the database engine. Current live malware detection tools such as anti- malware software are able to identify known malware, therefore, cybercriminals are continually developing new techniques for creating malware that are not detectable by AV engines. Once new malware is released, the AV engines will reactively update their signatures to combat the new malware. However, recent methods adopted by computer intruders, cybercriminals and malware are to target hidden and deleted data so that they could evade from virus scanners. As a result, some malware adopt circumvention techniques such as polymorphic and metamorphic obfuscations so that they cannot be detected through current live analysis techniques.

$$MD(P) = \begin{cases} Malware & if S \in p \\ Benign & otherwise \end{cases} \qquad (1)$$

Creating and producing malicious code is not done only by malware writers, but there are also in the market, malicious software kit vendors [9] such as Zeus, exploit kits, Flesta, MyPolySploit, Limbo2 and SpyEye, snd these kits are used to create highly effective malware. These kits serving as new offsprings of malware have caused serious threats and major problems. The new market for malware creation software on-sale is widely available on the internet and can be found easily using Google and other search engines. Apart from purchasing these kits, one could also buy the updates for the kit to ensure and guarantee it is a reliable business. Likewise, cybercriminals are being purchased in underground markets with even after sales services and guaranteed effectiveness of evading security countermeasures offered. As a result, cybercriminals update the construction kits to suit the needs of their client base to stay ahead of their contenders. Malicious software kit vendors or 'crime ware' is being offered for sale on underground trading forums and IM for negotiation.

"Full ZeuS Souurce code of last v2.0.8.9 (includes everything). Requires MSVC++ 2010. You can create your own HWID licenses and much more."

According to the Internet Crime Complaint Center $(IC3)^2$ in 2010 malicious codes are evolving rapidly. For instance, a study conducted by University of Maryland?shows?that on an average, a?computer?connected to?the?Internet? may experience an attack every 39 seconds [10]. Equally important in the first quarter of 2010, another experiment conducted by the San Diego Supercomputer Center (SDSC) shows that an average of 27,000 hacking attempts were made per day. Similarly, when PSINet Europe purposely built an unprotected server and connected it to the internet their results were staggering: in the first 24 hours and the server was maliciously attacked 467 times [11]. More recently, these figures have grown exponentially [3], [5].

Types of malware such as worms, rootkits viruses, script viruses, trojans, macro viruses, backdoors, spyware, key loggers, etc. are being recycled [12] to produce new variants of old malware. In 2006, BitDefender Antivirus [12] published that it had over 270 thousand malware signatures in its database. Symantec Internet Security threat published report in 2010 [13] announced that malicious code activity continues to grow at a record pace, and there are over 2.8 million new malicious code signatures, mostly developed in 2009. Other sources show the infection rates through experiments performed by Kaspersky Labs that identified almost 120 million servers in the first quarter of 2010 of which 0.64% was malicious [9]. Recently, McAfee Labs [5] identified almost 60,000 new pieces of malware per day and this shows the sophistication in malware is getting more difficult to detect and that cybercriminals are engaging in a growing number of targeted attacks.

3   Cybercrime

In many ways, cybercrime is no different than traditional crime [6]. Both crimes are involved in identifying targets, using surveillance and psychological profiling. The major difference is that the perpetrators of cybercrime are increasingly remote to the scene of the crime [7]. The traditional idea of a criminal gang loses its meaning as members can now reside on different continents without ever having to actually meet.

In this 21st Century, a bank robber does not require a gun, a mask, a note, or a getaway car. Data has become more valuable than money. Hence, accessing bank data gives cybercriminals repeated access to the money. Research studies relating to credit card fraud detection has steadily increased over the recent years [5] [10] [11] [12] [13] [14]. Moreover, use of botnets, VOIP and mobile SMS in attacks are expected to rise. Globally, 30,000 phishing attacks are reported each month and at least 3% of phishing attempts are successful. Although phishing alone is not directly responsible for all online banking fraud, Singh (2007)'s statistics indicates that 900 online bank accounts get compromised each month from phishing alone. In general, online banking fraud includes all unauthorized transactions conducted without the legitimate account holder's knowledge and (usually) resulting in loss of funds from the account.

4   Obfuscated Malicious Code Types

Criminals today have sophisticated service providers and high-tech expertise to fully take advantage of their current targets. Furthermore, the exploit servers used can be changed to avoid detection and countermeasures.

4.1   Polymorphic Malware

Anti-malware vendors are confronting a serious problem of defeating the complexity of malwares. Polymorphic malware uses encryption and data appending/ data pre-pending in order to change the body of the malware, and further, it changes decryption routines from infection to infection as long as the encryption keys change, making it very difficult to create antivirus signatures to block infections. Crime-ware tool kits such as CRUM Cryptor Polymorphic, PoisonIvy Polymorphic Online Builder and Mariposa, use polymorphic code and obfuscation techniques to avoid detection, and are available on black-market for a price range 50−10000 depending on the features included. As result, this will lead to anti-malware experts to develop different scanning techniques from simple byte sequence matching to combine of the difficulty of antivirus engines to block it and its numerous propagation techniques. In early 2011, Symantec Internet Security

Threat Report stated that detecting polymorphic malware such as w32.Polip and w32.Detnat is much more difficult and complex than any other type of Malware. The use of simple virus scanners has made this type of obfuscation prolific and continues to pose a major threat [14].

4.2 Metamorphic Malware

Metamorphic malware changes the code itself without the need of using encryption. In general, there are four techniques commonly used for metamorphic obfuscation. These are, i) Dead-code Insertion which is meant to do nothing such as a sequence of NOPs (No Operation Performed), ii) Code Transposition that changes the instructions such as using JMP instructions so that the order of instructions is different from the original one, iii) Register Reassignment such as replacing push ebx with push eax to exchange register names, and iv) Instruction Substitution which replaces the instructions with different instructions that have the same result, and some authors use a database dictionary of equivalent instruction sequences to make the replacement easier and faster.

4.3 Packer

Packers are commonly used today for code obfuscation or compression. Packers are software programs that could be used to compress and encrypt the PE in secondary memory and to restore the original executable image when loaded into main memory (RAM). Cybercriminals do not need to change several lines of code to change the malware signature mainly because, changing any byte sequence in the PE results in a new different byte sequence in the newly produced packed PE. For instance, Themida (www.oreans.com), Obsidium (www.obsidium.de), ASPack (http://www.aspack.com) and Armadillo (www.siliconrealms.com) are all commonly used packers and malicious code authors are using such packers to produced new codes. Packers have the essential features of reducing the size of malware, making malware easier to transfer, and thereby producing malware more resistant to static analysis. Hence, packers being able to bypass detection engines have become the most favorite toolkits.

4.4 File System Vulnerabilities

Cybercriminals make use of file system vulnerabilities in order to infect more computers and guarantee effectiveness of evading security countermeasures. For instance, keeping the last modified date of an infected file unchanged to make it seem like it was uninfected was one of the first early techniques cybercriminals had adopted to thwart detection. Cybercriminals target a hidden area on the system structure to hide the malware. Since NTFS is predominantly used in most computer systems, and malware cybercriminals take advantage of NTFS weaknesses to hide malware, more computers get infected without being detected by commercial detection engines. They are capitalizing on the vulnerabilities of

NTFS to hide the malware from AV engines and further exploit the weaknesses of the present digital forensic techniques from being detected. From a preliminary investigation we had conducted on the hidden data of the $Boot file [2], we observe that a variety of tools and utilities have to be adopted along with manual inspections to identify unseen malware. It takes an enormous amount of time to analyse the data derived with such tools and most of the existing tools are complex and not easy to use. Moreover, not all computer infections are detected by forensic tools, especially intrusions that are in the form of hidden data in the $Boot file go unchecked. Hence, our study reveals that the existing forensic tools are not comprehensive and effective in identifying the recent computer threats that use obfuscated malware.

NTFS, Windows NT's native file system, is designed to be more robust and secure than other Microsoft file systems. The key feature to note in NTFS disk structure is that the Master File Table (MFT) contains details of every file and folder on the volume and allocates two sectors for every MFT entry. Since the Windows operating system does not zero the slack space, cybercriminals make use of MFT to hide malicious code without raising any suspicion. Our investigations have revealed that such limitations in NTFS have led to cybercriminals using different techniques such as disguising file names, hiding attributes and deleting files to intrude the system.

5   Case Study: The Zeus Botnet

The Zeus Trojan, a financial malware Zeus botnet, is a well-known banking Trojan also called Zbot, NTOS, WSNPOEM, or PRG, and forms the king of financial malware 'in wild', both in terms of infection size and effectiveness. Furthermore, it is the biggest and most sophisticated threat to internet security and to most of the detection engines such as Symantec and McAfee. The Zeus Trojan estimated to be responsible for about 90% of banking fraud worldwide [5] and found guilty in 44% of the banking malware infections [15]. Symantec Corporation describes it as *"Zeus, King of the Underground Crimeware Toolkits"*.

The Zeus Trojan software with a friendly interface toolkit that is available in underground online forums for $1,500-20,000US$ is causing a serious problem because it enables cybercriminals to configure and create malicious software to affect user systems, allowing them to take control of a compromised computer, harming the data, logging keystrokes, and executing unauthorized transactions in online banking. The name Zeus has created a panic in the world of computers and security experts today. Reports and studies [5] [12] [13] [14] show that since last year Zeus has been found embroiled in more than half of the banking malware infections in the world.

The Zeus Trojan carries a very light footprint and is designed to steal sensitive data stored on computers or transmitted through web browsers and protected storage. Once infected, the computer sends the stolen data to a bot command and control (C&C) server via encrypted HTTP POST requests, where the data is stored. Also, it allows cybercriminals to inject content into a bank's web page as it is displayed in the infected computer browser in real time. It is setup such that the stolen data is sent to a "drop server" controlled by an attacker called a botmaster and it allows cybercriminals to control the infected systems remotely. Moreover, Zeus is highly dynamic and applies obfuscation methods such as polymorphic encryption and metamorphic in a network of bots. In each infection, it re-encrypts itself automatically to create a new signature to defeat signature-based detection. Thus, Zeus poses a threat as it can successfully evade commercial detection engines and is able to hide malicious features such as string and API function calls. Zeus is still evolving with new plugin releases that can infect even latest operating systems such as Windows 7.

According to numerous research labs and hacker forums, the ZeuS botnet recently has combined [5] [16] [17] with the new release of 2010 'SpyEye Trojan' source codes to create more sophisticated bots and takes the new threat to a new level. This new toolkit is being reported that it is currently available for purchase in the underground market and version 1.4.1 has been published on January 11, 2011 [17]. The new version of the combination has two versions of a control panel used for committing fraud and managing compromised systems. These trends indicate that self-learning and self-updating by observing system anomalies and behavior patterns is much warranted in malware detection systems of the future [18].

6   Summary

Overall observation is that malicious code authors are producing unique threats using different obfuscation methods, and signature-based detection is of little defense to our present computing environments and such traditional anti-virus techniques are rapidly becoming obsolete. Therefore, Anomaly Detection (AD) should be more explored and used than signature-based detection since it has many limitation and proven inability against the new threats. Also, we believe that anamoly-based detection methods are required to be adopted to detect Zeus botnets and malicious activities that are increasing exponentially since the start of this year.

Cybercriminals are leveraging innovation at a pace to target many organizations that ecurity vendors cannot possibly match. Effective deterrents to cybercrime are not known, available, or accessible to many practitioners, many of whom underestimate the scope and severity of the problem. In our view the key for fast speed in malware growth is the lack of understanding of the various types of hidden malware and their capabilities to exploit file system vulnerabilities. Security breaches are increasing in frequency and sophistication. Through a preliminary investigation conducted in this research work, we have illustrated the abovementioned attacking trend with a view to identify the various behavior of hidden malicious code that could be categorized as distinct malware types. This paper has also identified and described Zeus botnet as the start of a new generation of malware and has highlighted the importance of anomaly detection to combat Zeus.

References

1. Herrera-Flanigan, J.R., Ghosh, S.: Criminal Regulations. In: Ghosh, S., Turrini, E. (eds.) Cybercrimes: A Multidisciplinary Analysis, pp. 265–308. Springer, Heidelberg (2010)
2. Alazab, M., Venkataraman, S., Watters, P.: Effective digital forensic analysis of the NTFS disk image. Ubiquitous Computing and Communication Journal 4, 551–558 (2009)
3. RSA: The Current State of Cybercrime and What to Expect in 2011. RSA 2011 cybercrime trends report (2011)
4. Venkatraman, S.: Autonomic Context-Dependent Architecture for Malware Detection. In: Proceedings of International Conference on e-Technology, International Business Academics Consortium, Singapore, pp. 2927–2947 (2009)
5. Alperovitch, D., Dirro, T., Greve, P., Kashyap, R., Marcus, D., Masiello, S., Paget, F., Schmugar, C.: McAfee Labs - 2011 Threats Predictions. McAfee, Inc. (2011)
6. Jahankhani, H., Al-Nemrat, A.: Global E-Security. Communications in Computer and Information Science. In: Jahankhani, H., Revett, K., Palmer-Brown, D. (eds.) ICGeS 2008. CCIS, vol. 12, pp. 3–9. Springer, Heidelberg (1974)
7. Jahankhani, H., Al-Nemrat, A.: Examination of Cyber-criminal Behaviour. International Journal of Information Science and Management, 41–48 (2010)
8. Alazab, M., Venkataraman, S., Watters, P.: Towards Understanding Malware Behaviour by the Extraction of API Calls. In: Second Cybercrime and Trustworthy Computing Workshop, pp. 52–59. IEEE Computer Society, Victoria (2010)
9. Komisarczuk, P.: Web Attack: WHO ARE WE FIGHTING? Dealing with threats is one thing, finding them is another. The manazine of the BSC security forum, ISNOW (Autumn 2010)
10. Cukier, M.: Study Documents Rate, Nature of Hacker Attacks. IT Pro. (2007)
11. Daniel, J.: Internet Security - the Threats Are Very Real. Educators' eZine (2007)
12. BitDefender Antivirus Technology, white paper (2010),
    http://www.bitdefender.com/files-/Main/file/
    BitDefender_Antivirus_Technology.pdf
13. Symantec Enterprise Security: Symantec Global Internet Security, Security Threat Report, Trend for 2009, vol. XV (2010)
14. Symantec Enterprise Security: Symantec Report on Attack Kits and Malicious Websites. White paper (2011)
15. Banking malware zeus sucessfully bypasses anti-virus detection (2011),
    http://ecommerce-journal.com/news/
    18221_zeus_increasingly_avoids_pcs_detection
16. SPAMfighter News: Seculert Finds Fresh Malware Combining Zeus And SpyEye (2011),
    http://www.spamfighter.com/
    Seculert-Finds-Fresh-Malware-Combining-Zeus-And-SpyEye-15773-News.htm
17. SPAMfighter News: Alliance of ZeuS-SpyEye Resulting in the Publication of First Toolkit in the Underground Market (2011), http://www.spamfighter.com
18. Venkatraman, S.: Self-Learning Framework for Intrusion Detection. In: Proceedings of The 2010 International Congress on Computer Applications and Computational Science (CACS 2010), Singapore, pp. 517–520 (2010)

Feeling Secure vs. Being Secure
the Mobile Phone User Case

Iosif Androulidakis[1] and Gorazd Kandus[2]

[1] Jožef Stefan International Postgraduate School
Jamova 39, Ljubljana SI-1000, Slovenia
sandro@noc.uoi.gr
[2] Department of Communication Systems, Jožef Stefan Institute
Jamova 39, Ljubljana SI-1000, Slovenia
gorazd.kandus@ijs.si

Abstract. In this work, we are comparing the subjective security feeling of mobile phone users to the (objectively agreed) best security practices. This was possible by statistically processing a large pool of 7172 students in 17 Universities of 10 European countries. We introduced a "mean actual security value", comparing their security practices to best practices. There was a clear negative connection between feeling secure and actually being secure. Users that feel that mobile phone communication is secure, tend to be less cautious in their security practices. Moreover, we extracted profiles of students according to their mobile phone communication security feeling. These profiles belong to well defined categories. Users, exhibit different values of a metric that we named "mean security feeling value" according to their age, field of study, brand and operating system of phone, connection type, monthly bill and backup frequency. These results can help both academia and industry focus their security awareness campaigns and efforts to specific subsets of users that mostly need them. Finally, as there are not available any already validated questionnaires in regards to this specific research topic, our research, apart from revealing the situation, aims at providing a basis for the formulation of similar questionnaires for future use.

Keywords: mobile phone security, user profiling, security practices, survey, mean security feeling value, mean actual security value.

1   Introduction

Mobile phones have become a vital part of daily life for billions of people around the world. Their presence is ubiquitous and most users report that their cell phone makes them feel safer, even sleeping with their phone on or right next to their bed [1]. Physical safety however is completely different than communication security. As such, in this paper, we are comparing the subjective security feeling of mobile phone users to the (objectively agreed) best security practices.

Since mobile phones are used from both experienced, security savvy users and from people that do not pay that much attention to security issues, there is a relevant

H. Jahankhani et al. (Eds.): ICGS3/e-Democracy 2011, LNICST 99, pp. 212–219, 2012.

distinction in the results of the survey. Users indeed, exhibit different levels of security feeling in regards to mobile phone communications. As a matter of fact, there are categories of users that face increased security risks due to their self-reassuring feeling that mobile phones are per se secure.

These categories need proper training and education, otherwise, a security incident will soon follow, harming in the long term the operators too. They must be protected from unauthorized third party access to their data and from economic frauds. Thanks to the statistical process concluded in this work, these specific user categories can easily be pinpointed by operators and handset manufacturers. This way they can offer better security training and intrinsically more secure products and services. It must also be noted that there are not available any already validated questionnaires for the specific research topic we examined. As such, our research aims at providing a basis for the formulation of such questionnaires for future use.

In the rest of the paper, in Section 2, related literature is examined. The methodology used for the survey is described in Section 3. Results are presented in Section 4, closing with conclusion and future work in Section 5.

2   Related Work

Although there have been quite many theoretical studies concerning mobile services and mobile phones, a significant means for investigating and understanding users' preferences is asking their opinion via specific questioning techniques. The vast majority of these surveys indicate the growing importance of mobile phones in everyday life and the increased popularity of new features [1][2].

In any case, the security of mobile phones is proven not to be adequate in many research papers. Modern smart phones, specifically, are vulnerable to more security risks [3]. There also exist several survey studies in this direction. Some of these surveys studies focus on mobile phone's security issues [4][5] while others on mobile phone services, touching also security issues [6].

More surveys [7][8] focused on mobile phones security issues and in which degree these issues concern the users. The conclusion was that a major part of the participants are extremely concerned about security and don't want any of their private data to be available to 3rd party unauthorized users. Furthermore, users are interested in mobile services adoption only if the prices are low and the security framework tight enough [9].

Despite the importance of security in the given field, cyber security and safety education is left out from the educational system [10]. Users, in turn, do not know if their phones are secure or not [11].

3   Methodology

A very useful evaluation method for surveying user's practices is the use of multiple-choice questionnaires (i.e. in person delivery or e-mail questionnaires) [12][13]. Our survey was conducted using in-person (face to face) delivery technique, with a total of

7172 respondents participating in this survey. This method was selected from other alternatives because is more accurate and has a bigger degree of participation from the respondents (e-mail questionnaires usually are treated as spam mail from the respondents plus there is the risk of misunderstand some questions). Indeed, the approximate ratio of participation was 80% since the researchers were able to answer the questions of participants regarding the scope and the purpose of the survey. There was also a pilot study, conducted in the University of Ioannina, Greece, before the questionnaire was administered to the sample, to ensure the reliability and validity of the questionnaire. As stated, there are not available already validated questionnaires for the subject. Data entry, finally, took place using custom software [14] while processing was done with SPSS.

The target group of the survey was university students from ages mostly 18-26, incorporating both younger and older youth segments because these ages are more receptive to new technologies. Given the fact that nowadays a very high percentage of young people is studying, the sample is not deemed limited and can be considered as representative of a large percentage of general youth population. Furthermore, since they are still studying, it would be easier to participate in security education programs, possibly implemented in Universities.

We correlated the answers using the last question: "Are you informed about how the options and technical characteristics of your mobile phone affect its security?" which had the following possible answers: "A Very Much, B Much, C Moderately, D Not too much, E Not at all". Apart from the statistical interpretations, a simple mathematical formula was developed in the analysis of the security knowledge to produce numerical values from the multiple choice questionnaires. We weighted the responses with the following weights: Very Much: 4, Much: 3, Moderately: 2, Not much: 1, Not at all: 0 and then divided by the number of occurrences, in order to get a mean value that we called "Mean Security Feeling Value (MSFV)".

In addition to MSFV which was based on subjective answers, another, objective, metric was introduced, the "Mean Actual Security Value (MASV)". MASV was calculated as following: we added one point for each of the following practices, which are objectively correct: Having IMEI noted down, knowledge of lack of encryption icon, having SIM PIN enabled, using a screensaver password, having Bluetooth disabled, not lending the phone, not downloading software to the phone, using antivirus, not saving passwords in the phone and not saving personal data in the phone. The maximum score would hence be 10, since there were 10 specific questions.

4   Results

The questionnaire was divided in two parts. In the first part participants were asked demographic questions including gender, age and field of studies as well as some economic data including mobile phone usage, connection type and budget spent monthly on phone service. In the second part we introduced security knowledge and practice questions. In the following sections we present the results of categorizing users in regards to their security knowledge using the correlation and the simple formula described earlier. All of the findings presented are statistically significant at the Pearson's Chi-Square test p<0.05 level.

4.1   Demographics

53% of the participants were females and 47% were males. The Mean Security Feeling Value MSFV was 2.26 in the scale 0 to 4 (0 not at all, 4 very much), with minimal differences among genders. Correspondingly, the Mean Actual Security value MASV was calculated to be just 3.55 out of maximum value 10.

Most of the respondents, in turn, were aged 18-26 (75%). The MSFV was found to be somewhat higher in younger ages. Examining the field of study we discovered that soon to be medical doctors are feeling the most secure. the most informed (MSFV 2.69). Mathematics and Natural Science students with MSFV 1.89 were in the other end of spectrum the most worried ones. Engineers were in the middle of the range, with MSFV 2.24.

4.2   Economics

Proceeding to economics, participants were asked whether they are using a pre-paid or post-paid (contract) mobile phone connection. 42.4% of students are using a contract based subscription, a rather high percentage, while 13.6% have both prepaid and post-paid SIMs (Subscriber Identity Module). Users having both types of connection seem to be more worried about security issues.

Answering how much money they spent monthly, student mobile phone users had a wide range of financial capabilities. The leading 36.7% spends 11-20 Euros (currency converted) monthly while 30.5% spend less than 10 Euros. Only 9% spend 31-40 Euros and some 6.3% spend more than 40 Euros per month. The MSFV shows an interesting trend. It progressively gets lower as the bills get higher, from 2.33 (<=10 Euros bill) to 2.05 (31-40 Euros bill). Then, for users that spend more than 40 Euros it grows a little to 2.12. This is quite logical, since the more users spend, the more are concerned about the security of communication and possible fraud.

4.3   Security Specific Questions

Our fundamental research question was how "secure" users feel that mobile phone communication is. The majority (36.9%) replied "moderately" followed by 28.6% "much" (Figure 1). On the other hand, some 21.36% felt not too much or not at all sure they are secure. Using the simple formula described in Section 3 (Methodology), the mean security feeling value (MSFV) was 2.26, in the 0-4 scale (0 not at all, 4 very much).

In addition, students answered whether they are informed about how the options and the technical characteristics of their mobile phones affect the security of the latter and whether they are taking the necessary measures to mitigate the risks. The majority (30.8%) states that they are "moderately" informed while a large 15.8% believes that they are "not at all" informed (Figure 2).

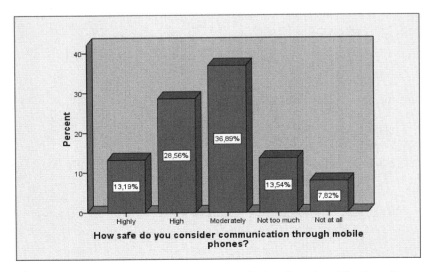

Fig. 1. How secure do you consider communication through mobile phones?

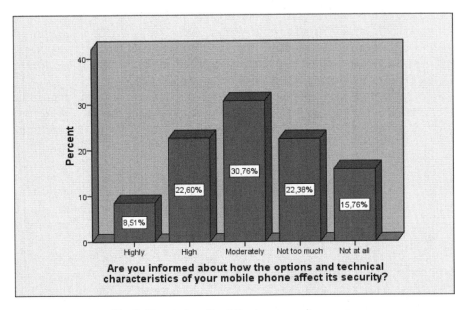

Fig. 2. Knowledge of mobile phone security aspects

Correlating MSFV value to awareness feeling (Figure 3), we see that there is an almost linear relationship between them. Users that feel very much informed believe that communication is very much secure. On the other end, users that do not feel informed are afraid that communication is not at all secure. At this point one can argue that excessive confidence can lead to "relaxation" of security practices. In addition, a campaign to enhance the security knowledge of users would lower their fear of communication insecurity, probably leading to greater phone usage and profits for the operators.

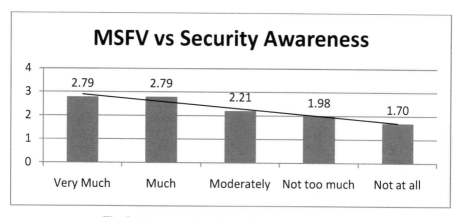

Fig. 3. Mean security feeling value vs. security feeling

There was an even better (negative) linear association between the subjective security feeling and the objective mean actual security value (Figure 4). Users that believe that mobile phone communication is very much secure have the lowest Mean Actual Security Value MASV (3.44). That is, there is a clear discrepancy between user opinions on security and actual security practices. The association grows linearly to the highest MASV of 3.84 for those that believe that communication is not secure at all. This group employs the most best practices, bit still fails in more than half (c.f. Methodology, where the maximum value of MASV is theoretically 10).

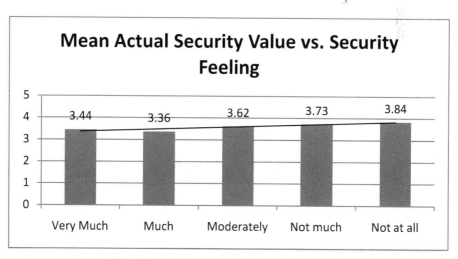

Fig. 4. Mean actual security value vs security feeling

Further correlating the responses to the type of operating system–O/S (advanced or not) proved that students owning phones with an advanced operating system believe they are more secure than those who actually own a phone without advanced O/S. There was a also a clear connection between increased backup frequency and security feeling.

At the same time, knowledge of the existence of the special icon that informs the user that his/her phone encryption has been disabled increased the safety feeling of users. In short, when A5 encryption is switched off or not supported, there is provision for handsets to display a special icon informing the user about the situation. Such an occurance can be attributed either to network's lack of encryption capability or to temporary failure/overloading. The same can happen when a malicious attacker is launching a man in the middle attack, impersonating network's base stations to deceit the handset into connecting with the fake base station instead of the legitimate one. The fraudster can then channel the communication through his own equipment, effectively intercepting it [15]. This finding is a clear explenation of how better User Interfaces can help enhance the subjective security feeling via an objective method.

5   Conclusion

As the findings of this survey support (using Pearson's Chi Square), users can be grouped in well defined categories according to the subjective statement of how secure they feel mobile phone communication is. These categories exhibit different values of a metric that we named "mean security feeling value". Further introducing a "mean actual security value", we counted how many "good" security practices they follow.

Comparing this (objective) value to their subjective security feeling we got very interesting results. There was a clear negative connection between feeling secure and actually being secure. Users that feel that mobile phone communication is secure, tend to be less cautious in their security practices, being actually less secure than they feel. This discrepancy between user opinions on security and actual security practices is a fact that should be addressed in order to minimize vulnerabilities and user exposure.

In regards to awareness, users that feel they are very much informed believe that communication is very much secure. On the other end, users that do not feel informed are afraid that communication is not at all secure. Excessive confidence could lead to "relaxation" of security practices while excessive fear certainly hinders technology adoption and especially mobile downloading.

As such, academia and industry should focus their security awareness campaigns and efforts in order to combat the false sense of security that users have. Moreover, given the growing usage of mobile phones to access the internet, it is of paramount importance to enhance the overall users' security levels that were found to be alarmingly low.

Closing, as there are not available any already validated questionnaires in regards to this specific research topic, our research, apart from revealing the situation, aims at providing a basis for the formulation of similar questionnaires for future use.

References

1. Lenhart, A.: Cell phones and American adults. Pew Research Center (2010), http://www.pewinternet.org (accessed: February 10, 2011)
2. Synovate: Global mobile phone survey shows the mobile is a 'remote control' for life. Synovate survey (2009), http://www.synovate.com (accessed: October 09, 2010)
3. comScore M:Metrics: Smarter phones bring security risks: Study (2008), http://www.comscore.com (accessed October 09, 2010)
4. Trend Micro: Smartphone Users Oblivious to Security. Trend Micro survey (2009), http://www.esecurityplanet.com (accessed October 09, 2010)
5. Goode Intelligence: Mobile security the next battleground (2009), http://www.goode/intelligence (accessed October 09, 2010)
6. Vrechopoulos, A.P., Constantiou, I.D., Sideris, I.: Strategic Marketing Planning for Mobile Commerce Diffusion and Consumer Adoption. In: Proceedings of M-Business 2002, CD (2002)
7. Androulidakis, I., Papapetros, D.: Survey Findings towards Awareness of Mobile Phones' Security Issues, Recent Advances in Data Networks, Communications, Computers. In: Proceedings of 7th WSEAS International Conference on Data Networks, Communications, Computers (DNCOCO 2008), pp. 130–135 (2008)
8. NCSA: 2010 NCSA/Norton by Symantec Online Safety Study (2010), http://www.staysafeonline.org (accessed: February 10, 2011)
9. Androulidakis, I., Basios, C., Androulidakis, N.: Surveying Users' Opinions and Trends towards Mobile Payment Issues. In: Techniques and Applications for Mobile Commerce - Proceedings of TAMoCo 2008. Frontiers in Artificial Intelligence and Applications, vol. 169, pp. 9–19 (2008)
10. National Cyber Security Alliance (NCSA): Schools Lacking Cyber Security and Safety Education (2009), http://www.staysafeonline.org (accessed October 09, 2010)
11. McAfee: Most Mobile Users Don't Know if They Have Security, McAfee-sponsored research (2008), http://www.esecurityplanet.com (accessed October 09, 2010)
12. Dillman, D.A.: Mail and Internet Surveys: The Tailored Design Method, 2nd edn. John Wiley & Sons (1999)
13. Pfleeger, S.L., Kitchenham, B.A.: Principles of Survey Research Part 1: Turning Lemons into Lemonade. ACM SIGSOFT Software Engineering Notes 26(6), 16–18 (2001)
14. Androulidakis, I., Androulidakis, N.: On a versatile and costless OMR system. WSEAS Transactions on Computers 4(2), 160–165 (2005)
15. Androulidakis, I.: Intercepting Mobile Phone Calls and Short Messages Using a GSM Tester. In: Kwiecień, A., Gaj, P., Stera, P. (eds.) CN 2011. CCIS, vol. 160, pp. 281–288. Springer, Heidelberg (2011)

A Collaborative System Offering Security Management Services for SMEs/mEs

Theodoros Ntouskas, Dimitrios Papanikas, and Nineta Polemi

Department of Informatics, University of Piraeus,
Karaoli & Dimitriou 80, 185 34 Piraeus, Greece
{tdouskas,papanik,dpolemi}@unipi.gr

Abstract. Although small, medium and micro enterprises (SMEs, mEs) play a decisive role in the European digital economy, they have been identified as one of the weakest links in information security. Identifying these security weaknesses and needs we parameterize our open collaborative environment STORM in order to offer a cost-efficient tool to the SMEs and mEs for self-managing their security.

Keywords: Collaboration, Security management, Vulnerability assessment, Risk Management, SMEs, mEs.

1 Introduction

Small, medium and micro enterprises (SMEs, mEs) play a decisive role in the European digital economy. Despite the increasing demand for their services as suppliers and sub-contractors in value chains of larger companies, they also have been identified as one of the weakest links in information security. Unable to comply with stricter security demands to the business value chains as established by large businesses and their customers, SMEs and mEs may find themselves losing business opportunities.

These enterprises (SMEs, mEs) cannot easily foster a more secure attitude in their business activities (causing them security problems and bridges) due to their peculiar characteristics [1]:

- Minimal resources on budget or time prevent SMEs and mEs to evaluate and ensure security and privacy as a continuing activity;
- Lack of trained and security educated personnel dedicated to the task of security and privacy;
- Education is considered as extra cost with no tangible benefit;
- Dependency on external security expertise, strong tendency to rely for their security / privacy strategy on external support, making sourcing decisions primarily on the basis of cost and vicinity;
- Lack of formal security policy and strategy, a plan determining the level of security needed as well as a policy outlining how to operate and maintain security is not a highly prioritized issue for management;

H. Jahankhani et al. (Eds.): ICGS3/e-Democracy 2011, LNICST 99, pp. 220–228, 2012.

- Lack of attention by their managers to address legislative or regulatory requirements, even if there is a penalty for not doing so;
- Lack of far-sightedness by the business managers thinking of themselves as of "no interest" from a global perspective ("We're too small - who would want to attack us?");
- Risk-agnostic of their ICT security risks involved, as well as the resulting business risks (e.g. operational loss, breach of statutory obligations, customer loss, and damage to reputation) and the extended risk to e-business as a whole.

Being the backbone of the economy and chief provider of jobs in many EU Member States, this may create severe damage to the innovativeness and competitiveness of European economy. Therefore, enhancing information security practices of SMEs and mEs has become an urgent need.

Existing well-defined and widely adopted security methodologies, standards and tools, are inadequate to meet the SMEs/mEs' basic characteristics. This paper contributes towards the urgent need to improve the current security and privacy level of these enterprises by adjusting an open, collaborative and trustful information security management system, STORM [2] considering the SMEs/mEs characteristics. In particular, the risk management methodology, STORM RM, is improved (originally presented by the authors in [3]) with a new step for practical vulnerability assessment (in order to achieve accurate vulnerability evaluations) and its main steps are customized targeting the SMEs/mEs characteristics. Also the enhanced STORM RM methodology [3] is implemented as a user friendly STORM service enabling the non security qualified SMEs/mEs personnel to use it in order to self-manage their security.

The rest of the paper is organized as follows: Section 2, assesses existing security management standards, methodologies and tools against SMEs and mEs security needs. Section 3, describes the STORM-RM enhanced methodology and service along with its basic modules, that are customized in order to help SMEs and mEs solve their particular security problems. Finally, Section 4 draws conclusions and future research directions.

2   Assessment of Security Management Approaches

Managing information security requires a continuous and systematic process of identifying, analyzing, mitigating, reporting and monitoring technical, operational and other types of security risks. This section assesses and outlines the weaknesses of the existing information security approaches when applied to SME/mEs.

A bundle of Security Management standards have been developed in order to help organizations to develop Information Security Management such as Cobit [4], ITIL [5], ISO-17799 [6] and ISO-27001 [7]. These standards define security requirements that cover many areas of the security lifecycle such as, ICT, operational, legal and organizational security requirements. Also, security standards have been developed to support the implementation of the required security controls, such as the ISO 27002 [8], Nist SP 800-53 [9]. Typically, setting up an Information Security Management System requires economic and human resources that are usually not available within the environment of SMEs/mEs who tend to consider security as a burden, rather than an asset in terms of profit. Although there exist automated tools to support security management lifecycle (such as ISO17799 Toolkit [10] or NetSPoC - Network Security Policy Compiler [11]), they are either too expensive for SMEs/mEs or in case of free tools, support capabilities for non-experts do not exist.

Existing RA/RM methodologies are targeted to bigger organizations and are too complex for mEs and SMEs since they do not possess the appropriate resources and expertise. The limitations of existing RA/RM methodologies can be summarized as follows:

- they are too complicated for the SMEs/mEs information systems requiring external, expensive, support. Simplifications and automated steps of the methodologies and the tools are still required to meet the SME/mEs characteristics;
- they are not supported by free of charge automated tools. Commercial tools supporting such methodologies are expensive and thus not likely to be used by micro and small enterprises;
- there is a lack of collaborative, multi-attribute, group-decision making approaches. More sophisticated approaches that enable collaboration, both within and between enterprises are required, especially for small and medium businesses with distributed IT systems.

Vulnerability assessment (VA) is yet another problem for the SME/mEs. Several initiatives have been launched releasing a set of methodologies and frameworks for VA. Some of these efforts emphasize on application security testing [12], [13] aiming at assessing and improving the security web applications while others mainly focus on network security testing by describing applied techniques and tools [14], [15], [16].

Also, open research communities have created open environments [17], [18], [19] that have been pre-configured to function as VA platforms. These platforms contain a set of open source/freeware tools that focus on testing information and communication systems. The main identified weaknesses of the existing VA approaches can be summarized as follows:

- there is a lack of VA methodologies, which would support the self implementation of a technical vulnerability assessment,
- although free of charge VA platforms and tools are in place, it is highly unlikely that SMEs and mEs will be able to trace, configure and utilize these tools, due to their lack of expertise and time availability. In addition, such open platforms do not usually come with instructions about how these environments have been configured or installation guidelines of the embedded tools.

There is an urgent need to develop targeted security management methodologies and tools addressing the SMEs/mEs characteristics and overcome the above mentioned obstacles.

3   STORM Security Management Service for SMEs/mEs

This section presents the targeted risk management service, STORM-RM, for the SMEs/mEs and its integration in the STORM environment.

STORM is an innovative, collaborative, cost effective and user friendly security consultancy environment (developed by the authors [2]) based on widely used collaborative web 2.0 technologies and can be used by different type of organizations in order to collaboratively manage their security, offering a pool of interactive services.

In order for SMEs/mEs to use STORM, the STORM Identity & Access Management system (STORM-IAM)[2] is customized in order to control the access to STORM services by SMEs and mEs users. Based on the STORM-IAM procedures and authentication mechanism, SMEs and mEs users will have access to the collaborative services, in order to cooperate and exchange information and ideas, work together in building open working groups, providing diverse opinions, thoughts and contributions and sharing information, experience and expertise. Notable components of these services are the Open and Private Forums and the Chat Rooms that support public and private discussions as well as the Open Knowledge area that acts as a knowledge source of security related information (e.g. security standards, specifications, reports, vulnerability assessment (VA) methodologies and frameworks, legal and regulatory directives and recommendations, open source and freeware tools and platforms, cases studies).

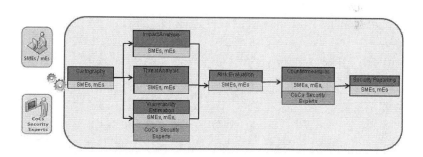

Fig. 1. STORM-RM Service for SMEs/mEs

Furthermore, the STORM Risk Management methodology (STORM-RM) (first presented in [3]) is enhanced, parameterized and implemented as a modular service (each step of the methodology is integrated independently and can be separately accessed depending on the users role/privileges reported in the STORM

IAM).The STORM-RM service (Fig. 1) consists of the following modules enabling SMEs/mEs to: capture all assets of their IT system (Cartography); identify their security critical asset(s) (Impact analysis); reveal their threats (Threat Analysis); estimate their vulnerabilities (Vulnerability Estimation) / risk levels (Risk Evaluation) of their assets and select the appropriate Countermeasures for their organization. The final collected outcome of the above modular steps is embedded in the Security Reporting.

Taking into account the specific characteristics (e.g. minimal resources / expertise) of the SMEs and mEs, STORM system is proposed to be hosted by an appropriate service provider (SP), e.g. the Chambers of Commerce (CoC). The CoCs are natural candidates to become STORM SPs since their fundamental responsibility is to serve the interests of their members (SMEs and mEs mostly). The CoCs mainly identify and underscore their members' needs by promoting, stimulating and supporting any initiative that aims at creating and developing innovative business services for them (and security is definitely a business driver). Their existing security team will embrace the STORM-RM service (Fig.1) which will be offered at low cost to their SMEs/mEs members.

In the following section, the STORM-RM enhanced methodology and the implemented service (in Fig.1) will be described.

3.1 STORM Risk Management Service (STORM-RM) for SMEs/mEs

STORM-RM service integrates and implements the STORM-RM methodology [3], which is based on Analytic Hierarchy Process, AHP [20] and is customized in order to address the specific characteristics of the SMEs and mEs. All the steps of STORM-RM methodology are implemented in an automated, self explanatory, user friendly manner by making use of interactive screens, online forms and help menus. The distinctive steps of the STORM-RM methodology are implemented as independent modules of the STORM-RM service (see Fig. 1). The autonomous modules of the STORM-RM service are:

Module 1 - Cartography: This module is implemented using online forms and consists of four (4) phases. In the *first phase*, all assets of ICS (e.g. servers, rooters, applications, users etc.) are reported and categorized in four main groups (hardware, software, services and participants). In the *second phase*, each service is associated with its interactive hardware, software and participant(s), in order to report the interdependencies and interconnection of assets. In the *third phase*, installed security controls (e.g. back-ups/ access control policies) (if any) are reported. The appropriateness of these controls are assessed against the ISO-27001 [7] proposed controls as well as their implementation maturity (e.g. fully, partly or not implemented). In the *fourth phase*, weights (opinion priorities) of all participants (administrators, managers, end users) are calculated, according to their role in the organization and the services that they use. To summarize the output of this module will be: all assets categorized in four groups (hardware, software, services, participants) with technical and operational characteristics;

all assets interconnections; all already installed controls and their assessment in terms of appropriateness and maturity; opinion weights of the organization participants (these weights will be used in the impact and risk analysis).

Module 2 - Impact Analysis: Distinct online questionnaires, stored in the STORM Content Management System (CMS), evaluating the security importance (taking into consideration the consequences of security loss i.e. loss of availability, integrity, confidentiality) for each asset are assigned automatically by the STORM tool to different groups of participants depending on their organizational role (administrators, managers, end users) and their access rights provided by the STORM-IAM. The group impact level is calculated by the STORM-RM automated multi-criteria algorithm [3], taking into account the weight of each participant of the organization. The output of this module is a list with all the assets, A_i, and their Impact security levels, $I(A_i)$, with possible values: Very Low = VL, Medium= M, High = H, Very High = VH.

Module 3 - Threat Analysis: In this module, the stored list in the STORM CMS with all possible threats categorized accordingly (e.g. physical, technical etc.) and correlated with different type of assets (e.g. server, application, router etc.) is used as follows: Each participant prioritizes the listed threats, corresponding to an asset, using online forms and then these priorities are taken into account in order to calculate the final group threat level for each asset. The threat priorities are calculated by the automated STORM-RM algorithm which in return estimates the Threat value, $T(A_i)$, of each asset, A_i. The results of this module are depicted with interactive screens that help participants to view which threats are more possible to occur for every asset of the organization.

Module 4 - Vulnerability Estimation: In this module the Vulnerability Assessment (VA) and the estimation of the Final Vulnerability level (FV) for each asset A_i are calculated using four (4) distinct phases. *Vulnerability Identification:* During this phase, every threat is connected with corresponding vulnerabilities and each asset A_i is examined in terms of the vulnerabilities revealed from their correlated threats. *Theoretical Vulnerability Level:* Every user u_j compares, in this step, the vulnerabilities assigned to each asset A_i in order to calculate its Theoretical Vulnerability level, $TV_{u_j}(A_i)$ which in turn are collected within the STORM group decision tree [18] in order to calculate the Group Theoretical Vulnerability level (the resulting level from all u_j' s for a specific A_i), $TV(A_i)$. *Practical Vulnerability (PV) Level:* Taking into consideration the list of assets and their Impacts levels, A_i, $I(A_i)$, from Module 2, PV assessment is executed only for the assets with very high Impact level, i.e. $I(A_i)$=VH. Depending on the asset type (e.g. hardware, software etc.), STORM-RM suggests the appropriate open source, online, vulnerability assessment (VA) tool(s), stored in the STORM-CMS, to be used by the users; these VA tools are stored in the STORM-CMS. Security consultants of the service provider assess the results, which are exported by security testing tools, and estimate the Practical Vulnerability, PV (A_i), level of each tested asset A_i. *Final Vulnerability Level:* In this final phase, the Final Vulnerability Level, $FV(A_i)$, is calculated for each asset A_i with Impact level $I(A_i)$= VH, as the maximum between the Theoretical

Vulnerability Level, TV(A_i), and the Practical Vulnerability Level, PV(A_i); for these assets A_i with Impact level I(A_i) < VH, the Final Vulnerability Level, FV(A_i), equals with the Theoretical Vulnerability Level, TV(A_i), as described in the following formula:

$$FV(Ai) = \begin{cases} \max(TV(A_i), PV(A_i)) & if I(A_i) = VH \\ TV(A_i) & if I(A_i) < VH. \end{cases} \tag{1}$$

Module 5 - Risk Evaluation: After collecting all values for Impact, I(A_i), Threat, T(A_i), and Final Vulnerability, FV(A_i), levels, the risk value, R(A_i), of each asset, A_i, is calculated here as the product:

$$R(A_i) = I(A_i) * T(A_i) * FV(A_i) \tag{2}$$

SMEs/mEs participants have the capability to see through online forms the results of STORM-RM risk analysis for all assets and decide which is the risk threshold (e.g. if R(A_i) > 6 then A_i is security critical) in order to continue with the next module of the security countermeasures' selection.

Module 6 - Countermeasures: There is a list of different type countermeasures (e.g. technical, physical etc.) that are appropriate for different type of asset (e.g. servers, rooters, application) stored in the STORM -CMS. SMEs/mEs participants are able to view all choices and select (using on-line forms) the appropriate countermeasures that wish to implement, taking into account different criteria (e.g. economical, business, legal, technical, performance) from their own business perspective. Each user of the above groups gives priorities through on-line judgments for all the recommended countermeasures of each asset. The final selection of countermeasures is the result of the automated AHP algorithm that STORM-RM uses [3], according to the participants' priorities. The outcome of this module is a list of the selected appropriate countermeasures that is implemented in order to minimize the identified risks.

Module 7 - Security Reporting: All security reports (produced in each module) can be generated as online growing documents in various representation formats and with personalized content (e.g. risk reports for all assets with characteristics, threats and risks interconnected with a particular service).

4   Conclusions and Future Work

SMEs and mEs have to take a more strategic comprehensive view of information security. They should treat it as a factor that guarantees and enhances their viability in a competitive, turbulent and diverse globalized e-market. In this context, STORM system, via the provision of a bundle of innovative security and privacy services offers these enterprises several benefits, such as increasing their competitiveness by strengthening their ICT security and data privacy level of their electronic services in a demonstrative way; respecting the regulations and standards and thus offering them competitive advantage in the area of trustful e-business in a cost-efficient, economic and collaborative way. In addition,

STORM-RM service improves their business processes by providing a simplified, integrated and comprehensive framework for the identification, assessment and treatment of security and privacy risks improving their ICT-based business processes.

Future work includes the integration of theoretical and practical vulnerability assessment on an upper level. Also STORM RM service will be implemented at the S-PORT system [21] and will be tested by three Greek commercial Ports (Piraeus Port Authority S.A., Thessaloniki Port Authority S.A, Municipal Port Fund Mykonos).

Acknowledgements. This work has been performed in the framework of the GSRT/SYNERGASIA/S-Port project (09SYN-72-650) (http://s-port.unipi.gr).

References

1. Reynolds, D., Rabey, K., Polemi, N.: Analysing mes needs and expectations in the area of information security. ENISA report (2008),
   http://www.enisa.europa.eu/act/sr/reports/
   micro-enterprises/files/wg-micro-report
2. Ntouskas, T., Pentafronimos, G., Papastergiou, S.: STORM - Collaborative Security Management Environment. In: Ardagna, C.A., Zhou, J. (eds.) WISTP 2011. LNCS, vol. 6633, pp. 320–335. Springer, Heidelberg (2011)
3. Ntouskas, T., Polemi, N.: STORM-RM: A collaborative and multicriteria risk management methodology. Int. J. Multicriteria Decision Making 2(2), 159–177 (2012)
4. COBIT4.1: It governance control framework. IT Governance Institute (2007),
   http://www.isaca.org
5. Clinch, J.: Itil v3 and information security, ogc white paper (May 2009),
   http://www.best-managementpractice.com
6. ISO/IEC:17799: Information technology - security techniques - code of practice for information security management (2005), http://www.iso.org
7. ISO/IEC:27001: Information technology - security techniques - information security management systems - requirements (2005), http://www.iso.org
8. ISO/IEC:27002: Information technology - security techniques - code of practice for information security management (2005), http://www.iso.org
9. NIST SP800-53: Recommended Security Controls for Federal Information Systems and Organization. NIST Special Publication 800-53,
   http://csrc.nist.gov/publications/PubsSPs.html
10. ISO17799: Toolkit, http://www.iso17799-made-easy.com/
11. NetSPoC: Network Security Policy Compiler, http://netspoc.berlios.de/
12. Agarwwal, A., Bellucci, D., Coronel, A., DiPaola, S., Fedon, G., Goodman, A., Heinrich, C., Horvath, K., Ingrosso, G., Liverani, R.S., Kuza, A., Luptak, P., Mavituna, F., Mella, M., Meucci, M., Morana, M., Parata, A., Su, C., Sureddy, H.S., Roxberry, M., Stock, A.: Owasp testing guide v3.0 (2008),
    http://www.mare-system.de/whitepaper
13. Stock, A.V.D., Lowery, D., Rook, D., Cruz, D., Keary, E., Williams, J., Chapman, J., Morana, M.M., Prego, P.: Owasp code review guide v1.1 (2008),
    https://www.owasp.org

14. NIST SP800-42: Guideline on Network Security Testing - Recommendations of the National Institute of Standards and Technology. NIST, http://www.iwar.org.uk/comsec/resources/netsec-testing/sp800-42.pdf
15. NIST SP800-115: Technical guide to information security testing and assessment. NIST, http://csrc.nist.gov/publications/nistpubs/800-115/SP800-115.pdf
16. Orrey, K., Lawson, L.J.: Penetration testing framework(ptf) v0.21, http://www.vulnerabilityassessment.co.uk
17. Backtrack, http://www.backtrack-linux.org/
18. Net Tools 5.0, http://www.mabsoft.com/nettools.htm
19. Samurai Web Testing Framework, http://samurai.inguardians.com/
20. Saaty, T.L.: Decision making with the analytic hierarchy process. Int. J. Service Sciences 1, 83–98 (2008)
21. S-PORT: S-port project, http://s-port.unipi.gr/

A Situational Awareness Architecture for the Smart Grid

Anastasia Mavridou and Mauricio Papa

Institute for Information Security,
Computer Science Department, University of Tulsa,
800 S. Tucker Dr., Tulsa, OK 74104, USA
{anastasia-mavridou,mauricio-papa}@utulsa.edu

Abstract. Components of the electric power grid that were traditionally deployed in physically isolated networks, are now using IP based, interconnected networks to transmit Supervisory Control and Data Acquisition (SCADA) messages. SCADA protocols were not designed with security in mind. Therefore, in order to enhance security, access control and risk mitigation, operators need detailed and accurate information about the status, integrity, configuration and network topology of SCADA devices. This paper describes a comprehensive system architecture that provides situational awareness (SA) for SCADA devices and their operations in a Smart Grid environment. The proposed SA architecture collects and analyzes industrial traffic and stores relevant information, verifies the integrity and the status of field devices and reports identified anomalies to operators.

Keywords: Cyber Security, Smart Grid, Situational Awareness, SCADA.

1 Introduction

The electric power grid is responsible for reliably and efficiently delivering electricity from generation to the end consumer. Three major components make up the grid: electricity generation sources, transmission system and distribution system. Electric power transmission refers to the bulk transfer of electrical energy, 100 kV and above, from power plants to distribution substations located close to population centers. On the other hand, electric power distribution, which is the final stage of the delivery network, refers to the delivery of electricity from distribution substations to end consumers. Since no energy storage mechanism is used, electric energy requires that system operators control electricity flow, by balancing power generation and consumption, using SCADA systems [1]. Hence, the electric infrastructure is highly dependent on SCADA systems that are responsible for monitoring and controlling all functions in the grid.

The current power grid is based on requirements written in 1950 and it is already considered to be an outmoded, inefficient, vulnerable infrastructure. There have been at least five massive blackouts over the past 40 years that illustrate

H. Jahankhani et al. (Eds.): ICGS3/e-Democracy 2011, LNICST 99, pp. 229–236, 2012.
© Institute for Computer Sciences, Social Informatics and Telecommunications Engineering 2012

problems associated with the power grid [2]. These blackouts have occurred mainly due to faults at power stations, damage to power lines and substations, unusually high demand and others. Also, a cyber attack may have a huge impact on the functionality of the power grid that can result in a blackout. In fact, the massive North East blackout of 2003 has been linked to the propagation of the MSBlaster worm [3] [4].

The need to address these issues, as well as higher demand for quality and availability, penetration of renewable energy resources and the increased threat of terrorist attacks has given birth to the Smart Grid. The Smart Grid is expected to deliver electricity from multiple suppliers to end consumers using two-way communications, involving multiple distributed intelligent entities and including large-scale real-time data collection capability [5]. This large-scale, accurate, and timely data collection and fusion of the monitored processes of the Smart Grid can provide SA. In particular, NIST states that "the goals of situational awareness are to understand and ultimately optimize the management of power-network components, behavior, and performance, as well as to anticipate, prevent, or respond to problems before disruptions can arise" [6]. This paper describes a SA architecture intended to provide Smart Grid operators with a detailed view of the network topology along with information about the configuration, status, critical states and traffic of SCADA devices.

2   Smart Grid Architecture

As technology continues to advance, the power grid is being upgraded with new technologies and additional IT systems and networks. The importance of upgrading the current electricity network is emphasized in President Obama's speech: "...my administration is making major investments in our information infrastructure: laying broadband lines to every corner of America, building a smart electric grid to deliver energy more efficiently..." [7]. The National Energy Technology Laboratory (NETL) [8] outlined the functionalities of this new electric grid. According to NETL [9], the Smart Grid self-heals, motivates and includes the consumer, resists physical and cyber attacks, increases power quality, accommodates all generation and storage options, enables new products, services and markets, optimizes assets and operates efficiently.

Smart grid modernization is an ongoing process. Smart meters are currently being installed on buildings that enable two-way communication between the utility and end customers. Also, other smart components are added to provide the system operator with SA and the ability to reroute electricity in case of problems in transmission lines. As a result, operators can react and solve system problems in a timely manner to minimize any negative impacts. The main components of a Smart Grid (Figure 1) are electric power generators, electric power substations, transmission and distribution lines, controllers, smart meters, collector nodes, and distribution and transmission control centers [10]. Power generators and electric power substations use electronic controllers to control the generation and the flow of electric power.

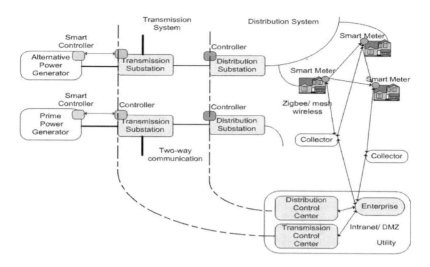

Fig. 1. Block diagram of typical smart grid components and connections

End consumers and collector nodes may communicate through a Zigbee or similar mesh wireless two-way communication network. Two-way communication paths are also used between collectors and the utility. Collector nodes communicate with the utility mostly using the Advanced Metering Infrastructure (AMI) [11] possibly via the Internet. A utility's intranet includes a Demilitarized Zone (DMZ) to provide extra protection. Additionally, communication between the transmission and distribution substations and the utility's control center facilitates operation. Like existing power grids, a Smart Grid includes a control system that accommodates intelligent monitoring mechanisms and keeps track of all electric power flowing in a more detailed and flexible way.

3 Security and Reliability Standards and Requirements

The new functionalities provided by the Smart Grid also introduce new security risks due to the transition from legacy (closed) to IP-based (open) networks. In the past, industrial systems were considered to be secure mainly due to the use of proprietary controls and limited connectivity. Smart Grid expands the number and the exposure of SCADA systems, therefore making the protection of these systems a major concern [12].

The National Institute of Standards and Technology (NIST) Cyber Security Coordination Task Group (CSCTG) was established to ensure consistency. NIST, especially after the publication of the NISTIR 7628 document [13], continues to play an important role in shaping Smart Grid Cyber Security research. According to NISTIR 7628, increasing the complexity of the grid through interconnected networks could increase the risk of private data exposure to potential adversaries and unintentional user errors.

The Federal Energy Regulatory Commission (FERC) [14] is responsible for protecting the reliability of the high voltage transmission system. Its mission is to "assist consumers in obtaining reliable, efficient and sustainable energy services at a reasonable cost through appropriate regulatory and market means". In early 2008, FERC approved mandatory critical infrastructure protection reliability standards designed to protect the nation's bulk power system against potential disruptions from cyber security threats.

These reliability standards were developed by the North American Electrical Reliability Corporation (NERC) [15], which FERC has designated as the Electric Reliability Organization (ERO). These standards specify the minimum requirements to support the reliability of the electrical system. NERC's authority is limited to the electrical generation resources and transmission lines. The set of standards addressing cyber-security in the power grid are known as NERC Critical Infrastructure Protection (CIP) standards [16]. NERC requires power transmission companies to be compliant with reliability standards. Table 1 lists and briefly describes the CIP Reliability standards as of June 2011.

Table 1. NERC CIP reliability standards

Number	Title	Description
CIP-001-1a	Sabotage Reporting	Entities are required to maintain procedures for recognizing and making appropriate personnel aware of sabotage attempts.
CIP-002-4	CS-Critical Cyber Asset Identification	Creates risk-based assessment methods for identifying Critical Cyber Assets within a bulk power system facility.
CIP-003-4	CS-Security Management Controls	A cyber security policy ensuring compliance with the other CIP standards must be created and implemented.
CIP-004-4	CS-Personnel and Training	On-going awareness program to reinforce security practices.
CIP-005-4a	CS-Electronic Security Perimeter	Every critical cyber asset must be within an electronic security perimeter (ESP) with documented access points.
CIP-006-4c	CS-Physical Security of Critical Cyber Assets	Requires an annually reviewed security plan approved by a senior manager or delegate for a physical security perimeter (PSP).
CIP-007-4	CS-Systems Security Management	Test procedures must be created to ensure that changes to cyber assets do not adversely affect existing cyber security controls.
CIP-008-4	CS-Incident Reporting and Response Planning	Requires annually reviewed security incident response plans.
CIP-009-4	CS-Recovery Plans for Critical Cyber Assets	Requires the creation and annual review of recovery plans.

Furthermore, SA is recognized as a key enabling functionality for the Smart Grid by FERC [17]. Table 2 summarizes the SA requirements that should be satisfied according to [18].

Table 2. Situational awareness requirements

	Requirement	Description
1	Situation perception	Be aware of the current situation. Situation recognition and identification.
2	Impact assessment	Be aware of the impact of the attack. Vulnerability analysis.
3	Situation tracking	Be aware of how situations evolve.
4	Trend and intent analysis	Be aware of actor (adversary) behavior.
5	Causality analysis	Be aware of why and how the current situation is caused.
6	Quality assessment	Be aware of the quality of the collected situation awareness information items.
7	Future assessment	Assess plausible futures of the current situation.

4   Situational Awareness Architecture

The proposed SA architecture provides operators with comprehensive knowledge of the topology and status of SCADA devices and their operations in a Smart Grid, and also allows detection of suspicious incidents. Electric power substations, which are important components of the Smart Grid, contain a number of critical assets such as transformers, circuit breakers, SCADA devices and safety devices. Optimizing the maintenance of these assets is a challenging task. The Critical Infrastructure Lab at the University of Tulsa designed and constructed a scaled-down electric power substation prototype to validate the approach and test functionality.

The design of the substation prototype closely resembles the topology of a ring-type substation with redundant lines. The substation uses power transformers rated at 3KVA and has two three-phase inputs at 240 VAC that are subsequently transformed to 208 VAC. Furthermore, the substation uses Programmable Logic Controllers (PLCs) that communicate over Ethernet using the Distributed Network Protocol (DNP3) protocol [19]. According to Electric Power Research Institute (EPRI) [20], over 75% of North American electric utilities employ DNP3 to control their power systems. DNP3 is an insecure industrial protocol and as a result, security and access control in DNP3 implementations is a major concern.

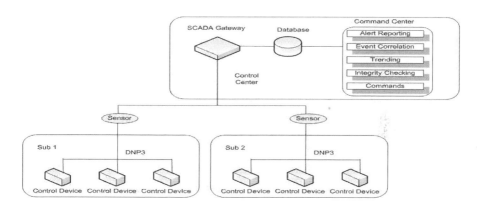

Fig. 2. Situational awareness architecture

The proposed SA architecture (Figure 2) incorporates a SCADA gateway, a database and a command center located in the control center and a number of network sensors placed at strategic points in the field.

Network Sensors. The network sensors operate in promiscuous mode to capture network traffic of interest. As a result, the sensors receive information about network topology, unit configuration, functionality and state of the devices, requested operations, function codes and other important pieces of information.

The sensors timestamp the collected traffic, analyze it and forward relevant information to the SCADA gateway. In addition, they may also help in locating attack signatures to identify malicious traffic. Therefore, simple attacks can be detected where the intent is to interfere with the state of a single field device. Additionally, the sensors receive commands from the command center through the SCADA gateway. Upon receiving a specific command, a sensor may configure its network interface, start and stop scanning activities or generate a traffic analysis report.

SCADA Gateway. The SCADA gateway collects the data gathered by sensors, translates them from different protocols into a canonical format and then forwards them to the database. Communication may also flow in the opposite direction to forward commands concerning configuration settings, scanning and generating reports from the command center to the sensors.

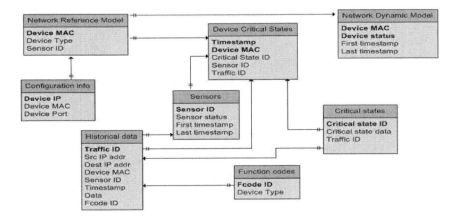

Fig. 3. Database scheme

Database. The database provides a buffering interface between the SCADA gateway and the command center. The traffic stored in the database is used by the command center to provide state based traffic analysis. The database scheme (Figure 3) includes information about system configuration, historical data, the critical states, the network reference model and the network dynamic model. The configuration info contains the configuration settings of the devices such as network addresses, protocols and function codes. Historical information, indicative of inter-task communications data exchange, is stored in the historical data table. In general, network transactions are stored indefinitely for post incident retrieval since they may help in further causality analysis and impact assessment. The network reference model contains, time invariant information such as the network topology. Its counterpart, the dynamic network model includes real time information related to the actual and current status of the field devices.

The critical states table contains the rules that describe all these states, as well as other fault conditions of the system.

Command Center. The command center is a collection of applications that provide facilities for alert reporting, event correlation, integrity checking, trending and command generation. State based traffic analysis is achieved by event correlation and prior knowledge of the critical system states. The command center verifies whether the system may enter into a critical state, as defined by the associated table in the database, and raises an alert. This approach will allow security practitioners to detect complex and coordinated attacks on industrial control systems that may have a negative impact on overall availability and integrity. Time stamps are key elements in supporting the development of an accurate incident timeline from stored transactions. This will help operators in the command center to better recognize adversary intents, capabilities and trends, understand system vulnerabilities and identify new threats.

5   Conclusions and Future Work

A SA architecture designed for SCADA systems in a Smart Grid environment was presented. The proposed architecture combines traditional signature-based techniques and a state analysis technique. More specifically, the architecture aims at satisfying the requirements included in Table 2 in terms of situation recognition (requirements 1 and 6), situation comprehension (requirements 2 and 5) and situation projection (requirements 3, 4 and 7) [18]. Furthermore, Table 3 describes areas in which the proposed SA architecture can help with NERC CIP 001 through 009 compliance efforts.

Table 3. Compliance with the NERC CIP standards

NERC standard	SA architecture
CIP-001-1a	Identifies incidents in real-time monitoring, classifying and alarming on attacks.
CIP-003-4	Provides reporting that helps operation management, security and compliance related decision making.
CIP-004-4	Enhances personnel training by providing situational awareness. Covers areas of awareness that personnel usually cannot.
CIP-005-4a	Monitors the ESP and identifies changes on ESP devices while enhances access control. Alerts upon detecting unauthorized access and correlates detected vulnerabilities with other data to provide cyber vulnerability assessments.
CIP-006-4c	Enhances physical access controls by monitoring the access systems.
CIP-007-4	Monitors and correlates incident data across all devices and enhances Systems Security Management by providing a centralized view of the system.
CIP-008-4	Provides a centralized system for collecting, reporting and responding/alarming on critical events.
CIP-009-4	Provides early warning system failures that may improve response time and diagnostic abilities.

Further research objectives include modeling, simulating and experimentally verifying the behavior of the electric substation control system and providing methods to link the physical and cyber assets of the system. As the architecture is moved from design to implementation, test strategies for validating security and reliability properties of the modeled assets will have to be developed.

References

1. National Communications System: Supervisory Control and Data Acquisition (SCADA) Systems, Technical Information Bulletin NCS TIB 04-1 (2004)
2. U.S. Department of Energy: The Smart Grid: An Introduction (2008), http://www.oe.energy.gov/1165.htm
3. Carnegie Mellon University's Computer Emergency Response Team: Advisory CA-2003-20 W32/Blaster Worm (2003)
4. Verton, D.: Blaster Worm Linked to Severity of Blackout, Computerworld (2003)
5. National Energy Technology Laboratory for the U.S. Department of Energy Office of Electricity Delivery and Energy Reliability: The NETL Modern Grid Initiative Powering our 21st-Century Economy: A Compendium of Smart Grid Technologies (2009)
6. National Institute of Standards and Technology: NIST Framework and Roadmap for Smart Grid Interoperability Standards Release 1.0, NIST Special Publication 1108 (2010)
7. President Obama: Remarks by the President on Securing our Nation's Cyber Infrastructure (2009), http://www.whitehouse.gov/the_press_office/Remarks-by-the-President-on-Securing-Our-Nations-Cyber-Infrastructure/
8. National Energy Technology Laboratory, http://www.netl.doe.gov/about/
9. National Energy Technology Laboratory for the U.S. Department of Energy Office of Electricity Delivery and Energy Reliability: The NETL Modern Grid Initiative Powering our 21st-Century Economy: Modern Grid Benefits (2007)
10. U.S. Department of Energy Office of Electricity Delivery and Energy Reliability: Study of Security Attributes of Smart Grid Systems – Current Cyber Security Issues (2009)
11. National Energy Technology Laboratory for the U.S. Department of Energy Office of Electricity Delivery and Energy Reliability: Advanced Metering Infrastructure (2008)
12. Electric Power Research Institute: Report to NIST on Smart Grid Interoperability Standards Roadmap, Contract No. SB1341-09-CN-0031-Deliverable 7 (2009)
13. National Institute of Standards and Technology: Guidelines for Smart Grid Cyber Security, Vol.1, Smart Grid Cyber Security Strategy, Architecture, and High-Level Requirements, NISTIR 7628 (2010)
14. Federal Energy Regulatory Commission, http://www.ferc.gov/about/ferc-does.asp
15. North American Electric Reliability Corporation, http://www.nerc.com
16. North American Electric Reliability Corporation: Reliability Standards for the Bulk Electric Systems of North America (2010), http://www.nerc.com/files/Reliability_Standards_Complete_Set.pdf
17. Federal Energy Regulatory Commission: Smart Grid Policy (2009)
18. Barford, P., Dacier, M., Dietterich, T.G., Fredrikson, M., Giffin, J., Jajodia, S., Jha, S., Li, J., Liu, P., Ning, P., Ou, X., Song, D., Strater, L., Swarup, V., Tadda, G., Wang, C., Yen, J.: Cyber SA: Situational Awareness for Cyber Defense. In: Jajodia, S., Liu, P., Swarup, V., Wang, C. (eds.) Cyber Situational Awareness, pp. 3–13. Springer (2010)
19. Curtis, K.: A DNP3 Protocol Primer, Technical report. DNP Users Group (2005), www.dnp.org/About/DNP3%20Primer%20Rev%20A.pdf
20. Electric Power Research Institute: DNP Security Development, Evaluation and Testing Project Opportunity (2008)

Alleviating SMEs' Administrative Burdens: The Rural Inclusion Initiative

Maria Ntaliani, Constantina Costopoulou, and Alexander B. Sideridis

Informatics Laboratory, Agricultural University of Athens, 75 Iera Odos St.,
11855 Athens, Greece
{ntaliani,tina,as}@aua.gr

Abstract. Reducing the administrative burdens of businesses and citizens comprises a major area of e-government benefit. Reducing SMEs' efforts to find information on particular public services is a challenge for the European Union. This aim can be achieved through semantic services along with an innovative training approach for public administration employees and SMEs. The paper presents the preliminary results of the administrative burden measurement for rural SMEs in the Spanish region of La Rioja, as well as planning and tools for collaborative training of public authorities in using three platforms (eGovTube, RuralObservatory 2.0, and eGovPortal) for the administrative simplification of public services in European rural regions.

Keywords: Electronic government, rural SMEs, administrative burdens, learning objects, collaborative training.

1   Introduction

Regulation encumbers citizens and businesses with costs that are connected with the following actions: finding which regulations are needed for compliance, understanding regulation and finding ways to comply with it, and complying with regulation [1]. Administrative burdens are costs incurred by businesses for collecting information for their action or production so as to meet legal obligations. With Small and Medium Enterprises (SMEs) comprising the backbone of European economy, European Union's (EU) concern on the reduction of their administrative burdens has been increased over the last decade. Administrative burdens comprise a significant business constraint, particularly today that SMEs have fewer resources and need to invest to remain competitive [2].

It is a fact that among others, SMEs' administrative burdens are closely related with their efforts to find information on particular public services. A great part of this information regards the informational phase, namely things that an SME should know before executing a particular public service. For instance, the informational phase concerns the SME's eligibility to perform a service; the Public Authorities (PAs) that are responsible for it; and what kind of documents the SME should adduce so as to apply for it. The process of searching for and retrieving this knowledge, either

H. Jahankhani et al. (Eds.): ICGS3/e-Democracy 2011, LNICST 99, pp. 237–244, 2012.

performed by the SME or by an expert (e.g. accountant, lawyer) on the SME's behalf, costs in terms of time and money. In many cases, this process can be repeated several times throughout a year, due to change of laws and regulations or in need of clarifications [3]. It has been estimated that SMEs spend on average 27,500 USD per year so as to comply with tax, employment and environmental regulations, which is about 4% of their annual turnover and incurs a cost of 4,000 USD per employee [1].

Already, various projects and initiatives from various countries have aimed at measuring and reducing administrative burdens. Such examples include: the "Measurement Project" in the UK for measuring the administrative burdens of businesses in complying with tax regulation; the "Bureaucracy Reduction and Better Regulation" program in Germany for reducing the administrative burdens of SMEs by 25% by the end of 2011; and the new initiative by EURinSPECT (www. eurinspect.eu) for the elimination of obstacles of cross-border procedures in the healthcare sector and the cross-border collaboration between hospitals in the Netherlands, Belgium and Germany [2].

In this context, "Rural-Inclusion (RI): e-Government Lowering Administrative Burdens for Rural Businesses" (www.rural-inclusion.eu) a project supported by the European Commission under the Competitiveness and Innovation Framework Programme has been launched. It aims at deploying an innovative infrastructure (e.g. software, models, and services) that will facilitate the offering of semantic Web services by PAs in rural areas for the informational phase. In particular, RI aims at addressing PAs' longstanding challenges, such as easing the discovery of public services by users-rural SMEs, personalizing the service that the user needs to have access to, providing all necessary information for the execution of the particular service and checking the eligibility of the user for receiving the service. Also, RI proposes a collaborative training for helping PAs in implementing e-government services for supporting the informational phase.

For succeeding these objectives, RI adopts, adapts, and deploys in a rural setting the Service Oriented Architecture (SOA) paradigm, implemented through state-of-the-art semantic Web technology and supported by rigorous and reusable public administration domain analysis and modelling. In the context of RI, the administrative burdens imposed to businesses when performing particular public services are alleviated through the implementation of an online dialogue of the public services.

The users of the RI services are in five European rural regions, rural Spain, the Greek island of Chios, rural Latvia, rural France and overseas, in the region of Martinique. At regional/national level, the directly involved user groups will be rural SMEs, PAs, and e-government service technology providers and innovators.

Thus, the scope of the paper is to present the RI approach for the administrative burden measurement, as well as planning and tools for PAs' training in using three platforms for the administrative simplification of public services. Therefore, the structure of the paper is as follows: in the next section the initial measurement of administrative burdens for the case of La Rioja SMEs is presented. In section 3, the approach for training PAs is apposed. Lastly, some conclusions are given.

2 Measuring Administrative Burdens of Spanish SMEs

Various initiatives in the EU and internationally for measuring and reducing the administrative burdens have been proposed. Nowadays, there is a continuously increasing interest and effort towards the particular issue by different bodies (public authorities, private organizations etc.) in terms of level of administration, aims and business sector, and models and tools. The most well know tool is the Standard Cost Model (SCM) (www.administrative-burdens.com). It enables the assessment of the cost of "red tape" and identification of the benefits by administrative cost reduction. It produces transparent measurements, which construct an essential tool against administrative burdens and complex legislation. It must be noted that the SCM has already been widely used globally, as well as by many EU countries. In the context of RI project the SCM has also been used.

In the first stage of the RI initiative, the administrative burdens measurement concerns "Measuring the Cost of Administrative Activities". It is twofold:

- Firstly, it depicts the profile of rural SMEs regarding the following: (a) ICT literacy (use of personal computers and the Internet), (b) ways of transacting with public agencies and (c) knowledge and use of e-government services at national and European level;
- Secondly, it measures the cost of all administrative activities performed by rural SMEs in order to comply with the obligations of the specific public services that have been selected to be measured.

It must be noted that this measurement will provide strong evidence on the significance of information cost of SMEs relevantly to the total cost of the public service. In order to fulfil the requirements of the measurement a specialized questionnaire has been prepared. Below, the questionnaire analysis for the case of La Rioja is presented and particularly for the "Provision of grant from SRE to unemployed persons for starting up a business" public service.

Servicio Riojano de Empleo (SRE) provides a subsidy to facilitate the financial capacity of unemployed people in becoming self-employed workers. Although the Spanish government provides various electronic services regarding the creation of a new business process (e.g. application submission, guidelines for filling out the application), citizens who want to start up a new business are not familiar with the different legal business types that exist and thus they are not able to choose among them [4].

The measurement has been conducted during the first semester of 2010. The sample consisted of thirteen SMEs, namely one medium, eleven small and one micro. They have been represented by owners, managers and internal professionals. Their line of business regards legal advice, tax and labour services, associationism, driving school, research and development, trade of building materials, health, dental clinic, technological centre, consulting and computer services, audiovisual production, constructions and development of management software. All SMEs acquire personal computers and Internet connection, used daily for searching for information, communicating and offering product information and possibilities for ordering them.

Face to face meetings, the Internet, the email and telephone are the main transaction ways with public agencies. More than 30% have some knowledge regarding the existence of online public services for SMEs at European level, namely services for receiving grants. Concerning national services, they are aware of many, such as receiving grants, tax and social security services, services provided by the Ministries of Science and Innovation, Industry, Tourism and Commerce availability, as well as training courses. Regarding the use of online public services, almost 40% uses some of them daily.

In order to receive grants from the SRE the following administrative activities have to be performed: (a) Delivery of Taxes forms; (b) Collection of forms from the Social Security; (c) Payment of fees; (d) Delivery of forms to Social Security; (e) Collection of documentation for new workplace; (f) Filling in forms; (g) Submission of forms; (h) Issuance of health permits; (i) Procurement of supplies; (j) Issuance of a license; and (k) Starting up of activity.

Regarding the difficulty of the collection, preparation and provision of information for the service, it is considered as moderate (60%). The main administrative burdens for collecting, preparing and providing information are the following:

- The number of different entities that must be visited;
- The difficulty in harvesting and completing the forms;
- The collection of information and reading of guidelines, since the language used is difficult to understand and identify what is eligible or not.

SMEs believe that if someone wants to speed up the process, it is necessary that their subcontracted counsellor has good relationship with the local economic development agency. The most burdensome activity is filling in the forms. The SMEs do not use the required information in another context. SMEs believe that they can reduce the costs by reducing the administrative processes and performing activities through the Internet. The relevant regulation is complicated. The particular service could be simplified by creating an electronic process through which someone can find specific help or by enabling the completion of the public service through the SRE portal.

3   Training Public Agency Employees

PAs are the responsible bodies for serving citizens' and businesses' needs regarding their transactions with government. In order to succeed this, PA employees have to be trained. RI offers an innovative training approach for training PA employees and rural SME personnel so that the RI services can be effectively introduced in rural settings.

The RI initiative provides formal training and activities through a multistage process developed as a series of living labs/workshops where PA employees are trained and guided in an experiential learning process that will be fostered and sustained by a collaborative learning experience through the use of the tools provided by the project. The main target participants of the training sessions are representatives of the local authorities and public service providers, who can also act as facilitators/observers. In this context, three main platforms will be used, namely the eGovTube, the Rural Observatory 2.0 and the semantic eGovPortal, creating an incubator (Fig. 1) described as follows:

- eGoveTube is a collaborative Web 2.0-oriented platform that aims at supporting PAs in sharing information and experiences, identifying innovative services and developing users' interest for them. Also, it supports users in sharing and exchanging ideas and experiences and using of innovative e-government supportive technology introduced through video communication, community and knowledge assets network(s) visualisation, rich profiling and other tools [5]. eGovTube will be used as core driver for sustaining the overall process, not only by giving room to the delivery of training content, but also by giving voice to all participants to share their ideas and experiences, so that the innovation diffusion process will be constantly challenged and assessed. This platform is able to deliver formal training content as well as informal, actionable learning-based activities;
- Rural Observatory 2.0 is an innovative sophisticated Web-based environment that will facilitate information retrieval, access, usage and exploitation of e-government services and relevant digital educational content [6], [7]. The use of the Rural Observatory 2.0 tool will allow to store and deliver more traditional training content for various topics;
- eGovPortal is a platform that offers an ontology-based structured dialogue for driving users in eliciting specific information for performing a public service. It offers the main bundle of semantic e-government services and undertakes the responsibility of alleviating the administrative burden for rural SMEs, in regard to their transactions with local authorities and regional public authorities.

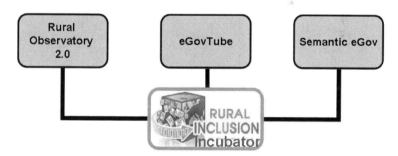

Fig. 1. The Rural Inclusion incubator

Two workshop sessions per PA will take place in 2011. Further workshops will be organized in order to address specific training needs that may emerge from the feedback and the input of the RI community posted in the eGovTube. The objectives of the workshops are to train the PAs in: (a) documenting and modelling public services using the RI methodology and tools; (b) using and exploiting the opportunities of eGovTube; (c) using and exploiting the opportunities of RuralObservatory 2.0; and (d) using and exploiting the opportunities of eGovPortal.

The organized workshops will allow to provide direct tutoring on the RI tools that will foster the reduction of administrative burdens related to public services and to gather insights from direct interaction from targeted users by the means of discussions and of hands-on sessions. It also concerns testing products and services in real time and real life environments, thus helping users to encounter, understand and solve problems, , and to detect the usable features that have to be promoted. Observation of the behaviour of the users will provide information about how to improve the usability of the tools and the users' ICT skills. Recommendations, thus, will be based in real life experiences of the target group, and therefore they will be context based and usable.

Training content is a very vital means so as to disseminate the RI knowledge to interested stakeholders. The training content will be used in the training workshop sessions that will be attended by the PA employees in the context of the RI project. In total, 21 learning objects/ activities have been determined. A learning object is any entity, digital or non-digital, that may be used for learning, education or training [8], [9]. The learning objects have been analyzed by a set of characteristics, which have been classified in three main categories, namely content characteristics, media type and format and usability and availability, as described below [3]:

(i) Content characteristics
- Subject coverage: The most important identification in regard to the training content is the different topics it covers. There are four main subjects, namely Public Service Modelling, Using eGovTube, Using RuralObservatory 2.0, and Using eGovPortal.
- Type: A learning object can be of one or more of the following types, namely application, assessment, case study, demonstration, educational, glossary, guide and lecture (course/seminar).
- Content use: In regard to the potential use of the content, two possible uses have been identified, namely informational use and use for training purposes.
- Quality procedures: An approach for evaluation of the content quality, including structured questionnaires and interviews.

(ii) Media type and format
- Format: Learning objects are in various formats (e.g. videos, PowerPoint presentations, and Word documents) so as to offer a variety of means and attract more participants.
- Size: The analysis of content in respect to the storage capabilities revealed that the total of content does not have excessive requirements for storage.

(iii) Usability and availability
- Ownership: For every learning resource the owner and creator/author have been identified.

The objective of training PAs on documenting and modelling public services using the RI methodology and tools has been achieved through the creation of fifteen learning objects. Three learning objects have been created so as to support the eGovTube tool. Also, two and one learning objects have been created for exploiting the possibilities of RuralObservatory 2.0 and eGovPortal correspondingly.

4   Conclusions

In the context of business to government innovations, current EU initiatives aim at building a strong European economic area with simplified government transactions. Although, various efforts and e-government initiatives at national/European level exist to enable electronic communication/ transactions between SMEs and PAs, complexity still exists.

In this light, the reduction of SMEs' administrative burdens is one of the issues to be studied. SMEs devote many resources and time to find information before executing a particular public service. The administrative burdens incurred by this process deprive SMEs of their ability to make more investments and enhance their dexterity. RI tries to address the problem of the alleviation of administrative burdens by easing the discovery of public services by rural SMEs, personalizing the service and providing all necessary information for its execution. Also, RI provides a collaborative training for helping PAs in implementing e-government services and rural SMEs in using them. Thus, RI boosts a transformational e-government dynamic by achieving a change in culture on how e-government services are designed by PAs and accessed by rural SMEs.

Acknowledgments. Part of the work presented in this paper has been funded by the European Commission, and the project No 238900 "Rural-Inclusion: e-Government Lowering Administrative Burdens for Rural Businesses" of the ICT Policy Support Programme. This publication reflects the views only of the authors, and the Commission cannot be held responsible for any use, which may be made of the information contained therein. The authors would like to thank all the consortium partners for their contribution in the design and implementation of this initiative.

References

1. Lau, E.: E-government and the Drive for Growth and Equity. In: Governance and Information Technology: From Electronic Government to Information Government. MIT Press, Massachusetts (2007)
2. Costopoulou, C., Ntaliani, M.: Measuring Administrative Burdens of e-Government Services for Rural SMEs. In: Lytras, M.D., Ordonez de Pablos, P., Ziderman, A., Roulstone, A., Maurer, H., Imber, J.B. (eds.) WSKS 2010. CCIS, vol. 112, pp. 435–442. Springer, Heidelberg (2010)

3. Ntaliani, M., Costopoulou, M., Luccini, M., Sideridis, A.: Collaborative Training for Agricultural Public Authorities for Innovative Provision of Information and Services. In: EFITA 2011 (2011) (in press)
4. Kalampokis, E., Tambouris, E., Tarabanis, K.: D2.3: Selection and Documentation of Public Services. Rural Inclusion Deliverable (2010)
5. Luccini, M., Angehrn, A.: eGovTube: Web2.0 Collaboration to Sustain Innovation Adoption in Rural Living Labs. In: 16th International Conference on Concurrent Enterprising (2010)
6. Manouselis, N., Tzikopoulos, A., Costopoulou, C., Sideridis, A.: Training Rural SMEs on Using e-Government Services. In: 6th Biennial Conference of the European Federation of IT in Agriculture on Environmental and Rural Sustainability through ICT (2007)
7. Karamolegkos, P., Maroudas, A., Manouselis, N.: Application Profiling for Rural Communities: eGov Services and Training Resources in Rural Inclusion. In: Sánchez-Alonso, S., Athanasiadis, I.N. (eds.) MTSR 2010. CCIS, vol. 108, pp. 46–56. Springer, Heidelberg (2010)
8. Patrikakis, C.Z., Koukouli, M., Costopoulou, C., Sideridis, A.B.: Content Requirements Identification Towards the Design of an Educational Portal. In: Lytras, M.D., Carroll, J.M., Damiani, E., Tennyson, R.D., Avison, D., Vossen, G., Ordonez De Pablos, P. (eds.) WSKS 2008. CCIS, vol. 19, pp. 253–260. Springer, Heidelberg (2008)
9. Costopoulou, C.Z., Manouselis, N., Ntaliani, M., Tzikopoulos, A.: Training Agricultural Tutors in Digital Learning Repositories. In: 3rd International Congress on Information and Communication Technologies in Agriculture, Food, Forestry and Environment, pp. 15–21 (2010)

Optimum Hardware-Architecture for Modular Divider in GF(2^m) with Chaos as Arbitrary Source Based on ECC

Azar Hosseini and Abolfazl Falahati

Department of Electrical Engineering (DCCS Lab)
Iran University of Science and Technology, Tehran
ahosseini@elec.iust.ac.ir, afalahati@iust.ac.ir

Abstract. The large-scale proliferation of wireless communications both inside and outside the home-office environment has led to an increased demand for effective and cheap encryption schemes. Now a new chaos based signals as arbitrary source and digital signals as main source make digits for Elliptic curve algorithm by 2 parallel-in (with pipelining), 1parallel-out and 1 serial-out to produce encrypted signals. For computing this scheme in application on MC-DS-CDMA transmitter and receiver, new algorithm of division with the least time consumption, is presented.

This algorithm is implemented in modular division over GF (2^m) without any considerable increase in hardware gate count. By considering appropriate circuit configuration, the simulation results are also presented.

Keywords: ECC, Chaos source, Proposed Divider, FPGA, MC-DS-CDMA.

1 Introduction

Finite fields GF (2^m) have several applications in such areas of communications as error-correcting codes and cryptography. In these applications, computing inverses or divisions in GF (2^m) is usually required. Since it is not efficient to perform such computations in real time on a general-purpose computer, hardware efficient architectures for inversion or division in GF (2^m) are highly desirable [2]. Computing inversion or division over GF(2^m) can be performed in one of the following forms:

1. Little Fermat's theorem, computed by a modular exponentiation: XY^{2m-2} mod p(x) [3];
2. Solution of a system of linear equations over GF(2^m) using Gaussian elimination [4,5];
3. The use of the extended Euclid's algorithm over GF(2^m) to perform iterative transformations of the GCD(Greatest Common Divisor) [2,6,7].

H. Jahankhani et al. (Eds.): ICGS3/e-Democracy 2011, LNICST 99, pp. 245–252, 2012.
© Institute for Computer Sciences, Social Informatics and Telecommunications Engineering 2012

The first and second schemes have area-time product of $O(m^3)$, but the last scheme has $O(m^2)$ [7]. So the last scheme is more desired than the first and the second schemes. But in the literature this kind of algorithms is usually considered as very slow [8]. On the other hand, due to the size of the field-m is not being constant it is desired to reduce its effect on the hardware design. In this paper a new and fast algorithm for division over GF (2^m) based on extended Euclid's algorithm scheme is developed that can perform a finite field division in m-1 clock cycles and its proposed hardware implementation of m. The rest of the paper is devoted to implement this modular in new scheme with chaos circuit as arbitrary source to ECC (Elliptic Curve Cryptosystem).

2   New Variant of Euclid's Algorithm for Division in GF(2^m)

Let $A(x)$ and $B(x)$ be two elements in GF (2^m), $G(x)$ the primitive polynomial used to generate the field and $P(x)$ the result of the division $A(x)/B(x)$ mod $G(x)$, where:

$$A(X) = a_{m-1}x^{m-1} + a_{m-2}x^{m-2} + \ldots + a_1x + a_0 \tag{1}$$

$$B(X) = b_{m-1}x^{m-1} + b_{m-2}x^{m-2} + \ldots + b_1x + b_0 \tag{2}$$

$$G(X) = x^m + g_{m-1}x^{m-1} + g_{m-2}x^{m-2} + \ldots + g_1x + g_0 \tag{3}$$

$$P(X) = p_{m-1}x^{m-1} + p_{m-2}x^{m-2} + \ldots + p_1x + p_0 \tag{4}$$

Each coefficient of the polynomials is in $(0, 1)$. $P(x)$ is called the inverse of $B(x)$ when $A(x) = 1$ [2].

A. *Reclaimed Euclid's Algorithm*
This algorithm needs a total of 2m iterations. This fact within the following is obtained [2]:

```
R = B(x); S = G = G(x); U = A(x); V = T = 0; state = 0; count = 0;
For i = 1 to 2m  do  R = x .R;  T = x .T  mod G; //key operations
   If state = = 0    then    count = count + 1;
      If rm = = 1 then R  <->   S; // rm : the coefficient of x^m in R
         R = R + S;   T= T + U;   T= U;   state = 1;   End
   Else    count = count - 1;
   If   rm = = 1    then     R = R + S;   T = T + U;   End
      If count = = 0   then    V= V + T;   u <-> v;   state = 0;   End
   End
End // V has  P(x) = A(x)/B(x)  mod G(x);   count = 0.
```

R is a polynomial with a degree of at most m, S is a polynomial with degree m, and U, V and T are polynomials with the degrees at most $m - 1$.

Table 1. An example of the claimed algorithm for division in GF(2^4) [2]

i	counter	state	R	S	U	V	T
0	0		x^3+x+1	x^4+x+1	x^3+x^2+x	0	0
1	1	1	x^2+1	x^4+x^2+x	x^3+x^2+x	0	x^3+x^2+x
2	0	0	x^3+x	x^4+x^2+x	x^3+x^2+x+1	x^3+x^2+x	x^3+x^2+x+1
3	1	1	x	x^4+x^2	x^3+x^2+x+1	x^3+x^2+x	x^3+x^2+x+1
4	0	0	x^2	x^4+x^2	$x+1$	x^3+x^2+x+1	x^3+x^2+1
5	1	0	x^3	x^4+x^2	$x+1$	x^3+x^2+x+1	x^3+1
6	2	1	x^2	x^4	$x+1$	x^3+x^2+x+1	$x+1$
7	1	1	x^3	x^4	$x+1$	x^3+x^2+x+1	x^2+x
8	0	0	0	x^4	0	$x+1$	x^3+x^2+x+1

B. Proposed Algorithm for Division

The main disadvantage of the above architecture is the required high number of clock cycles per a division over GF (2^m) i.e,. ($2m-1$ cycles). The proposed new algorithm merges two stages of the binary extended GCD algorithm over GF (2^m) to obtain the result of two stages simultaneously so that the whole stage can be done in one clock cycle, and in a way that the algorithm is directly proper to be implemented in hardware. It has been tried to obtain a relation between the registers (R, S, U and V) and states (count and state) of iteration with the corresponding registers and states of two previous stages.

$R = B(x); U = A(x); S = G(x); V == 0; (C1 = C2 = J) == 0;$
For $i = 1$ to $m - 1$ do
    If $C1 == 0$ then $C2 == 0$;
    If $C2 == 0$ then $C1 + +$;   Else $C1 - -$;
    If $((C2\&C1) == 0)$ then $J == 1$;   Else $J == 0$;
$R = R + [(!R[0]\&R[1])XOR(R[0]|R[1]))].S + [((R[0]\&!R[1])\&(R[0]|R[1]))].$
        $[(C2|!R[0]).S + (!(C2|!R[0]).R].X;$
$U = U + [(!R[0]\&R[1])XOR(R[0]|R[1]))].V + [((R[0]\&!R[1])\&(R[0]|R[1]))].$
        $[(C2|!R[0]).V + (!(C2|!R[0]).U].X;$
$S = (J|R[0]).R + [(!(C2|R[0]|R[1])XOR(C2\&!(J\&R[1])))].S + [((C2|R[0]|!R[1])$
        $XOR(C2 \& R[1] \& !J))].\frac{R+R[0].S}{X};$
$V = (J|R[0]).U + [(!(C2|R[0]|R[1])XOR(C2\&!(J\&R[1])))].V + [((C2|R[0]|!R[1])$
        $XOR(C2 \& R[1] \& !J))].\frac{U+R[0].V}{X};$
    If $((C2|!R[0])\&R[1] == 1)$ then $C2 == 1$;
    If $(!(C2|!R[0])|C2 == 1)$ then $C1 + +$;   Else $C1 - -$;
$R = \frac{R}{X^2}$
$U = \frac{U+R[0].X+R[1]}{X^2} + (R[0]|R[1]).\frac{S}{X} + (R[0]\&R[1]).\frac{S}{X^2}$
End.

As the result of the states are conditioned to the result of the registers after an iteration and also the registers are calculated respect to the status of the states, an extra state condition , J , is added to register the state in the middle stage. The following algorithm shows the result of the performed experience. In the above algorithm, the three parameters: C1, C2 and J, control the flow of the iterations and in each stage, the content of R, S, U and V are computed using these condition parameters along by the first and second bits of R in each stage (i.e. R[0], R[1]). At the end of each iteration a division by X^2 is performed that can be done just by a right shifting of the corresponding register. Although the proposed algorithm seems to be complex, its hardware implementation is very simple and just use logical gates and latches.

Table 2. An Example of Proposed Algorithm for Division in GF(2^4)

i	C1	C2	J	R	S	U	V
0	0	0	0	x^3+x+1	x^4+x+1	x^3+x^2+x	0
1	1	0	0	$x^4+x^3 \to x^2+x$	x^2+x+1	$x^3+x^2+x \to 1$	x^3+1
2	2	1	1	$x^2+x \to x$	x^2+x	$1 \to x+1$	1
3	1	1	0	$x \to x$	x+1	$x+1 \to x$	x+1
4	0	1		x		x	x+1

In table 2, first line shows initial polynomials, at first cycle (i=1) by state conditions (C1=1, C2=0) and with the equations for R, S, U and V, we would have new polynomials. In this cycle after calculating R and U, at the end of the program new values should be replaced (i=1, columns 5,7). This computation continues to i=4 and we can see the same value for V that had been obtained by i=3, thus for m-1 cycle will catch.

3   Hardware Implementation

The algorithm is designed so that it could be implemented by simple basic gates and latches for synchronization for the iterations. The proposed hardware consists of four separated modules. These modules are designed to calculate R, S, U and V registers that are exposed in a block diagram as follows. The calculation manner of control parameters, C1, C2 and J have been shown in program of proposed algorithm (VHDL language-section 2.B). The statements of $/X$ and $/X^2$

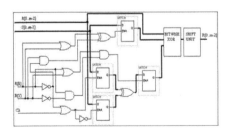   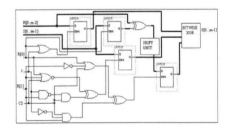

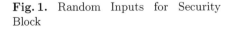

Fig. 1. Random Inputs for Security Block

Fig. 2. Outputs of Security Block with λ Digit

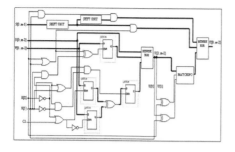
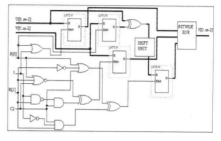

Fig. 3. Random Inputs for Security Block

Fig. 4. Outputs of Security Block with λ Digit

	Name	Value a 11.7 ns			
	A	B 000011		00001110	
	B	B 00001C		00001011	
	G	B 000010		00001001	
	V1	B 000000		00000001	

Fig. 5. The Result of new Algorithm for division

is implemented by shifted wiring of the corresponding data buses connecting to the latches. The module of R, S, U and V block in the new algorithm implementation are represented in Fig.1, Fig.2, Fig.3 and Fig.4 respectively. Also, the result of new algorithm for division is represented in Fig.5.

4   Encryption Scheme in Application on MC-DS-CDMA Transmitter and Receiver

Chaos was defined as process like random existing in the confirmed system. This process was non periodical, and it was stable on the whole and extensive on spot[1]. The chaos signal especially suited for secret communication because it has the characters of conceal, inscrutability, high complexity which are liable to achieve [9]. In this paper we offer simple chaos circuit that is combined with ECC to produce cypher. For this production, new algorithm for division helps that time consumption becomes the least. The basic character of the chaos motion [9] could be defined as follows for $n = 0, 1, 2, ...$ where:

$$x_{n+1} = k.x_n.(1 - x_n) \tag{5}$$
$$k \in (3.4688596, 4) \tag{6}$$
$$x_n \in (0, 1) \tag{7}$$

Assume that every symbol of one user is passed from serial to parallel block and we have $d_i^{(0)}(n)$, $i \in \{0, 1, ..., v-1\}$ with n bit-symbols in each line [10]. Suppose that bit-symbols of one line go to security block (Fig.6), at first the digits would change with Chaos algorithm, afterwards these are varied with based digits to make Elliptic curve algorithm input data (Fig.7).

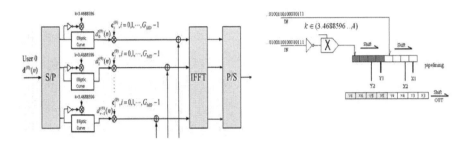

Fig. 6. Random Inputs for Security Block

Fig. 7. Outputs of Security Block with λ Digit

a_2, a_6 are calculated with each pair of $\{(x1, y1), (x2, y2)\}$ in Elliptic curve equation i.e., $(y^2 + x.y = x^3 + a_2.x^2 + a_6)$, and then:

If $a_6 \neq 0$ then

$x_3 = \lambda^2 + \lambda - x_1 - x_2 - a_2$; $// \ a_2 = \frac{y_1^2 + x_1.y_1 + x_2^3 - y_2^2 - x_2.y_2 - x_1^3}{x_1^2 - x_2^2}$

$y_3 = (x_1 - x_3).\lambda - x_3 - y_1$;

If $x_1 \neq x_2$ then $\lambda = \frac{y_1 - y_2}{x_1 - x_2}$; else $\lambda = \frac{3x_1^2 + 2a_2 x_1 - y_1}{2y_1 + x_1}$

If $x_1 = x_2 = 1$ then $a_2 = -0.5$;

If $x_1 = x_2 = 0$ then $a_2 = 0$.

The rest of the computation for output digits is adherence for equations above. Conversely at the receiver with cypher digits and λ, we could gain our initial values again. Decryption is calculated in the following:

$\lambda = \frac{(\sim x_1 - \sim x_2).k}{x_1 - x_2} = \sim k$;

if $(\lambda = \sim k)$ $x_1 \neq x_2$; else $x_1 = x_2$;

$y_1 = \sim x_1.k$; $x_1 = \frac{in(1,2) + (\lambda+1).in(1,1)}{\lambda - \sim k}$; $x_1 \propto x_2$.

In encryption, parallel symbols in each line are separated into 2 digits (x_1, x_2) so in decryption, at receiver we have in(1, 1) and in(1, 2) for each stage.

5   Simulation Results by MATLAB

In $d^{(k)}(n) = [d_0^{(k)}(n), d_1^{(k)}(n), ..., d_{v-1}^{(k)}(n)][10]$ if $v = 100$ we have 100 lines after S/P (Fig.6) and we assume 4-bit symbols for each input symbol (Matrix [100,4]). Every 2-bit symbols input to the security block have 2-bit outputs (Fig.7) that calculate with fourth section equations.

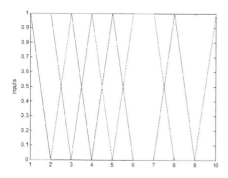

Fig. 8. Random Inputs for Security Block

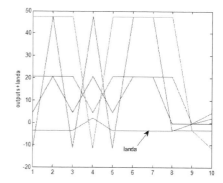

Fig. 9. Outputs of Security Block with λ Digit

6   Conclusion and Comparison

In this paper the algorithm of calculating modular division over GF (2^m) based on extended binary GCD is modified to improve the system implementation speed. The important differences between Reclaimed Euclid's algorithm[2] and proposed algorithm are throughput and latency with 1/2(m-1) and (5m-4) values respectively for first algorithm and 1/(m-1) and m-1 values respectively for second algorithm. Additionally an algorithm is designed and provided directly for the hardware so that as shown in Table 3, almost affiliation of the hardware are obliterated with the size of the field selected (i.e. the amount of m in GF(2^m)). Table 3 shows the compression of the proposed algorithm with the most commonly used algorithms of Kim [11] and Bruner [6] considering both in speed and area consumption. These comparisons show that proposed algorithm has the smallest latency. Of course, if the algorithm is implemented by the systolic architecture, it will result in better specifications in speed and cell delays as well as improvement in clock frequency. That is the future work of the author.

Table 3. Compression of the proposed algorithm with the most commonly used algorithms of Kim and Bruner, in speed and area consumption

	Bruner et.al	Kim et.al	Proposed algorithm
Throughput (1/cycles)	1/2m	1/2m	1/(m-1)
Latency (cycles)	2m	2m	m-1
Basic Components and their numbers	AND2:3M+log(m+1)	AND2 :3m+5	AND2:12
	XOR:3m+log(m+1)	XOR:3m+1	XOR:5m+12
	FF:4m+log(m+1)	FF:5m+2	FF:16
	MUX2:8m	MUX2:4m+4	OR2:8
		OR2:1	AND3:2
			OR3:2

The reclaimed Euclid's algorithm based on the COMPASS 0.6um CMOS is performed with maximum propagation delay 3ns and clock rate up to 167MHZ[2], while our proposed algorithm is implemented by MAX7000S series-FPGA is performed with delay time 1ns and maximum frequency 10000MHZ. In resumption, the algorithm of cryptography is security voucher with combination of two encryption algorithms to complete MC-DS-CDMA block. The results expose that finding relation between output-columns is impossible, because encryption equations are based on arbitrary environment such as Chaos algorithm with its random characters and Elliptic curve in cycloids too. The Fig.8 and Fig.9 show in-out and out-in encryption and decryption unit sequentially.

References

1. Murali, K., Yu, H., Varadan, V., Leung, H.: Secure Communication Using a Chaos Based Signal Encryption Scheme. IEEE Transaction on Consumer Electronics 47, 709–714 (2001)
2. Guo, J.-H., Wang, C.-L.: Hardware-efficient systolic architecture for inversion and division in $GF(2^m)$. In: IEE Proc.-Comput. Digit. Tech., vol. 145, pp. 272–278 (July 1998)
3. Jain, S.K., Song, L., Parhi, K.K.: Efficient Semi-Systolic Architecture for Finit Field Arithmetic. IEEE Transaction on VLSI System 6, 101–113 (1998)
4. Wang, C.L., Lin, J.L.: A Systolic Archtecture for Computing Inverses and Divisions in Finit Field $GF(2^m)$. IEEE Transaction on Computer 42, 1141–1146 (1993)
5. Hasan, M.A., Bhargava, V.K.: Bit-Serial Systolic Divider and Multiplier for Finit Fields $GF(2^m)$. IEEE Transaction on Computer 41, 972–980 (1992)
6. Brunner, H., Curiger, A., Hofstetter, M.: On Computing Multiplicative Inverses in $GF(2^m)$. IEEE Trans. Comput. 42, 1010–1015 (1993)
7. Wu, C.-H., Wu, C.-M., Shieh, M.-D., Hwang, Y.-T.: High-Spesd, Low-Complexity Systolic Designs of Novel Iteration Division Algorithms in $GF(2^m)$. IEEE Transaction on Computer 53, 375–380 (2004)
8. Fong, K., Hankerson, D., Lopez, J., Menzes, A.: Field Inversion and Point Halving Revisited. IEEE Transaction on Computers 53, 1047–1059 (2004)
9. Deng-Hong, Z.: Encryption design for the database under the VFP environment based on Chaos algorithm. In: IEEE, ICACTE (2010)
10. Chen, J.-D., Ueng, F.-B., Chang, J.-C., Hsien, S.: Performance Analyses of OFDM-CDMA Receivers in Multipath Fading Channels. IEEE Transactions on Vehicular Technology 58, 4805–4818 (2009)
11. Kim, C.H., Kwon, S., Kim, J.J., Hong, C.P.: A Compact and Fast Division Architecture for a Finite Field $GF(2^m)$. In: Kumar, V., Gavrilova, M.L., Tan, C.J.K., L'Ecuyer, P. (eds.) ICCSA 2003. LNCS, vol. 2667, pp. 855–864. Springer, Heidelberg (2003)

Sufficiency of Windows Event Log as Evidence in Digital Forensics

Nurdeen M. Ibrahim, Ameer Al-Nemrat, Hamid Jahankhani, and Rabih Bashroush

University of East London
School of Computing, IT and Engineering, UK
{u0947707,ameer,hamid2,rabih}@uel.ac.uk

Abstract. The prevalence of computer and the internet has brought forth the increasing spate of cybercrime activities; hence the need for evidence to attribute a crime to a suspect. The research therefore, centres on evidence, the legal standards applied to digital evidence presented in court and the main sources of evidence in the Windows OS, such as the Registry, slack space and the Windows event log. In order to achieve the main aim of this research, cybercrime activities such as automated password guessing attack and hacking was emulated on to a Windows OS within a virtual network environment set up using VMware workstation. After the attack the event logs on the victim system was analysed and assessed for its admissibility (evidence must conform to certain legal rules), and weight (evidence must convince the court that the accused committed the crime).

Keywords: Cybercrime, Digital forensics, Digital evidences.

1 Introduction

The proliferation of computer and network systems has brought forth the increasing spate of cyber crime [1]. The Windows operating system (OS) is the most prevalent; therefore, Windows users bear the brunt of most cyber crimes [2]. Criminals constantly devise a variety of technique to perpetrate crime; and are constantly updating their skills subsequently, the need for measures to investigate how computer crimes are committed and mechanisms for identifying suspects, in order to present evidence needed for successful prosecution is vital to mitigating cyber crime. The need for technology to combat cyber crime has therefore conceived computer forensics [3]. "Computer forensic can be summarised as the process of collecting preserving, analysing and presenting the computer-related evidence in a manner that is legally acceptable in court" [4]. Evidences gathered during forensic investigation could be used in criminal cases such as in intellectual property theft and other civil cases.

However, for evidence to be admitted in court it has to satisfy two test which is the admissibility (evidence must conform to certain legal rules) and weight (evidence should sufficiently convince the court that the crime is committed by the accused). The admissibility test requires that evidence conform to certain legal rules such as authenticity and reliability, best evidence rule and hearsay rule [5]. After evidence is admitted in court, its weight is assessed to determine its probative value [6]. The

H. Jahankhani et al. (Eds.): ICGS3/e-Democracy 2011, LNICST 99, pp. 253–262, 2012.

Windows OS preserves a pool of data from which investigators can obtain evidence pertinent to a case under investigation (StrathclydeForensics, n.d.). Evidence related to cybercrime activities can be found locations such as, Registry, Slack space and the Windows event log [7].

The Windows event log is the most important source of evidence during digital forensic investigation of a Windows system because the log files connect certain events to a particular point in time [8]. An event in Windows Event log is an entity that describes some interesting occurrence in a computer system [9]. For instance event log is generated when an OS starts, stops or fails, when a user attempts to access system resource or logged on to a computer etc. To the digital forensic investigator event logs is of enormous benefit as it provides a detailed step by step account of activities that occurred in a system. By investigating the event logs incidence response team could tell whether an attempt to intrude a system succeeded or not [10].

The objective of any investigation is to identify evidence that is needed to attribute a crime to the perpetrator. This can be achieved by unveiling information that links a crime to a suspect. It can be used to support or to refute the occurrence of a crime and also to provide useful information in proving the intent of committing a crime, which is a key to prosecution [6]. This paper therefore, aims to discuss legal requirements of evidence and then discuss the sufficiency of the Windows event log as source of evidence in digital forensics.

2   Legal Requirement for Evidence

The legal requirement for evidence is that it satisfies two tests: admissibility (evidence must be in conformity to certain legal rules) and weight (must be understood and convincing enough to the court).

2.1   Admissibility

The general standard for admissibility of evidence is to prove that the evidence is relevant, authentic and reliable It is also required that evidence satisfy the best evidence rule and does not contain hearsay unless if it is classified as an exception to the hearsay prohibition rule before it is admitted as evidence in court [11].

2.1.1   Authentic and Reliable
The requirements for the authentication of evidence to satisfy the court are:

- The evidence was not altered during collection and
- It actually comes from the claimed source – human or machine.
- Supplementary information such as date of record to be used as evidence is accurate

Two steps are involved in authenticating digital evidence. The first step involves the examination of the evidence to determine whether it is what the proponent purports and that it originates from the claimed source. Authenticity of digital evidence can be verified if the person who has collected the evidence testifies that the integrity of the evidence has been maintained and that the evidence originates from the claimed source. The second step of the authentication process involves analysis of the evidence to ascertain its probative value [6]. Digital evidence is acceptable in court if a witness who is versed in computer operation can testify that the evidence is authentic and reliable [11].

After evidence is authenticated and accepted in court its reliability is evaluated to ascertain its probative value. The evidence must be cogent and understandable [5]. Doubts regarding the integrity of evidence reduce the weight of evidence in court Digital evidence is acceptable in court if the party presenting it can prove that the information is reliable and the reliability can be verified by the opposing party in court [12].

2.1.2   Satisfy the Best Evidence Rule

Writing - The best evidence rule requires that original evidence to be provided before evidence is acceptable in court. Evidence in the form of writing is required to satisfy the best evidence rule. However, because exact and accurate copies of the original evidence can be made, duplicate copies are now acceptable and since computers are capable of producing an accurate copy of the digital evidence, printout of digital evidence are usually acceptable in court.

Hearsay – the rule of hearsay is applicable to all evidence unless it falls within exception to the hearsay prohibition. According to Casey 2004 pp179 "Evidence contained in a document is hearsay if the document is produced to prove that a statement made in court is true". For example, e-mail message may be used to demonstrate that an individual made a statement but it cannot be used to prove the veracity of the content of the e-mail [6]. Digital evidence is classified as computer generated or computer stored or hybrid.

Computer generated- this is evidence consisting of output from a computer program e.g., ATM receipt phone records. Courts admit computer generated record providing an expert witness testifies that the computer that generated the record produced an accurate result and was functioning properly [11].

Computer Stored- Computer stored evidence are electronic data consisting the writing and statement of an individual e.g. e-mail, business correspondence. Computer stored evidence has more ambiguous standard of authenticity than computer generated. Requirements of some court are that the same standard of authenticating physical document be applied to computer stored – advocates must demonstrate firsthand knowledge of the evidence.

Hybrid- hybrid combines the features of both computer generated and computer stored. Computer generated records are classified under the business record exception to hearsay rule prohibition. Computer generated data are not regarded as hearsay as they do not consist of human statement rather they document an action [6].

2.2   Weight

The weight of evidence is a non-scientific concept. After evidence is accepted in court the next step of the evaluation process is to assess its weight. There isn't any classification of evidence that a court is compelled to accept. The differences between admissibility and weight are unclear especially in scientific evidence. In assessing the weight of evidence a number of features are put into consideration. Based on these features the weight evidence carries is determined.

2.2.1   Authenticity
The evidence is connected to the circumstances and the suspect.

2.2.2   Accuracy
Evidence must be convincing and error free; evidence must be acquired using standard accepted procedure by an expert who is able to explain the procedure [5].

2.2.3   Completeness
Evidence must be capable of telling in- its- term the whole event that occurred [5].

2.2.4   Clear Chain of Custody
In assessing the weight of evidence the manner in which evidence is handled right from collection to the time is presented to court put into consideration. All people who handled the evidence and actions performed on the evidence should be documented. The condition of the evidence at the time of collection   should be described.

2.2.5   Transparency of Forensic Procedure
The forensic procedures should be transparent such that a third party can follow the same method and arrive at the same conclusion [5].

3   Legal Standards Applied to Digital Logs

Because digital logs are used as evidence in court, it is therefore, required that the logs satisfy legal standards applied to evidence. As discussed earlier evidence are generally required to conform to certain legal rules before being admitted as evidence. The rules require that evidence is authentic, reliable and relevant. Also required is that evidence does not contain hearsay and that it satisfies the rule of best evidence.

3.1   Authentication and Log Evidence

It has been discussed earlier that evidence is authentic if originates from the claimed source and that its integrity has not been compromised. The rule applies to log evidence as well. As earlier discussed computer evidence is classified in court as computer-generated, computer stored or hybrid. Based on this classification the court determines how to scrutinize digital log before admittance. There is no over-arching prescription for classifying digital logs therefore; its admissibility is open to case by case decision. For computer generated record, Courts admit computer generated record providing an expert witness testifies that the computer that generated the record produced an accurate result and was functioning properly.

3.2   Log and Best Evidence Rule

As discussed earlier the best evidence rule requires that evidence is original before it is admissible in court. The standard is applied to ensure its credibility. In the case of computer record, printouts or other output that exactly represent that they are regarded as original. Therefore, accurate printout of computer records is accepted as evidence in court. Digital logs satisfy the best evidence rule if the MD5 hashes of the original and the copy matches.

3.3   Digital Log and Hearsay

The application of the rule of hearsay to digital logs depends on the way a court classifies the log- computer generated, computer stored or hybrid. As described earlier. Computer generated are classified under the business record exception to hearsay prohibition rule [11]. Computer generated records have been classified as non hearsay because its proponent have been able to demonstrate to the court that the records are merely the product of a computer operating under a set of programme with no human intervention [6].

4   Methodology

In order to achieve the objective of this paper, analysing the sufficiency of the Windows event log as evidence in digital forensic investigation, experiments were conducted within a virtual network environment. The virtual network was set up using VMware workstation. Within the virtual network configuration, cyber crime related activities were emulated to determine the sufficiency of the Windows event log in providing evidence of the attack. The cyber crime activity emulated involves password guessing attack with the aid of the Net Essential tools.

Essential Net Tools used to conduct the password guessing attack on the target system (Window Server 2003 domain controller). Net Essential tool contains a variety of network auditing tool, which includes NetBIOS Auditing Tool. NetBIOS Auditing Tool is used to audit a system that offers NetBIOS file sharing service. It also offers password guessing functionality. NAT is a GUI tool with an interface that requires

Fig. 1. A total of 181 passwords checked on target

Fig. 2. Administrator password found on victim computer

user to supply the starting IP address and the stopping IP address of the target system. NAT attempts to crack the target system by trying a combination of predefined username and password. Figures 1 – 2 displays result of the attack.

5   Analysis of the Event Logs for Evidence of Attack

The previous section shows that an automated password guessing attack was conducted on a Windows Server 2003 server using NetBIOS Auditing Tool (NAT). The attack involved connecting to an enumerated share (IPC$, C$) on a target (Windows Server 2003) domain controller and then attempting to crack the target with a combination of guessed username and password. During the attack process, a total of 181 passwords were checked (fig 1). On completion of the attack five shares including the C$ and ADMIN$ were enumerated on the victim system. A total of eleven users were enumerated. Passwords for administrator account and a user (nurex113) was discovered on the victim system (fig 2).

In this section, the event log is analysed for evidence of activities that occurred during the attack. The attack involved an automated password guessing, therefore, a series of username and password combination will be used by the attacker in attempt to authenticate and logon to the target system. As authentication and logon events are recorded under the account logon and logon events the analysis will be focused on the events generated under the account logon and logon category of the security log in the victim system.

5.1   Examination of the Security Log on the Victim Computer for Evidence of Failed Account Logon Events

As the victim computer is a Window Server 2003 domain controller, both account logon and logon events will be recorded in the security log of the victim computer. The account logon event logs only authentication events (Microsoft, 2011). Because the attack was conducted from a local account and Microsoft uses NTLM to authenticate local accounts; Event ID 680 was filtered in order to search for failed NTLM authentication. A series of failed account logon event was discovered in the security log of victim system. A large number of failed authentications appearing in the security log of the victim computer is a clear sign that the computer was under an automated password guessing attack. In order to obtain more information on the attack, some of the entries were examined to find any correlation between the events as shown in fig. 3.

Fig. 3. Event ID 680 recorded when the attacker logon to the victim system

5.2   Examining the Victim System for Evidence of a Successful Authentication (Account Logon)

As shown above, the attacker hacked into the passwords of the administrator (Administrator) and the user (nurex113) accounts; subsequently the attacker successfully authenticated to the victim. In Windows Server 2003, Event ID 680 is used to record both failed and successful NTLM authentication. Event ID 680 with success audit was recorded in the security log of the victim system as shown in fig 4. The event logs generated in fig. 4 also provides evidence that the attacker has successfully guessed two passwords from the target system.

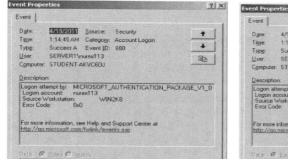 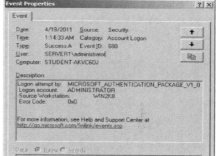

Fig. 4. Event ID 680 recorded when the attacker successfully guessed and logon with the user account nurex113

5.3   Examining the Victim System for Evidence of Failed Logon Events

Logon event is generated when a user is attempting to access a resource on a computer. Before a user can logon to a computer the user must be authenticated. If the authentication (account logon) succeeds then the user is granted access (logon) to a system. If, however, the authentication fails the user is denied access to the system. The authentication process and the resulting event generated have been discussed in the previous section. This section discusses the evidence provided by the Windows event log due to failed logon. A large number of failed logon events are also recorded in the security log of the victim system and they are an indication that an unauthorised person is attempting to logon to the target system. After filtering for Event ID 529 in the security log, a large number of failed logon events were revealed. A security log full of failed logon events is a sign that the computer is under an automated password guessing attack..However, In order to obtain more information on the failed logon, some of the entries was viewed and examined as shown in fig 5.

5.4   Examining the Victim System for Evidence of Successful Logon Events

As demonstrated above, the attacker has successfully obtained the password for two accounts, the administrator account and the user account (nurex113) and subsequently logon with their credentials. This results in an Event ID 540 to be logged in the victim computer. Event ID 540 indicates that the attacker logged on from a network. Figures 6 and 7 below show event generated as a result of a successful logon.

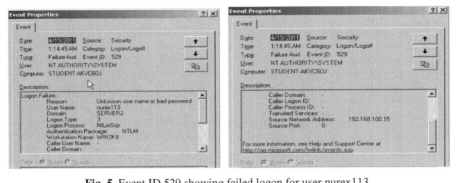

Fig. 5. Event ID 529 showing failed logon for user nurex113

Fig. 6. Event ID 540 showing successful logon for administrator

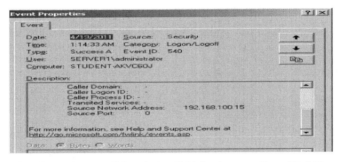

Fig. 7. The bottom of description field for the same Event ID 540

6   Evaluating the Sufficiency of the Windows Event Log as Evidence

In the previous sections, the security log of the victim system has been examined and analysed for evidence of the cyber crime activities emulated. In this section the evidence obtained are analysed to determine whether they satisfy the legal standard applied to digital logs and evidence in general. It has been mentioned earlier that evidence is required to satisfy two test (admissibility and weight).The admissibility requirement is that evidence satisfy some legal rule such as authenticity, best evidence rule and the hearsay rule. The weight of evidence is assessed based on how the evidence is able to convince the court that the accused is guilty.

6.1   Admissibility of the Windows Event Log as Evidence

Authenticity of the Windows Event Log: Evidence provided by the Windows event log is admissible if it can be proven that the evidence is from the claimed source. This can be confirmed by examining the logs generated from the attack. The computer field of each of the events generated shows that the logs were generated by the victim system (STUDENT_AKVC0J).This proves that the logs were authentic and actually originates from the source.

The Windows Event Log and the Hearsay Rule: Log evidence is classified as computer generated. Computer generated records are classified as an exception to the hearsay prohibition rule [11]. Therefore, the Windows event log falls under the classification of the hearsay exception prohibition as it is generated by a computer that is operating under a set of program.

The Windows Event Log and the Best Evidence Rule: It has been discussed earlier that log evidence satisfy the best evidence rule and because the Windows event log falls under the category of log evidence, it therefore satisfies the best evidence rule.

6.2   Weight

As discussed earlier, the criteria used in assessing the weight of evidence is that the evidence provides sufficient information needed to convince the court that the crime was perpetrated by the accused [5]. Therefore, in this section the weight of the evidence provided by the Windows Event log after each of the attacks is evaluated.

Evaluating the Weight of the Windows Event Log for the Password Guessing Attack: Evidence carries much weight if it can be linked to the circumstances and the suspect and also, if can tell in its own term the whole story of the activities performed by the attacker [5]. This section will therefore analyse whether the evidence provided by the Windows event log can be linked to the circumstances of the crime and whether it tells the details scenario needed to reconstruct the events that occurred during the incident. After the examination and analysis of the password guessing attack demonstrated above, it was discovered that the Windows event log tells the complete story of the attacker's activities. It provides the following information:

1. From the security log of the victim system a series of failed authentication activities and failed   logon activities were discovered and this provides evidence that the victim system was under a password guessing attack.
2. Careful examination of the logs further revealed that the attacker has enumerated some user account on the victim system and attempted to logon with their credentials. This evidence was obtained from viewing the entries of failed account logon and logon events.
3. It also provided evidence that the attacker successfully cracked the victim system and discovered passwords for 2 users as previously discussed. This evidence was obtained from the successful logon and account logon events.

4. It provided the attacker workstation as WIN2K8
5. It provided the IP address of the attacker as 192.168.100.15

In conclusion, the analysis of the Windows event log proves that it provides all the evidence needed to reconstruct the activities performed during the password guessing attack and also to link the attack to the actual perpetrator. Hence, it will carry much weight in court.

7   Conclusion

This paper has investigated the question of sufficiency of windows event logs in serving as digital forensics evidence that could be accepted in the court of law. it has been discussed that evidence must satisfy two the admissibility and weight test The admissibility test requires that evidence conform to certain legal standard such as authenticity, reliability and that the evidence most not contain hearsay. After evidence is admitted in court its weight is accessed to determine its probative value. In evaluating the weight evidence, what is most considered is that the evidence be able to convince the court that the offence was perpetrated by the accused. cyber crime activities were emulated on a Windows Server 2003. The cyber crime activities emulated involved password guessing attack and exploitation of the Windows network service.

References

1. Wang, S.J.: Measures of retaining digital evidence to prosecute computer-based cyber-crime 29(2), 216–223 (2006)
2. Dashora, K., Tomar, D.S., Rana, J.L.: A practical approach to evidence gathering in Windows environment 5(8), 21–27 (2010)
3. Wang, G., Cannady, J., and Rosenbluth, J.: Foundation of computer forensics: A technology for the fight against cyber-crime 21(2), 119–127 (2005)
4. Abdullah, M.T., Mahmood, R., Ghani, A.A.A., Abdullah, M.Z., Sultan, A.M.S.: Advances in computer forensics 8(2), 215–219 (2008)
5. Sommer, P.: Intrusion detection as evidence 31(23-24), 2477–2487 (1999)
6. Casey, E.: Digital evidence and computer crime: forensic science computer and internet, 2nd edn. Academic press, London (2004)
7. Steel, C.: Windows forensic: The field guide for corporate computer Investigations. John Wiley and Sons (2006)
8. Schuster, A.: Introducing the Microsoft vista event log file format 4(1), 65–72 (2007)
9. Stallings, W., Brown, L.: Computer security: principle and practice. Pearson Education Inc., NJ (2008)
10. StrathclydeForensics, (n.d) Windows forensics,
    http://www.strathclydeforensics.co.uk/windows_forensics.htm
    (accessed: March 12, 2011)
11. Kenneally, E.E.: Digital logs-proof matters 1(2), 94–101 (2004)
12. Ryan, D.J., Shpantzer, G.: Legal aspect of digital forensic (2002),
    http://euro.ecom.cmu.edu/program/law/08-
    732/Evidence/RyanShpantzer.pdf (accessed: March 25, 2011)

An Evaluation of the Initiatives and the Progress Made on e-government Services in the EU

Alexander B. Sideridis[2], Elias Pimenidis[1], Loucas Protopappas[3], and M. Koukouli[2]

Agricultural University of Athens, Iera Odos 75, 118 55, Athens, Greece
e.pimenidis@uel.ac.uk, {as,mkou}@aua.gr,
loucas.protopappas@gmail.com

Abstract. The European Union (EU) member states have over the past decade been actively developing their e-government services. These services cover a whole range of Public Administration activities aiming to integrate digital interaction between government agencies, government and citizens, as well as government and businesses. This paper provides a review of the criteria used in evaluating e-government services worldwide. Emphasis is given on the progress made by EU States as well as their commitment in meeting European Commission's requirements. Furthermore, the degree of European stakeholder's (citizen, business and organisations) satisfaction is estimated and compared to the availability of these online services.

Keywords: e-government, e- services, e-democracy, e-government indicators, Public Administration.

1   Introduction

Availability of e-Government services in modern societies, with complex day to day activities, is a prerequisite not only for meeting citizen's needs but also in creating the background for the development of knowledge based economies. This observation had lead the European Commission (EC) to very significant decisions for the information society and media, aiming at further enhancing the contribution of Information and Communication Technologies (ICT) to societies and citizens' life on one hand and, on the other, to the global economy as a whole [1].

Ambitious plans of accelerating the whole process of e-Government *"for all"* in the member states of the EU, with so diverse political, social and economic systems, are not easily implemented and, quite often, fail to meet their targets, despite of the available resources both of national and community public expenditure. Furthermore, the economic crisis prevalent in Europe during the time of writing, has led to considerable changes of plans due to severe restrictions in expenditure.

The main aim of the EC decisions towards e-Europe was in reducing bureaucracy among the twenty seven states. Adding to the existing national bureaucratic procedures, bureaucracy imposed by the policies, directives and regulations of Brussels made the task of simplifying, homogenising, integrating and automating

H. Jahankhani et al. (Eds.): ICGS3/e-Democracy 2011, LNICST 99, pp. 263–270, 2012.
© Institute for Computer Sciences, Social Informatics and Telecommunications Engineering 2012

public administration procedures rather more difficult [2], [3]. Indeed, national diversity is a characteristic of plurality and should be encouraged to exist. Nevertheless, many horizontal activities exist in the EU. Examples of difficulties in systems unification and integration appear in taxation, insurance and public health. The present crisis in Economy, starting from Greece and the fears to be spread all over Europe, and the inability of European organisations to deal with this problem is another demonstration of the lack of cohesiveness within the administrative mechanisms of the member states.

In spite of the negative economic climate, there has been some progress towards e-government development and integration recently. Two successive e-Europe Action Plans [4], [5] focusing on "eEurope – an Information Society for All" have be finally integrated by the i2010 e-Government Action Plan [6]. Low uptake of ICT innovations has led the EC to the Digital Agenda for Europe 2020 [7].

In section 2 of this paper, the aims of these plans are described in brief. The whole effort on ICT developments that had a direct effect to the implementation of e-Government services is described in section 3. Section 4 considers existing e-readiness assessments and the indicators for e-government readiness evaluation. Finally, in section 5 the authors propose ideas and views for strengthening the whole effort towards a successful implementation of e-government services satisfying today's citizen needs.

2   Information Society: The European Initiatives

By the end of the 20th century, figures regarding Internet usage in Europe were disappointing and presenting a large disparity among the EU member states [8], particularly so in the south of Europe. In response to this data, a multilingual major project was launched aiming at the PROMotion of Information Society in Europe (PROMISE). Its main objectives over a five year plan were to: (i) increase awareness and appreciation of the public to the degree of influence of the Information Society and its implications to day-to-day practices, (ii) alert societies in making full use of socioeconomic benefits, and (iii) stimulate the role of EU in the global aspect of the Information Society [11].

In promoting Internet usage and combining this with the "people and skills" investment, the Action Plan strongly supported, at a priority level, projects for improvement of networks of scientific research communities. Information Society Technologies (IST) Programme was then launched by the EC [12] within the 5th Framework Programme for Research, Technology Development and Demonstration (FP5).

The EU's ambitious plans were fully documented in an Action Plan [13] published early in the year 2000. The aim was for a knowledge based society that would guarantee dynamic growth of the economy and a full range of services for all European citizens provided by the information society. All these should have been achieved by the year 2010!

The strategy was focusing on a uniform deployment of Internet and web capabilities throughout Europe. Taking into account the existing diversity on the available network infrastructures between the south, central and north Europe, and the longstanding eminent computer illiteracy in remote areas of Europe, the whole process had to start from scratch.

The e-Europe 2005 Action Plan was launched aiming at encouraging the development of e-services for both the public administrations and private enterprises. It was a rather refocusing programme for research, putting a framework for online services in Europe financed by the 6th Framework and eTEN programmes [9], [10]. It primarily targeted new projects in e-government, e-health, e-inclusion, e-learning and e-trust/security available by the year 2010, taking into account the enlargement of the EU.

Concrete actions for online services in relation to their contributing factors had been also suggested by the EC, with emphasis on the adoption of copyright EU legislation, provision of distance marketing services and financial services (e-taxation, e-money) and jurisdiction on electronic services. Similarly, the EC had specified actions and provisions for secure application of online e-health systems and services.

Despite all efforts, Internet usage in the EU in 2005 had reached a figure nearly 37% well below North America's 68% and well above the 14.6% penetration rate of the world [15]. In response to the above, the i2010 initiative [16] was launched in an effort to implement the new Lisbon strategy towards a sustainable growth of a fully inclusive information society. The i2010 initiative was actually a strategic framework for the information society and media. Digital economy and competiveness should be using ICT as "...a driver of inclusion and quality of life" [5]. As a result, by the year 2010 [16] in improved figures (doubled compared to the year's 2005) of Internet usage [14], and broadband Internet access in Europe to 70% and 60% by the European households and individuals respectively [17].

Concurrently, with the i2010 initiative, the EC issued an Action Plan on e-Government, aiming at increasing and updating the efficiency of public administration services in an effort to comply with the needs of citizens and businesses [6]. In summary, this plan demanded, effective public services, provision of secure services, higher quality of services, reduction of bureaucracy, and cross boarder integration of public services for sustainable citizens' mobility.

In meeting the objectives above, EC's plan contained five priorities: (i) No barriers should exist to any group of citizens in relation to accessibility of online services. By the year 2010 all citizens (eAccessibility and eInclusion major programmes) should enjoy e-Governemt services. (ii) The digital divide should be further eliminated and the member states should reduce administrative burden using innovative e-Government services by the year 2010. (iii) E-Government priority is given to high impact horizontal cross-border services. E-procurement and public contracts are such public services that should be carried out electronically by 2010. (iv) e-Government services should be optimized. Interoperability in identification management, document authentication and e-archiving procedures, and secure systems of mutual recognition of national websites identifiers are a few key enablers of such an improvement. (v) e-Democracy via e-Government services and increased ICT use for significant citizen participation in decision-making and public debates is of significant importance [18].

By the year 2010 the world economic crisis necessitated the need for new measures, raising the "Digital Agenda for Europe". Since there still was a very low degree of adapting ICT innovations in the productivity lines, in public administrations and day-to-day activities, the EC proposed the Digital Agenda for Europe 2020 [19]. This agenda was an effort to "wider deployment and more effective use of digital technologies" thus improving competiveness, providing better health services, improving environmental conditions, creating more opportunities, spurring innovation and, through all of them, help economic growth. Growth could be achieved by taking steps towards smart (i.e. education, innovation, knowledge and digitization), sustainable (i.e. competiveness and resource efficient production) and inclusive (i.e. skill acquisition, participatory and all in one effort) growth. In order to achieve year's 2020 goals, the EC fosters seven priority areas one of which is the *Digital Agenda for Europe*.This Agenda pursues the availability and connectivity of all Europeans to high speed Internet, on which a Digital Single Market should be based [20], [21], [22].

3   EU e-government Services in Relation to ICT Action Plans

One of the most important sources for evaluating the success of the initiatives discussed in section 2 is "Eurostat". It publishes surveys based upon data gathered from statistical services of the member states with regard: (i) to the availability of online public administration services, (ii) to the connectivity to Internet and its Web services both of businesses and households, (iii) to the state' s network infrastructures, and (iv) to various ad-hoc studies [22].

e-Government service development indices are closely related to and indicate the general ICT impact and developments on information societies. On the other hand it is also evident that e-Government service development indices are implying economic and social progress made. Therefore, the various initiatives taken by the EC aiming to diminish heterogeneity of the ICT services provided to the European citizens throughout Europe, are finally aiming at improving knowledge based economy and quality of life of each member state.

In developing e-government, lots of services have been implemented nationally, aiming at providing tools for saving time and effort in their interaction with public sector procedures to the citizens. In a multi national society's environment as that of the EU, with such a tremendous variety of social, financial and environmental conditions, life of Europeans and particularly those of young age is becoming more demanding and complex. The numbers of young people moving from one State to another, either for studies or looking for jobs or, even if for a better future, are constantly increasing. If to the reasons of increasing complexity of services offered to Europeans the economic crisis is added, then the necessity of improved multilingual e-government services becomes apparent. Of course, the economic crisis that hit many European countries over the last three years has slowed down the efforts and expenditure for the implementation of e-government services, needed by the citizens. As a result, the existing e-government services fail to meet the current needs not only of citizens or business in a Government to Citizen (G2C) or Government to Business (G2B) mode but also the needs of interaction between government organizations, departments and local authorities in a Government to Government (G2G) mode.

4   Evaluation of Implemented e-government Services

In evaluating e-government services, a key question has to do with the *completeness* or the *maturity* of this existing service. And then, a second serious question is raised of "How *sophisticated* the existing e-service is?", immediately followed by the another of "How is sophistication related to usability?".

The confusing questions above are due to the lack of a uniformly used benchmarking model. This lack allows the use of various benchmarks and methodologies with various interpretations based upon different weighting variables and different evaluation criteria of each model. Apart from these variations, other important and not taken into account causes of deficiencies in benchmarking may be due to the negligence's of the interrelationship of an e-government service to the organizational structure and the back-office processes [23], [24].

4.1   E-readiness Assessment

As it has been discussed in previous sections e-readiness of the citizens to use the offered services varies in accordance mainly to social and cultural local developments and idiosyncrasies. E-readiness motivation programmes and projects have been funded and many researchers and international organisations have developed models and indices for assessing worldwide e-readiness in various ICT advances like broadband networking and services, e-business for market economy integration and global digital inclusion [23], [24], [25], [26], [27].

4.2   E-government Readiness

e-Government readiness is basically evaluated taking into account a considerable number of indicators, the most significant of which are: (i) existence of the appropriate ICT infrastructure, (ii) maturity of online services (i.e. transactional services fully covering citizen's needs), and (iii) support in providing advisory and decision making services. The variation of the full set of these indicators is used for assessing e-government readiness for different countries.

Amongst the more coherent systems for estimating e-readiness is that of the UN-DESA. It employs 16 "core" indicators, the first 13 of which cover telecommunication network infrastructure, human capacity development and online presence. Three additional indicators were added later concerning e-Participation, the e-Information, e-Consultation and e-Decision Making indicator [28], [29].

In evaluating state of the art or the progress made on e-readiness in Government services aggregate indices make comparison easier but do not help for diagnostic purposes. Benchmarking necessitates the use of unanimously accepted indicators in analysing e-Government readiness worldwide, while taking into consideration particularities and local conditions of each country [30].

5   Discussion and Conclusions

By the end of the '90s, the EC announced its strategy towards e-Europe. Framework programmes adapted to the information age were launched aiming at transiting Europe to a knowledge based economy enjoying higher growth, job availability and e-services to all citizens. EC's initiatives towards Europe's transition to a knowledge based economy, known as the "eEurope initiative", have been developed in phases and have been successively dictating new action plans in an effort to realise the potential benefits of the information age, i.e. exploitation of ICT innovations, Internet and Web services for all citizens, public administrations and businesses. Actually, eEurope was a policy framework with no funds but directives of how to use and reallocate public expenditure in order to fulfil directives provided. Thus, the e-Europe 2002 Action Plan focusing to a faster, cheaper and "open to all" Internet was quite impatiently followed by the e-Europe 2005 Action Plan, focussing on broadband technologies and their full use for online services for all citizens and in both the public and private sector. In continuation, the i2010 EC initiative was announced in 2005 promoting ICTs' impact to the societies, the quality of life and the global economy. Well before i2010 initiative's expiration in 2009, the Digital Agenda for Europe 2020 had followed.

Although eEurope framework programmes were rather expressing EU strategy and did not provide extra funds but needed to reallocate public funds from existing expenditure, the EU member states had followed these policies. Also, the EC seemed to have achieved the aims of its first initiative Action Plan to improve Internet connection indices throughout Europe and support the member states in adopting the appropriate legal frameworks in liberalizing communication networks, applying new business practices like e-commerce and enjoying e-government services in rural areas like e-health. Nevertheless, in spite of the money spent and the sophistication of certain e-government services, as it has been shown in the previous sections, the results are not satisfactory in terms of broadness and general applicability. There was a large discrepancy from state to state as far ICT systems adaptation by public administrations is concerned. That is why by its second initiative, the EC tried to encourage quality network infrastructures, development of attractive applications and services and organisational transformations. Another goal of the EC should be on new initiatives to join efforts so that the member states could exchange knowledge and know-how, providing support to each other through more effective joint public administration activities.

Although the EC has continued with persistent plans, framework programmes and horizontal ICT and e-government project support, there are still rural areas in EU with poor network infrastructure, citizens not enjoying or at least taking advantage of e-government services, businesses not been integrated to wider markets and, in general, the EU that is not competitive on the grounds of a knowledge based economy. Moreover, worldwide economic crisis has hit weak economies of the EU and unemployment figures are continuously growing. In parallel, corruption figures, in spite of the well declared transparency and lucidity ICT guaranties, are running high for a number of member states.

In general, the EU Member States have initiated major projects in trying to further develop their e-Government services and, on average, are successfully competing technologically advanced countries of the rest of the world. Nevertheless, there are member states with low performance on the availability of e-Government services. Member states like Greece should focus their effort in redesigning their major national priorities in the e-Government services development. In particular, based on our experience, effort should also be made in the field of attracting citizens and promoting the use of e-Government services. Obviously, countries of low performance on e-Government services, should give emphasis to firstly improve their general ICT indices. Further efforts are needed to improve their broadband networks, as well as initiate major projects for the elimination of the still existing digital divide. The inequality has reached high scores in rural areas of EU and still creates problems of less privileged EU citizens.

Measurements and evaluation of the progress made of e-Government services in general should be considered very cautiously since respective studies and publications are using different models, indicators, weights, data collection methodologies and target groups. Also, since these services are closely related to many complex and broad governmental fields, a comparison and careful combination of the various benchmark results is necessary prior to an evaluation of the progress made on e-Government services of a particular country.

The complexity, disparity and variability of existing e-Government indicators has lead to the establishment of a partnership task group including leading organisations like ECA (coordinator), ECLAC, ESCAP, ESCWA, ITU, UNCTAD, UNDESA, OECD, EuroSTAT and the World Bank. The objective of this task group is to develop "conceptually clear, methodologically feasible, and statistically sound set of e-government indicators, which also focus on essential features of e-government in the context of development"[31], [32], [33].

References

1. Commission of the EU: i2010 eGovernment Action Plan: Accelerating eGovernment in Europe for the Benefit of All SEC(2006) 511, Brussels (2006)
2. Sideridis, A.B.: e-Government – Useful Management. In: Conference on ICT Developments, UoII, Corfu (2006)
3. Sideridis, A.B.: Developments on e-Government Services. T/R 187, Infolab (2010); Also presented in Inauguration Day of Dept of Informatics' Appls in Management & Economics, TEIII, Lefkas (2010)
4. Commission of the EU: eEurope 2005: An information society for all. An Action Plan presented to the Sevilla European Council, Brussels (2002)
5. Communication from the Commission to the Council, the European Parliament, the European Economic and Social Committee and the Committee of the Regions, COM(2005) 229 final: i2010 – A European Information Society for growth and employment, Brussels (2005)
6. Communication from the Commission: i2010 eGovernment Action Plan - Accelerating eGovernment in Europe for the Benefit of All COM(2006) 173 final - Not published in the Official Journal, Brussels (2006)
7. Communication from the Commission to the Council, the European Parliament, the European Economic and Social Committee and the Committee of the Regions, COM(2010) 743: The European eGovernment Action Plan 2011-2015 Harnessing ICT to promote smart, sustainable & innovative Government, Brussels (December 2010)
8. Commission of the EU: eEurope – an Information Society for All. Communication on a Commission Initiative (COM 1999/687), Brussels (1999)
9. OECD, http://www.oecd.org/dataoecd/38/57/1888451.pdf
10. Council Decision 98/253/EC: Adopting a multiannual Community programme to stimulate the establishment of the Information Society in Europe (Information Society), Brussels (1998)
11. European Commission, http://ec.europa.eu/information_society/eeurope/2002/index_en.htm

12. Council Decision 182/1999/EC. The Information Society Technologies Programme, Brussels (1999)
13. Council and the European Commission: eEurope 2002, An Information Society For All, Action Plan prepared for the Feira European Council (2000)
14. European Commission, http://ec.europa.eu/cip
15. Internet World Stats News: Internet Growth 2000-2011, The Internet Big Picture, World Internet Users and Population Stats, Monthly Newsletter (March 2011)
16. Commission of the EU, http://ec.europa.eu/information_society/ eeurope/i2010/index_en.htm
17. Seybert, H., Lööf, A.: Internet usage in 2010 – Households and Individuals, Eurostat, Data in focus 50, Luxembourg (2010)
18. Cimander, R., Hansen, M., Kubicek, H.: Electronic Signatures as Obstacle for Cross-Border E-Procurement in Europe. Lessons from the PROCURE-project. Institut fór Informations management, Bremen GmbH (2009)
19. Euroactiv, http://www.euroactiv.com/infosociety/ digital-agenda-put-eu-back-gear-news-286500
20. Communication from the Commission to the Council, the European Parliament, the European Economic and Social Committee and the Committee of the Regions, COM(2011) 11 final. Annual Growth Survey: advancing the EU's comprehensive response to the crisis, Brussels (2011)
21. Commission of the EU, http://ec.europa.eu/eu2020/index_en
22. i2010 High Level Group, Benchmarking Digital Europe 2011-2015 a conceptual framework (2009)
23. Ojo, A., Janowski, T., Estevez, E.: Determining Progress Towards e-Government -What are the Core Indicators? UNU-IIST Report No. 360 (2007)
24. United Nations Department of Economic and Social Affairs: e-Government Readiness Assessment Methodology (2003), http://www.unpan.org/dpepa-kmb-eg-egovrandaready.asp
25. Bridge.org, http://www.bridges.org/ereadiness/report.html
26. Bakry, S.: Toward the development of a standard e-readiness assessment policy. International Journal of Network Management 13, 129–137 (2003)
27. Alghamdi, I.A., Goodwin, R., Rampersad, G.: E-Government Readiness Assessment for Government Organizations in Developing Countries. Computer and Information Science 4/3, 3–17 (2011)
28. United Nations Department of Economic and Social Affairs: Public Governance Indicators: Literature Review, New York (2007)
29. United Nations Department of Economic and Social Affairs: United Nations e-Government Survey 2008 From e-Government to Connected Governance, New York (2008)
30. Molla, A.: The Impact of eReadiness on eCommerce Success in Developing Countries: Firm-Level Evidence, Institute of Development Policy and Management, Paper Nr 18 (2004)
31. ITU: Partnership on Measuring ICT for Development, Core ICT Indicators, International Telecommunication Union, Geneva (2010b)
32. ITU: Partnership on Measuring ICT for Development, Core ICT Indicators, International Telecommunication Union, Geneva (2010c)
33. ITU: Partnership on Measuring ICT for Development: Core list of science, technology and innovation indicators. Proposal of e-Government Indicators, Geneva (2011)

Improved Awareness on Fake Websites
and Detecting Techniques

Hossein Jahankhani, Thulasirajh Jayaraveendran, and William Kapuku-Bwabw

School of Computing, Information Technology and Engineering
University of East London, UK
h.jahankhani@uel.ac.uk, thulasirajh@gmail.com,
wbkapuku@yahoo.co.uk

Abstract. Fake website pages use the similar page layout, font style and picture to mimic legitimate web pages in an effort to convince internet users to give their personal sensitive information such as bank account number, passwords, personal details etc and also sell fake products like fake ticket, duplicate brand cloths, medication etc. There are many available techniques in the market to identify the fake websites. This paper provides an efficient awareness on detecting fake websites. A novel technique or tool will be proposed, implemented and analysed. This technique visually compares a suspected fake website page with legitimate web page by capturing the snapshot of the fake page and identifies it using the assigned identity pixels which are in the legitimate webpage.

Keywords: cybercrime, scammers, fake websites, URL.

1   Introduction

Fake website is one form of phishing, usually scammers create a fake website whose appearance is similar to the page of a real website in order to trick the internet users to divulge their credentials and identities which scammers will use to commit identity theft and fraud for instance they may open bank accounts, take credits from financial institutions etc. also the scammers are able to sell their fake products. Perpetrators of fake websites always use the current or seasonal trend of business. For Example scammers create a fake website and sold fake tickets to the top sporting and entertainment events.

It is obvious that there are lots of computer and internet users who lack online security skills and are not aware of fake websites; hence they would easily fall into the scammers trap. Once they enter their personal sensitive information into a fake website, this information is used by fraudsters for illegal transactions [9] in their article "Bank to rights, we smash dodgy migrant's £1m credit card racket" stated that recently in East London a man was arrested for fraud by Met Police. The detainee person used websites to acquire victim's credit cards information and illicitly use or sell them. Furthermore, nowadays websites are powerful media which easily assist people to communicate with others and facilitate people to perform transactions online. It is noticeable that rumors are quickly created and easily spread to the public

H. Jahankhani et al. (Eds.): ICGS3/e-Democracy 2011, LNICST 99, pp. 271–279, 2012.

via fake websites. In the light of all the above, it is obviously that fake websites effectively causes concerns for law and public order. The research has noticed that the followings major factors:

- Lack of user awareness regarding online security
- Authentic design of the fake websites (high quality and professional designing)
- The belief by some victims that the law enforcement agencies will not act if they report computer-related crime.
- Lack of education in online security
- It is easy and cheap to create a fake websites
- Individuals are scared and reluctant to report incidents to the police through embarrassment.

2   Background

The method of crime is shifted from traditional methods to electronic methods. Hence this has turned out to be a biggest challenge issue to the modern world especially to the law enforcement agencies. Thus it is imperative to find an effective solution to eradicate this growing virtual method of committing crimes which is cybercrime. There is considerable debate surrounding what the term 'cybercrime' means. The Association of Chief Police Officers (ACPO) has recently defined e-crime as 'the use of networked computers or Internet technology to commit or facilitate the commission of crime" [1].Cybercrime is a crime that takes place within cyber space, which could be said to represent the virtual environment within which networked activity takes place [17]. According to surveys, the scale and the volume of the crimes are too large so technical complexities make almost impossible to identify the criminals, since there is a large volume of data to be scanned to identify perpetrators and bring them to justice. Cyber criminals have the belief that the implementation and enforcement of the law is difficult in the online world, therefore they perform their illicit acts without any fear.

2.1   Use of Internet

Over the past 15 years there has been an immense increase in internet usage by individuals of all age. According to the report there were 1.97 billion internet users; 475.1 million in Europe and 825.1 million in Asia. The same survey stated that there was over 14% increase from previous year. [12]. Furthermore "www.symbolic.com" was first domain registered in the world in 1985; there were more than 255 million websites on internet and 152 million blogs –net craft's web server survey December 2010[18]. Cyber criminals use complicated Fake website technical methods when designing fake websites. And these methods are really hard to detect. Some of the methods are:

- Add suffix to the domain name
- Use the mimic link different from visible link

- Use the redirect bugs to redirect the link to the fake pages.
- Replace the certain characters in target URL with similar characters [3]
- Cover the address bar to scam users into believing they are in correct page. It is achieved by adding some script or image to fake the address bar.
- Use the visual based content like image, flash, java applet.
- Use the downloaded WebPages from the real website to make the fake web pages which appear and react exactly as the legitimate web pages.

This paper is attempts and intends to answer the following research question: How best can the public and law enforcement agencies detect fake websites? For examples; in august 2008, Olympic game was held in china, for those games some of the websites sold fake tickets. For instance this site http://www.beijingticket.com was selling fake tickets and committing fraud with other people from all around the world. Reports said that the people who have bought tickets from this website are mostly from America, Australia, New Zealand, Britain etc. Furthermore on this website rate of opening ceremony of Olympic were $1750 to $ 2150. This website named http://www.beijing-ticket2008.com was also closed on 23rd July 2008. It is reported that there are many fake websites offering tickets regarding of Olympic Tickets [19]. There is a highly lucrative market for ticketing; scammers are becoming sophisticated, using encryption on fake websites to lure the potential purchaser into a false sense of security. (BBC News, 4 March 2011) [8]. The HM Revenue and Customs (HMRC) has provided some details about the fake web sites so that the consumer may be aware of those and can act accordingly of fake web sites is found .generally the phishing sites target the personal details of the consumer and using those personal details they may go for gaining some profits in improper way, so this leads to theft and fraud [20]. Website www.uk-tiffancyonline.com,which advertised 85% offer. And that site exactly looks like the original tiffancy.com site, and also scammer put this fake site on the Google ad sense. So Google can be paid £5 every time user clicks on that link [7]. Financial institutions and their customers remained the target of phishing attacks over half the time, according to the report. Other specific attack targets included auctions, online payments and government organizations. The top countries for phishing URLs are Romania at 18.8%, the United States at 14.6%, China at 11.3%, South Korea at 9.8% and the United Kingdom at 7.2%. In tracing the origin of phishing emails, IBM research shows India is tops at 15.5%, Russia at 10.4%, Brazil at 7.6%, U.S. at 7.5% and Ukraine at 6.3%. [5, 13]. "Top countries hosting phishing URLs and top targeted sectors in EMEA" - Symantec Corporation [13]. "11% of the online British population has been a victim of online identity fraud in the last 12 months." - YouGov survey, March 2010 [10]. "1 in 5 businesses has been a victim of an internet scam". "Over a quarter of UK internet users are more afraid of being a victim of online crime than they were 12 months ago".-Get Safe Online Report, 2008 [14].

2.2   Fake Website Spreading Techniques

There are so many ways follow by the scammers to spread their fake website into the internet .some of them are:

Semi-Fake Websites: Cyber criminals place a fake popup window in the legitimate website, when a customer accesses the legitimate website; the fake window popup then appears on the body of the legitimate website requesting user to enter his/her details.

Tab Nabbing: Tab nabbing is another technique which is used to launch a fake website. This gathers the user's frequent visits to web pages by means of CSS history mining. And then uses little bit of JavaScript to create a multiple tabs and launches the fake web page in one of the tab. As the user scans their tabs, the fake web tab acts as a strong visual cue memory making the user to simply open that tab and provides their credential in the fake webpage [4].

Evil-Twins Technique: This is method of launching fake website is the very hard to detect. Cyber criminals create a fake website and wireless network that looks similar to the public network, then they establish the network near the coffee shop, hotels etc. Whenever an ordinary user accesses their network, cyber criminals capture his/her sensitive details into a fake website which was hosted in the fake wireless network.

URL Tricking: Cyber criminal registers a fake website with a similar name of a legitimate website to trick the user to disclose hi/her classified data into a fake webpage. For instance, HSBC Bank has customer's transaction site as "http://instancebanking.hsbc.com", cyber criminals have also set up a server using any of the below similar names to obfuscate the real destination host "http://instancebanking.hsbcc.com or http://instancebanking.hssbc.com".

Sub Domain Concept: Some fake websites are registered with the domain name as similar as the legitimate websites domain name. For example, Barclays bank received the phishing scam which used domain name "http://www.barclayze.co.uk". Other examples include using a sub-domain such as "http://www.barclays.validation.co.uk", where the actual domain is "validation.co.uk" which is not related to Barclays Bank as described by Fraud Watch International [6]. Consider this site http:/unibank.onlinebankingcenter.com (Fig.1).

Legitimate website: "http:// www.unibankghana.com";

Fake Website: http://www.unibank.onlinebankingcentre.com [21]

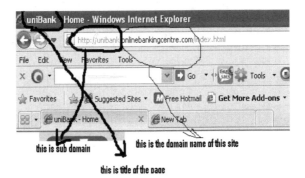

this is sub domain   this is the domain name of this site

this is title of the page

Fig. 1. Sub domain concept

In this page original domain name is onlinebankingcenter.com, sub domain is Unibank and title of the page also Unibank. At a glance, people would think that is a legitimate page of the UNIBANK. Sub domain is the one of the part of main domain, no need of registration required for adding sub domain to the exiting domain. Sub domain and domain is separated by a single dot (.). Scammers utilise this feature and make a fake website in this format. New versions of the browsers are clearly display the URL of the page in the address bar. User easily point out the difference of the domain and sub domain. The fake has a tab for open an account that lead to a form.

URL Encoding Method: Using the "@" symbol to confuse the user, for example login URLs are allowed for the complex URLs to include authentication information such as a login name, passwords. Generally such information is achieved in the format "http://username:password@hostname/pathof the domain page." scammers have a chance to substitute the password and user ID fields for detail associated with the concern. Sample model: **http://hsbc.com:instancebanking@internatiional.com/login.htm** Here, scammers used the login URL concept to mimic the user. Hsbs.com is used as user ID and instance banking used as password and scammers substitute the respective fields. Scammers successfully attract many users into their site, because users think that they are actually visiting a legitimate page. In order to avoid this method, users should use the new version of the browsers and also trusted browsers.

Host Naming Tricks: Most of the internet users are familiar with the fully qualified domain name to navigate to the required websites but at the back of this scene there is a process of converting such domain name to IP addresses. Scammers utilised this feature and obfuscate the destination address and by pass the content filtering server. For example URL: http://hsbc.com:instancebanking@internatiional.com/login.htm. Could be entered as: http://hsbc.com:instancebanking@207.10.10.95/login.htm.

2.3   Use Legitimate Website's Content for Fake Web Page

When analysing the objects of the suspected page, scammers often used the objects from legitimate site, for example, they use a picture, flash objects, streaming videos etc.. Most of the scammers create a frame in the web page and simply link to the legitimate domain. That web page looks like a real web page. But fake website only contains a home webpage and pages such as about us and contact us. This means that fake websites often contain hyperlinks that links to legitimate web site (domain is different from one page to another) [16].

In this case, scammers used the most popular and trusted company logo. Also they provide some tips to detect fake websites, and then users believe that the site they visit is legitimate as they are provided with tips to spot a fake websites. To confirm their details it is advisable not to click on the link provided for verification, users have to visit the trusted network company sites (ABTA, IATA and VERISIGN) and from that site verify the suspected site [6].

URL Spoofing of Address Bar: This method involves removal of the original address bar and then introducing the fake address bar with the help of images and texts. the link is send to a legitimate user through e-mail and when the user clicks on the link it will open a new browser window, which closes and re-opens without the address bar, sometimes status bar, The new window uses HTML, HTA and JavaScript commands to construct a false address bar in place of the original. In order to avoid this cyber attack: since it uses scripts it can be able to stop by disabling active x and java scripts in browser settings.

To Avoid Scam Websites:

- User should be more careful before entering into payment by noting the letters "https" on the web address.
- Buy from trusted pages which were linked from official web pages,
- A sponsored link on a search engine or other website offers no guarantee of authenticity (Sunday times, 2010) [7]
- Spend more time to analyse a suspicious website before making any transactions.
- Look for UK limited company details and a VAT number, if one, or both are absent, this may raise suspicions
- Go to the WHOIS website and check the status and registered details of that page (don't click any link says "who is look up" from the same website)
- Some fake whois website also available in internet.
- If more tabs are open in browser means, don't do any transaction, close all the tabs whichever not necessary at that time and do the transaction.
- Don't leave any credential data request/access page inactive for long time. And also don't access the page if it has inactive for a long period.
- Always check the address bar, whether it shows known domain name, don't do any transaction if there is suspicious URL.
- @, more (.), - symbol found means be alert and verify other factor to ensure that site is legitimate [13,6,8].

3   Implementation of Proposed System

3.1   Proposed System

The improved toolbar is proposed for the purpose of providing awareness regarding a fake website and also differentiating a fake website from legitimate website (fig.2). The system proposes three different levels of detection process involved in detecting a fake website:

Level 1 (Minimal) - URL Identity Check: This level of protection will check URL itself and advise whether it is legitimate or not. This check is achieved by analysing suspected symbols in the URL (for example '@' more dot (.) symbols). This level is very basic.

Analyse the URL and display the URL to the user- this creates user awareness. User is able to identify the URL. Fake address bar and other URL will be cleared in this level of detection. Message box clearly displays the original link which the user is visiting at that time.

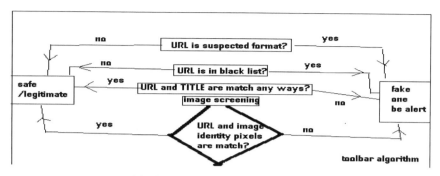

Fig. 2. Improved toolbar is proposed

Level 2 (Medium)-Black List Check: This level of protection will check the list of black list and white listed base for fake website URL. If URL is in the black list, it will show the warning to user as fake site. (Black list are obtained from the common anti-phishes database). Additionally at this level, tool will compare the title of the webpage and the URL, if anything is suspicious the system will alert the user.

To perform this test we have to maintain two data base column, black list and white list. Data base tables have to be updated periodically and the black list information may be gathered from some of the site monitoring forum. In the case of new sites which are not in both lists, there will be a massage box alerting the user to do further investigations on a suspected site.

Additionally compare the URL on the address bar and title of the webpage, if URL is completely different from the title of that page then massage box will alert the user as "page title and URL doesn't match – site may be suspicious".

Level 3 (Maximum) - Image Based Screening: The system captures the current page and checks the image pixel with the already stored pixels. If the pixels are matched with the database pixel for the given URL then that one is legitimate. If it is not then tool will alert the user. For a better result of this detection, the secure pages should be designed with various identity points (pixel) all over the page, so identity pixels contain little colour difference than adjacent pixels. (Example: page with white background and colour value for white is 00000, then identity point's colour value is 000001).

At this level, a database stores the identity pixels detail of the webpage and updates the pixel information periodically, below we use the windows application to update the pixel information to the database. This application is designed for the purpose of updating the pixel information to the database. This application captures the screen short of the webpage by means of buffer memory and then picks the pixel from that image (fig.3).

While performing the level 3 detection, client side webpage will convert as image and particular pixels will be taken from that webpage image (client side) and compare against pixels stored in a database. If there is match in the identity pixels in a URL, this means that image belongs to that URL. A message will be displayed as "current loaded page is legitimate" otherwise the display massage will show "current loaded page is fake".

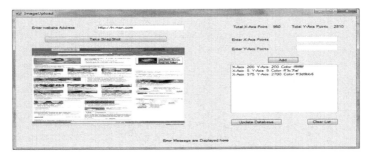

Fig. 3. Shows image based screening with different colours

4   Conclusion

This paper provides an efficient awareness in detecting a fake website. Providing concept of fake website and its spreading method itself creates a big awareness among the internet users. No matter what security measures fitted in a device to protect online information, users should be regularly made aware of new approach to fight cyber crimes. In this paper we have attempted and intended to propose, implement and analyse a new improved tool which assists to detect fake website. Furthermore it creates the awareness on fake website detection.

References

1. http://www.acpo.police.uk/asp/policies/Data/Ecrime%
   20Strategy%20Website%20Version (accessed October 17, 2010)
2. Amoo, D.I.P., Thomson, N.: ACPO e-crime Strategy, Version 1.0 ACPO, the Association of Chief Police Officers of England, Wales and Northern Ireland, e-Crime Strategy (2009)
3. Fu, A.Y., Deng, X., Liu, W.: A Potential IRI Based Phishing Strategy. In: Ngu, A.H.H., Kitsuregawa, M., Neuhold, E.J., Chung, J.-Y., Sheng, Q.Z. (eds.) WISE 2005. LNCS, vol. 3806, pp. 618–619. Springer, Heidelberg (2005)
4. http://www.azarask.in/blog/post/
   a-new-type-of-phishing-attack
5. Messmer, E.: 31.03.2011 kl 22:52 I Network World (US),
   http://news.idg.no/cw/art.cfm?id=90A7235F-1A64-6A71-
   CEF6A16B1DEE1DC1
6. http://www.fraudwatchinternational.com/phishing-
   fraud/phishing-web-site-methods/#content
7. Internet bank fraud statement, Sunday times (January 09, 2010),
   http://www.met.police.uk/fraudalert/docs/
   internet_bank_fraud.pdf
8. http://news.bbc.co.uk/1/hi/uk/8189905.stm
9. News of the world (2011),
   http://www.newsoftheworld.co.uk/notw/_news/1280300/
   Webcatch-Nigerian-crime-boss-who-cons-Brits-out-of-millions-
   of-pounds-each-year-online.html

10. YouGov survey commissioned by VeriSign Authentication, Cifas report (March 2010)
11. Phishing Activity Trends Report-APWG Q1/2010
12. http://royal.pingdom.com/2011/01/12/internet-2010-in-numbers
13. Symantec Corporation report,
    http://www.nortoninternetsecurity.cc/2011/04/
    symantec-internet-security-threat.html
14. UK Internet Security: State of the Nation - Get Safe Online Report (November 2008),
    http://www.getsafeonline.org/media/GSO_Report_2008.pdf
15. http://www.velocityreviews.com
16. http://www.wiki-news.com/fakewebsites
17. Wall, D.S.: Cybercrime: Transformation of crime in the information age. Polity Press,
    Cambridge (2008)
18. web server survey (December 2010),
    http://news.netcraft.com/archives/2010/12/01/
    december-2010-web-server-survey.html
19. Amit ranat, http://www.groundreport.com (August 07, 2008)
20. Simon frediction, http://www.shopsafe.co.uk (August 16, 2010)
21. http://www.unibank.onlinebankingcentre.com

Study of the Perception on the Biometric Technology by the Portuguese Citizens

Daniela Borges[1], Vítor J. Sá[1], Sérgio Tenreiro de Magalhães[1], and Henrique Santos[2]

[1] FaCiS, Universidade Católica Portuguesa, Campus Camões, 4710-362 Braga, Portugal
[2] DSI, Universidade do Minho, Campus de Azurém, 4800-058 Guimarães, Portugal
minagalhaesborges@hotmail.com,
{vitor.sa,stmagalhaes}@braga.ucp.pt, hsantos@dsi.uminho.pt

Abstract. This article presents the results of a systematic inquiry about the perception of the Portuguese on the biometric technology, which involved 606 citizens. It is presented the principal biometrics and the main concepts on its evaluation. Following a simple method consisting in a survey by questionnaire, the most relevant conclusions are presented.

Keywords: biometrics, reliability, security, cognitive biometrics.

1 Introduction

Because of the needs that have occurred in recent times, in respect to security, biometrics technology is expanding year after year. It consists in the recognition of the individual based on one or more physical or behavioral characteristics and, therefore, some people believe that biometrics is a threat to privacy. Other people do not know the technology at all and others are poorly informed about their capabilities. Due to the lack of consensus, and as a starting point to some potential research in the field, it is useful to have concrete values of these disparities of opinions. With this purpose we conducted a study of acceptance of Portuguese adults to discover the level of familiarity with this type of technology.

In the next section we present the basic concepts and the main biometrics, in section 3 we describe how a biometric system is evaluated, for acceptance or comparison purposes, in section 4 we present the methodology that was followed, including the survey questions, in section 5 we describe the results obtained from the data analysis and, finally, in section 6 some conclusions are drawn.

2 Biometric Technologies

The word biometrics comes from the Greek bios (life) + metron (measure), meaning "measure of life". It is the science that makes the verification of identification of an individual's own characteristics, that is, the automatic recognition of the individual.

In general, access control can be made with the following methods, with its respective advantages and disadvantages:

H. Jahankhani et al. (Eds.): ICGS3/e-Democracy 2011, LNICST 99, pp. 280–287, 2012.

— Card: this is something an individual "has", which can be stolen, forgotten, copied, broken, demagnetized, eventually expires, and has no cogency;
— Password: this is something an individual "knows", which can be copied, must be changed periodically and should not have personal data, and has no cogency that can causes problems in the case of forgetting;
— Biometric technology: this is something an individual "is", which does not lose validity, is not forgotten, is difficult to be copied, is true, is not transferable and is permanent.

The main components of a biometric system are the following: capture (capture of an image or basic information of biometric characteristics), extraction (through a biometric reader, geometric points are extracted, e.g., which will characterize the individual), comparison (matching with stored information) and authentication (decision about the veracity of the recognition).

Biometric technologies are classified into two main categories: those that are related to physical body shape, and those that are related to the behavior of an individual. They can also be classified as collaborative, if they require the user be aware of their existence and consciously participate in the process, or as stealth, if they can be used without the knowledge of the individual that is being identified or authenticated [1].

Recently, a new trend has been developed that merges human perception in a kind of brain-machine interface. This approach has been referred to as cognitive biometrics. Cognitive biometrics is based on specific responses to stimulation of the brain. Currently, cognitive biometrics systems are being developed to utilize the brain's response to stimuli (e.g. the facial expression to the perception of odor). Some systems are based on the functional Transcranial Doppler[1] (fTCD) and functional Transcranial Doppler spectroscopy (fTCDS) to obtain brain responses [2].

In the next subsections, we describe some of the most widely used biometrics.

2.1   Facial Recognition

Facial recognition is a natural method of biometric identification, having as a start point the capture of an image of the face. The identification is not easy because of the constantly changing facial appearance. Causes for different facial expressions are the following: hair style, head position, mustache, angle, lighting conditions, etc. The facial recognition uses distinctive facial features, including contours of the cheeks, sides of mouth and location of the nose and eyes.

2.2   Hand Geometry

Hand geometry is the measurement of the shape of the hand of an individual, which include length, width, thickness, curvature and surface of the hand and fingers. In this method the hand may be well positioned, i.e., the hand must always remain in the same position on the reader device, otherwise the measurements may differ. It is one

---

[1] Test that measures the velocity of blood flow through the brain's blood vessels.

of the oldest methods that exist, but it is not very precise. It is a fast way of identification and has low cost.

2.3   Fingerprint

The fingerprint is a method that yields great accuracy at low cost, and it is simple and widely used. Fingerprints are unique for each finger of one individual. This method consists in capturing the formation of grooves in the skin of the fingers and palms of an individual. For recognition there are basically three types of technology: optical - to read the fingerprint it is needed a light source; capacitive – consists in the measurement of the temperature that comes from printing and; ultra-sonic – the fingerprints are obtained by using sound signals.

2.4   Iris Recognition

This method is based on reading the colored ring that surrounds the pupil of the eye. Modern systems can be used even in the presence of eyeglasses and contact lenses, and this technology is not intrusive. An important characteristic is that the iris does not change with the person age.

2.5   Retinal Recognition

The reading of the retina is the analysis of blood vessel formation in the back of the eye. It is used a light source to measure the patterns of retinal blood vessels. This method is complex and costly.

2.6   Voice Recognition

The voice recognition works through the spelling of a phrase that acts as a password. The features in voice recognition are based on shape and size of vocal cords, mouth, lips and nasal cavity. This method is associated with the behavioral biometrics, is sensitive because of the person's emotional state and the environment noise, and has a low cost.

2.7   Keystroke Dynamics

This technique is based on the person's behavior when typing text into a keyboard, or the measurement of typing speed. There are several ways to measure the dynamics of typing: the time interval between successive keystrokes; the time a key is pressed; the frequency of typing wrong keys and; the habit of using different keys on the keyboard. This technique has a low cost, due to not require special equipment.

2.8   Signature

The signature is a type of identification that is based on comparing the signature written by an individual with the signature stored in the database, but especially in the dynamics when an individual is signing relatively to its writing speed, direction, movement pressure, rhythm, among others. It's used in banks, although no one signs it the same way, allowing a margin for errors.

3   Evaluation of Biometric Systems

The evaluation of a biometric system suitable for a certain type of application is a complex method that involves different factors. In general the parameters are extracted from the application requirements, being essential to choose the most suitable technology [3]. The assessment can be made between various parameters such as degree of reliability, cost of implementation, level of comfort and acceptance.

The degree of reliability of a biometric system is made by comparing two values: the FRR (False Rejection Rate) and FAR (False Acceptance Rate). These variables are dependent but cannot be both minimized. When the FRR and FAR rates are equal, a balance point was found, which is known by CER (Crossover Error Rate) or EER (Equal Error Rate). The level of comfort and acceptance are user subjective standards but this parameter is crucial for a biometric system. Overall the system is more acceptable as it is less intrusive.

The cost of implementation is a key factor and covers many different factors, some of which are often neglected [4]:

- Hardware
- Software
- Integration with hardware/software available
- Training of users
- Database maintenance staff
- System maintenance

The choice of the method(s) to be used depends on the risk analysis that must necessarily be made relatively to the information/infrastructure to be protected [1].

4   Methodology

Scientific research is a process of systematic deductions that provide information to solve a problem or answer complex questions. This is a systematic and rigorous method. In social sciences, the inquiry produces systematic and accurate research. With a set of relevant social data, explanations can be provided from hypothesis made in advance [5].

The construction of questionnaires is not a simple task. Spending some time and effort in their structure may be a favorable factor in the "growth" of any researcher.

In this work, the choice for data collection and processing falls on the quantitative analysis, since it is more objective, more reliable and more accurate. The quantitative analysis focuses on the use of instruments that quantitatively describe a phenomenon. It also provides a more objective and accurate analysis of the phenomenon, because it uses more standardized techniques for phenomena measurement [6].

One of those techniques is the survey by questionnaire, which was what we used for data collection. According to Raymond Quicky [6], the survey by questionnaire is advantageous because it has the ability to quantify a variety of data and to proceed to a large analysis of correlations.

A questionnaire is a research tool that aims to gather information based, commonly in the inquisition of a representative group of the population under study. This is still extremely advantageous when a researcher wants to collect information on a specific topic within a relatively short time. The questionnaire can be used directly and indirectly. It is used indirectly when the investigator considers the answers that are provided by the respondent and directly when is the proper respondent who fills it.

In order to study the perception on the biometric technology by the Portuguese citizens a survey was prepared and 606 citizens from the Portuguese mainland answered to it. We started to collect some data on the citizen, like living region, gender, age and occupation, and the questions in the survey were the following:

-    Do you know the biometric technology?
-    From the following types of biometrics indicate which ones do you know?
-    Do you think useful to adhere to the biometric technology?
-    Have you ever used the biometric technology?
-    Do you consider the biometric technology a high-security technology?
-    Do you know what cognitive biometrics are?
-    If you answered "Yes" to the above question please indicate which ones do you known.

5   Results Obtained

The population in study is represented by 606 respondents. They were mostly females, about 329, while only 277 were male, as Fig. 1 shows. In Fig. 2 we note that the major part of respondents, 215, is from the Southern Region, that 212 represent the Central Region, and 177 correspond to the Northern Region.

As a starting point for any future research on biometric technologies, the conclusion extracted from the next data is relevant, because it demonstrates that most

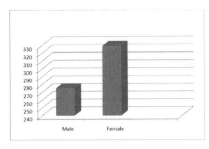   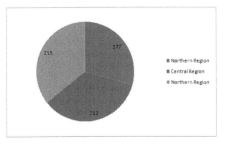

Fig. 1. Number of respondents by gender   **Fig. 2.** Number of respondents by region

of the people, 362, don't know what this kind of technology is about. Only 241 respondents are aware of this (Fig. 3).

The analysis of the types of biometrics that respondents know suggests that fingerprint (215), signature (209), voice recognition (143) and facial recognition (119) are the best known. Likewise, only 97 respondents know the hand geometry, 81 respondents know the retinal recognition and 61 of the respondents know the iris recognition. Finally, 35 respondents know the stroke dynamics, which represents the smallest proportion of individuals (Fig. 4).

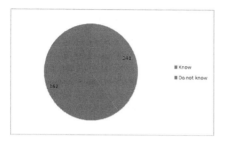
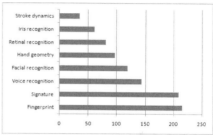

Fig. 3. Who knows biometric technology   **Fig. 4.** Types of known biometrics

From the analysis of Fig. 5, below, we can see that 220 of the inquired individuals find it advantageous to adhere to the biometric technology, 38 individuals do not find advantageous to adhere to this technology, and the majority, about 368, chose not to answer this question, which is nevertheless a curious fact.

About the real experience with this kind of technology, most of the respondents already had some contact with biometric recognition. 142 have already used, against 122 that have never used it (Fig. 6).

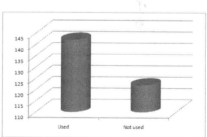

Fig. 5. Respondents that find it advantageous   **Fig. 6.** Respondents who already used

Regarding the level of security deposited by the Portuguese people in the biometric technologies, as shown in figure 7, 64% of the responses consider that they are high security technology, while 36% consider they are not (Fig. 7).

Finally, not less important because it is currently a hot topic in this field, the questionnaire has a question about cognitive biometrics. Without surprise the great majority of the Portuguese people refer that they don´t know what it is, about 246 responses, while only 19 respondents know what this specific group of biometrics is. Fig. 8 shows the correspondent graphic.

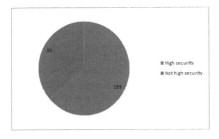

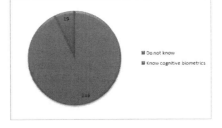

Fig. 7. Biometrics as high security   **Fig. 8.** Who knows cognitive biometrics

6   Conclusion

Throughout this paper, taking into account the amount of collected data, we conclude that respondents, which can represent the Portuguese citizens, did not know the biometric technology in a representative percentage, despite being in a modern country with regard to technological advances. Even being aware of these advances, there are still people (although a small proportion) that do not consider the biometric technology for high security. These can be to the fact that they only had contact with biometrics working on common use devices, like fingerprint or signature, the most well known as shown in Fig. 4. Talking about more specific and new ones, like the cognitive biometrics, the scenario is extreme with a knowledge rate of only 7%.

Other studies of acceptance shows that even in situations where the benefit of such technologies is known, it has no effect on the decision to adopt a biometric technology, because environmental and other organizational characteristics have a major impact in technology adoption [7]. The key consideration in biometric technology adoption is the user acceptance. Alhussain and Drew, 2009, conducted a study that indicated the significant digital and cultural gap between the technological awareness of employees and the preferred authentication solutions promoted by management. It is recommended that an awareness and orientation process about biometrics should take place before the technology is introduced into an organization [8].

We can conclude that something must be done not only in the development and refinement of new security technologies, but also in making people aware of the resulting benefit, and even the real necessity, in many situations.

References

1. Magalhães, P.S., Santos, H.D.: Biometria e autenticação. In: Conferência da Associação Portuguesa de Sistemas de Informação, Porto (2003)
2. Bishop, C., Powell, S., Rutt, D., Browse, N.: Transcranial Doppler measurement of middle cerebral artery blood flow velocity: a validation study. Stroke 17(5), 913–915 (1986)

3. Pinheiro, J.M.: Biometria nos Sistemas Computacionais: Você é a Senha. Ciência Moderna (2008)
4. Liu, S., Silverman, M.: A practical guide to biometric security technology. IT Professional 3(1), 27–32 (2001)
5. Birou, A.: Dicionário das ciências sociais. Dom Quixote, Lisboa (1982)
6. Quicky, R., Campenhoudt, L.: Manual de Investigação em Ciências Sociais. Gradiva, Lisboa (1998)
7. Uzoka, F.-M.E., Ndzinge, T.: Empirical analysis of biometric technology adoption and acceptance in Botswana. Journal of Systems and Software 82(9), 1550–1564 (2009)
8. Alhussain, T., Drew, S.: Towards User Acceptance of Biometric Technology in E-Government: A Survey Study in the Kingdom of Saudi Arabia. In: Godart, C., Gronau, N., Sharma, S., Canals, G. (eds.) I3E 2009. IFIP AICT, vol. 305, pp. 26–38. Springer, Heidelberg (2009)

Author Index